The Hangman's Record

Volume Three 1930 – 1964

To Lorraine hope you enjoy the books best wishes

STEVE FIELDING

Chancery House Press

Chancery House Press

15 Wickham Road, Beckenham,

Kent, BR3 5JS, England

ISBN   0 900246 81 2

Published by   Chancery House Press
                             15 Wickham Road
                             Beckenham
                             Kent
                             BR3 5JS
                             UK
                             tel 020 8650 7745
                             fax 020 8650 0768

Cover design & logo   Simone Riley
                             www.her-nibs.co.uk
Pictures

                             Whilst every effort has been
                             made to trace copyright on the
                             pictures, in some cases it has not
                             been possible to find and credit
                             the holders.

Also by Steve Fielding from Chancery House Press:

The Hangman's Record Volume 1: 1868-1899   ISBN 0 900246 65 0
The Hangman's Record Volume 2: 1900-1929   ISBN 0 900246 77 4

Other Chancery House Press publications:

Adhesive wafer seals: A transient Victorian phenomenon
by Michael Champness & David Trapnell   ISBN 0 900246 78 2

St. Petersburg - The Imperial Post:
its postmarks and other postal markings 1765-1914
by Ian L.G. Baillie & Eric G. Peel   ISBN 0 900246 89 8

The Poacher's Lawyer by Hunter Adair   ISBN 0 900246 90 1

Chancery House Press

Chancery House Press is an imprint of the well established and respected publishing house, CBD Research Ltd.

Its aim is to provide an outlet for non-fiction publications of an esoteric or specialist nature, to assist serious researchers and the dedicated hobbyist.

We welcome any proposal – in the form of a preliminary letter or e-mail – for reference works of a singular nature that will extend what is intended to be a diverse and eclectic range of publications.

Contents

Author's Preface   vii

Corrections   ix

Acknowledgments   xi

Introduction: Development of the Scaffold   xiii

The Executioners   xli

The Cases: 1930-1964   1

Victim Index   263

Method Index   305

Executioner Index   323

Hanged Index   351

v

Author's Preface: Why The Hangman's Record?

As with the first two volumes of The Hangman's Record, this book is intended to fill a void in the subject of British executions. A number of attempts have been made over the years to copy the formula for this book but this is the first time a reference book of this depth of information has been made available.

This volume carries on where Volume Two ended, covering the period from 1930 to 1964, and chronicles all those executed in Great Britain and Ireland, including executions sanctioned by both the civil and military courts. It includes details of all persons executed under the Treachery Act during the Second World War and the American servicemen hanged at Shepton Mallett.

There are a number of executions not listed in the text such as that of the German soldier executed by firing squad in the Tower of London in 1941, several cases from Ireland in the early 1940s that resulted in death by firing squad, and the military executions carried out overseas.

As with the earlier volumes, readers with any additional information, comments or enquiries are welcome to contact me through my publishers or direct through my website listed below.

Steve Fielding
Bolton
Lancashire
England
2005

www.stevefielding.com

Errata

These pages list omitted entries from Volume 1 of The Hangman's Record and corrections to locations of hangings.

Erroneous dates of hangings, and names of victims, executioners and people hanged, have been corrected in the relevant indexes. For easy reference, updated entries include the information as originally given, *shown in italics.*

The Victim Index includes some names which were not available when Volumes 1 and 2 were published. These names also appear *in italics.*

Omissions

1869, September 6th: William Dixon (28)   Winchester

A soldier convicted of the murder of Corporal James Brett who was shot dead at Aldershot on 21 July.

Sentenced to death by Mr Justice Smith at the Central Criminal Court on 18 August, it was alleged that Dixon had been aggrieved at some duties he had been made to carry out by Brett, and that while drunk he had picked up a rifle and shot him in the head.

Hanged by Calcraft.

1870, December 26th: Patrick Durr (28)   Manchester

Durr and his wife Catherine were seen out together on the evening of 17 August, close to their home in Manchester. Later that evening they were seen together very drunk. When they returned it was alleged that Durr had strangled his wife because he was angry at her pawning various items from their home to buy drink.

Sentenced to death by Mr Justice Brett on 5 December, the judge adding that drink was no excuse for carrying out the crime and hoped it would act as a warning to others.

Hanged by Calcraft.

1871, April 12th: John Gregory (55)   Downpatrick

The first private execution in Ireland. Gregory

served with the army in the Crimea for 20 years. On Friday 29 July 1870 he visited a John Gallagher who like Gregory was employed on the Seaforde estate. Part of Gallagher's duties was to deliver the workers' wages and he had completed this task a short time before Gregory called at 5pm.

Gregory asked his friend to accompany him on a walk along the road and when Gallagher failed to return home after some hours, friends began searching for him. He was found shot dead in a wood close to his home. When the police searched Gregory's house they found a money bag which had been stolen from Gallagher. Gregory was arrested and during his trial the jury heard how he had bought powder for a gun which he had borrowed and failed to return. The trial lasted for two days and the jury found him guilty of the murder.

Hanged by Calcraft.

1876, May 1st: Henry Webster (61)   Norwich

Convicted at Norfolk Assizes on 10 April for the murder of his wife Sarah (53) at Cranworth on 17 September 1875.

They had lived together unhappily for a while before she was found stabbed to death by a policeman who had been summoned to the house by neighbours after they heard sounds of a disturbance.

Hanged by Marwood.

Location Corrections

1873, August 19th: Edward Walsh   Castlebar

1876, April 10th: George Hill   Hertford

1886, March 1st: Thomas Nash   Swansea

1886, March 2nd: David Roberts   Cardiff

1889, August 7th: Lawrence Hickey   Tralee

1892, January 12th: James Heaney   Sligo

Acknowledgements

I would like to thank the following people for help with illustrations, photographs and information received during the research of this book.

Thanks in the main to Matthew Spicer, whose knowledge and database of 20th Century criminology has been a priceless asset in reconciling information; and to Tim Leech and Tony Homewood, who have both kindly supplied rare photographs and information and have offered help and support from the conception of The Hangman's Record.

Thanks to Linda Towers for supplying the photograph of her father Robert Leslie Stewart, and to Doris Allen for allowing me to use a photograph of her late husband Harry Bernard Allen. I also acknowledge the help and encouragement given to me by the late Syd Dernley, retired executioner, whose willingness to chat and share information was vital in getting the project off the ground. Thanks also to retired prison officer Frank McKue for information on executions in Scotland and information on Albert Pierrepoint and Jock Stewart.

A lot of the research was compiled many years ago so belated thanks must go to Professor J Robert Lilly who supplied much of the information relating to the execution of American servicemen during the Second World War, to Mrs Annette Mingay who helped with information on several Scottish cases, and to David Mossop and Wilf Gregg who both helped with information on a variety of cases.

Michelle Marsh-Giles helped with research on a number of Liverpool cases and some data inputting, and Janet Buckingham helped with information on some Durham cases and proof reading. Peter Goodall and Alan Constable helped with information on Swansea Gaol and Winchester Gaol respectively.

Thanks also to the staff at Bolton Library's Archives and Local Studies Department, also the staff at Manchester Central Library and Colindale Newspaper Library. Thanks as always to Lisa Moore for her constant help and support.

My sincere apologies to anyone who contacted me offering information that has since been used in the compiling of this book, and whom I haven't credited. In the time span between publication of the second and third volumes some of the names have been misplaced.

Finally, thank you to everyone who has waited patiently for this final volume. I hope you will find it worth the wait.

Introduction: Development of the Scaffold

By the early 1930s the number of prisons housing apparatus to conduct executions was almost half what it had been at the turn of the century. London still housed two prisons divided geographically, so that persons convicted of crimes to the north of the River Thames were housed at Pentonville, while those convicted south of the river were taken to Wandsworth. Nationwide, each county now tended to just have one centre of execution, with some counties sending convicted criminals to an adjacent county for execution. Those condemned in Cumbria, for example, would usually be sent to Liverpool and those convicted in North Wales to Shrewsbury or Manchester.

Execution sheds were still the norm in many prisons, but gradually a blueprint was produced to bring all prisons in line with a set-up that housed the execution chamber in the wing of a prison. It comprised a three-storey block of cells: the middle cell being the actual gallows room, with the floor housing the large trapdoors. The cell below was the pit into which the executed person dropped. It was usually adjacent to a mortuary room where a jury would view the body after execution and prior to post mortem. The upper of the three cells housed the beam room to which the hangmen would shackle the ropes and chains.

The press still witnessed executions at some prisons; this was usually at the discretion of the governor or under-sheriff, and press reports still carried dramatic accounts of the last moments of those condemned. This was eventually curtailed and the press were admitted to view their last execution at Wandsworth in 1934.

The Sentence of Death (Expectant Mothers) Act 1931 now decreed that pregnant women were no longer to be hanged after giving birth. This had last happened in 1873 when Mary Cotton had her baby taken from her shortly before execution. In 1933, the Children and Young Persons Act prohibited the death sentence for persons under 18 at the time of the crime and in 1938 the Infanticide Act (1922) was amended to remove the death penalty for women who killed their babies in the first year of life.

The Select Committee on Capital Punishment 1929-1930, which debated abolition of the death penalty, had an effect on the number of executions carried out. As the data shows there was an average of nine executions per year during the 1930s; approximately 50% of those sentenced to death. The ratio increased dramatically during the Second World War when a large number of foreign spies and American servicemen were hanged in British prisons. The rise in death sentences being carried out also increased, due in the main to the climate of the time. It is perhaps surprising that the peak year for executions in Great Britain during modern times was 1952, when 25 people were hanged out of a total of 39 convicted (64%). Only once, in 1903, was there a larger annual total of executions carried out.

By the 1950s, nearly all prisons had adopted the modern execution suite and by the time of abolition only Bedford prison still had an execution shed. At Leeds prison, Steve Wade, the hangman for Yorkshire, found his earning powers reduced when for a 12-month period persons convicted at Leeds were sent across the Pennines for execution at Manchester's Strangeways Gaol while the Leeds gallows was updated. At the Winter Assizes in 1953, Wade again found his income suffering when an unprecedented number of death sentences at one sitting (seven) meant that Leeds didn't have enough condemned cells to house the prisoners. Four of those condemned were transferred to Strangeways Gaol and the request to carry out the executions thus went to Albert Pierrepoint, the regular hangman at Manchester.

It's interesting to note the way prison governors and under-sheriffs selected their executioners. Readers of Volumes 1 & 2 of The Hangman's Record will have read how certain counties chose their own hangman regardless of who the country's chief executioner was. Much of this came down to the residence of the hangman and the expense of bringing a man 200 miles to carry out an execution if it could be done by a man living less than a quarter of that distance away.

Some hangmen with decades of service found that they were never called upon at certain prisons. Durham and Leeds, two of the prisons at which an above average number of executions were carried out, each employed Albert Pierrepoint only once. Despite being a hangman for 40 years, Tom Pierrepoint was only employed at Pentonville on a handful of occasions, with a gap of 30 years between his first and second execution there. For a long period through the twenties and thirties the chosen hangman for London prisons was Baxter, the hangman living in the Home Counties.

The north-south rivalry between the hangmen that had begun in the 1920s went on until right up to the start of the Second World War, when the bias shifted firmly to the north. From January 1941 until abolition in August 1964, every execution bar one was carried out by a chief executioner living in the north of England.

It was always the norm to have an assistant at an execution. Besides gaining experience by watching an experienced hangman at work, his role was usually just to help secure the prisoner's arms in the condemned cell and to strap his legs on the drop. Although these duties were deemed relatively simple, more than one assistant was dismissed for failing in this task. Occasionally, at the judgment of the hangman, the legs were not strapped, for example if the prisoner had put up a fierce struggle en-route to the drop.

It was usual to have two or three assistants at a double execution; the number was often at the discretion of the authorities, as more assistants meant more expense. For a projected double execution at Liverpool in 1943, the governor wrote that he was concerned at the behaviour of one of the prisoners and requested another assistant be employed. He also made a rider that the more experienced assistant should carry out the same role as the chief executioner, in strapping the arms in the cell, leading the man onto the drop and placing the cap and noose around the prisoner's neck. This, he said, would cut the time of the execution dramatically, lessen the chance of a violent scene on the drop and avoid the necessity of the second condemned man viewing the other man noosed and waiting. On this occasion it never happened as one of the men was reprieved at the eleventh hour.

In the 1949-1953 Royal Commission Report, similar observations were made, but they were never carried out to the extent the Liverpool Governor suggested. The senior assistant was given the responsibility of leading the man onto the drop, but placing the cap and noose was the duty of the chief executioner alone. It was the hangman's, not the assistant's responsibility to place the noose and pull the lever. On one occasion in the 1950s, a debut executioner's career was curtailed when, in trying to emulate the speed of other hangmen, he slightly misplaced the noose over the white cap resulting in it fouling the knot, causing the execution to go less cleanly than planned.

One of the outcomes of the 1949-1953 report was the ending of double executions. For a time during the mid-1940s an experiment was made with carrying out single executions on the same day instead of a double execution. They still engaged two assistants although one would have been sufficient as they were technically now single executions. This new procedure was short-lived and double executions again became the usual way to hang two people on the same day. In October 1945, five Germans were executed on the same day at Pentonville. Neither the prison records, nor the hangmen's diaries, make note of the timings of these executions; evidence suggests they were hanged in five single executions. Experts on the subject debate that they would have been hanged in two doubles and one single, and I tend to agree with that theory.

It was procedure for the condemned man to be left to hang on the rope for one hour after execution. This dated back to the days of public executions when incidents were recorded of people being taken down and found to still be alive. During the post-war executions carried out in Germany, the sheer number of executions carried out daily necessitated a shorter time for the body to hang before being taken down. With hanging supposedly producing instantaneous death it was decided in 1953 to allow a period of around fifteen minutes before the body was removed from the rope. On one occasion in 1959, when a body was removed after the allotted time, the doctor noted that the blood had began to circulate again. The body was re-suspended and henceforth it was decided to allow the body to hang for 45 minutes.

The biggest change in the execution procedure and protocol took place with the passing of the Homicide Act (1957). Prior to this act the mandatory sentence for murder was death by hanging. This was regardless of whether the murder was un-premeditated, the result of a drunken quarrel for example, or the result of a calculated plot. The high profile executions of Bentley (Jan 1953), Christie (July 1953) and Ruth Ellis (July 1955) and the arbitrary way reprieves were handed down eventually led to a revising of the whole structure of the legal system relating to capital punishment. From March 1957 liability to the death penalty for capital murder was reduced to those convicted of:

(a) any murder done in the course or furtherance of theft;

(b) any murder done by shooting or explosion;

(c) any murder done in the course or for the purpose of resisting or avoiding or preventing a lawful arrest, or of affecting or assisting an escape or rescue from legal custody;

(d) any murder of a police officer acting in the execution of his duty or of a person assisting a police officer in so acting;

(e) in the case of a person who was a prisoner at the time when he did or was a party to a murder, any murder of a prison officer acting in the execution of his duty or of a prison officer so acting.

One of the other changes brought about by the new Act was a change to the wording of the death sentence used in court. Instead of the lengthy wording about being removed to a place of lawful execution etc., the wording now simply stated the prisoner would 'suffer death in the manner authorised by law'. The practice of posting notices on the prison gates also ended; instead a short notification was inserted in the London Gazette and other national newspapers such as The Times.

Double executions, which had stopped three years earlier in 1954, were now officially outlawed. On the three occasions during the time of the Homicide Act, when two convicted killers were hanged for the same crime, their executions were carried out at different prisons at the same hour. This resulted in there not being one person officially and historically named as the last to hang in Great Britain.

There were 65 capital murder convictions after 1957 in England and Wales and of that number 29 (45%) were executed, a rather lower percentage than in the pre-Homicide Act days.

The newly elected Labour Government came to power in October 1964 with the promise to abolish the death penalty. In July, while the last two to hang were in the condemned cell awaiting their fate, Ronald Cooper had committed murder during the course of theft in Barking. When Cooper was sentenced to death at The Old Bailey in December, he knew that he would not hang.

The last death sentence passed in Great Britain was by Mr Justice Havers at Leeds Assizes, on 1st November 1965, when David Stephen Chapman was convicted of committing a capital murder at Scarborough.

A week later, on 8th November 1965, the Murder (Abolition of Death Penalty) Act was passed, which effectively abolished capital punishment but provided for another vote on it 'within five years'. High treason, piracy with violence and arson in Royal Dockyards remained capital crimes. In December 1969, Parliament confirmed abolition of capital punishment for murder.

The last working gallows kept tested and in readiness in England was at Wandsworth Gaol in south London. It was dismantled in 1992, in the same week that the last death sentence was pronounced in the Isle of Man. The sentence wasn't commuted as was expected. The Manx Appeal Court ordered a re-trial, carried out in 1994, and by the time the jury came to the same conclusion as at the first trial, hanging had been removed from the Isle of Man Criminal Code. The new sentence was therefore life in prison. By the end of the last century just one gallows still remained: at Perth Gaol in Scotland.

In early 1998 the death penalty was abolished for crimes committed under military jurisdiction. On 20th May that year, on a free vote during a debate on the Human Rights Bill, MPs decided by a large majority (294 to 136) to adopt provisions of the European Convention on Human Rights outlawing capital punishment for murder except 'in times of war or imminent threat of war'. The Bill incorporates the European Convention on Human Rights into British law. On July 31st 1998, high treason and piracy with violence ceased to be capital crimes.

On 27th January 1999 the then Home Secretary, Jack Straw, formally signed the 6th protocol of the European Convention of Human Rights in Strasbourg, on behalf of the British Government. This formally abolished the death penalty in the UK.

Memorandum of Conditions to which any Person acting as

Assistant Executioner is required to conform

(An Assistant Executioner will not be employed by the
Governor without the concurrence of the High Sheriff)

1. An Assistant Executioner is engaged, with the concurrence of the
High Sheriff, by the Governor of the prison at which the execution is to
take place, and is required to conform with any instructions he may receive
from or on behalf of the High Sheriff in connection with any execution
for which he may be engaged.

2. A list of persons competent for the office of Assistant Executioner
is in the possession of High Sheriffs and Governors; it is therefore unneces-
sary for any person to make application for employment in connection with
an execution, and such application will be regarded as objectionable
conduct and may lead to the removal of the applicant's name from the list.

3. Any person engaged as an Assistant Executioner will report himself
at the prison at which an execution for which he has been engaged is to
take place not later than 4 o'clock on the afternoon preceding the day of
execution.

4. He is required to remain in the prison from the time of his arrival
until the completion of the execution and until permission is given him
to leave.

5. During the time he remains in the prison he will be provided with
lodging and maintenance on an approved scale.

6. He should avoid attracting public attention in going to or from
the prison; he should clearly understand that his conduct and general
behaviour must be respectable and discreet, not only at the place and time
of execution, but before and subsequently. In particular he must not
reveal to any person, whether for publication or not, any information about
his work as an Assistant Executioner or any information which may come his
way in the course of his duty. If he does he will render himself liable
to prosecution under the Official Secrets Acts, 1911 and 1920.

7. His remuneration will be £2.12s.6d. for the performance of the
duty required of him, to which will be added £2.12s.6d. if his conduct
and behaviour have been satisfactory. The latter part of the fee will
not be payable until a fortnight after the execution has taken place.

8. Record will be kept of his conduct and efficiency on each occasion
of his being employed, and this record will be at the disposal of any
Governor who may have to engage an assistant executioner.

9. The name of any person who does not give satisfaction, or whose
conduct is in any way objectionable, so as to cast discredit on himself,
either in connection with the duties or otherwise, will be removed from
the list.

10. The apparatus approved for use at executions will be provided at
the prison. No part of it may be removed from the prison, and no
apparatus other than approved apparatus must be used in connection with
any execution.

11. The Assistant Executioner will give such information, or make
such record of the occurrences as the Governor of the prison may require.

H.B. Allen

xix

MEMORANDUM OF INSTRUCTIONS FOR CARRYING OUT AN EXECUTION

1. The trap doors shall be stained a dark colour and their outer edges shall be defined by a white line three inches broad painted round the edge of the pit outside the traps.

2. (a) A week before an execution the apparatus for the execution shall be tested in the following manner under the supervision of the Works Officer, the Governor being present:-

The working of the scaffold will first be tested without any weight. Then a bag of dry sand of the same weight as the culprit will be attached to the rope and so adjusted as to allow the bag a drop equal to, or rather more than, that which the culprit should receive, so that the rope may be stretched with a force of not more than 1,000 foot-pounds. See Table of Drops. The working of the apparatus under these conditions will then be tested. The bag must be of the approved pattern, with a thick and well-padded neck, so as to prevent any injury to the rope and leather. Towelling will be supplied for padding the neck of the bag under the noose. As the gutta percha round the noose end of the execution ropes hardens in cold weather, care should be taken to have it warmed and manipulated immediately before the bag is tested.

(b) On the day before the execution the apparatus shall be tested again as above, the Governor, the Works Officer and the executioner being present. For the purpose of this test a note of the height and weight of the culprit should be obtained from the Medical Officer and handed to the executioner.

3. After the completion of each test the scaffold and all the appliances will be locked up, and the key kept by the Governor or other responsible officer; but the bag of sand should remain suspended all the night preceding the execution so as to take the stretch out of the rope.

4. The executioner and any persons appointed to assist in the operation should make themselves thoroughly acquainted with the working of the apparatus.

5. In order to prevent accidents during the preliminary tests and procedure the lever will be fixed by a safety-pin, and the Works or other Prison Officer charged with the care of the apparatus prior to the execution will be responsible for seeing that the pin is properly in position both before and after the tests. The responsibility for withdrawing the pin at the execution will rest on the executioner.

6. Death by hanging ought to result from dislocation of the neck. The length of the drop will be determined in accordance with the attached Table of Drops.

7. The required length of drop is regulated as follows:-

(a) At the end of the rope which forms the noose the executioner should see that 13 inches from the centre of the ring are marked off by twine wrapped round the covering; this is to be a fixed quantity, which, with the stretching of this portion of the rope, and the lengthening of the neck and body of the culprit, will represent the average depth of the head and circumference of the neck after constriction.

(b) While the bag of sand is still suspended, the executioner will measure off from the painted line on the rope the required length of drop and will make a chalk mark on the rope at the end of this length. A piece of copper wire fastened to the chain will now be stretched down the rope till it reaches the chalk mark, and will be cut off there so that the cut end of the copper wire shall terminate at the upper end of the measured length of drop. The bag of sand will

The chain will now be so adjusted at the bracket that the lower end of the copper wire shall reach to the same level from the floor of the scaffold as the height of the prisoner. The known height of the prisoner can be readily measured on the scaffold by a graduated rule of six foot six inches long. When the chain has been raised to the proper height the cotter must be securely fixed through the bracket and chain. The executioner will now make a chalk mark on the floor of the scaffold, in a plumb line with the chain, where the prisoner should stand.

(c) These details will be attended to as soon as possible after 6 a.m. on the day of the execution so as to allow the rope time to regain a portion of its elasticity before the execution, and, if possible, the gutta percha on the rope should again be warmed.

8. The copper wire will now be detached, and after allowing sufficient amount of rope for the easy adjustment of the noose, the slack of the rope should be fastened to the chain above the level of the head of the culprit with a pack-thread. The pack-thread should be just strong enough to support the rope without breaking.

9. When all the preparations are completed the scaffold will remain in the charge of a responsible officer until the time fixed for the execution.

10. At the time fixed for the execution, the executioner will go to the pinioning room, which should be as close as practicable to the scaffold, and there apply the apparatus. When the culprit is pinioned and his neck is bared he will be at once conducted to the scaffold.

11. On reaching the scaffold the procedure will be as follows:-

    (a) The executioner will:-

        (i) Place the culprit exactly under the part of the beam to which the rope is attached.

        (ii) Put the white linen cap on the culprit.

        (iii) Put on the rope round the neck quite tightly (with the cap between the rope and the neck), the metal eye being directed forwards, and placed in front of the angle of the lower jaw, so that with the constriction of the neck it may come underneath the chin. The noose should be kept tight by means of a stiff leather washer, or an india rubber washer, or a wedge.

    (b) While the executioner is carrying out the procedure in paragraph (a) the assistant executioner will:-

        (i) Strap the culprit's legs tightly.

        (ii) Step back beyond the white safety line so as to be well clear of the trap doors.

        (iii) Give an agreed visual signal to the executioner to show that he is clear.

    (c) On receipt of the signal from his assistant the executioner will:-

        (i) Withdraw the safety pin.

        (ii) Pull the lever which lets down the trap doors.

12. The body will be carefully raised from the pit as soon as the Medical Officer declares life to be extinct. Then the body will be detached from the rope and removed to the place set aside for the Coroner's inspection, a careful record having first been made and given to the Medical Officer of both the initial and final drops. The rope will be removed from the neck, and also the straps from the body. In laying out the body for the inquest the head will be raised three inches by placing a small piece of wood under it.

Records of an Execution carried out in

Particulars of the condemned Prisoner.	Particulars of the Execution.
Name	The length of the drop, as determined before the execution. feet inches. 6 7
Register Number 2006	The length of the drop, as measured after the execution, from the level of the floor of the scaffold to the heels of the suspended culprit. feet inches. 6 8 $\frac{1}{4}$
Sex Male	Cause of death [(a) Dislocation of vertebræ, (b) Asphyxia.] Fracture dislocation between 3rd & 4th Cervical vertebræ with tearing of the cord.
Age 23	
Height 5'6"	
Build Spare but muscular.	Approximate statement of the character and amount of destruction to the soft and bony structures of the neck. Fairly considerable bruising to soft tissues of neck but relatively little to skin, apart from bruise behind left ear. Bone damage entirely localised to site of fracture dislocation.
Weight in clothing (to be taken on the day preceding the execution) 150.	If there were any peculiarities in the build or condition of the prisoner, or in the structure of his neck, which necessitate departure from the scale of drops, particulars should be stated
Character of the prisoner's neck Muscular, thick set.	

Records respecting the Executioner and his Assistants (if any).

—	Name and Address, in full, of the Executioner.	Name and Address, in full, of the 1st Assistant to the Executioner (if any).	Name and Address, in full, of the 2nd Assistant to the Executioner (if any).
	A. Pierrepoint 303 Manchester Rd Hollinwood Nr. Manchester Lancs.	Stephen Wade Edendale Doncaster Rd Edenthorpe Nr. Doncaster Yorks Sidney Dernley 10 Sherwood Rise Mansfield Woodhouse, Mansfield, NoHS.	Harry Kirk ℅ Black Horse Inn Elton Peterborough Northants 3rd assistant Herbert Allen 352 Alwold Rd Selly Oak Birmingham

OPINION of the Governor and Medical Officer as to the manner in which each of the above-named persons has performed his duty.

. Has he performed his duty satisfactorily ?	1.	1.	1. 1
2. Was his general demeanour satisfactory during the period that he was in the prison, and does he appear to be a respectable person ?	2.	2.	2. 2
3. Has he shown capacity, both physical and mental, for the duty, and general suitability for the post ?	3.	3.	3. 3
4. Is there any ground for supposing that he will bring discredit upon his office by lecturing, or by granting interviews to persons who may seek to elicit information from him in regard to the execution or by any other act ?	4.	4.	4. 4
5. Are you aware of any circumstances occurring before, at, or after the execution which tend to show that he is not a suitable person to employ on future occasions either on account of incapacity for performing the duty, or the likelihood of his creating public scandal before or after an execution ?	5.	5.	5. 6

Marshall A.B. Fenton
M.O.

LIST OF CANDIDATES REPORTED TO BE COMPETENT FOR THE OFFICE OF EXECUTIONER, OR WHO HAVE ACTED AT EXECUTIONS

Name and Address	Remarks
Thomas William Pierrepoint Town End Clayton Bradford Yorks	Has satisfactorily conducted executions, has assisted at executions, and has been practically trained at Pentonville Prison
Robert Orridge Baxter 10 Balfour Street Hertford Herts	Has satisfactorily conducted executions, has assisted at executions, and has been practically trained at Pentonville Prison
Robert Wilson 15 Barnard Road Gorton Mount Estate Gorton Manchester	Has assisted at executions, and has been practically trained at Pentonville Prison
Thomas Mather Phillips 208 Albert Road Farnworth Bolton Lancs	Has assisted at executions, and has been practically trained at Pentonville Prison
Lionel S Mann 91 Milkstone Road Rochdale Lancs	Has assisted at executions, and has been practically trained at Pentonville Prison
Henry Pollard 15 Longfield Street Blackburn Lancs	Has assisted at executions, and has been practically trained at Pentonville Prison
Alfred Allen 2 Park Street South Blakenhall Wolverhampton	Has assisted at executions, and has been practically trained at Pentonville Prison

Dated March 1930

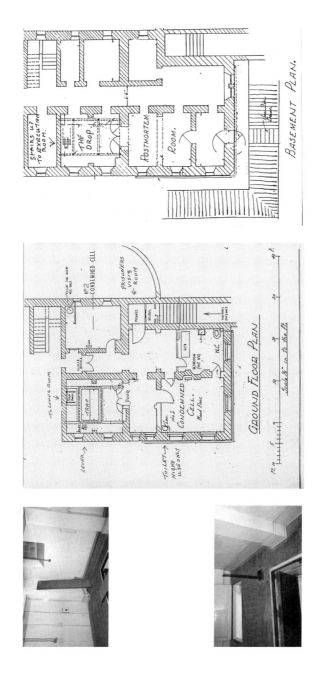

The execution chamber at Wandsworth prison, and plans of a typical 20th century execution suite

LIST OF CANDIDATES REPORTED TO BE COMPETENT FOR THE OFFICE OF EXECUTIONER, OR WHO HAVE ACTED AT EXECUTIONS

Name and Address	Remarks
Albert Pierrepoint 303 Manchester Rd, Hollinwood Nr Manchester, Lancs	Has satisfactorily conducted executions, has assisted at executions, and has been practically trained at Pentonville Prison
Stephen Wade Edendale Doncaster Road, Edenthorpe Nr Doncaster Yorks	Has satisfactorily conducted executions, has assisted at executions, and has been practically trained at Pentonville Prison
Harry Kirk Black Horse Inn Elton Peterborough Northants	Has assisted at executions, and has been practically trained at Pentonville Prison
Harry B Allen Rawson Arms Hotel Farnworth Bolton Lancs	Has assisted at executions, and has been practically trained at Pentonville Prison
Sydney Dernley 10 Sherwood Rise Mansfield Woodhouse, Mansfield Notts	Has assisted at executions, and has been practically trained at Pentonville Prison
Herbert Allen 352 Alwold Road Selly Oak Birmingham	Has assisted at executions, and has been practically trained at Pentonville Prison

Dated July 1950

LIST OF CANDIDATES REPORTED TO BE COMPETENT FOR THE OFFICE OF EXECUTIONER, OR WHO HAVE ACTED AT EXECUTIONS

Name and Address	Remarks
Harry Bernard Allen Junction Hotel, Whitefield Nr Manchester, Lancs	Has satisfactorily conducted executions, has assisted at executions, and has been practically trained at Pentonville Prison
Robert Leslie Stewart 2 Birchenlea Street Chadderton, Oldham Lancs	Has satisfactorily conducted executions, has assisted at executions, and has been practically trained at Pentonville Prison
Royston Lawrence Rickard x x x Kent	Has assisted at executions, and has been practically trained at Pentonville Prison
Harry Frank Robinson x x x Staffs	Has assisted at executions, and has been practically trained at Pentonville Prison
Samuel Barrass Plant x x x Berks	Has assisted at executions, and has been practically trained at Wandsworth Prison
John Edward Underhill x x Berks	Has assisted at executions, and has been practically trained at Wandsworth Prison

Dated August 1964

<u>Execution of No: 5194 - Roy Gregory @ 9 a.m. on 3/1/34.</u>

The Staff will come on duty at 7-0 a.m. and the usuual winter
time table will be observed.

Officer McWean and Temporary Officer Lilley will come on duty at
7-0 a.m. and remain on duty in the Condemned Cell until 8-25 a.m. when
they will go off duty. The Former will return about 10-30 a.m. to
settle with the Steward, and return to Feltham on the 12-5 p.m. London
train.

All prisoners will go to exercise except the sick, none of whom
will remain in "D" Wing or the South Side of "A" Wing.

At 8-25 a.m. Officer Adams and Hospital Officer Lilleywhite
will take over the charge of the condemned convict and remain with him
until the Execution is over.

The following Officers will be detailed for duty as follows:

Engineer Morris will come on duty at 7-0 a.m. and take over the
charge of the scaffold and remain there until the execution is over. He
will see that the Executioner and Assistant Executioner do not enter the
Prison except via the Officers' Mess Room.

Chief Officer will first satisfy himself that the Door leading
from "D" Wing to Condemned Cell is treble locked and that it is not used.
He will then proceed to the condemned cell via the Officers' Mess Room
and see that all is in order and shortly before 9-0 a.m. he will report
to the Governor that all is in readiness. He will then return to the
Condemned Cell and await the arrival of Governor, Sheriff and others
attending the Execution. On instructions from the Sheriff he will then
open the Condemned Cell for the Executioner to enter.

After the Execution he will see that all doors leading to the
Scaffold etc. are safely locked and will be present when the body is

xxviii

of the Prison.

Officer Boocock will be responsible that no prisoner is anywhere
in the vicinity of the Condemned Cell from 8-45 a.m. till after the body
is taken down at 10-0 a.m..

Hospital Officer Blake will be in attendance on the Medical
Officer, *at 10-0 am, will stretched*.

Officer Lightfoot will attend at the Gate at 8-45 a.m. to await
the arrival of the Sheriff and conduct him to the Governor's Office.

Officers Worsnop and Hughes will attend the Scaffold at 10-0 a.
and carry out the duties laid out in standing orders 185 (1) and subsequently attend the funeral. *(1)+(2)*

The Gatekeeper will be instructed that no one will be admitted
to the Prison under any circumstances *after 8.50 am other than* the Sheriff
~~until after his departure.~~

The Inquest will be held at 11-0 a.m. and shortly before that
hour the Chief Officer will attend at the Gate and take charge of the
Coroner's Officer and the Jury.

The funeral will take place at 2-0 p.m. and shortly before tha
hour the Rev. D. Tudor Jones will be in readiness at the Chief Officer's
Office and on receipt of a message from one of the burial party will
proceed to the door leading from underneath the Centre to "B" Exercise
Yard from whence the funeral will proceed.

The door leading from the Kitchen Stokehold – opposite the
Officers' Mess Room will be double locked at ~~6-30~~ *7-0* a.m. and remain so
locked until 3-0 p.m..

The Chief Officer will impress upon all members of the Staff
that nothing should be done to give the prisoners the impression that

<u>Witness, of First Execution</u>

November 26<u>th</u> 1940

Name.

    William Henry Cooper.

Height.   5 Feet 5½ inches.

Age.   24 years, Weight. 136 lbs

Drop. 8 Feet - 1. inch.

    <u>Remarks.</u>

Very good and a clean
job carried out at Bedford
by Mr Thomas W. Pierrepoint

    <u>Personell</u>
The culprit had to be
carried to the scaffold owing
to faintness and loss of
curage but met untill the
same morning, He played dominos
and cards untill 10.0 PM the
proceeding night with the wa.ders.

XXX

'Capital Punishment Amendment Act, 1868'

(31 & 32 *Vict. c. 24, s. 7*)

The sentence of the law passed

upon _DEREK WILLIAM BENTLEY_

found guilty of murder, will be

carried into execution at _9_ a.m.

to-morrow.

C R Wigan Under Sheriff of _THE COUNTY OF SURREY_

Governor.

27th JANUARY. 1953

WANDSWORTH Prison.

No. 278

(C23368—6) 100 3/48

xxxi

CERTIFICATE OF SURGEON

(31 Vict. Cap. 24)

I, _Samuel Hunter Lee doel_ the Surgeon of His Majesty's Prison of _WANDSWORTH_ hereby

certify that I this day examined the Body of

DEREK WILLIAM BENTLEY, on whom Judgment of

Death was this day executed in the said Prison;

and that on that Examination I found that the

said _DEREK WILLIAM BENTLEY_ was dead.

Dated this _28ᵗʰ_ day of _JANUARY, 1953_

(Signature) _Jas H. un. doel._

No. 279

(40317) Wt.47776/20 250 8/50 A.& E.W.Ltd. Gp.685

DECLARATION OF SHERIFF

AND OTHERS

(31 Vict. Cap. 24)

We, the undersigned, hereby declare that

Judgement of Death was this Day executed on

DEREK WILLIAM BENTLEY in ~~His~~ *Her* Majesty's Prison of

WANDSWORTH _____ in our presence.

Dated this 28ᵗʰ _____ day of JANUARY, 1953 _____

C.N.B. ~~jan Undon~~ /Sheriff of COUNTY OF SURREY

_____ Justice of the Peace

_____ for _____

_____ Governor of the said Prison.

_____ Dep/Chaplain of the said Prison.

No. 280

(40317) Wt.47776/20 250 3/50 A.& E.W.Ltd. Gp.685

All Communications
to be addressed to
G. L. B. LIGHTFOOT,
UNDER SHERIFF

TEL. NOS.—23525-6
YOUR REF.:
MY REF.:   GLSL

UNDER SHERIFF'S OFFICE
21 CASTLE STREET
CARLISLE

9th July, 1957

Dear Sir,

          3900 John Willson Vickers
                Capital Murder

          With reference to my letter dated 3rd June, I have now
been informed that the Court of Criminal Appeal has dismissed
the prisoner's appeal.

          In these circumstances the High Sheriff of Cumberland
has fixed the execution for Tuesday 23rd July 1957 at
9 a.m. at Durham Prison and I shall be glad to know that
you can undertake the duties of executioner. On this
assumption, I enclose two copies of a Memorandum of
Conditions to which any person acting as executioner is
required to conform. On the back of one copy is an
acknowledgment that you have received it. I shall be glad
if you will sign and date this acknowledgment and return
it to me in the enclosed stamped addressed envelope.

          Provided there is no reprieve the High Sheriff and
myself will be arriving at the prison on the afternoon of
22nd July and no doubt I shall have an opportunity of
seeing you in order to ascertain that everything is in
order.

          Should there be a reprieve I shall at once notify you
by telegram when the matter will, of course, be cancelled.

                    Yours faithfully,

                    Lionel Shipyard

Mr H.B. Allen,
Junction Hotel,
Whitefield,
Nr. Manchester.

Notice of execution posted outside Manchester Prison, 1936

H.M. Prison **Leeds**

26th April 19 **61**

Register No. **38131**   Name   **Zsiga PANKOTAI**

Court and Place   **Leeds Assize**

Date   **26/4/61**

Crime   **Capital Murder**

Date of Reception on conviction   **26/4/61**

Probable date of carrying out sentence   *Provisionally arranged for 17.5.61, but Pankotai appealed on 28.4.61.*

1.

The Commissioners,

I beg to report that the above-named prisoner has been received into this prison under sentence of death, and to request that I may be furnished with the list of candidates reported to be competent for the office of executioner, together with copies of the records as to the conduct and efficiency of each of them, with a view to their transmission to the High Sheriff, as directed in Standing Orders. I beg also to apply for a copy of the memorandum of instructions for carrying out the details of an execution; also for a copy of the table of drops.

Govern~~o~~r.

2.

The Governor,

_____ LEEDS _____ Prison.

(a) Your attention is specially directed to the Memorandum dated 26.10.36, in the enclosed packet of forms, and also to Standing Order 170(2). Any unused forms should be returned to this office.   11-1(2)

The object of supplying the information to the Secretary of State is to help in reviewing the case. Everything should be done, therefore, to supply every detail; and the Medical Officer should report on the mental and physical condition of the prisoner while under his observation, calling attention to anything which may have been brought forward at the trial bearing on the prisoner's condition.

The Commissioners desire you personally to satisfy yourself that the instructions are carefully and promptly carried out in every detail.

(b) The services of   *hm. H. F. Robinson*   are recommended for employment as Assistant Executioner.

(c) If the execution is to take place at 9 a.m., the Commissioners request that you will arrange for the usual prison routine to be followed during the time of execution so that prisoners will be scattered over the prison at their respective tasks. Their minds will be occupied; and any noise caused by the trap-doors should pass unnoticed.

The following arrangements are suggested:-

Early morning exercise as usual; associated labour at 8.35 a.m. Prisoners normally employed near the execution shed given a period of additional exercise in a yard remote from it and the prison clock chime disconnected for the hour of nine. The executioners lodged so that they neither have to enter the prison nor cross the yards.

(d) If the Medical Officer considers any Young Prisoner in your custody is likely to be affected adversely by the execution, he should submit a report on the prisoner stating fully his reasons for such an opinion in order that the Commissioners may consider the advisability of transferring the prisoner.

(e) Please inform the Assistant Executioner that he will be eligible for reasonable travelling expenses. Taxi fares will only be payable when public transport is not available.

Please inform the Assistant Executioner that he will be eligible for reasonable travelling expenses. Taxi fares will only be payable when public transport is not available.

With reference to A.1939/86 dated 11.1.55. please note that during the past twelve months Mr. H.B. Allen has been employed five times and Mr. R.L. Stewart nil times.

for Establishment Officer.
28/4/61.

<u>ORDERS FOR EXECUTING DEATH SENTENCE</u>

ON 15 AUGUST 1963

331/63 HENRY JOHN BURNETT 21 YEARS

<u>SENTENCED TO DEATH AT ABERDEEN HIGH COURT ON 25 JULY 1963</u>

1. <u>CONDEMNED CELL</u>

    As per instructions issued.

2. <u>EXECUTIONERS</u>

    On arrival of Mr Allen and Mr Plant, they will be accommodated in the Chief Officers Room. They will not leave the Prison till after the execution.
    The Engineer Officer will assist the Executioners in their preparation (See SO 177 for detail of particulars required to be supplied).

    A quantity of alcoholic refreshments will be supplied by Aberdeen Corporation.

3. <u>ROUTINE FOR DAY OF EXECUTION</u>

    The duty roster for the day will be adjusted to meet requirements. Normal routine will be followed as far as possible but the following adjustments will be made:-

    Double staff on gate duty till 10 am.
    All liberations will be made before 7 am.
    All prisoners, including cooks and works prisoners (locked up by 7.30 am).
    It is expected that normal work will commence about 9.30 am.
    Orderly room will be held at 12 noon.
    The CO and PO will arrange their duties for the day to fit requirements.
    Prisoner Burnett's own clothing will be put to the Condemned cell, the night before (except collar and tie).

4. <u>STAFF PRESENT AT EXECUTION</u>

    The Governor.
    The Medical Officer.
    The Chaplain.
    Chief Officer.
    Engineer Officer.
    Nurse Officer.
    Escort - 2 Officers (Aberdeen Prison Staff) to take over at 7.30 am.

    The Chief Officer will check the exact time.

5. <u>STIMULANTS</u>

    At about 7.30 am the prisoner may be offered a stimulant on the Medical Officer's instructions.

6. CITY MAGISTRATES ATTENDING

The officials attending (Baillies Stephen and Middleton and Deputy Chief Constable McQueen) will assemble in the Governor's Office and will be conducted to the Execution chamber at 7.57 am.
After the execution they will be conducted back to the Governor's Office.
Should a stimulant be required Aberdeen Corporation will provide.

The Chief Officer will look all entrances to Execution Chamber.

7. BURIAL

The grave will be dug by free workmen as arranged with the Engineer Officer and the Superintendent of the Links and Parks. Work will commence at 2 pm on 14 August 1963 and will be supervised by the EO. The grave will be dug in the recess between the pit room and the staff room toilets.
The same free workmen will attend the Prison at 8.30 am on the day of the execution to complete the burial.
Prisoner will be buried in his own clothes.
The Engineer Officer will arrange for Officers to carry the coffin to the grave.

It is the responsibility of the Governor to arrange for the coffin. Town Clerk will advise.

8. MOTOR CARS AT GATE

No cars will be permitted to park on the entrance drive from 7.30 am till 9 am. Cars carrying officials will enter the Prison and park inside.

9. EXCUSED DUTY OFFICERS

Officer on loan to be returned to their respective Prisons at a convenient time after the last tour of duty.

The 2 Officers who act as escort at the execution will be excused further duties for the day.

10. PRISONERS PROPERTY

All letters and papers (other than legal documents eg. a will) will be destroyed by burning in the furnace.

Prisoner's other property, less clothing in which he was buried will be disposed of in accordance with SO 14.

11. REPORTS   The Department in Accordance with SO 14

To Procurator Fiscal for Public Enquiry to be held in Sheriff Court on the afternoon of 15 August. Governor, Medical Officer and Chief Officer called to attend.

Robert Orridge Baxter

Thomas William Pierrepoint

The Executioners

At a time when Parliament was discussing whether to abolish capital punishment, the first execution in the new decade was one of the most notorious, when Sydney Fox went to the gallows for the murder of his mother. Long serving hangman **Robert Orridge Baxter** of Hertford carried out the sentence, the last at Maidstone prison. Baxter carried out one execution in Gibraltar in July 1931 and was still living in the Hertford area when he left the list of approved hangmen in 1935. Research suggests that ill health and failing eyesight brought about the end of his career. He died in a nursing home in the early 1960s.

Thomas William Pierrepoint was in his 24th year as a hangman when the 1930s began, and for twenty years he had been serving as a chief executioner. In a rare interview in February 1930 during a debate on abolition, Pierrepoint said: '*Why should a murderer be nursed for the rest of his life? I think it would be encouraging people to murder if the death penalty were abolished. It makes no difference to me either way.*'
It was Pierrepoint who hanged most of the infamous criminals in the years prior to the Second World War . He also hanged many of the spies captured during the war and all the American servicemen hanged at Shepton Mallet, but by the end of the war it was clear that his young nephew had taken over his role as chief.

Tom Pierrepoint retired in 1946, shortly after the death of his wife, Lizzy. He was 76 years old when he hung up his ropes, evidently much against his will. He participated in around 300 executions, over 260 as chief executioner. It was reported that he became surly in his old age and more than one Governor's report after an execution mentioned this. Tom had been working in a local foundry since his sixtieth birthday, after giving up his carter's business. He died on 10th February 1954, at the home of his only daughter.

Thomas Mather Phillips had been an assistant hangman since 1922. During the 1930s he was present at a number of infamous executions before he graduated to chief executioner in 1939. He assisted Tom Pierrepoint in the execution of the two IRA men in 1940 and was at the helm again a month later, when he was assisted by Albert Pierrepoint. It appears his conduct was questioned by the Governor at this execution, carried out at Wandsworth in March 1940, who reported that Phillips demanded more beer on the night prior to the execution, and he became surly and angry when his request was refused. A report was sent to the Home Office and Phillips's career as a hangman ended. He had moved to London from his home in Bolton, shortly before the war, but returned north during the blitz, with his hanging days over, settling in Rochdale where he died aged 51, one year to the day after his last execution.

Thomas Mather Phillips

Of all the assistant hangmen on the list in 1930, the one with the shortest amount of service was **Alfred Allen** of Wolverhampton, yet it was he who was the first to be promoted when he carried out an execution as chief in November 1932. Records show that Fred, as he was known, had assisted at barely a dozen jobs before his promotion. He reverted back to assistant throughout the mid 1930s but was twice more called to officiate, once in 1936, and again a year later. He carried out his last job in August 1937 and then disappeared. Relatives are uncertain when he died, but it is thought to have been around 1938.

Robert Wilson had been on the list since 1920 and was to serve for a period of eighteen years without rising to chief executioner. Few of his later jobs made the national headlines and although his name appears on a list of hangmen for 1939, his last recorded execution was in the spring of 1937, and I am led to believe that he died around this time.

Lionel S. Mann had been on the list since 1925. In 1931, his employers at a Rochdale factory told him that his 'other job' was holding back his chances of promotion. His most famous execution was probably assisting Baxter at the execution of Sydney Fox in April 1930. A year later, after helping Baxter hang Newman and Shelley, he tendered his resignation.

Henry Pollard was a native of Blackburn and had joined the list at the same time as Mann. Pollard lasted on the list until 1937 when he too died without ever rising above rank of assistant. Pollard's most infamous customer in the later years was probably Reginald Hinks, but his best days had been in the previous decade when he helped to dispatch many notable villains.

In 1932 two men graduated from Pentonville's hangman's training school. Fulham born **Stanley William Cross** was the elder of the two and the first to be called into action as a second and non-participating assistant in November 1932, in what was Fred Allen's first execution. Cross gained regular work throughout the country, including such engagements as child killer Frederick Nodder, George Brain and the two IRA men hanged in 1940.

Cross received promotion in July 1940 when he hanged Udham Singh at Pentonville. Cross was back in action in December 1940, when he carried out a double execution at Pentonville, with Albert Pierrepoint again amongst his assistants, and he also hanged another spy a week later. He assisted Tom Pierrepoint on several jobs throughout 1941 and I believe that he died later that year opening the door for his training partner, **Albert Pierrepoint.**

Albert Pierrepoint was born in Clayton, Bradford, in 1905. He decided at an early age to follow in his father's footsteps and applied to join the list of approved executioners in 1931. Pierrepoint first assisted his uncle at Dublin shortly after Christmas 1932 and carried out his first job (as 2nd assistant) at Birmingham in February 1933 when he helped his uncle and Robert Wilson hang Jeremiah Hanbury. Pierrepoint refers to Hanbury as Gerald Hutchins in his book.

It is fair to say that Albert Pierrepoint did get more than his share of work leading up to the war, but much of it was at the personal invitation of his uncle who was allowed to select his own assistant over in Ireland. Pierrepoint carried out his first senior execution on 31st October 1941, when he hanged London gangster Antonio Mancini at Pentonville.

Albert Pierrepoint

Albert Pierrepoint has gone into the history books as the most famous modern day executioner. It is true that the total count of his executions, over 400, far outnumbers that of his contemporaries; this is due to him carrying out a great deal of work in mainland Europe after the war crimes trials.

Pierrepoint left the list in July 1955 and the reason for his departure has long been the subject of speculation. Numerous reasons for his leaving have been bandied about, many ridiculous such as that he was removed from the list so he could not reveal the last words of Ruth Ellis, or that he was asked to resign after word reached the Home Office that he had agreed to accept a hefty payment for his memoirs. Once it was learned that he planned to write his life story, steps were taken to limit the contents as he was still bound by the official secrets act.

The main reason for his resignation was that Pierrepoint was engaged to execute a man at Manchester prison in early January 1956; the journey from his home at Much Hoole, Preston, to Strangeways was a little under 20 miles. After rigging the drop and settling into his quarters word reached the prison that the man had been reprieved. Regulations at the time meant the hangman did not receive any fee for a reprieve. Pierrepoint objected and wrote to the Home Office. They made an offer of money for expenses which Pierrepoint dismissed as derisory and he tendered his resignation in February 1956, shortly before the newspaper serialisation began.

He published his life story in book form in 1974 when he came down on the side of the abolitionists. He appeared on television on a number of occasions and was good for a few column inches in the popular press whenever the subject of capital punishment was raised. (He retired from running a public house in the late 1960s and moved to a bungalow in Southport.) He died in a Southport nursing home in July 1992.

Doncaster motor coach dealer **Stephen (Steve) Wade** was Pierrepoint's only rival between the late 1940s and 1955. Wade had applied for the position in 1918, after coming out of the army, because, in his words, he hated murder. He was twenty-one at the time and was told by the prison authorities that he was too young for the position. Resolutely, he made subsequent applications through the next 20 years before finally being accepted for training shortly after the outbreak of the war, presumably following the deaths of Wilson and Pollard.

'I was never nervous,' he once wrote, 'it's a job which needs a special type of temperament. You're either fit to do it or you're not. And you soon find out!'

Wade attended a training course at Pentonville in the summer of 1940 along with three other would-be hangmen, all of whom went on to have long careers on the list. He witnessed his first job in the winter of 1940; among the first of his engagements was to help hang George Armstrong, the first Briton hanged for treason during the war.

Three months later he assisted Albert Pierrepoint on his first job as senior executioner and he also assisted Albert a few weeks later when they hanged Karel Richter, the spy whom Pierrepoint later recalled had given him his most difficult experience on the scaffold. This is Wade's account of this execution.

Execution good in the circumstances. 8.58am.
On entering cell to take prisoner over and pinion him he
made a bolt for the door. I warded him off and he then
charged the wall at a terrific force with his head. This
made him even more violent. We seized him and strapped

his arms at rear.

This new strap was faulty, not enough eyelet holes and he broke away from them. I shouted to Albert he is loose and he was held by warders until we made him secure. He could not take it and again charged for the wall screaming 'help me!'

Had to drag him to the scaffold and he then tried to get to the opposite wall over the trap with legs splayed. I drew them together and could see Albert going to the lever. I shouted 'wait - strap on legs and down he goes'. As the rope was fixed around his neck he shook his neck and the safety ring – too big – shifts. Noose slackens and in the drop the eyelet catches underneath his nose. Neck broken immediately. 9-15am hanged. I said I would not miss this execution for £50 and well worth it!

Steve Wade

In March 1946 Steve Wade was promoted to number one when he replaced Tom Pierrepoint as the hangman for Durham prison. He was also the assistant on Tom Pierrepoint's last job in England. Wade took over as the regular number one at Leeds in the following year and was a regular assistant to Albert Pierrepoint in Scotland. Once Wade had gained promotion he stopped receiving letters to assist, and for some years during the early 1950s he was called into action on only one or two occasions.

Wade was promoted to the country's chief executioner when Albert Pierrepoint resigned in February 1956, but a combination of illness, failing eyesight and the temporary suspension of all executions saw the end of his career. He retired through ill health in the spring of 1956 and died in December of that year, aged 59.

Herbert Morris was a Blackpool man who had joined the list in

1938. I am led to believe he worked as a taxi driver during the war and he was present on a couple of jobs per year up to 1946. It appears he retired in 1946 and I have seen a letter written by one hangman to another, dated 1951, which states: ' I see that Morris has applied and been re-instated on the list'. This is contrary to Albert Pierrepoint's claim that once a hangman left the list, for whatever reason, he was never again invited back. This may have applied in his case, but it is clear that other men did rejoin the list.

Morris briefly came out of retirement and assisted at the execution of Griffin at Shrewsbury in 1951, but this was his last job and he disappeared from the list soon after.

Another northern assistant who appeared on the list prior to the war was Mancunian **Alexander Riley**. Riley had a lean start, only carrying out one job per year in the early war years before he was offered one of the most prestigious jobs in the post-war years when he helped dispatch traitor William 'Lord Haw-Haw' Joyce. He carried out a handful of other jobs and finished in 1946. I am told he was a deeply religious man who would often pray before carrying out an execution.

Henry William Critchell had passed out from the same intake of trainees as Steve Wade in 1940. He lived at Pimlico, London and was present at many infamous cases throughout the war years. Critchell helped Stanley Cross hang the first of his spies and assisted both Tom and Albert Pierrepoint. His last job was to help assist Steve Wade in 1948, after which it was recorded that for some reason he was sacked. He told a fellow assistant shortly before the end of his short but hectic career that: 'the damage this job has done me, no doctor can repair'. He gave a newspaper interview prior to the execution of Ruth Ellis and claimed he was now anti-hanging.

Like Steve Wade and Henry Critchell, **Harry Kirk** also graduated from Pentonville in the summer of 1940. Kirk was a publican from Elton, near Peterborough, and ran the Black Horse between 1942 and 1954. Kirk's

Henry William Critchell

first official engagement was as an observer in October 1940, and he was present as a working assistant for the first time later that year.

After a quiet start Kirk was a busy assistant during the war, helping both Pierrepoints on many occasions. Kirk later claimed that he helped hang 22 Yanks in one morning at Shepton Mallett, but research has shown that this was untrue. He was also used as an assistant when Albert Pierrepoint went over to Gibraltar to hang two saboteurs, but his best known executions were assisting Albert Pierrepoint at the hangings of Neville Heath and John Haigh.

During the late 1940s, Kirk became the most senior assistant and in November 1950, when both Albert Pierrepoint and Steve Wade were engaged elsewhere, he was promoted to number one for an execution at Norwich. Trying to emulate the speed of Pierrepoint, Kirk misplaced the white bag over the condemned man's head and as a result it became caught up in the noose when the drop fell. Kirk's assistant recalled that the hanged man made a groaning noise from the pit, but otherwise the execution was carried out satisfactorily and the prisoner died from a broken neck. Kirk never officiated again after this incident and died of cancer in 1967.

There was another influx of would-be hangmen in 1949, when three trainees passed out together from the Pentonville training school. The first to receive a call into action was **George Dickinson**, a Manchester-based chemical worker. Dickinson was present at the double execution at Swansea at the beginning of August, and according to Pierrepoint the job had traumatised him to the extent that he became ill on the journey home. Possibly as a result of this experience, he rejected the offer to hang John Haigh a week later and swiftly retired from the list. He later emigrated to Canada.

Herbert Allen was a Wolverhampton based ice-cream man who succeeded in becoming an assistant after making many unsuccessful applications. Although he shared the same surname and home town as a hangman from the 1930s, Alfred Allen, I have been unable to find out if they were related. Research suggests not. Neither were they related to the other Mr Allen, Harry, who became chief executioner in the 1950s.

During the next 18 months Herbert Allen assisted both Albert Pierrepoint and Steve Wade on half a dozen jobs before being told by his employers that 'ice-cream and hangings don't mix!' He resigned and then made an unsuccessful attempt to become re-instated. His most famous execution was that of Herbert Mills, which also appears to be his last.

Sydney Dernley was a Mansfield collier who also became a hangman in 1949. Most people interested in this subject will have read Syd's excellent autobiography The Hangman's Tale, published in 1989, which gives a terrific insight into the training of a would-be hangman. Freed from many Home Office restrictions, following a change in the secrecy laws, Syd and his co-author recount the crimes and last moments of many condemned men in a way Pierrepoint never could.

Syd Dernley's last execution was in 1952 and although he received offers of engagements up to 1954, Syd believed his career as a hangman effectively ended when he made a tasteless remark after an execution. His career ended in fact when he was convicted of a minor offence at Nottingham Assizes in April 1954. During the 1960s he became a postmaster in his home town of Mansfield and regularly appeared at lectures and on television promoting his book after his retirement. He died at his Mansfield bungalow on 1 November 1994.

Sydney Dernley

Harry Smith became a hangman in 1950. He lived for a time in the same Doncaster street as Steve Wade and it is not unreasonable to assume that friendship between the two may have been instrumental in Smith applying to join the list. Smith carried out his first execution in the summer of 1951 and in the following year he was present at five executions assisting both Pierrepoint and Wade.

The highlight in Smith's 10-year career took place in July 1953 when he helped Pierrepoint hang Christie at Pentonville, while most of his other work was with Wade at Leeds prison. He assisted at executions in Cyprus and resigned in 1959.

Harry Smith and Harry Allen
at an execution in Cyprus

Two new assistants were added to the list in 1953: Yorkshireman **John Broadbent** and **Royston Rickard** of Kent. Broadbent assisted at just a handful of jobs, the most notable of which was Whiteway 'The Teddington Rapist', before his short career ended sometime during 1954, when he offered his resignation. He was still alive in the late 1990s.

I am led to believe that Rickard was a publican and of all the latter-day assistants, his record of engagements is second to none. Amongst the names in his diary are such notorious killers as Hepper; Ruth Ellis; police killer Podola; and Forsyth, 'The Hounslow Footpath Murderer'. Rickard was also in action in August 1964 and his career was only ended when the Government abolished the death penalty. He too may still be alive and living in retirement.

Harry Bernard Allen had been an assistant hangman for 15 years before he was promoted following the resignation of Albert Pierrepoint. He was born in Yorkshire in 1911, but grew up in Ashton-under-Lyne, Manchester. He received his training alongside Wade, Critchell and Kirk and carried out his first jobs in early 1941.

For a period during the war Harry Allen left the list, presumably due to his other wartime work as a bus driver, but he was invited back in 1945. This gap put him behind Steve Wade and Harry Kirk who both rose to the top of their profession before Harry.

Harry Bernard Allen

On 25 October 1955, Harry Allen was promoted to chief executioner and his first jobs as chief were in Cyprus when a number of executions were carried under the authorisation of the British Government. He carried out his first job in Great Britain at Durham in July 1957 when, after an 18 month period, hanging was brought back for certain types of murder under the newly passed 'Homicide Act'. As the entries in the book show, Harry Allen carried out the vast majority of latter day executions and was still on call up to the late 1960s before the abolition bill was finally passed. He continued to receive offers to carry out executions throughout the commonwealth until the late 1970s, but his last execution was at Manchester in 1964.

Like several of his predecessors Harry Allen was also a publican, running a number of successful houses in the Lancashire area. He retired to Fleetwood with his second wife Doris, making the occasional television appearance. He was also the last hangman to model for Madame Tussuards and for many years his wax figure stood in the '*chamber of horrors*' next to several of his customers, including the A6 murderer Hanratty.

Harry Allen at Madame Tussaud's in the 1960s. The murderers include Neville Heath (1946), James Hanratty (1962), John Haigh (1949), Buck Ruxton (1936) (seated)

Harry Allen died after a short illness in August 1992. There is no truth in the popular misconception that he collapsed while dressing to attend Albert Pierrepoint's funeral. Press reports from the late 1950s and early 1960s state that Harry was often assisted by his son, **Brian Allen**. During research into his father's background I spoke at length with Brian Allen and he has denied that this was the case. Newspaper reports in Scotland however, name him as the assistant hangman at the execution of Peter Manuel.

Harry Allen's chief rival during the late 1950s was Edinburgh born **Robert Leslie Stewart**. Jock, as he was known to his fellow hangmen, had joined the list at the same time as Harry Smith in 1950. Stewart had had a long-standing ambition to be a hangman and when his wife took a job at Albert Pierrepoint's public house, the two became friends and Pierrepoint advised him of the appropriate steps to take to achieve his goal.

Stewart assisted Pierrepoint regularly throughout the 1950s, most notably on the execution of Mrs Merrifield. Coincidentally, he was the assistant on both Albert Pierrepoint and Steve Wade's last jobs. On

29 March 1956, he was promoted following the retirement of Steve Wade, but during his short time as number one he was limited mainly to engagements at which Allen could not officiate. This was no criticism of his

Robert Leslie Stewart

skill as a hangman, as the testimony of a prison governor following his first execution showed that in his opinion he had never seen a more efficient execution carried out. Stewart emigrated with his family to South Africa in the mid 1960s, where he found work as an aircraft engineer. He died after a short illness on 1 November 1989.

John Robert Barker of north London graduated from Pentonville in the summer of 1955 and was present as an observer at the execution of Wilkinson at Leeds in August. A long period of inactivity seemed to have caused him to re-think. He was offered the role of assistant executioner in 1958, but wrote back saying he had tendered his resignation to the Home Office.

There were just a handful of assistant executioners who made it onto the official list following the Homicide Act of 1957. **Thomas Cunliffe** of Wigan joined the list in late 1956. He graduated out of Pentonville with another trainee **Harry Frank Robinson**, who was from the Black Country. They were the only two men successful out of six applicants, and both were present as non-participating observers at an execution in Birmingham in 1957. Cunliffe assisted at just four jobs before an unfortunate incident occurred at one execution when he failed to strap the legs of the prisoner and his name was removed from the list. He died at the age of 68 in the 1980s.

Robinson received many engagements, most of which were reprieved, throughout the following years, being regularly paired with Jock Stewart. By the turn of the century he was living in retirement, his past life on the scaffold a secret from even his immediate family.

Thomas Cunliffe

From 1960, would-be hangmen were henceforth trained at Wandsworth and the last two graduates were both from the Berkshire area.

John Edward Underhill was a former soldier who had experience at executions during active service overseas. Opportunities were few once he had joined the Home Office list, although I am told his actual experience surpassed even that of Jock Stewart, having carried out many jobs as chief executioner in the Far East during the 1950s. In the late 1990s Underhill was still alive and living overseas.

The other assistant was **Samuel Barrass Plant**. He too carried out just a handful of jobs, but was present at executions in both Scotland and Northern Ireland. He was not involved in the last executions in England.

All the remaining hangmen and assistants stayed on call until well into the 1960s and none were ever informed that their services would no longer be needed. The last men convicted of capital murder were removed from the death cells in November 1965 and capital punishment was finally abolished in 1969.

Of the former executioners known to be still alive, there is probably only Underhill, in his mid-seventies, who could realistically be called upon to resume his duties should capital punishment be returned to the statute book. Yet despite repeated media calls for its re-introduction, the chances of this happening, one would have to imagine, are very slim indeed.

Steve Fielding
January 2005

1930

Cases where no executioner is recorded are multiple executions, and readers are asked to refer to the entries before or after for details of the hangman.

April 8th: Samuel William CUSHNAN (26)   **Belfast**

A farm labourer sentenced to death on 9 March, by Mr Justice Moore at Antrim Assize Court, for the murder of James McCann, a Toomebridge postman, who had been found shot dead in a lonely lane on 16 May 1929. His postbag, containing over £60 in pension money, had been rifled.

Cushnan was convicted largely on circumstantial evidence, but betrayed himself while on remand, when he wrote a letter to his brother from his cell mentioning that a fellow prisoner was going to help him dispose of the money.

He was allowed two trials. At the first, lasting four days, the jury failed to reach a verdict, whilst at the second trial he was sentenced to death twice! When the Lord Chief Justice passed sentence he announced that Cushnan was to be 'hanged on April 8th 1929'. The prisoner was taken from the dock to a holding cell before a court official noticed the mistake. Cushnan was then brought back into court and re-sentenced. He appealed for a reprieve on the grounds of mental anguish at the debacle over the sentencing, but it was quickly dismissed.

Hanged by Tom Pierrepoint and Robert Wilson.

Sydney Harry Fox

April 8th: Sydney Harry FOX (31)   **Maidstone**

A homosexual con-man convicted of the murder of his mother Rosaline (63), who was found dead in a smoke filled room at the Metropole Hotel, Margate, on the night of 23 October 1929. At 20 minutes to midnight, Fox raised the alarm and as fellow guests rushed to help, someone pulled Mrs Fox from the room. She died a few minutes later.

The coroner recorded a verdict of misadventure, but Fox raised suspicions by immediately making efforts to claim insurance monies from a number of policies in his mother's name. One insurance broker noticed that Mrs Fox seemed to have died just in time for her son to claim on an insurance premium he had taken out with their company; it was due to expire the next day. He refused to pay out and contacted the police. After a short investigation they ordered that the body be exhumed.

Pathologist Sir Bernard Spilsbury was called in and he declared that Mrs Fox had died as a result of being strangled. Fox was subsequently charged with her murder.

Fox was tried at Lewes Assizes on 12 March, before Mr Justice Rowlatt. His defence challenged the findings of Dr Spilsbury, who suggested that Fox had got his mother drunk before strangling her in a chair, stuffing newspaper underneath the chair, dousing it with petrol and setting it alight. Fire investigation officers confirmed the fire had been started in this way.

Fox was one of the few people who chose not to appeal against conviction and he was hanged by Robert Baxter and Lionel Mann, allegedly having to be half-carried to the gallows after collapsing through sheer terror.

William Henry Podmore

April 22nd: William Henry PODMORE (29)   **Winchester**

A motor mechanic and small time criminal who battered to death with a hammer Vivian Messiter (58), the owner of a small garage in Southampton, in October 1928. Messiter was an agent for an oil company and it was alleged he was killed after discovering that Podmore, who he knew as Mr Thomas, was defrauding the company. Podmore worked on commission and it was found he was making fictitious sales, earning the commission, and then tampering with the books to cover his tracks.

Messiter's body was found in the locked garage on 10 January 1929, and at first glance it appeared that he had been shot in the head. Pathologist Sir Bernard Spilsbury was called in and later confirmed that Messiter had been battered by the hammer found beside the body. A search of the victim's lodgings found a note with the name of W.F. Thomas, a man already suspected of robbery. Thomas's hideout was traced and police found evidence that suggested his real name was Podmore, a man wanted by the police in Manchester for a similar fraud.

Podmore was arrested and though evidence linking him to the murder was not conclusive, he was strongly suspected. Police charged him with fraud and he was sentenced to six months in prison. Meanwhile police built up a case against him and upon his release he was arrested for murder.

Podmore was convicted before Lord Chief Justice Hewart on 8 March and hanged by Tom Pierrepoint and Alfred Allen, protesting his innocence to the end.

June 11th: Albert Edward MARJERAM (23)   Wandsworth

A labourer sentenced to death for the murder of Edith May Parker (23), who he stabbed to death on Dartford Heath on 11 April, as she was out walking with her sister.

He had never met either girl before and claimed after his arrest, later that same day, that he committed the murder for gain, although it was later found that he hadn't actually stolen anything. He made a statement claiming that he had just purchased a knife for two shillings when he spotted the two girls approaching. 'I never spoke to them - I just up and did it with the knife.... I forget to add the motive, it was robbery. I was out of work and wanted money'.

At his trial at the Old Bailey, before Mr Justice Humphreys, on 22 May, his defence was insanity. Evidence was shown that Marjeram had previously confessed to a murder he hadn't committed. Despite his mother claiming he had endured severe childhood trauma as a result of having an abscess on the brain, the insanity plea was rejected.

He had a history of petty crime and had previously been imprisoned at Maidstone gaol, being released on 5 April, three days before Fox's execution. Hanged by Tom Pierrepoint and Henry Pollard, 60 days after committing a pointless murder.

1931

Cases where no executioner is recorded are multiple executions, and readers are asked to refer to the entries before or after for details of the hangman.

January 3rd: Victor Edward BETTS (21)   Birmingham

Convicted along with Herbert Charles Ridley (21), of the murder of William Thomas Andrews (63), a messenger for a drapery firm in Aston, Birmingham, whom they had planned to rob as he was taking a large sum of money (over £900) to the bank.

On 24 July 1930, they hired a car and with Ridley at the wheel they waited. As Andrews approached, Betts climbed out of the car and tailed him to the street corner adjacent to the bank. He then pushed him to the ground and snatched the takings. Andrews died three days later from a fractured skull sustained in the fall.

A witness gave police a description of the car, which was traced to Ridley whose name was on the hire agreement. It was found soon after and contained the empty money bag; the two men were arrested in Brighton a short time later.

At their trial on 5 December, Ridley's counsel argued that had he known Betts would use force in the robbery Ridley would have played no part in it. Regardless, they were sentenced to death by Mr Commissioner Mitchell-Innes at Warwickshire Assizes.

Both appealed unsuccessfully, but three days before the scheduled double execution Ridley was granted a reprieve, seemingly because, as he was still in the car when the crime was committed, he was not deemed directly responsible for the murder.

Hanged by Tom Pierrepoint and Alfred Allen.

February 4th: Frederick GILL (26)   Leeds

A trolley bus driver convicted on circumstantial evidence of the murder of Oliver Preston, an elderly money lender who was found mortally wounded in his office at Keighley on 25 July 1930. He had been severely beaten with a blunt instrument and died three days later. Missing from the office was over £80, in one pound notes, which had been drawn from the bank the previous day.

Gill, a regular customer of Preston's and recently the subject of a summons for failing to repay money owed, was known to be short of money; but at the end of July he was able to pay back rent and take his girlfriend on holiday to Whitehaven, where he was arrested shortly after the crime was discovered.

The defence at his trial at Leeds Assizes, on 10 December before Mr Justice Talbot, were able to call three witnesses who had seen the victim alive after the time that the prosecution claimed the crime was committed. After a four-day trial Gill was found guilty and sentenced to death.

Hanged by Tom Pierrepoint and Robert Wilson.

March 10th: Alfred Arthur ROUSE (36)   **Bedford**

The Blazing Car Murderer. Rouse was a travelling salesman, convicted of the murder of an unknown man whose body was found inside a burnt out car at Hardingstone, Northamptonshire, on 6 November 1930.

Two young men saw a man walking away from a blaze they assumed was a bonfire. As they approached they found that it was a car ablaze and the heat made it impossible to get near. Fire officers were called and when the fire was extinguished they found the charred remains of a man on the front seat. Despite the car being a burnt out shell, the registration plate was hardly damaged and the car was traced to Rouse who lived in North London. He had travelled to Wales to be with a girlfriend, but when police named him in the newspapers he returned home and offered an explanation.

Alfred Arthur Rouse

Rouse said that he was giving a hitch hiker a lift to Leicester when they ran out of fuel. He then said that he asked the passenger to fill the tank from a spare can of fuel in the boot. Previously the man had asked Rouse for a cigar, and despite being a non-smoker he happened to have one in his pocket. Rouse said he had walked a little way down the road intending to relieve himself behind a bush when he saw the car explode in flames. He said he then panicked and fled, but not before realising that this accident had given him a chance to lose his identity and free himself of his many debts and tangled love life. He then fled to his mistress in South Wales.

At his trial before Mr Justice Talbot at Northampton Assizes, he maintained that the fire was an accident, but on 31 January he was convicted after evidence suggested that the car had been tampered with. His wife stood by him throughout the trial, believing his pleas of innocence. Although not revealed at the time, it was known to the Home Office that Mrs Rouse knew of the plan to commit murder so they could both benefit from a £1,000 insurance policy.

He was hanged by Tom Pierrepoint and Tom Phillips, and his confession appeared in the following morning's paper.

April 16th: Francis LAND (41) Manchester

A boiler fireman from Rochdale, convicted of the murder of Mrs Sarah Ellen Johnson (24) who was found dead in his flat.

In January 1930, Mrs Johnson had separated from her husband and had moved in with Land. On 2 December, she had left him due to him viciously ill-treating her, arriving at a friend's house 'half-dead'. After spending the night there she went to stay with another friend.

On 12 December, Mrs Johnson agreed to meet Land to try to reconcile their differences. At 9pm, they were seen by a friend strolling arm-in-arm, but later that night Sarah was found dead in Land's bedroom with her throat cut. Land had reported the murder, saying he had gone out and returned to find her dead.

At his three-day trial before Mr Justice Charles at Manchester Assizes on 23-25 February, Land claimed he had an alibi for the time of the murder, and this was supported by several witnesses, but he was found guilty.

His appeal on the grounds that the jury had been misdirected was heard at the end of March, but rejected.

Hanged by Tom Pierrepoint.

June 3rd: Alexander ANASTASSIOU (23) Pentonville

A Cypriot waiter sentenced to death at the Old Bailey by Mr Justice Swift on 27 April, for the murder of Evelyn Victoria Holt (22), a waitress from Shepherd's Bush, who was found dead in a room in Warren Street, off Tottenham Court Road, on 26 February.

His defence claimed her death was an accident through self-defence, stating that Miss Holt was an intensely jealous woman and that, following a series of quarrels, Anastassiou had broken off the engagement. On the night of her death she had attacked him with a razor, after he told her he planned to emigrate to America. He said she had sustained her wounds by accident.

The pathologist Sir Bernard Spilsbury was called by the Crown and said that the wounds could not have been self-inflicted, nor was there evidence to suggest anything other than wilful murder. The prisoner then pleaded insanity, but was convicted and sentenced to death.

He lodged an appeal against the conviction - on the same day that William Wallace, the Liverpool man accused of murdering his wife, had his conviction quashed. Anastassiou's appeal was not so fortunate and a few weeks later he was hanged by Robert Baxter and Henry Pollard.

July 31st: Thomas DORNAN (46)   Belfast

A farmer convicted of the murder of two sisters, Isabella and Margaret Aitken, at Newtoncrommelin, Ballymena, County Antrim on 22 May.

Dornan was a married man, an industrious farmer and well-respected member of the community. He had long been friendly with the Aitkens, a neighbouring farming family, and in particular with the youngest daughter 'Bella'. In December 1929, Bella, then aged 18, became pregnant and when the child was born, Dornan admitted to being the father. He agreed to pay a weekly amount of money (six shillings) for the child's upkeep, but almost from the start he was regularly behind with the payments.

It was alleged that on the day of the crime, Dornan had watched the sisters at work before returning home for his gun. Unaware that they were being watched, the girls stacked turf in a field on their farm. Dornan, who it appears was angry after receiving a solicitor's letter regarding the maintenance payments, then walked into the field and fired his gun. James Aitken, their brother, watched helplessly from the opposite field as the two girls tried to flee the advancing Dornan. He hurried to the scene, but as he entered the field he could see Dornan firing shot after shot into their lifeless bodies. Margaret (30) had been shot six times; her younger sister four times.

Dornan was tried before the Lord Chief Justice at Antrim Assizes on 8 July, where it was contended that he committed the crime under 'uncontrollable impulse'.

Hanged by Tom Pierrepoint and Robert Wilson.

August 4th: David O'SHEA (33)   Dublin

On Sunday night, 8 February, Ellen O'Sullivan (24) failed to return to her home at Rathmore, near the Cork and Kerry border. A search failed to find her, but five days later her body was found beneath a bush. Her clothing was ripped away and she had been raped. A pathologist told police she had been a virgin before being battered over the head with a heavy stone and raped, the killer continuing to have sex with her long after she had died.

A trail of her personal belongings was found scattered in adjacent fields, and a month later a bundled parcel, including her underwear, was found near a house owned by O'Shea. Once Ellen's boyfriend had been able to satisfy police of his innocence (by his own admission he had been one of the last to see her alive), suspicion turned to O'Shea, a bachelor farmer who was known to the victim. An item of clothing thought to belong to O'Shea was recovered from close to the body.

O'Shea made a statement saying he had seen a couple walking close to where the girl was found, but did not recognise them. He said he was in bed by 9pm, the time the pathologist deduced was the earliest the murder could have taken place. O'Shea also had scratches on his hand which were thought to have come from the bush used to conceal the body.

He was tried before Mr Justice Hanna on 18 June and after a three-hour deliberation the jury found him guilty, but added a rider that they thought the murder was not premeditated and had been committed during a period of mental abnormality.

Hanged by Tom Pierrepoint.

August 5th: Oliver NEWMAN (61)   Pentonville
William SHELLEY (56)

Two labourers, known as 'Tiggy' (Newman) and 'Moosh' (Shelley), were charged with the murder of Herbert William Ayers (45), known as 'Pigsticker', whose charred body was found on 30 May on a burning refuse dump in Edgware, London.

The two men lived alongside the refuse dump, among a vagrant community who mostly worked as railway labourers or down the nearby sewers. They were constantly in trouble with the police and feared and despised by the local community. Newman and Shelley lived in a rather grand hut for the area, but it was nothing more than a timber shack covered with tarpaulin. They both worked a few miles from the dump and would only return home after drinking themselves into a stupor in the nearby pub.

On 1 June, a resident noticed a human hand protruding from a smouldering pit. He called the police and the remains of a middle-aged man were retrieved from the ashes. The corpse was badly charred but identification was possible due to a distinctive tattoo on one arm that had not been destroyed by the flames. The victim was identified as a man known as 'Pigsticker' and when the pathologist Sir Bernard Spilsbury conducted a post-mortem he found the death had been due to severe blows to the head, possibly with an axe.

A witness, Jack Armstrong, told police that he had been 'dossing' in Newman and Shelley's shack when he was awoken by the sound of a quarrel. Peeping through a crack in the wall, he saw the two men beating Ayers, who cowered on the ground. They had caught him with some food stolen from their hut. When questioned by detectives, they admitted hitting Ayers but maintained that it had been a fist fight. A search of the dump by the police uncovered a bloodstained axe hidden under the floorboards of their hut.

Their trial, before Mr Justice Swift at the Old Bailey on 25 June, was memorable mainly for a comical outburst from the dock. The defence had challenged the evidence by Armstrong as to the time he had seen the prisoners beating Ayers, saying that at the time Armstrong saw two men attacking Ayers, the accused were both elsewhere and had a witness to confirm this. When asked if there was a clock in the hut, the witness said 'There was, but there isn't now.' 'Why is that?' he was asked. 'Because I have it here.' he said, to much laughter in the gallery, as he withdrew it from his pocket. 'Look, Tiggy,' Shelley exclaimed to further laughter, 'he's pinched our clock.'

When the inevitable death sentence was passed and they were asked if they had anything to say before sentence was carried out, Newman said: 'Yes, it should have happened 20 years ago!'

The two old men were hanged together by Robert Baxter, assisted by Tom Phillips, Lionel Mann and Robert Wilson.

August 12th: William John CORBETT (32)   Cardiff

An unemployed colliery worker sentenced to death by Mr Commissioner Hollis-Walker at Glamorgan Assizes, on 2 July, for the murder of his wife, Ethel Louise Corbett (39).

They lived in a small bungalow in Caerphilly and on 25 March there was a row between Corbett and his step-daughter Florence after it was alleged he made a pass at her. Ethel sided with her daughter and in a rage Corbett struck them both. The row flared up again later that afternoon and Corbett again struck his step-daughter. As his wife tried to intervene, Corbett picked up his shaving razor and slashed her across the throat.

Corbett tried to commit suicide following the murder by cutting his own throat with the razor, but was nursed back to health to face trial. His defence argued that since losing his job in November of the previous year he had undergone a drastic change of character and claimed Corbett was insane when he carried out the crime. This was backed up by claims that his wife had been to see
the police on the day before her murder, saying she was worried for her safety as her husband was acting very strangely.

Hanged by Robert Baxter and Henry Pollard.

December 10th: Henry Daniel SEYMOUR (52)   Oxford

A vacuum-cleaner salesman charged with the murder of Mrs Anne Louise Kempson (54), a widow and one of his regular customers.

On 1 August, she was found murdered in her ransacked home in Oxford. Pathologist Sir Bernard Spilsbury ascertained that she had been beaten with a hammer, and that a chisel had then been rammed through her throat.

Police learned that a salesman named Seymour had been seen calling at the house on the day of the crime, and a neighbour came forward who said that she had given him a bed for the night after he had told her a pitiful tale of having his money stolen. In the room police found tiny fragments of a label which they found had come from a hammer, and a local ironmonger was traced who had sold a hammer to a man matching the description of Seymour.

He was arrested in Brighton two weeks later and sentenced to death after a five-day trial, before Mr Justice Swift on 25 October.
Hanged by Tom Pierrepoint and Alfred Allen.

Henry Daniel Seymour

December 15th: Solomon STEIN (21)   **Manchester**

On Sunday morning, 4 October, the body of Annie Riley (28) was found in a room at the Station Temperance Hotel, adjacent to Victoria railway station, Manchester. She had been strangled with a brown tie.

Friends of the victim told police they had seen her in the company of a man whose description matched that of Stein, a waterproof machinist from Hightown, Salford; the police knew that he had arranged a date with her for that night. They had checked into the hotel as man and wife, although it was later discovered that the woman, who worked as a prostitute, had also arranged another date that night. Stein surrendered to the police on the following day. He claimed that he had strangled her after waking to find she had stolen some money from him while he slept.

He pleaded guilty at his trial before Mr Justice Finlay on 25 November. After making his plea, his counsel interrupted and said, 'I think he means not guilty, your honour.' 'No, I mean guilty.' Stein reiterated.

Stein was due to be hanged alongside another Manchester murderer named McVay who had also pleaded guilty, but a few days before the execution date, it was announced that McVay was to be reprieved. There was no such mercy for Stein and he became only the third Jew to be hanged at Strangeways Gaol.

A crowd of over 1,500 Jews gathered outside the prison gates as Stein, who had committed the murder on his 21st birthday, was hanged by Tom Pierrepoint. It was reported that just five seconds elapsed from the pinioning to the drop.

1932

Cases where no executioner is recorded are multiple executions, and readers are asked to refer to the entries before or after for details of the hangman.

January 13th: Edward CULLENS (28)   **Belfast**

A Jewish American ex-motion picture operative and fairground entrepreneur convicted of the murder of Turkish-born fellow fairground business man Achmet Musa (26).

The two men were engaged in the exploitation of a Turkish fairground freak, Zara Agha, who was billed as being 156 years old. On 4 September 1931, Musa was found shot dead in a field outside Carrickfergus. He was naked, but was wearing a woman's blue and white bathing cap. Police initially believed that it was a 'mafia style' killing, but a tip-off led police to Cullens, who a witness claimed had had a similar bathing cap in his car.

The trail led across to Liverpool and evidence that the crime was planned there was compounded when a pre-dug grave was discovered in the garage of a house in Wavertree that Cullens had rented. He was arrested in Hyde Park, London, and taken back to Ulster.

His three-day trial took place before the Lord Chief Justice at the Antrim Assizes at the beginning of December 1931. The defence contested that there was a lack of motive but the prosecution, who had been able to match the bullet taken from the victim with a gun found in Cullen's possession, was able to convince the jury of his guilt.

Hanged by Tom Pierrepoint and Robert Wilson.

February 3rd: George Alfred RICE (32)   **Manchester**

An unemployed labourer, of Rusholme, convicted of the murder of Constance Inman (9), who was found dead at Victoria Park, Manchester, on Tuesday evening, 22 September 1931.

She had died of asphyxiation caused by attempted rape. Rice, whose garden backed onto the park, was questioned after several children playing in the streets had given police a description of a man seen talking to Constance a few hours before she disappeared.

Rice denied the crime and claimed that he had been at the cinema that evening, offering a ticket as evidence. Police checked the ticket and found that it had in fact been issued in February that year, and faced with this evidence, Rice confessed. 'Give me a cup of tea and I will tell you all about it', he told officers at the station.

At his trial before Mr Justice Finlay at Manchester Assizes on 15 December, Rice's counsel claimed that while he had admitted killing Constance Inman, it had been an accident and the charge should be one of manslaughter. The harrowing evidence of the attempted rape was relayed in court and after the jury had considered their verdict, they returned a verdict of guilty of murder. Rice, who had lost an eye several years ago, collapsed as sentence of death was passed, and Mr Justice Finlay, feeling the strain of the trial, wept as he passed sentence.

On the day before his execution Rice was visited in the condemned cell by friends and he told them that he would die bravely. It was a false boast, for when Tom Pierrepoint entered his cell he broke down completely and had to be carried, an inert and broken man, to the gallows.

February 23rd: William Harold GODDARD (25)   Pentonville

On 30 November 1931, Goddard, an Ipswich-born mate serving on the sailing barge SS Speranza, walked into an Ipswich police station and confessed he had accidentally killed the skipper.

Detectives boarded the vessel moored on the River Thames, and found the body of Captain Charles William Lambert (57), of Grays, Essex. He had a fractured skull and a rope was knotted around his neck.

Goddard claimed that three days earlier, while berthed in Woolwich, they had quarrelled after a disparaging remark Lambert had made about Goddard's fiancée. In the ensuing fight Lambert had attacked him with a hammer and Goddard had fatally wounded the skipper in self-defence. He had then attempted to fake a robbery, and had tied the rope around Lambert's neck.

At his two-day trial before Mr Justice Finlay at the Old Bailey on 19 January, the claim of self-defence was dismissed by evidence that Lambert had been strangled before being beaten and then robbed, which contradicted Goddard's account of events. Goddard had eight previous convictions for theft and drunkenness.

Hanged by Robert Baxter and Tom Phillips.

March 9th: George Thomas POPLE (22)   Oxford

A private in the 2nd battalion, South Wales Borderers, stationed at Portsmouth, convicted of the murder of Mrs Mabel Elizabeth Matthews (56), who had been found dying from severe head injuries on the main Oxford to Cheltenham road at Burford on 19 December 1931.

Police originally thought she had been in collision with a car but they noticed signs of a struggle and later found that Mrs Matthews' bicycle lamp was missing. Items belonging to Mrs Matthews were found further along the road, as was a man's mackintosh with a sandwich in the pocket.

On the following day, a policeman spoke to Pople who was cycling in Abergavenny. He denied being anywhere near the scene of the crime, but aroused enough suspicion for detectives to visit him at his home in Brecon later that day. Pople confessed that he was on a cycling holiday while on leave from his unit and that while passing through Burford his lamp became defective. He was walking in the twilight when he saw Mrs Matthews approach and when he attempted to snatch her lamp she fell from her bicycle and sustained fatal injuries.

At the two-day trial before by Mr Justice Roche at Gloucester Assizes on 1 February his counsel claimed that it was manslaughter as the killing was not intentional, but medical evidence showed that the victim had injuries consistent with being strangled and kicked.

Hanged by Tom Pierrepoint and Henry Pollard.

April 27th: George Emmanuel MICHAEL (49)   Hull

A seaman who, on New Year's Eve 1931, in full view of a local policeman, stabbed to death Danish-born Mrs Teresa May Hemstock (47), to whom he was bigamously married.

Michael had stabbed both her and her daughter on a previous occasion and was sentenced to 11 months imprisonment for wounding. She took him back on his release but later, because of his brutal treatment of her, gave herself up to the police for bigamy. She was released on bail a few days before Christmas, and when Michael finally tracked her down he stabbed her to death.

He admitted at his trial before Mr Justice Humphreys on 4 March that he had committed the crime because her confessing to bigamy meant that he would have to go back to prison.

Hanged by Tom Pierrepoint and Henry Pollard.

April 28th: Thomas RILEY (36)   Leeds

On 16 December 1931, Riley, an Irishman, formerly of Wigan, but living at Lepton, Huddersfield, walked into his local police station and confessed that he had murdered his landlady.

Officers called at the house and found Mrs Elizabeth Castle (53) lying on the pantry floor. Nearby was a bloodstained hammer with which Riley said he had struck her after she called him 'an Irish bastard' during a quarrel.

His defence of insanity failed and he was sentenced to death at Leeds Assizes, on 9 March, by Mr Justice Humphreys. The Judge, after handling the murder weapon, said that because of its weight and size only a plea of self-defence from someone wielding such a weapon would have stood any chance of a verdict other than guilty of murder. In 1925, Riley had been charged with the murder of a woman and her illegitimate child by pushing them into a canal. The charge was dropped through lack of evidence.

April 28th: John Henry ROBERTS (27)   Leeds

An unemployed Pudsey labourer sentenced to death at Leeds Assizes on 11 March for the murder of Alfred Gill (55), a Bradford grocer and pig farmer.

On 11 December 1931, Gill was found battered to death at his farm at Tyersal, near Pudsey. Roberts, a casual employee at the shop, was seen with Gill as he went about his rounds and was soon interviewed. He made a number of statements denying the murder, but eventually said that he had struck Gill after he had insulted his mother and even then it was in self-defence.

At his trial before Mr Justice Humphreys it was alleged that the victim had been beaten to death with a hammer and a brick. The Crown dismissed the plea of self-defence and said the motive for the crime was robbery and that the killer had then stolen over £40. Roberts was found to be in possession of a large sum of money despite having had to sign on the dole on the day of the murder.

Hanged alongside **RILEY** in a double execution carried out by Tom Pierrepoint assisted by Tom Phillips and Alfred Allen.

May 4th: Maurice FREEDMAN (36)   Pentonville

Freedman was a former policeman who earned his living by gambling and borrowing money. Although married, he had been having a relationship with Miss Annette Friedson (31), a typist, but her parents, unhappy at the situation, told her she must break off the romance.

For several weeks the relationship between the two was fraught and, fearful that Freeman might make an attack on her, she was regularly accompanied to work in the city by her brother.

At lunchtime on 26 January, Freedman met her inside the building and during a heated quarrel she received a fatal wound to her throat. Freedman was soon arrested, but claimed her death was accidental. A bloodstained razor, in a patent holder, was discovered on a London bus, and identified as the murder weapon from traces of Annette's rare blood group.

Freedman's defence, at the two-day trial before Mr Justice Hawke at the Old Bailey on 8 March, was that she inflicted the wounds herself during a struggle and that the weapon found was not his. The conductor on the bus identified Freedman as a passenger, and a pathologist stated it was almost impossible for the wound to be self-inflicted.

Hanged by Robert Baxter and Robert Wilson.

May 18th: Charles James COWLE (18)   Manchester

An unemployed labourer, of Darwen, Lancs, convicted of the murder of Naomi Farnworth (6), daughter of his next door neighbour.

Naomi would often run errands for Cowle and when she failed to appear for afternoon school on 22 March, enquiries led police to him. They called at his house after she had been missing for two days and he immediately showed the officer up to his bedroom where the child's body was concealed in a trunk. She had been raped and then strangled.

Cowle, who had been sent to borstal for attempted murder at the age of nine, was convicted at Manchester Assizes before Mr Justice Humphreys on 26 April.

His appeal on the ground of insanity failed and he was hanged by Tom Pierrepoint.

November 23rd: Ernest HUTCHINSON (42)   Oxford

On 14 September, the body of Mrs Gwendoline Annie Warren (36) was found hidden beneath a mattress at her home in Maidenhead. She had parted from her husband earlier that year and had been living with

Hutchinson, as Mr and Mrs Warren. A neighbour noticed that she had not been seen for several days and became suspicious. She forced the door and found the body, under a heavy mattress piled with bedding.

A doctor stated that death had taken place four days earlier and a nationwide search was launched for Hutchinson who was arrested in a boarding house at Southend on 15 September.

At his three-day trial, before Mr Justice Mackinnon at Reading Assizes on 13 October, it was alleged that they had quarrelled frequently because Hutchinson was out of work and there was little money coming into the house. The pathologist Sir Bernard Spilsbury said that it appeared that the victim was knocked unconscious with a blow to the head and the mattress and bedding were then placed upon her. He said that death was due to suffocation.

Hutchinson said that he and Gwen had quarrelled and she had stormed out of the bedroom saying she would sleep on the sofa. He then said that when he went downstairs on the following morning he found her body and panicked, thinking he would be blamed for the murder.

The jury needed just over an hour to convict him of murder and after sentence of death was passed upon him, Hutchinson, with 16 charges of larceny and having served almost 20 years in prison, burst out laughing in the dock. An appeal was launched on the grounds that the Judge had misdirected the jury but this was dismissed by Lord Hewart, who claimed the grounds were 'rubbish'.

Hanged by Alfred Allen carrying out his first execution, assisted by Henry Pollard. Stanley Cross was also present as a trainee observer.

December 29th: Patrick McDERMOTT (26)   **Dublin**

A farmer convicted of the murder of his brother John McDermott (30), in Rosmoylan, County Roscommon.

In the early hours of Monday 4 September, John McDermott was found shot in the gateway to his home seven miles from Roscommon. Hearing two gunshots, his brother and sister, with whom he lived, rushed from the house and found John dead from wounds seemingly inflicted with a double-barrelled shotgun.

John was eldest of the children and all three had separate rooms in the house. Their father had died two years earlier and John had taken charge of the farm, worth £700. The other two children were left £100 each. On the night of the murder John had left the house and gone to visit a friend. He was shot as he returned home. Detectives investigating the crime asked Paddy whether he had seen a flash of fire when he heard the shots, and he said that he could not see the spot where his brother died from his window. This was found to be untrue. He denied having a gun, but a friend told police that he had recently borrowed his gun, allegedly to shoot crows which were attacking crops. Three days after the murder of his brother, police charged Paddy McDermott.

At his four-day Dublin trial before Mr Justice Hanna, the motive was alleged to be so that Patrick could inherit the farm, which he intended to sell, and emigrate to America. On 14 November, after retiring for almost four hours, the jury returned a guilty verdict.

A large crowd demonstrated outside Mountjoy as Tom Pierrepoint, assisted for the first time by his young nephew Albert, carried out the execution.

1933

Cases where no executioner is recorded are multiple executions, and readers are asked to refer to the entries before or after for details of the hangman.

February 2nd: Jeremiah HANBURY (49)   **Birmingham**

On the afternoon of 17 October 1932, Hanbury, a widower and unemployed puddler, entered the house of Mrs Jessie Payne (39), the mother of four young children, at Newtown Brockmoor, and struck her two blows with a hammer, knocking her unconscious. Hanbury then cut her throat so severely she was almost decapitated. He then gave himself up to a policeman.

At his trial before Mr Justice Humphreys at Birmingham Assizes on 8 December, it was alleged that Hanbury and Mrs Payne had been having an affair, but in July of that year she had ended the relationship and refused to see him. As a result he became depressed and, as his counsel, offering a defence of insanity, suggested, it was during this depression he had committed murder.

Hanged by Tom Pierrepoint and Robert Wilson. Albert Pierrepoint was also present as a trainee observer.

April 7th: Harold COURTNEY (23)   **Belfast**

On 3 August 1932, a group of schoolchildren stumbled across the body of a woman hidden in some bushes. Police identified the body as that of Minnie Reid (23), a domestic servant of Derryane, County Armagh. Her throat had been cut, and police found a bloodstained razor nearby.

Investigations led police to Courtney, a lorry driver. He admitted that he had known the victim for the last four years, but denied that they had ever been lovers. He had no alibi for the time police believed she was murdered and forensic officers in London were able to find traces of her blood on some of his clothing.

At his trial it was suggested that Minnie had become pregnant and told him he was the father. As he was already engaged to another girl he killed her, hoping that the trail would not lead to him. His counsel claimed that Courtney had agreed to a meeting with the girl and when he told her he did not want any further contact with either her or the baby, she committed suicide.

Hanged by Tom Pierrepoint and Albert Pierrepoint.

June 8th: Jack Samuel PUTTNAM (32)   **Pentonville**

A boot repairer convicted of the murder of his aunt, Mrs Elizabeth Mary 'Betts' Standley (44), at Finsbury Park on 4 March.

When her husband became unemployed, Betts Standley solved their money problems by selling her house in Highbury. The house had been left to her in a will, and part of the money was used to pay off their mortgage, part to buy her husband a coffee-stall near King's Cross Station. £150 was held awaiting suitable investment and what money remained was used to rent a flat.

When police found the body, she had been battered about the head, strangled with a flex and stabbed ten times with a sharp instrument.

Her clothing had been arranged to suggest a sexual motive, but this was not the case.

Among the first suspects was her nephew who ran a printing business with his brother. Word reached police that he had asked her for an investment which she had refused, and they had quarrelled. She was also pressing him to pay back a small loan. A neighbour told police that on the morning of the murder she had heard someone call at the flat and heard the name 'Jack' mentioned. A bus driver, stuck in traffic, saw a man emerge from the flat and picked out Puttnam from a identity parade.

When questioned, Puttnam confessed that he had killed his aunt, but claimed that he had stabbed her with a skewer he had picked up from a table after losing his head during a struggle. This was disproved when it was found the sharp weapon was a printer's gimlet, which suggested he had taken the weapon to the house, destroying his argument that it was picked up in the heat of the moment.

At his three-day trial, before Mr Justice Hawke at the Old Bailey on 3 May, Puttnam retracted his confession and claimed he was covering up for a relative.

Hanged by Robert Baxter and Stanley Cross.

June 20th: Richard HETHERINGTON (36)   Liverpool

Hetherington, a farmer of Great Strickland, Westmorland, had been involved in a long running dispute with his neighbours Joseph Dixon (76), and his wife Mary Ann (75). The quarrel was over money owed for work done by Hetherington on the Dixons' farm for which the old man was refusing to pay. Matters came to a head in February when the police were summoned by Dixon after he had received threats. On 20 February, the bodies of Mr and Mrs Dixon were discovered in the burnt out shell of their bungalow at Newby.

When arrested, Hetherington had in his possession money and papers belonging to the dead couple, and he made a full confession when charged by the police. At his three-day trial, held before Mr Justice MacNaughton at Westmorland Assizes on 29 May, the prosecution put forward a strong case for wilful murder. Hetherington, who had been badly wounded in the war, put forward a defence of insanity. It was rejected and he was found guilty after the jury deliberated for almost four hours.

Hanged by Tom Pierrepoint and Albert Pierrepoint assisting for the first time as a bona fide assistant.

July 25th: Frederick MORSE (34)   Bristol

Although she was not yet in her teens, Dorothy Brewer (12) easily passed for a mature young woman. Local rumour held that she was the result of an incestuous relationship between Frederick Morse and his married sister Lily Brewer.

Dorothy did not live with her mother, but stayed with her

grandparents and aunts and uncles in a small over-crowded cottage near Taunton. Early in February, Dorothy was showing clear signs of pregnancy, which her doctor confirmed. 'Uncle Fred' Morse accompanied her to the doctors.

On 23 February, Morse returned home from work in the local quarry and tried to persuade Dorothy to return to school, which, being pregnant, she was reluctant to do. When he failed to persuade her to go to school, he asked if she wanted to go to a nearby village where he had laid some rabbit traps. They were seen riding on his bicycle, and in a pub during the afternoon.

That evening, a neighbour spoke to Morse in her kitchen. He was soaking wet, and had clearly been more than just caught up in the recent light rain. The forthright neighbour asked if it was he who had got Dorothy pregnant and he denied it. When asked why Dorothy had not returned with him, he said he had lost her in the village. The police were informed and Dorothy was found dead in a local river. She had traces of alcohol in her stomach and death was due to drowning. There was no sign of other injuries.

Under questioning by Scotland Yard detectives, Morse finally admitted killing Dorothy but claimed it had been part of a suicide pact.

This was clearly disbelieved by Mr Justice Goddard and the jury at Wells Assizes on 8 June, and he was sentenced to death.

Tom Pierrepoint carried out the sentence after the appeal had failed, assisted by Tom Phillips.

August 10th: Varnavas Loizi ANTORKA (31)   Pentonville

Antorka had arrived in London from his native Cyprus in 1928. He quickly learned to speak English and found work in a Soho restaurant as a silver washer. In the spring of 1933 he was working at the Bellometti Restaurant under head chef Boleshar Pankorski (35).

On 12 May, Antorka was told to warm some plates in an oven and when he refused to carry out the order Pankorski sacked him on the spot and ordered him to leave the premises. A short time later he returned, brandishing a gun, and demanded his job back. During the ensuing skirmish Pankorski was shot and fatally wounded. Another waiter was injured. Antorka was arrested at once and when the victim died on the following day, he was charged with murder.

His three-day trial before Mr Justice Humphreys ended on 30 June. It had been alleged that the crime was accidental and, returning a guilty verdict, the jury recommended mercy on the grounds that it was not a premeditated crime, despite it being shown in court that Antorka had returned to his flat earlier in the evening to get the gun.

Hanged by Robert Baxter and Henry Pollard.

October 11th: Robert James KIRBY (26)   Pentonville

Kirby, a Dagenham labourer, had been courting Grace Ivy Newing (17) for three months when he asked her to marry him after she became pregnant. She refused and on 7 July, while they were alone in her house at Beacontree, he strangled her with a cord. He then went home, woke his mother and told her he had 'done Gracie in'.

He was tried before Mr Justice Swift at the Old Bailey on 21 September, where his defence was insanity. Kirby refused his counsel's request to go into the witness box, and it was left for a doctor to say that Kirby sported a silly grin on his face when he talked about the crime. Several doctors who had examined him while awaiting trial reported that he showed no trace of insanity.

Hanged by Robert Baxter and Robert Wilson. Several years earlier Kirby's father had served a prison sentence for the attempted murder of his wife.

December 6th: Ernest Wadge PARKER (25)   Durham

A fruit seller, who murdered his sister Lily (36) at their home in West Stanley, County Durham, on Sunday 25 June.

Parker, a twin, lived unhappily with his father and elder sister, the mother of a young daughter, above the family's fruit shop. He frequently assaulted both his father and sister and in the previous December he was bound over by a court for assault.

In April 1933, Parker was sentenced to two months' hard labour for beating his sister and upon his release he told a neighbour: 'if they start their impudence up again, I will do them both in.' Returning home, his conduct was such that the police had to be called to escort him away.

On the day of the murder Parker called at the house. While his sister rested in her room her daughter heard a cry. She entered the room and saw Parker standing over the bed wielding an axe. After battering his sister about the head, Parker ran into the street and told a neighbour that he had 'fettled her this time!'

Lily Parker was rushed to Newcastle Infirmary where she died in the early hours. Upon his arrest, Parker told the officer: 'I hope she is dead, I want the rope.'

At his trial at Durham Assizes on 14 November before Mr Justice Humphreys, his defence was inherited insanity based on the fact that his mother was declared insane before the birth of Parker and his twin brother Sydney. Despite the brutal nature of the crime, over 20,000 people signed a petition for a reprieve.

It was in vain and he was hanged by Tom Pierrepoint.

December 19th: William BURTOFT (47)   Manchester

On 19 July, Mrs Francis Levine (61), a wealthy Jewess, was found battered to death at her home in Cheetham Hill, Manchester. Police believed she had disturbed someone robbing the house.

One week after the murder, Burtoft, a one eyed, out of work sailor and meths drinker, of no fixed abode, was arrested and taken into custody at Hyde and charged with drunkenness. Burtoft fitted the description of the man wanted for the Cheetham Hill murder and he was questioned by officers dealing with this case. Under interrogation it was alleged that Burtoft confessed to committing the murder.

At Burtoft's trial, before Mr Justice Atkinson on 13 November, his defence counsel claimed that the evidence against their client was very suspect. Apart from Burtoft's admitting to being in the area there was little other evidence, other than his 'confession', linking him to the crime, and they also maintained that, judging from the state of the bloodstained house, if Burtoft had committed the murder his clothes would show traces of blood. No traces of blood were found on any of his clothes.

The prosecution also pointed out that the confession was the only real piece of evidence, and other than showing that Burtoft had spent a little money after the murder, when before he was short, there was little else to connect him to the crime. His defence asked the jury to acquit the prisoner as there was no case to answer, but he was convicted on the evidence of his supposed confession, the jury evidently believing the police version of events.

Hanged by Tom Pierrepoint. Burtoft had previous convictions for housebreaking and attacking women.

December 28th: Stanley Eric HOBDAY (21)   Birmingham

In the early hours of 27 August, Charles Fox (24), was stabbed to death after disturbing someone robbing his house at West Bromwich. The killer fled after leaving footprints in the soil outside the house, and spots of blood from a cut probably sustained whilst gaining entry to the house.

Later, another burglary was committed at nearby Newton, and this time the thief left a set of fingerprints traced to Stanley Hobday, a local electrician already known to the police as a petty thief.

Hobday had also used a needle and thread at this house, presumably to repair a tear in his clothing. Later that night a stolen car was recovered in Cheshire, this also had Hobday's fingerprints on the steering wheel. Detectives used the BBC to appeal for information on the whereabouts of Hobday and three days later he was arrested at Gretna Green.

Questioned back in the Midlands, Hobday's jacket was found to have been repaired with the black cotton from the house at Newton, and on his arm, beneath the tear, was a freshly healed cut. The most damning evidence against Hobday was the footprints left at the murder scene. Plaster casts made of these found they were from a size four shoe, an unusually small size for an adult. Hobday wore size four shoes.

Sentenced to death by Mr Justice Talbot at Staffordshire Assizes on 16 November, he was hanged by Tom Pierrepoint and Albert Pierrepoint.

1934

Cases where no executioner is recorded are multiple executions, and readers are asked to refer to the entries before or after for details of the hangman.

January 3rd: Roy GREGORY (28)   **Hull**

A Scarborough boot-repairer, convicted of the murder of his step-daughter Dorothy Addnall (2), whose battered body was found buried under the cellar floor at Gregory's house, six months after she had disappeared.

Police were tipped off and the house searched after Gregory gave neighbours differing accounts of what had become of the child. He told one neighbour she was being looked after by a commercial traveller in London, and another that she was being cared for by people in Yorkshire.

At his trial before Mr Justice Humphreys at Yorkshire Assizes on 21 November, defence counsel claimed that on 9 March 1933, Gregory had pushed her against a wall when she wouldn't stop crying and in panic, upon finding he had killed her, he buried her in the cellar. The prosecution alleged that he had struck her with a hammer as she lay asleep in bed. He was looking after the child as her mother was in hospital having another baby.

Hanged by Tom Pierrepoint and Tom Phillips.

January 5th: John FLEMING (32)   **Dublin**

A shoe salesman from Drumcondra, who murdered his wife Ellen (42) by battering her with a blunt instrument, because she stood in the way of his romance with a young waitress.

Fleming made a number of attempts to administer poison to his wife during March 1932, and after the third attempt, his brother-in-law became suspicious and threatened to call the police if anything happened to her.

On Wednesday 26 July, Ellen had a half-day holiday from her job as a shop assistant and she was last seen alive later that afternoon. Around this time Fleming spoke to a neighbour and said he had been swimming at a nearby beach, although his hair was not wet and he had neither towel nor costume with him.

Later that evening Ellen Fleming was found battered to death in the kitchen at her home. Fleming was arrested that same night and despite his protestations of innocence he was charged with murder.

At his seven-day trial before Mr Justice Creed-Meredith KC in Dublin, it was shown that Fleming had been having an affair with a teenage girl who believed him to be unmarried. She had become pregnant and as he was the father of the baby he promised to marry her. It was alleged that he had killed his wife to be free to marry his mistress.

Hanged by Tom Pierrepoint. No assistant was recorded as being present at the execution, but almost certainly Robert Wilson assisted.

February 6th: Ernest BROWN (35)   **Leeds**

On 5 September 1933, Frederick Ellison Morton (28), a wealthy cattle merchant, went out for the day, leaving his wife at their home at Saxton Grange, a remote farmhouse in Towton, Yorkshire.

Also at the farm was groom Ernest Brown, recently reinstated after a row with Morton. Unbeknown to Morton, Brown had been having an affair with his wife Dorothy, but their relationship was fraught with fits of violence and quarrels. With Morton away for the day, Brown set about a terror campaign: cutting the telephone wires and firing a shotgun at the house as Mrs Morton and her housekeeper sat terrified behind the locked door.

In the early hours an explosion occurred in the garage and when the fire died down, the body of Frederick Morton was found inside a burnt out motor car. He had been shot dead.

Brown was charged with the murder, which he was alleged to have carried out after a fit of jealousy, and out of resentment at the lowly position he held at the farm. Sentenced to death by Mr Justice Humphreys after a three-day trial at Leeds Assizes on 14 December 1933, and hanged by Tom Pierrepoint and Robert Wilson.

Asked on the scaffold if he wished to confess, Brown made an utterance. The drop fell before he could clarify if he said 'ought to burn' or 'Otterburn' which may have been a confession to the murder of a young woman at Otterburn three years earlier.

April 6th: Lewis HAMILTON (25)   **Leeds**

Hamilton, a Bradford slaughterman, married his wife Maude in July 1933 and a short time later she gave birth to their first child. By December that year they were living at his mother's house, when they parted after a quarrel and she went back to her own mother's. A few days before Christmas, Hamilton received a summons to go to court regarding a separation order.

On Boxing Day he waited for her in the yard at her mother's house. Maude (23) was next door having a drink with a neighbour. As she left he dragged her into her mother's house and cut her throat with a knife.

A large crowd gathered outside the house and eventually someone broke down the door. Hamilton was almost lynched by neighbours before he was rescued by the police.

He offered a defence of insanity through epilepsy at his trial but medical evidence refuted any such claims and on 15 March, he was sentenced to death by Mr Commissioner H. H. Joy at West Riding Assizes. The jury added a strong recommendation for mercy. An appeal failed, as did a petition with over 30,000 signatures.

Hanged by Tom Pierrepoint and Alfred Allen.

May 3rd: Reginald Ivor HINKS (32)   **Bristol**

Sentenced to death by Mr Justice Branson at the Old Bailey on 11 March, for the murder of his father-in-law James Pullen (85).

Hinks was a petty criminal with a number of convictions for theft. In 1933 while working as a vacuum cleaner salesman in Bath he met Constance Pullen, a divorcee with a young child. They married after a brief courtship, Hinks no doubt attracted as much by his wife's father's wealth as by her looks.

James Pullen lived in Bath, tended to by a male nurse. Once Hinks had wed Constance they moved in with her father and Hinks, declaring he would care for the old man, dismissed the nurse.

Within a short time Hinks had obtained some £900 from his father-in-law which he used to buy a house, but further attempts to obtain money were curtailed when Pullen's solicitors put the money out of Hinks's reach.

Hinks planned to get the money at any cost and decided to speed up Pullen's demise by taking him on exhausting walks and abandoning him on busy streets, hoping that the old man would have an 'accident'. When these plans failed, his patience ran out and he committed murder in the hope that it could be made to look like suicide.

On 1 December Hinks called the fire brigade and told them that his father-in-law was lying with his head in the gas oven. 'Any bruises you find on his head happened when I tried to pull him from the oven.' he told police investigating the apparent suicide.

Hinks was charged with murder after it was found that the victim was already unconscious when his head was placed inside the gas oven. This could only mean murder.

Hanged by Tom Pierrepoint and Henry Pollard. Had Hinks not been so consumed with greed, and been prepared to wait for the frail old man to die, he would have eventually have received a share of the large inheritance, and become a very wealthy man.

May 4th: Frederick William PARKER (21)   **Wandsworth**
           Albert PROBERT (26)

On the night of 13 November 1933, Joseph Bedford (80) a shopkeeper, was found with head injuries on the floor of his general store at Portslade. Taken to hospital, it was soon apparent that the old man had not fallen as was at first thought, but had been struck over the head. He died from his injuries the following morning.

Witnesses reported seeing two men near the shop on the evening of the murder and the following day detectives questioned two men who had been picked up for loitering.

Parker, a small time criminal, bully and casual labourer from Hove, and Probert, a fitter from Dover, were questioned separately and, unaware that Bedford had since died, Parker admitted helping his friend to rob the shop but was insistent that Probert had committed the assault. 'I wish it had been a bigger job.' he confessed, adding that the total of the haul yielded just £6. Despite Probert denying any involvement, both men were then charged with murder.

Sentenced to death at Sussex Assizes by Mr Justice Roche on 16 March, they were hanged together by Tom Pierrepoint, assisted by Tom Phillips, Stanley Cross and Albert Pierrepoint. It was the last execution which members of the press were allowed to witness.

October 9th: Harry TUFFNEY (36)   **Pentonville**

Tuffney, a twice-married mechanic, had been living in a house on Star Street, Paddington, with Edith 'Kate' Longshaw (38). On the morning of 30 June, he walked into Marylebone police station and told the desk sergeant, 'I have killed my girl,' adding that he had made a failed attempt to gas himself.

Police returned to Star Street and found Kate Longshaw lying dead on the bed. She had been beaten about the head with an axe. Tuffney claimed he had struck her as she slept.

He stood trial before Mr Justice Atkinson at the Old Bailey on 11 September and offered a defence of insanity. The prosecution claimed that the motive for the killing was jealousy. The court heard that shortly before the murder, Tuffney had proposed marriage and she had accepted. Later, he was advised against this by friends who warned him that she was seeing other men. On 29 June, he had found a letter from a man making an appointment to meet her. In a rage, it was alleged, Tuffney then bought the axe and killed her as she slept.

Hanged by Robert Baxter and Alfred Allen.

November 14th: John Frederick STOCKWELL (19)   **Pentonville**

On the morning of 7 August, Dudley Henry Hoard (40), the manager of the Eastern Palace Cinema, Bow Road, London, was found severely beaten in his flat above the cinema. His wife Maisie had also been attacked but while she regained consciousness, her husband died in hospital.

A large sum of money was taken from the safe and a search of the cinema found a bloodstained axe hidden beneath the stage. This suggested to detectives that the killer was someone who knew the hiding place, reasoning that a stranger would not waste time looking for somewhere to hide the murder weapon.

A list of current and former employees contained the name of John Stockwell who was found to be missing from his lodgings. A letter bearing a Lowestoft postmark reached detectives which suggested that Stockwell had committed suicide by drowning.

Unfortunately for Stockwell, his clothes were discovered on the beach before the letter reached the police and to add to his misfortune he signed the hotel register in his hideaway as 'J.F Smith. Luton, Hertfordshire'. The manager, who was suspicious of the young man, knew that Luton was in Bedfordshire and informed the police that one of his guests might be the wanted murderer. Stockwell was arrested in his hotel room and on the journey back to London he made a full confession.

He pleaded guilty at his trial before Mr Justice Goddard at the Old Bailey on 22 October. Prior to his execution Stockwell said to his girlfriend: 'I can't imagine what made me do it except that I wanted money to get on in the world.'

Hanged by Robert Baxter and Robert Wilson.

John Frederick Stockwell   Ethel Lillie Major

December 19th: Ethel Lillie MAJOR (42)   **Hull**

On 22 May 1934, Arthur Major (44) complained of stomach pains after eating corned beef and was in agony until he died two days later. The death certificate stated the cause of death as due to *status epilepticus*. Mrs Major, the daughter of a Lincolnshire gamekeeper, soon arranged the funeral, but in the meantime the police had received a letter urging them to investigate the death, as a neighbour's dog had died after eating a meal prepared by Mrs Major. The funeral was halted at the eleventh hour.

When police questioned Mrs Major she made a fatal slip by showing she knew her husband had died of strychnine poisoning although no mention had been made up to this point of the cause of death.

Sentenced to death by Mr Justice Charles on 1 November after a three-day trial at Lincoln Assizes and hanged by Tom Pierrepoint and Albert Pierrepoint. Ethel Major was the last person hanged at Hull Gaol and her ghost is still said to haunt the prison.

1935

Cases where no executioner is recorded are multiple executions, and readers are asked to refer to the entries before or after for details of the hangman.

January 1st: Frederick RUSHWORTH (29)   Leeds

A farm labourer from Gellpool, near Middleham, Yorkshire, convicted along with Mrs Lydia Binks (24), at York Assizes for the murder of their un-named month-old baby girl.

Rushworth and Binks lived together, and in the summer of 1933 she became pregnant.   In January 1934, she obtained employment at a holiday camp near Wensleydale, a camp that contained both caravans and chalets.

On 1 March, Lydia Binks, who was described as simple and below average intelligence, gave birth to a daughter, concealing the birth from the camp owner.   When he heard the baby crying, Binks told him she was looking after it for a friend who was in hospital.   The owner told her he did not want a crying child disturbing holidaymakers and she said she would return it to the mother.

On 25 March she was seen with the child cycling away from the camp.   She had a rendezvous that day with Rushworth, whom she told she wanted the child to be looked after by a nurse.   He told her they couldn't afford to do this and suggested they 'put it away quietly'.   She refused to consent to this idea and alleged that as they walked through a field, Rushworth snatched the child and buried the child alive in a hole he dug with a spade.

At the trial Rushworth claimed he that thought the child was dead when he buried it and he had only done it to help her out.   They were both sentenced to death by Mr Justice Porter on 21 November.   Lydia Binks was reprieved three days before she was due to die; Rushworth was hanged by Tom Pierrepoint and Stanley Cross.

February 7th: David Maskill BLAKE (24)   Leeds

On Wednesday 17 October 1934, waitress Emily Yeomans (23) was found strangled in Middleton Wood, Leeds.   Witnesses told police that they had seen Emily in the company of a man later identified as David Blake, an unemployed steel worker.

Emily had been with Blake on Tuesday evening, despite the fact that he was due to be married next day.   When the body was found Blake talked enough about it to draw suspicion to himself and when the police asked to see his clothes they found hairs from the dead woman's cat.   Blake was also in possession of a powder compact identified as belonging to Emily.

Sentenced to death by Mr Justice Goddard at Leeds Assizes on 16 December.   Whilst serving in the army in 1930 Blake had raped a woman after offering to walk her home when she had missed her bus.

Hanged by Tom Pierrepoint and Alfred Allen.

March 13th: George Frank HARVEY (37)   Pentonville

Also known as Charles Malcolm Lake, sentenced to death at the Old Bailey by Mr Justice Atkinson on 24 January for the murder of George Hamblin, who was beaten to death at The Westminster Institute, a Chelsea workhouse, on 26 October 1934.

Hamblin, a bookmaker, was accused by Harvey of stealing some money from him, and in rage Harvey picked up a blunt instrument and beat him about the head. He then went to a nearby public house and confessed to a girlfriend that he had committed the crime. She later informed the police and Harvey was arrested.

His plea of insanity was rejected and he was hanged by Robert Baxter and Henry Pollard; his execution marking the first appearance outside a gaol of Mrs Van Der Elst, the wealthy anti-hanging campaigner.

April 2nd: Leonard Albert BRIGSTOCK (33)   Wandsworth

A stoker of Chatham, who murdered Chief Petty Officer Hubert Sydney Deggan (36) by cutting his throat on board a monitor ship, HMS Marshal Soult, at Chatham on 19 January.

On the previous day Brigstock had been reported by Deggan, and ordered to report to the Master-at-Arms on the following morning. He did so, and after Deggan made a statement, Brigstock was ordered to appear before the Captain when he returned from his weekend leave.

On the first night of his leave, Brigstock went into a public house and got very drunk. He then returned home, collected his razor and made his way back to the ship. Deggan was asleep in the mess as Brigstock crept in and cut his throat with such force that he almost decapitated him. He then went into another mess room and told someone what he had done.

At his trial before Lord Chief Justice Hewart, at Kent Assizes on 19 February, his defence was insanity based on hereditary mental illness. The prosecution maintained that what Brigstock had done did not fall within the scope of insanity and he was convicted.

Hanged by Robert Baxter and Robert Wilson.

April 16th: Percy Charles ANDERSON (21)   Wandsworth

In the late afternoon of 25 November 1934, Anderson, a Brighton mechanic, was seen in the company of his girlfriend, Edith Constance Drew-Bear (21), a restaurant cashier, heading towards the downs at the back of East Brighton golf links. Her body was later found in a water tank on the links. She had been shot and then strangled.

Witnesses saw Anderson, wet and barefoot, as he caught a bus to his home, and he told them he had fallen into the sea. He was questioned by detectives and claimed he could not remember what had happened except that they had quarrelled.

Percy Charles Anderson

At Anderson's four-day trial, before Lord Chief Justice Hewart at Sussex Assizes on 7-10 March, his counsel said he could offer no defence because Anderson had no recollection of events that evening. A defence of insanity was also offered but this too failed.

Hanged by Robert Baxter and Alfred Allen.

May 9th: John Stephenson BAINBRIDGE (26)　　　　　　　　**Durham**

A soldier of the Durham Light Infantry, sentenced to death by Mr Justice Goddard at Durham Assizes on 8 March, for the murder of Edward Frederick Herdman (75), a solicitor's clerk, in Bishop Auckland.

Mr Herdman was battered to death and his throat cut during a robbery on New Year's Eve 1934. Three days later, a letter addressed to a soldier in the same regiment as Bainbridge contained a sum of money which included some bloodstained notes. The handwriting on the envelope matched that of Bainbridge and he was arrested.

He admitted that he had sent the money but said that he had been given it by a woman on the day before the murder, although he refused to say who she was. Following conviction, the woman wrote to Bainbridge's mother claiming she had lent him the money. Attempts to postpone the execution failed and he was hanged by Tom Pierrepoint.

May 30th: John Harris BRIDGE (25)　　　　　　　　**Manchester**

A Salford warehouseman sentenced to death by Mr Justice Hilbery on 3 May for the murder of his fiancée Amelia Nuttall (26).

It was alleged at the trial that Bridge had fallen in love with another girl and tried to break off the engagement, but each time he broached the subject Amelia was able, by becoming hysterical, to make him change his mind. On 14 April, he called at her house and following a quarrel he struck her with a poker then cut her throat with a bread knife. Bridge then scattered things about the room to make it look like a robbery had taken place.

Hanged by Tom Pierrepoint.

June 25th: Arthur Henry FRANKLIN (44)   **Gloucester**

Franklin lived with his brother on a smallholding at Hanham Woods, near Bristol. In November 1933, their neighbour Mrs Gladys Bessie Nott (28), left her husband and went to live with Franklin as his wife, but at the beginning of May 1935, she told Franklin that she was going to go back to her husband.

On 8 May, as she was walking towards her husband's bungalow, Franklin shot her in the back with a shotgun. As her husband came rushing out he shouted 'You too, you rat', and fired the gun, wounding him.

He pleaded guilty at his trial, lasting just six minutes, before Mr Justice McNaughton on 5 June.

Hanged by Tom Pierrepoint and Robert Wilson.

Walter Osmond Worthington

July 10th: Walter Osmond WORTHINGTON (56)   **Bedford**

A retired engineer and poultry farmer of Broughton, Huntingdon, convicted of murdering his third wife, Sybil Emily Worthington (28) by shooting her after a row about her infidelity.

They had married in 1932 but soon the age difference began to tell. Worthington, the father of 13 children, was fond of staying home in the evenings while his wife preferred to go out. She became friendly with the son of the landlord of the local pub and often went for rides on his motorcycle.

On the evening of 9 March, Sybil told her husband she was going out. He had heard rumours she was over-friendly with the landlord's son and told her not to go. They quarrelled and in a jealous rage he pulled an old blunderbuss off the wall and threatened her with it. He claimed he thought it was empty but when he pulled the trigger there was shot inside and his wife fell down dead.

The murder was witnessed by two of his sons and immediately after committing the crime he walked to the local vicarage and confessed to the vicar who in turn called the police.

Sentenced to death by Mr Justice Hawke on 20 May and hanged by Tom Pierrepoint and Albert Pierrepoint.

July 16th: George HAGUE (23)   Durham

Hague, an unemployed bus driver of Langley Park, County Durham, was the former sweetheart of Amanda Sharp (20) and during their relationship he had given her a brightly coloured handkerchief as a love token.

On 6 May, he waited until she had finished work at the local hospital and asked her for the love token back. During the quarrel, when she refused to accompany him to a bonfire to celebrate the King's Silver Jubilee, he cut her throat with a razor.

He was sentenced to death at Durham Assizes by Mr Justice de Parcq on 29 June, after a plea of insanity failed.

Hanged by Tom Pierrepoint.

October 29th: Raymond Henry BOUSQUET (30)   Wandsworth

Although married with three children, Bousquet, a French-Canadian cruiserweight boxer who fought under the name of Del Fontaine, had been seeing Hilda Meek (19) regularly until she told him she had found a new boyfriend and wanted to end the affair.

On 10 July, he called at her mother's house and, after a quarrel, shot Hilda dead as she fled into the street. Hilda's mother followed them outside and Bousquet then shot her in the stomach. She later recovered in hospital. He then waited for Hilda's father to return, whereupon he unloaded the gun and told him to fetch the police.

At his six-day trial before Mr Justice Porter at the Old Bailey on 10 September, his defence claimed that Bousquet earned a living as a not very successful prize fighter and consequently he had become punch drunk.

It was claimed that the injuries he had sustained in the boxing ring had rendered him insane.

Hanged by Robert Baxter and Tom Phillips.

Raymond Henry Bousquet

October 30th: Allan James GRIERSON (27)   **Pentonville**

Mrs Louise Berthe Gann (63) was the caretaker of a smart flat in Gloucester Road, Regent's Park. Her daughter Mary befriended Grierson, a sometime gardener and the son of a wealthy Southampton solicitor, who was a petty thief and layabout.

Grierson persuaded the Ganns to let him lodge with them but after a few days he stole some items from the flat which he pawned. When the theft was discovered he wrote an apologetic letter and asked for forgiveness. They agreed and he was allowed to move back in.

Shortly afterwards he returned and told them he had found a job as a car salesman and had the use of a company car. Grierson suggested a trip to Torquay and while her mother could not go, Mary accepted. He arranged to meet her after work on the following afternoon, 22 June. When he failed to turn up at the appointed time, Mary returned home and found her mother severely beaten in the flat. She died the next day.

Grierson was arrested after a nationwide hunt that included an appeal on BBC radio. He protested his innocence and claimed that he was scared to go the police because of his previous record.

Allan James Grierson

At his eight-day trial before Mr Justice Porter on 10 September, Grierson pleaded not guilty. There was little to prove otherwise until dramatic last-minute evidence was produced in the form of a silver cruet set that could only have been stolen on the day of the murder, and which a witness proved was sold to him by the accused shortly afterwards.

Hanged by Robert Baxter and Henry Pollard.

1936

Cases where no executioner is recorded are multiple executions, and readers are asked to refer to the entries before or after for details of the hangman.

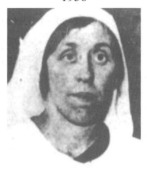

Dorothea Nancy Waddingham

April 16th: Dorothea Nancy WADDINGHAM (36)   Birmingham

Following the death of her husband, Waddingham posed as a qualified nurse and set up an old people's home in Nottingham which she ran with the assistance of her lover Ronald Sullivan (39).

In January 1935, Mrs Louisa Baguley (89) and her daughter Ada (50) arrived on the recommendation of Nottingham Council as their first patients. On 6 May, the daughter, who was obese and bedridden, instructed her solicitor to change her will in favour of Nurse Waddingham who had promised to care for both women till the end of their days.

On 12 May, the old lady died, followed a few months later by her daughter.   In her haste to have Ada cremated, Waddingham alerted the attention of the doctor who had signed the death certificate of the mother and he asked for an autopsy to be carried out. When this revealed an excessive amount of morphine, an exhumation was ordered on Mrs Baguley's body, which was also shown to contain morphine.

Waddingham and Sullivan were charged together, and stood trial before Mr Justice Goddard at Nottingham Assizes at the end of February 1936. It was decided there was not enough evidence to proceed with charges against Sullivan and he was acquitted.

On 27 February, after a two-week trial, 'Nurse' Waddingham was convicted on overwhelming evidence, with the jury surprisingly recommending mercy when returning a guilty verdict.

Hanged by Tom Pierrepoint and Albert Pierrepoint.

May 21st: Buck RUXTON (37)   Manchester

A Parsee doctor, born Bukhtyar Rustomji Ratanji Hakim, convicted of the murder by strangulation of his wife Isabella (34), and her maid, Mary Rogerson (20), in Lancaster.

When the women disappeared in September 1935, Ruxton told relatives that his wife had taken Mary away to have a pregnancy terminated.

The search for their whereabouts coincided with the discovery of two dismembered bodies in a ravine in Dumfriesshire, wrapped in a copy of a Sunday paper available only in Lancaster and Morecambe.

The family house was searched and traces of blood were found in the bathroom suggesting he had dismembered them there. Conclusive proof was supplied by some brilliant forensic work and items of Mary's clothing, recovered from the ravine and positively identified by her mother.

Ruxton was convicted at Manchester Assizes on 13 March and sentenced to death by Mr Justice Singleton.

Hanged by Tom Pierrepoint. Ruxton left behind a sealed note to be opened after his execution containing a confession to the murders. He said he killed his wife through jealousy at her supposed infidelity, and had to silence Mary after she inadvertently witnessed the crime.

Buck Ruxton

June 30th: Frederick Herbert Charles FIELD (32)   Wandsworth

In October 1931, the body of Norah Upchurch was found by workmen in an empty building on Shaftesbury Avenue. She had been strangled. Field was a suspect because he had a key to the building, which he claimed that he had lost. The coroner recorded an open verdict.

In 1933, while serving in the RAF, Field came to an arrangement with a newspaper that they would pay the costs of his defence if he confessed to the murder of Norah Upchurch. After retracting his confession he was unable to tell the police anything they did not already know about the case, and his trial at the Old Bailey ended with an acquittal.

In 1936, while absent without official leave from the airforce, he was picked up by the military police to whom he immediately confessed to the murder of Beatrice Vilna Sutton (48) who had been suffocated in her flat in Clapham on 4 April.

On 13 May, he was tried for the murder before Mr Justice Charles at the Old Bailey, and as before he retracted the confession. This time he let slip information only known to the killer and was convicted.

Hanged by Alfred Allen and Stanley Cross. Detectives investigating the case remarked that if Field had not confessed to the murder it was doubtful whether he would have been arrested.

Frederick Herbert Charles Field

July 14th: George Arthur BRYANT (38)   **Wandsworth**

On the evening of 21 May, police, acting on information received, called at a house on London Road, Dover, and found the body of Mrs Ellen Margaret Whiting (36). She had been strangled with a stocking after being beaten about the head with a bottle. She had moved from Folkestone to the house in Dover since parting from her husband of 14 years, earlier that year.

On the following day, Bryant, a labourer of Cheriton, Folkestone, was charged with the murder after walking into a police station and confessing. He pleaded guilty at his trial before Mr Justice Hilbery at Kent Assizes on 24 June.

Hanged by Tom Pierrepoint and Henry Pollard.

July 15th: Charlotte BRYANT (34)   **Exeter**

An Irishwoman who had met her husband-to-be Frederick John Bryant (39) while he was serving in Londonderry in the Black and Tans. She followed him back to Coombe, Dorset, where she quickly became disillusioned with life on a farm and soon began to have a steady stream of affairs which it seemed her husband chose to ignore.

In 1933, Leonard Parsons moved in with the Bryants and their five children and began to live with her as man and wife. Amazingly, Parsons and Fred Bryant became good friends. In December 1935, after the lodger had moved out, Charlotte's husband began to complain of stomach pains and when he died on 22 December an inquest was ordered. It was discovered that he had died of arsenic poisoning and a tin found to have contained arsenic was discovered in the garden.

Charlotte was sentenced to death by Mr Justice Mackinnon at Dorchester Assizes on 30 May. It was alleged that her striking black hair turned white as she awaited execution. Her letter to the King: 'Mighty King. Have pity on your afflicted subject. Don't let them kill me on Wednesday', failed to save her.

Hanged by Tom Pierrepoint and Tom Phillips.

August 5th: Wallace JENDEN (58) Wandsworth

On 23 May, Alice Whye (38) left her mother's house in Croydon and was never seen alive again. She had been seen in a public house with Jenden, a slaughterman of Wandle Park, Surrey, and later in a hut on his allotment.

Police interviewed Jenden about her disappearance and not being satisfied with his answers, kept him under observation. An officer saw him enter another hut and, following him inside, was able to prevent Jenden cutting his own throat. On the floor of the hut was the body of Alice Whye. She had been stabbed.

Jenden, who had been drinking, made a statement that amounted to a confession, saying that he had done it with his knife. When he sobered up he retracted this confession, but was charged with murder.

He was convicted before Mr Justice Hilbery at Surrey Assizes on 3 July after his defence of insanity failed. An unsuccessful appeal was launched, based on the Judge's misdirection on the evidence of drunkenness and the claim that the forensic evidence concerning the blood found on the knife was misleading.

Hanged by Tom Pierrepoint and Robert Wilson.

December 16th: Christopher JACKSON (24) Durham

Jackson was a labourer from Rotherham, living in lodgings in Chester-le-Street. He owed rent arrears and other money to his landlady's family, although he was not being pressed to re-pay. On 30 June, he left his lodgings, telling them he was going to collect a debt from a friend in Catterick, and returned later that day with enough money to settle his debts.

On the following day he was questioned about the death of his aunt, Mrs Harriet Linney (61), who had been battered to death with a bottle and coal rake at her home in Sunderland. He told police he had been in Catterick but later confessed to the murder.

Jackson said that he had travelled to Sunderland to see his aunt and uncle to ask for a loan. A few months earlier he had asked them for a loan and had been given a small sum. On the day in question he called at the house and found that his uncle was away at Carlisle races, but his aunt let him wait in the house until he returned. He said she began to insult and push him. He claimed he lost his temper, punched her and then hit her first with a coal rake, then battered her about the head with a bottle.

His counsel pleaded for manslaughter on the grounds of provocation but he was found guilty of murder and on 4 November at Durham Assizes, Mr Justice Goddard sentenced him to death.

Hanged by Tom Pierrepoint and Albert Pierrepoint.

1937

Cases where no executioner is recorded are multiple executions, and readers are asked to refer to the entries before or after for details of the hangman.

February 4th: Max Mayer HASLAM (23)   **Manchester**

Haslam was born in Heywood, Lancs, in 1913, with a crippling bone disease that left him unable to walk until he was nine, by which time he had grown bow-legged. By the time he reached his twenties he stood a little over four feet tall. His disability caused him to become a surly loner and he struggled at school. He found work in the cotton mills, but when made redundant in the economic decline of the mid-thirties, he turned to a life of crime.

After a number of convictions and prison terms for bungled robberies, he was released from Strangeways Gaol in May 1936 and moved into a lodging house at Burnley. Amongst his fellow tenants were a couple of small-time crooks and they soon began to plan jobs together.

On Friday 19 June, Haslam broke into the house of Miss Ruth Clarkson (74), a wealthy recluse, who lived alone with her dog on Clayton Street, Nelson. Despite the house looking like any other in the grim mill town, Miss Clarkson was a wealthy woman who owned property and collected antique jewellery.

On 22 June, word reached police that a dwarf was selling some stolen jewellery in Nelson and when police called at the house on Clayton Street, they were greeted by a fearful sight. Lying on the floor in the ransacked front room was the body of Miss Clarkson. She had been battered 17 times with a bloodstained tyre lever found beside the body. Upstairs, suspended from the headboard of the bed, was the body of her pet dog.

Haslam stood trial at Manchester Assizes before Mr Justice Lawrence on 8 December. In the face of a wealth of evidence, including witnesses who had seen him outside the house shortly before the murder, Haslam's alibi that he was at a cricket match when the crime was committed failed to convince the jury and on the the third day of the trial he was convicted.

He was due to be hanged alongside George Royle, a Stockport man who had killed a woman in the 'East Lancs Road Murder', but just hours before the scheduled double execution Royle was reprieved and Haslam alone faced hangmen Tom and Albert Pierrepoint.

February 10th: Andrew Anderson BAGLEY (62)   **Leeds**

In October 1932, Bagley's wife and mother to his six children died, leaving him with large debts. He refused to pay the debts and moved around Yorkshire changing his name to avoid his creditors who were pressing him to pay.

In August 1936, along with his mentally ill son, Bagley went to stay with his daughter and her family at Rotherham. It appeared that he soon became unnaturally close to his 16-year-old granddaughter Irene Hart, and there was an incident later that summer when he flew into a jealous rage when she went to the cinema with a boyfriend.

On 12 September, Bagley was sitting with Irene in the kitchen when her mother went out. She returned before lunch and found the old man alone in the kitchen saying that he had given Irene some money to go to the shop for him, but she had failed to return. He added that he thought she had run away, and said that he was going to Sheffield.

Later that day, Mrs Hart noticed that the attic door was open and inside was a trunk containing the still warm body of the missing girl. She had been strangled with the rope still knotted around her neck and her underclothing was missing. It was later found she had had sexual intercourse shortly before being strangled.

At his trial before Mr Justice Goddard at Leeds Assizes on 1 December, Bagley persisted with the story that Irene was still alive and in the company of a young man called Tom when Bagley left the house to go for a walk.

Hanged by Tom Pierrepoint and Robert Wilson.

June 17th: John HORNICK (42)   Dublin

On 25 January, Mary Redmond discovered the decomposing body of her brother James Redmond (45), in his caravan at Taghmon, County Wexford. He had extensive head injuries caused by the butt of a shotgun.

Despite living in a caravan, Redmond had worked hard all his life and had amassed savings of over £300, a considerable sum in those days. The receipt for the money was missing from the caravan; that suggested robbery as a motive for the killing, which police believe had taken place up to a fortnight before the body was discovered.

Hornick, a farmer from Kilgarvin, close to where Redmond kept his caravan, came under suspicion when Redmond's bicycle was found hidden on his land and when it was discovered that he had been spending money freely despite having recently had serious financial difficulties. He was charged with murder after being identified as the man who had cashed the missing receipt.

Sentenced to death by Mr Justice O'Byrne at Dublin Assizes on 15 April and hanged by Tom Pierrepoint and Albert Pierrepoint.

July 27th: Philip Edward Percy DAVIS (30)   Exeter

An engineer of Tuckingmill, Camborne, sentenced to death by Mr Justice Lawrence on 15 June at Bodmin Assizes for the murder of his wife Wilhelmina Vermadell Davis (33) and their niece Monica Rowe (15), at Camborne, Redruth.

Adjacent to the house Davis shared with his wife and niece was a garage which, on 24 April, he asked the landlord if he could rent to use as a workshop. His request was accepted and he was given the keys. Next day he told workmates his wife had left him, taking the niece and telling him not to try to find her.

At the end of April the landlord asked for the keys back and when he looked into the inspection pit he saw that it had been filled in with earth. He dug down a few inches and found the bodies of Mrs Davis and her niece.

Davis was questioned and confessed that he had battered them with a hammer after a quarrel.

His defence of insanity failed, despite his having previously been confined to an asylum. Hanged by Tom Pierrepoint and Tom Phillips.

August 12th: Horace William BRUNT (32) Manchester

On Saturday night, 24 April, Kate Collier (54) was found shot dead in her farmhouse at Bradley Wood, Ashbourne, Derbyshire. Her husband and daughter discovered the body when they returned from the market. The police were called and it was found that Kate had been blasted with a shotgun from a distance of just six feet.

Asked by detectives if they could think of anyone who might be responsible for the murder, the first name to spring to mind was Horace Brunt, daughter Elsie's boyfriend of five years whom her parents both disliked. He was arrested on suspicion but denied the allegations.

He then made a statement saying that he had gone to the house to try to discover why Kate disliked him so, and that she had attacked him with a poker and had pulled the shotgun off the wall and threatened him with it. He claimed it went off accidentally.

His version of events was disbelieved when it was proved that the gun could not have gone off by accident and it was also found that some money had been stolen from the kitchen.

Sentenced to death by Mr Justice Singleton at Derby Assizes on 2 July and hanged by Tom Pierrepoint.

August 13th: Leslie George STONE (24) Pentonville

Stone, a sandpit labourer of Heath and Reach, Bedfordshire, and Ruby Anne Keen (23) began courting seriously in 1931, when Stone was serving as a soldier in the Royal Artillery. He was later posted to Hong Kong and within a few months they had lost touch. By 1936, when he was discharged, she had become engaged to a policeman.

In April 1937, Stone met Ruby in a public house and tried to get her to give up her fiancé and become his girlfriend. They met up again on Sunday 11 April in a public house and were seen by some locals heading off into a lovers' lane later that night.

She was found strangled the next morning. Stone claimed to have left her around 10.15pm on the previous night and witnesses came forward to say they had seen her in the arms of a policeman at 10.45pm.

Detectives asked for clothing of all the suspects, including officers from Bedfordshire Constabulary and Leslie Stone, to be checked by forensic officers. Ingrained into the knees of Stone's trousers was a deposit of soil that proved it was his imprints found beside the body and because it was the first time he had worn the suit, he could not say that he had come into contact with the soil at another time.

He was tried before Lord Chief Justice Hewart at the Old Bailey on 28-29 June. The case against him rested on the slender forensic evidence but Stone made the fatal error of changing his version of the events of the night midway through the trial. In the second version of events he claimed that he was responsible for her death, but it was accidental.

Hanged by Tom Pierrepoint and Alfred Allen.

August 17th: Frederick George MURPHY (53)   Pentonville

In July 1927, Murphy, an odd-job man from Islington, was charged with the murder of a woman with whom he was having an affair. When the case came to trial it was decided that there was not enough evidence to proceed and he was acquitted.

On 12 May - Coronation Day - 1937, Murphy strangled Rosina Field (49), a prostitute, and left her body in the furniture shop at Islington where he worked. He then showed the body to a woman and asked her what to do, saying he had found the body there and was scared he would be implicated in the murder. He suggested that he should bury it. Unbeknown to Murphy, the woman, a Mrs Marshall, had seen Murphy and the prostitute enter the shop on the previous day and she suggested he gave himself up.

His trial before the Lord Chief Justice at the Old Bailey took place immediately after **Leslie STONE** had been convicted (see **August 13th**). He claimed that the police had bullied a confession out of him, saying that if he admitted to killing the woman he would be only charged with manslaughter.

Hanged by Alfred Allen and Tom Phillips. It was Allen's third and final job as chief executioner and the last time he attended an execution.

November 18th: John Thomas ROGERS (22)   Pentonville

In August 1937, Lillian Maud 'Lily' Chamberlain (25) worked as a barmaid in North London. She had married the previous summer and shared a flat with her husband at Northwood. Her husband's job as a railway steward meant he had to be away from home for several days at a time and it was while he was working away, on Tuesday 25 August, that his wife was strangled and battered to death.

Her body was found on the following morning when she failed to turn up for work. Also absent from work was John Rogers, the live-in barman, and when he was later questioned by detectives he was found to have bloodstains on his clothing.

At his two-day trial, before Mr Justice Charles at the Old Bailey from 18 October, it was shown that witnesses had seen Rogers outside the flat. In his defence, it was suggested that late in the evening he had called to see Lily, who had asked him to take 'glamour' photographs of her. Finding her battered to death, he had panicked and fled, scared that he would be implicated.

Hanged by Tom Pierrepoint and Henry Pollard. Although he had maintained his innocence throughout the trial, he confessed to guards on the night prior to his execution. It had also been revealed at the trial that Rogers' mother had been convicted of the manslaughter of his father in 1919.

December 7th: Ernest John MOSS (26)   **Exeter**

A former policeman at Brixham, Moss became a taxi driver when his marriage collapsed and moved to Exeter where he met Kitty Constance Bennett (18). The two became lovers and took lodgings at Ilfracombe before settling into a bungalow at Woolacombe.

He soon realised he no longer wished to live with Kitty and decided that the easiest way to end the relationship would be by committing suicide. Puzzling over what to do, Moss picked up a shotgun, battered her to death, then confessed to the police.

Moss insisted on pleading guilty to the charge and was sentenced to death by Mr Justice Hawke at Devon Assizes on 15 November.

Hanged by Tom Pierrepoint and Albert Pierrepoint.

Frederick Nodder

December 30th: Frederick NODDER (43)   **Lincoln**

Mona Tinsley (10) disappeared from her home in Newark on 5 January. She had been seen in the company of a man and the police routinely questioned Nodder, a motor driver, married with two children, who had lodged with the Tinsley family during the previous year.

Nodder, known to Mona as 'Uncle Fred', was wanted by police for failing to pay maintenance money to his estranged wife, and when put up for identification he was picked out by all the witnesses as the man seen with Mona on the day she disappeared. He claimed to have escorted the girl to Sheffield where she had gone to visit an aunt but could only corroborate parts of his statement and was charged with abduction. At his trial at Warwick in March, he was sentenced to seven years' imprisonment.

On 6 June, the body of a young girl, identified as Mona Tinsley, was washed up in the River Idle, 20 miles from Newark. She had been strangled. On 23 November, Nodder was taken from his cell to the dock of Nottingham Assizes and convicted of the murder.

Passing sentence of death, Mr Justice MacNaughton told Nodder: 'Justice has slowly, but surely, overtaken you.'

Hanged by Tom Pierrepoint and Stanley Cross.

1938

Cases where no executioner is recorded are multiple executions, and readers are asked to refer to the entries before or after for details of the hangman.

March 8th: Walter SMITH (34)   **Norwich**

  Albert Edward Baker (28) was the skipper of the barge 'East Anglia'. On the morning of 22 October 1937, it was moored at Felixstowe to unload a cargo of barley. That afternoon, Smith, a mate on the barge, went ashore. He spent the day in various public houses spending money lavishly on drinks.

  Next day, Baker's body was found in his cabin. He had been shot three times: once in the head and twice in the heart. His two wallets, which had contained over £10, were lying empty. Smith convicted himself when routinely questioned by police. 'You say the old man was shot dead?' he asked, when up to that time no mention had been made as to how Baker had died.

  At his trial before Mr Justice Singleton at Ipswich Assizes on 22 January, his defence of insanity through drink: *'mania a potu'*, was rejected.

  Hanged by Tom Pierrepoint and Tom Phillips.

April 20th: Charles James CALDWELL (49)   **Manchester**

  On 11 February, Caldwell, an unemployed hawker, followed his Swiss-born wife Eliza Augustine (40) as she headed for her new home in Rochdale. She had left home, on the advice of one of her workmates, when Caldwell became a heavy drinker and took out his anger at being unable to find work on his wife.

  He pleaded with her to go back with him, and when she repeatedly refused he stabbed her in front of several witnesses including his teenage son. He was arrested immediately and taken into custody, where he made a failed attempt to cut his throat.

  Sentenced to death by Mr Justice Tucker on 14 March, he declined to appeal saying he wanted to die.

  Hanged by Tom Pierrepoint and Albert Pierrepoint.

May 26th: Robert William HOOLHOUSE (21)   **Durham**

  In 1933, the Hoolhouse family were evicted from the cottage they rented from a farmer named Dobson, at High Grange, Wolviston, County Durham. On 18 January 1938, the farmer's wife, Mrs Margaret Jane Dobson (67), was found stabbed and sexually assaulted close to her home.

  Hoolhouse, a farm labourer of Haverton Hill, was one of many people questioned about the crime. He had a possible motive: eviction; a few scratches on his face, and roughly fitted a description of a man seen in the area. Despite the slender circumstantial evidence, he was charged with murder.

At his three-day trial before Mr Justice Wrottesley at Leeds Assizes on 30 March, the prosecution tried to show him as a callous killer who had taken a girlfriend to the cinema within hours of committing a brutal crime. His defence contested that there was no real case against him. However, evidence that supported his innocence was not produced in court, although a footprint found at the scene of the crime was proved not to match that of the accused. The jury however, found him guilty.

A petition of over 14,000 signatures failed to bring about a reprieve and in County Durham many people to this day believe an innocent man went to the gallows.

Hanged by Tom Pierrepoint.

June 8th: Jan MAHOMED (30)   **Liverpool**

An Indian seaman sentenced to death by Mr Justice Tucker at Manchester Assizes on 27 April for the murder of Aminul Hag (20), a trimmer aboard the SS Kabinga, at Gladstone Dock, Liverpool.

On 15 March Hag had been attacked Mahomed with an iron bar on board the ship. On 11 April, Mahomed returned to the ship and waited three hours for Hag to appear, and then attacked him with a large iron file. Hag fell down a metal ladder, caught his feet in a rung and hung suspended from his feet, bleeding to death.

The defence claimed that Mahomed had killed Hag in self-defence during a fight after Mahomed had gone to the ship to make peace, and that after being attacked Mahomed had picked up the first weapon at hand to fight him off. The prosecution disputed this by saying that if this were the case, Mahomed would not have crept unseen onto the ship and hid from the crew.

He spent his last days in the cell playing dominoes and draughts. On the morning of his execution he asked if he could play one last game. After keeping up his unbeaten record the draughts were put back in their box and Mahomed was led to the scaffold.

Hanged by Tom Pierrepoint and Albert Pierrepoint.

July 12th: Alfred Ernest RICHARDS (38)   **Wandsworth**

On 30 May, Kathleen Richards (37), a cinema usherette, was late returning to her home at Welling, Kent. She quarrelled with her husband, an illiterate mill hand, and when she told him she was going out with a workmate in two days' time he became angry. They were upstairs when her relatives heard her cry, 'Do something quick, he is strangling me!' After carrying out the murder, he left the house and confessed to a policeman.

He pleaded insanity at his trial before Mr Justice Humphreys at Kent Assizes on 25 June. Returning a guilty verdict, the jury added a strong recommendation for mercy.

Hanged by Tom Pierrepoint and Albert Pierrepoint.

July 19th: William James GRAVES (38)   Wandsworth

A labourer of Dymchurch, Kent, convicted of the murder of his 14-month-old illegitimate son, Tony Ruffle, whose body was found strangled in a hedge near Dover.

Graves was paying foster parents for the upkeep of his child, but when he became short of money he told the mother that he had found alternative arrangements for the child's upkeep. Instead he killed the child and tried to hide the body.

He pleaded insanity at his trial before Mr Justice Humphreys at Kent Assizes, on 27 June, and claimed he had no recollection of carrying out the attack. A senior medical officer at Brixton prison said he could find no sign of insanity, either now or previously.

Hanged by Tom Pierrepoint and Tom Phillips.

July 26th: William PARKER (25)   Durham

A golf caddie and ex-coalminer of Forest Hall, Newcastle, convicted before Mr Justice Atkinson at Newcastle Assizes on 17 June, for the murder of his wife Jane Ann (24).

On 25 April, Parker confessed to the police that he had murdered his wife at their home in Forest Hall, three days earlier. During these three days he had gone to work as normal, caddied at Northumberland Golf Club and slept at his mother's house.

He told police he had arrived home and found their two children had been strangled, and that it was his wife who killed the children and then attacked him with a hammer. He had then killed his wife in self-defence, battering her with the hammer.

The prosecution claimed that there was no evidence that his wife had killed the children, and that she had not died as he claimed. A pathologist stated cause of death as strangulation before she was struck nine times with a hammer.

Hanged by Tom Pierrepoint, almost certainly assisted by Alex Riley participating for the first time.

November 1st: George BRAIN (27)   Wandsworth

In the early hours of 14 July, the body of a prostitute, Muriel 'Rose' Atkins (30), was found lying in a road at Wimbledon. She had been battered over the head with a car starting-handle, and tyre marks on her body suggested she had been run down.

The woman had been seen shortly before her death climbing into a green van, and the tyre marks found on her were the type used on Austins and Morrises. The police contacted all local owners of green vans.

A boot-repairer came forward who claimed that two days after the murder, his van had disappeared along with the driver, George Brain of

Richmond, Surrey. Ten days later the van was located, and inside was the dead woman's handbag with bloodstained fingerprints that matched those of the missing driver. Other bloodstains inside the van suggested that it was the vehicle used in the crime. Two weeks later Brain was arrested at Sheerness after a massive manhunt.

At his trial before Mr Justice Wrottesley at the Old Bailey on 20 September, it was proved that Brain had stabbed the woman with a knife found in the van, then stolen her handbag before pushing her into the road to make it look like an accident. Missing from her handbag was just four shillings. He claimed that he had killed her after she accepted a lift home and tried to blackmail him. The jury took just 15 minutes to find him guilty.

Brain was due to be married a week after the murder. He had no previous criminal convictions and it was suggested he had panicked when faced with a compromising situation.

Hanged by Tom Pierrepoint and Stanley Cross. Herbert Morris was present as a trainee observer.

1939

Cases where no executioner is recorded are multiple executions, and readers are asked to refer to the entries before or after for details of the hangman.

January 7th: Dermot SMYTH (35)   Dublin

A well-educated farmer of The Rushes, Wolfhill, Leix, County Laois, sentenced to death at the Dublin central criminal court in December 1938, for the murder of Cornelius Dennehy, a butter buyer who was found shot dead in his car on 17 August 1938. The car was parked three miles from Smyth's farm.

At his trial Smyth declared his innocence and his defence claimed he was insane, with hereditary insanity in the family coupled with head injuries received in a fall several years earlier.

Hanged by Tom Pierrepoint and Albert Pierrepoint.

February 8th: John DAYMOND (19)   Durham

A farm worker from Northside, Workington, sentenced to death by Mr Justice Croom-Johnson at Cumberland Assizes on 19 January, for the murder of James Irwin Percival (68), of Aikhead near Wigton.

Daymond had worked for Percival as a casual farm worker during the summer, but was out of work and living rough in the area. On 9 December 1938, he attacked Percival and his son James (38) with a hammer, leaving them both for dead. Daymond was found hiding in a barn on the farm later that morning.

The defence at his trial claimed that Daymond was guilty but insane and called witnesses to testify that during a full moon he had funny moods.

Hanged by Tom Pierrepoint.

March 25th: Harry ARMSTRONG (38)   Wandsworth

On 2 January, the body of Peggy Irene Pentecost (17) was found in a Lambeth hotel room. She had been strangled and a bed quilt had been forced into her mouth.

From items found in the room, police ascertained the identity of the victim and learned that on New Year's Eve she had checked into the hotel with a man, signing the register Mr and Mrs Armstrong of Seaford. Armstrong was traced. He was found to be a parlour-man of Seaford, with a number of previous convictions, including attempted murder. Armstrong, who had become engaged to Peggy shortly after Christmas, was arrested on the following day.

At his two-day trial before Mr Justice Humphries at the Old Bailey, from 1 March, it was alleged that he had killed Peggy after a jealous quarrel. It was revealed at the trial that she was also seeing another man.

Armstrong denied the charges against him, offering an alibi that was easily discredited. After being sentenced he said he did not wish to appeal but asked for a reprieve on medical grounds.

Hanged by Tom Phillips, his first time as chief executioner, assisted by Albert Pierrepoint.

March 29th: William Thomas BUTLER (29)   Wandsworth

On Christmas Eve 1938, Ernest Percival Key (64), was found unconscious in his lock-up jeweller's shop at Surbiton. He had been stabbed 31 times and died on the way to hospital. Missing from the shop were a sum of money and items of jewellery.

Butler, a motor driver of nearby Teddington, left behind his bowler hat which was linked to him by traces of hair. He was also identified as a man who had called for hospital treatment for a cut hand. He gave differing accounts as to how he had received the wounds.

Sentenced to death by Mr Justice Singleton at the Old Bailey on 16 February. His defence claimed Butler had acted in self-defence and asked the court to reduce the charge to manslaughter.

Hanged by Tom Pierrepoint and Tom Phillips.

June 7th: Ralph SMITH (41)   Gloucester

Smith was a locomotive fireman with the Great Western Railway who lodged with a Mrs Beatrice Delia Baxter (53) in Swindon. He was infatuated with his landlady, who was single, and became jealous whenever she went out with other men.

On 4 March, he was seen talking to his landlady and during the conversation she was overheard telling Smith she was going to a dance with another man. Later Mrs Baxter was heard screaming and witnesses found her bleeding to death from a deep wound to the back of her neck.

Smith was tried before Mr Justice Atkinson at the Old Bailey on 3 May. His defence of manslaughter was rejected and he was sentenced to death. He lodged an appeal saying that the judge had misdirected the jury with regards to the issue of provocation and manslaughter, but it was rejected.

Hanged by Tom Pierrepoint and Albert Pierrepoint.

October 10th: Leonard George HUCKER (30)   Wandsworth

Mary Alice Maud Fullick (60), was stabbed to death in her basement flat at Victoria Villas, Kilburn, on 16 August. Hucker, a wood machinist, had gone to the house to try to patch up the broken romance between himself and Beatrice Moncrief, Mrs Fullick's daughter. It was alleged that during a row, when they both became angry, he picked up a knife to frighten her, and when she went towards him he stabbed her. Hucker then walked to the local police station and gave himself up.

61

At his trial before Mr Justice Oliver at the Old Bailey on 22 September, the defence claimed that the crime was not premeditated and that Hucker had picked up the knife on the spur of the moment after being attacked. This was disproved when a witness testified that Hucker had purchased the knife the previous day. He then admitted he had bought the knife to take his own life, but lacked the courage to go through with it.

Hanged by Tom Pierrepoint and Herbert Morris.

October 25th: Stanley Ernest BOON (28)   Wandsworth

On the morning of 5 July, the body of Mabel Maud Bundy (44) was found on a footpath near the staff entrance at the Moorlands Hotel, Hindhead, where she worked as a maid. She had a broken nose, severe bruising around her left eye and brain damage caused by a heavy blow to the chin.

Witnesses saw her drinking with a number of soldiers from Thursley Camp in a nearby hotel on the previous evening. The camp housed the 2nd Battalion North Staffordshire Regiment and at an identity parade held later that day, Boon was picked out as the man seen talking to the victim.

Asked to account for his movements, Boon, a private, said he was drinking with two soldiers, Private Goodwin and Private Arthur Smith, and left the bar at closing time. Smith said that he had left with Mabel Bundy and that she had consented to have sex with him, and while this was going on Boon and Goodwin approached. Goodwin said he had only followed because Boon seemed very drunk and aggressive.

At the nine-day trial before Mr Justice Oliver in September it was alleged that the two soldiers had followed behind intending to spy on the couple, but when she became aware of their presence she resisted and they battered her to death as she struggled. It was alleged that Boon had struck the woman as Smith held her and that both had raped her. Goodwin was found not guilty and acquitted, Boon and Smith were convicted and on 21 September both were sentenced to death. Boon chose not to appeal against conviction.

Hanged by Tom Pierrepoint and Stanley Cross.

October 26th: Arthur John SMITH (26)   Wandsworth

See above. Unlike Boon, Smith chose to appeal, but it was dismissed and he was hanged by Tom Pierrepoint and Tom Phillips.

1940

Cases where no executioner is recorded are multiple executions, and readers are asked to refer to the entries before or after for details of the hangman.

1940

February 7th: Peter BARNES (32)   **Birmingham**
James RICHARDS (29)

In the summer of 1939, the IRA formulated the 'S' Plan, a bombing campaign on the British mainland, aimed at focusing attention to the requests for the withdrawal of British troops from Ulster.

In July that year, Richards, also known as McCormack, travelled to the mainland and lodged with Irishman Joseph Hewitt and his family on Clara Street, Coventry. The house quickly became a terrorist HQ, where explosives were stored and prepared.

On 21 August, Barnes travelled to Clara Street, and over the next few days Hewitt's mother-in-law purchased a suitcase whilst Richards and another man obtained a bicycle from a Coventry shop.

On 24 August, Richards made a bomb in the front room of the house and on the following day the bicycle was left on the busy Broadgate, Coventry, where it exploded at 2.32 pm. Five people were killed in the explosion, amongst them being Elsie Ansell (21), who was due to be married in a few days' time.

The serial number found on the bicycle led police to Richards. Arrests in London later that night led to Barnes and later five people were arrested and charged with murder.

At the four-day trial before Mr Justice Singleton at Birmingham Assizes on 11 December, three were acquitted of the charges while Barnes and Richards were convicted of the murder of Elsie Ansell. Although there was no direct evidence that Barnes had planted the bomb, there was enough incriminating evidence against him to prove he had participated in the outrage.

Hanged together by Tom Pierrepoint assisted by Tom Phillips, Stanley Cross and Albert Pierrepoint.

March 27th: Ernest Edmund HAMERTON (25)   **Wandsworth**

A kitchen porter sentenced to death at the Old Bailey by Mr Justice Wrottesley on 8 February, for the murder of Elsie May Ellington (28), the assistant manageress at Lyon's Cafe, Camberwell Green.

Early in January 1940, Hamerton left his native Lancashire to live in London and be near his sweetheart, Elsie Ellington, who lived in lodgings at Walworth, and whom he hoped to marry. Hamerton took a room in the same house, but almost as soon as he arrived in the city they began to argue and matters came to a head on 14 January when they had a massive quarrel. On the following day he asked her to accompany him to the cinema, but she refused and he went alone.

On the following morning, they quarrelled at breakfast. The main grievance Hamerton bore was the fact that Elsie did not seem to appreciate that he had given up his job to be near her. She said their relationship was over. He told her he had given up a good job in Lancashire to be with her and in a rage picked up a knife and stabbed her 24 times, leaving the knife stuck through her heart. Hamerton left London by train, but was arrested as he arrived at Manchester.

Hanged by Tom Phillips and Alex Riley. Records note that Phillips was censured for his behaviour (aggressive and smelling of drink) and this may have led to dismissal. Either way, it was his last execution after 18 years as a hangman.

April 24th: William Charles COWELL (38)   Wandsworth

On 21 September 1939, hospital maid Annie Farrow Cook (34) left her quarters at the Brighton Officers hospital. She was never seen alive again. She had arranged to go to the circus with Cowell, a married man who worked as an orderly at the same hospital, but when questioned by detectives he said Annie had turned up late in a bit of a state and borrowed some money, saying she was going to London.

A month later her body was found in a wood at Albourne and Cowell, whom witnesses had seen leaving the wood, was charged with her murder. At his trial before Mr Justice Lawrence at Lewes Assizes on 8 March, Cowell claimed that they had bought a bottle of spirits and gone into the wood together. Whilst drunk they had quarrelled and he had smashed the bottle over her head, fatally wounding her. He then covered the body with twigs. It was alleged that Cowell visited the scene every day for a week to make sure the body had not been discovered.

Hanged by Tom Pierrepoint and Stanley Cross.

July 11th: William APPLEBY (27)   Durham
Vincent OSTLER (24)

In the early hours of Friday 1 March, Police Constable William Ralph Shiell (28) was on duty at Coxhoe, County Durham, when he was alerted to a break-in at a nearby Co-op store. He called at the premises with several colleagues and when two men made their getaway, PC Shiell gave pursuit. He was closing in on the men when one said: 'All right, let him have it!' A shot rang out and the constable fell, fatally wounded. He gave fellow officers a vague description of his killers before he died. Clues left near the scene included a stolen Vauxhall motorcar.

A newspaper appeal brought reports that a similar car had been in the possession of two local criminals, Appleby and Ostler. Appleby, a joiner, was questioned first and confessed that that he had taken part in the robbery, unaware that his accomplice, whom he named as Ostler, an ice cream man, was carrying a gun. Policeman's son Ostler, a father of four, was interviewed, unaware that his friend had confessed. He denied any knowledge of the murder.

They were tried before Mr Justice Hilbery at Leeds Assizes. Appleby denied PC Shiell's deathbed claim that he had shouted 'Let him have it!', instead insisting he told Ostler to 'Give him a clout!' On 10 May, after a four-day trial, both were sentenced to death, with the jury giving Appleby a strong recommendation for mercy.

Hanged together by Tom Pierrepoint assisted by Stanley Cross, Albert Pierrepoint and Alex Riley.

July 31st: Udham SINGH (37)   Pentonville

On 13 March, a meeting was held at London's Caxton Hall. Chaired by Lord Zetland, the debate was on Afghanistan, and on the platform was Sir Michael Francis O'Dwyer (75). In 1919 O'Dwyer was the Lieutenant-Governor of the Punjab, where, under the command of General Dyer, many Indians were killed as riots were brutally suppressed.

As the meeting came to its conclusion, a Sikh pulled out a revolver and fired six shots at the platform. Sir Michael was killed instantly, others received gunshot wounds, but were not seriously injured.

The killer gave his name as Singh Azad, but he was usually known as Udham Singh. From papers taken from his room, it seemed that he had mistaken his victim for General Dyer.

At his trial before Mr Justice Atkinson at the Old Bailey on 4-5 June, Singh, who had been on a 42-day hunger strike prior to his trial, claimed that the shooting was an accident and that he had meant to fire into the ceiling. The prosecution alleged that he had travelled to England to avenge the deaths of relatives, killed in the Amritsar riot in 1919.

Hanged by Stanley Cross carrying out his first engagement as chief executioner, assisted by Albert Pierrepoint.

August 8th: George Edward ROBERTS (28)   Cardiff

On 3 February Arthur John Allen (38), a ship's steward, had attended a party in Cardiff. Amongst the forty or so guests was Roberts. At the end of the night Allen asked for change to make a call from a nearby phone box, Roberts offered to help and the two men left.

In the early hours of the following morning, Roberts struck Allen over the head with an iron bar and stole his wallet, which contained five one pound notes. Although seriously injured Allen told police that Roberts had robbed him and his empty wallet was found at Roberts's house. The stolen pound notes were found hidden in a cigarette packet in Roberts's pocket. Allen died from his injuries on 9 April whereupon Roberts was charged with his murder.

He was sentenced to death by Mr Justice MacNaughton at Glamorgan Assizes on 17 July.

Hanged by Tom Pierrepoint and Stanley Cross.

September 10th: John William WRIGHT (41)   **Durham**

On 22 May, Mrs Alice Wright (44) was found severely beaten at her home, a former inn in Toronto, Bishop Auckland, by her children returning from school. She was taken to the nearby hospital where she died from her injuries. Wright, an unemployed brick-worker, told police that his wife had been fit and well when he had left home earlier that day. He was arrested after police found traces on blood on his clothes and a butcher's cleaver hidden nearby.

Sentenced to death by Mr Justice Stable at Yorkshire Assizes on 19 July. It was alleged that he had killed her in order to claim money on an insurance policy

Hanged by Tom Pierrepoint and Albert Pierrepoint.

October 31st: Stanley Edward COLE (23)   **Wandsworth**

Shortly after midnight on 23 August, Cole, a wood-machinist, walked into Wimbledon police station and confessed he had stabbed a woman. Police went to a house and found the body of Mrs Doris Eugenie Girl (29), whose husband was serving overseas.

Sentenced to death by Mr Justice Hallett at the Old Bailey on 12 September. The motive was never made clear. Cole had been very friendly with both Doris and her husband but may have been on intimate terms with her while her husband was away. He claimed to have been drunk when he committed the crime, but no evidence of any quarrel was offered and Cole declined to give any evidence at the three-day trial.

Hanged by Tom Pierrepoint and Herbert Morris. Henry Critchell and Harry Kirk were present as trainee observers.

November 26th: William Henry COOPER (24)   **Bedford**

On 5 July, farmer John Joseph Harrison (69) was found dying from head injuries on a farm he owned at Thorney, on the Isle of Ely. He had been battered about the head with a bottle.

Cooper, from Peterborough, a former horse keeper at the farm who had been dismissed in April, was arrested on a charge of assault and then charged with murder when the old man died on 21 July.

At Cambridge Assizes on 17 October, it was claimed that Cooper had called at the farm to ask Harrison why he had dismissed him, and that the victim had attacked him with a hammer. Cooper claimed he picked up the bottle in self-defence. The prosecution suggested that Cooper had beaten the old man in revenge for his dismissal and that he had then stolen a sum of money.

He appealed against conviction, saying that the trial judge, Mr Justice Singleton, had not guided the jury sufficiently on the defence's plea of manslaughter.

Hanged by Tom Pierrepoint and Albert Pierrepoint. Harry Allen and Steve Wade were present as trainee observers. Cooper collapsed in terror when the hangmen entered the cell and he had to be carried to the scaffold.

December 10th: Karl Heindrich MEIR (24)   Pentonville
Jose WALDBERG (25)

On 2 September four enemy agents set out for the English coastline. They split into pairs and landed in Kent. Meir and Waldberg, both German-born, were arrested shortly after landing. Both had been drinking prior to landing, and to quench their thirst they called into a pub at Lydd where, ignorant of the British licensing laws, they asked to buy a glass of cider. The suspicious licensee, warned to be on the look out for spies, called the police and they were arrested later that afternoon.

Like all subsequent spies caught during the war, they were tried under the 1940 Treason Act. The trials were held '*In Camera*' (in secret) so that the enemy would be unaware of their capture. Evidence was heard in court that the two men had sent back radio messages prior to their arrest.

Hanged by Stanley Cross, assisted by Albert Pierrepoint, Henry Critchell and Harry Kirk.

December 17th: Charles Van Der KEIBOOM (25)   Pentonville

Van Der Keiboom was born in Japan with a Japanese mother and Dutch father. He landed with another spy, Dutchman Sjoerd Pons, at Dymchurch, Kent, in the early hours of 3 September. Both were arrested almost at once by patrolling soldiers.

Van Der Keiboom attracted attention by virtue of his marked oriental features and the fact that he carried a large suitcase. It is alleged that Pons immediately turned King's Evidence and testified against both his fellow countryman and the two Germans who had arrived by the same boat.

Both stood trial on 22 November, along with Meir and Waldberg (see above) and were convicted of treason. Pons was sentenced to life imprisonment, the others sentenced to death.

The three spies were due to be hanged together but Van Der Keiboom appealed, the only one to do so, and as a result his execution was postponed to hear his plea. He claimed that he had been blackmailed into spying by the Germans after threats had been made against his family. The appeal rejected this, stating that it was the most common plea for such a charge and there was nothing to substantiate it.

Hanged by Stanley Cross and Herbert Morris.

December 24th: Edward SCOLLEN (42)   **Durham**

Scollen, a labourer, lived with his wife Beatrice Barbara (35) in Middlesbrough. It was the second marriage for them both and up until spring 1940, they had lived happily together. In July, his wife left him after a quarrel, but they patched things up, only to split up again in August.

During the afternoon of 12 August, Scollen went out drinking, and after consuming 12 pints he was unable to go into work that evening. He then called at a relative's house where his wife was staying and during a quarrel he tried to drag her back home. He then fatally stabbed her before cutting his own throat and making an attempt to hang himself.

Sentenced to death by Mr Justice Cassels at York Assizes on 6 November. His failed defence was manslaughter through provocation.

Hanged by Tom Pierrepoint and Henry Critchell after it was deemed that his injuries would not prevent the execution being carried out.

1941

Cases where no executioner is recorded are multiple executions, and readers are asked to refer to the entries before or after for details of the hangman.

January 7th: David DOHERTY (29)   Dublin

On 20 April 1940, the body of Hannah Margaret Doherty (28) was found on a mountainside less than 200 yards from her home at Ballyhillon, near Malin Head, County Donegal. She had been missing since the previous night. Cause of death was severe head injuries caused by her being struck with a large rock.

Investigations led police to believe that Hannah had left her home on a secret assignation and amongst the strongest suspects was Doherty, her second cousin. He was a married man who lived close by, but he gave an alibi for the time of the murder, claiming he was attending to a sick horse. His clothes were examined and when asked to explain bloodstains on the trousers he claimed he had had a fight in the previous week and suffered a nose bleed.

He was finally trapped when he lied to police about the clothes he wore on the night of 19 April. Doherty could not produce them as they had been burned. Although this was highly suspicious, police could not break the man's alibi until finally, after persistent interviews, Doherty elaborated a little too much and contradicted things he had said in earlier statements.

At his four-day Dublin trial before Mr Justice Maguire in November, it was alleged that the cousins had been lovers and that Hannah had fallen pregnant. He was asked to obtain the necessary medicines to procure an abortion and when he turned up at the rendezvous without them, they quarrelled. Doherty, fearful that her shouting would attract attention, strangled his cousin and then battered her about the head with a boulder.

Hanged by Tom Pierrepoint and Albert Pierrepoint.

February 11th: Clifford HOLMES (24)   Manchester

Returning home on leave, Holmes, a driver in the Royal Engineers, found that his wife, the mother of his two young children, had been unfaithful while he was serving overseas. They quarrelled and she told him to pack his bags.

On 8 October 1940, Irene Holmes (23), applied for a separation order, and two days later, hearing what she had done, Holmes called at their flat in Longsight, Manchester. Unable to gain entry, he shouted for his wife to open the front door and when she refused, he went to the back door, drew his rifle and blasted the lock.

Hearing the gunshot, and thinking her husband was trying to get in the front way, she ran down the stairs and turned to exit the house via the back door. Finding himself face to face with his adulterous wife, Holmes pointed the rifle and fired. The shot missed and as he reloaded his wife cowered behind the kitchen door crying for mercy.

Holmes then picked up a kitchen knife and stabbed her. As she lay dying on the floor, he reloaded the gun with the intention of shooting himself. 'I lacked the courage to do it myself.' he later stated at his trial. The commotion brought witnesses rushing to the house, whereupon Holmes was detained and later charged with murder.

Insanity was to be his defence at the trial before Mr Justice Stable on 16-17 December, where evidence was shown that Holmes's brother was a certified mental defective.

Hanged by Tom Pierrepoint and Harry Allen.

March 6th: Henry Lyndo WHITE (39)   Durham

On 19 January, a young man saw two people arguing in a South Shields street. He recognised them as Henry Lyndo White, a miner, and Emily Wardle (34). White seemed to be trying to throttle his companion, but on crossing the road the youth was told there was nothing to worry about, and that it was no more than a lovers' tiff. He turned away and moments later White cut the woman's throat. White then cut her across the forehead and blood gushed down her clothes as she screamed in agony.

The stricken woman was taken to a nearby shop, followed by the callous White. 'I told you I'd kill you, you bugger, meeting someone else and double-crossing me.'

Tried before Mr Justice Charles at Durham Assizes on St Valentine's Day, White's weak defence of provocation failed, the jury being satisfied that there was clear premeditation in a man walking around with a shaving-razor.

Hanged by Tom Pierrepoint and Harry Allen.

April 4th: Samuel MORGAN (28)   Liverpool

On 2 November 1940, the body of Mary Hagan (15) was found in a concrete blockhouse at Seaforth, Liverpool. She had been raped and strangled. Found beside the body was a bandage, smeared with zinc ointment and shaped to cover a thumb wound.

Investigations into the assault of another girl in the area led police to question Morgan, who lived nearby but was stationed in the south. When questioned Morgan was found to have a fleshly healed scar on his thumb. A search of his house found a piece of identical bandage which, due to a manufacturing fault, was conclusive proof that the one found beside the body belonged to Morgan.

Sentenced to death by Mr Justice Stable at Liverpool on 18 February. His appeal was dismissed on 25 March.

Hanged by Tom Pierrepoint and Herbert Morris.

April 23rd: Henry GLEESON (39)   Dublin

On 21 November 1940, the body of Mary McCarthy (40) was discovered in a field at Marl Hill, County Tipperary. She had severe head injuries which were found to have been caused by a shotgun. The body was discovered by Gleeson, a neighbour, who was subsequently charged with her murder.

He was condemned before Mr Justice Maguire at Dublin in February. It has been since alleged that Mary McCarthy worked as a prostitute and had been executed by the IRA for anti-social activities and that Gleeson was framed for the murder. Witnesses who could have testified as to his innocence were intimidated and warned against giving evidence. The real identity of the killer was suggested to be George Plant, a member of the IRA who was executed by firing squad in March 1942.

Hanged by Tom Pierrepoint and Albert Pierrepoint.

July 9th: George Johnson ARMSTRONG (39)   Wandsworth

A Newcastle born ship's engineer who served in the navy between 1939-1940. During this time he offered his services to the German Secret Service through the Consul at Boston in the USA.

Armstrong had previously made known his pro-nazi leanings and watch had been kept on his movements for many months. Briefed as to what information he should report back, he returned to his ship, but on 23 February, as it docked at Cardiff, he was placed under arrest.

Sentenced to death by Mr Justice Lewis at the Old Bailey, he was described as a 'rank amateur' in the field of espionage.

Hanged by Tom Pierrepoint and Steve Wade, he was the first British traitor to go to the gallows during the war.

July 23rd: David Millar JENNINGS (21)   Dorchester

On 26 January Jennings, a Warrington born soldier stationed at Dorchester, received a 'Dear John' letter from his fiancée. Coming off duty that night he rounded up some friends and went out on a massive drinking spree. Jennings was alleged to have downed ten pints and seven whiskeys that evening and on returning to camp realised he had blown all his savings.

He then changed uniforms, picked up his rifle and ten bullets and set out to commit a robbery. Jennings selected the NAAFI as his target. Patrolling the building was Albert Edward Farley (65), an ex-soldier who had just taken up the post of nightwatchman. Jennings attempted to force entry by shooting at the lock, but was unable to aim straight. Noticing a light come on inside the building, he fired another round of shots and then turned to walk back to barracks.

Arriving back at camp, he told an officer what he had done and investigations found the body of the watchman slumped behind the door.

He was convicted at Dorset Assizes before Mr Justice Charles on 3 June. An appeal failed, as did numerous petitions including one to the king.

Hanged by Tom Pierrepoint and Alex Riley.

1941

July 31st: Edward Walker ANDERSON (19)   **Durham**

On 11 June 1941 an old blind man, William Anderson (63), was discovered, seriously injured, at his home in Belmont, County Durham. He had been brutally battered with an axe and the house ransacked. Missing from the house was a large amount of money that had been well hidden and unlikely to have been discovered by a burglar unless he had prior knowledge.

With William Anderson held in intensive care, police inquiries centred on the family and in particular Edward Walker Anderson, his great-nephew, who had previous convictions for theft. Earlier that year Edward Walker Anderson had been employed as a porter at a hotel in Tynemouth, and investigations revealed that he had visited there on 7 June and admitted to having no money.

On 13 June police visited Edward Walker Anderson's home in Hull where they found items stolen from William Anderson's house including a fountain pen, shoes, and a raincoat. Edward Walker Anderson confessed that he had attacked his uncle and when the old man died on 19 June he was charged with murder.

Sentenced to death at Yorkshire Assizes by Mr Justice Croom-Johnson on 12 July, he made no appeal and was hanged by Tom Pierrepoint just 42 days after the death of his great uncle.

Werner Heinrich Walti

August 6th: Karl Theo DRUEKE (35)   **Wandsworth**
Werner Heinrich WALTI (25)

After the failure of the first spies (see **1940, December 10th: Karl Heindrich MEIR and Jose WALDBERG**), German Intelligence launched their next mission in the north of Scotland. On 30 September 1940 a plane carrying three agents left Norway and landed near Buckie. They paddled ashore and separated.

German born Drueke (spelt Drucke in some sources, also known as Robert Petter) and a female companion, Vera Erikson, immediately attracted the attention of the Portgordon station master when he enquired in

75

broken English for the next train to London. The police were called and they were arrested and charged with espionage. Walti, a Swiss national, travelled as far as Edinburgh, where he was arrested at Waverley Station on going to reclaim his luggage. He made a number of failed suicide bids following his arrest.

All three were questioned by agents from the Special Branch, but only the two men stood trial before Mr Justice Asquith on 12 June.

Hanged by Tom Pierrepoint, assisted by Albert Pierrepoint, Steve Wade and Harry Kirk.

September 4th: John SMITH (32)   Manchester

Smith had been keeping company with Margaret 'Ellen' Knight (28) for over four months, when she became pregnant. Smith, a member of the Home Guard based at Shawford, near Rochdale, was delighted at the news and proposed marriage. Ellen, however, was aghast. 'I'd rather die than marry him,' she told her mother.

One afternoon in May, Ellen broke off their relationship and made plans to terminate her pregnancy. On 17 May, she and a friend attended a meeting at a local Salvation Army hostel. Smith sat a few rows behind with his rifle on his knee. As the two women left he followed them into the road and pointing the rifle at Ellen's back, he fired. She fell to the ground dead as Smith rushed over shouting 'It's an accident'. He later claimed that he had intended to fire over her head to frighten her into going back with him.

The trial before Mr Justice Hallett on 8 July was remarkable only in the fact that the chief defence witness was Smith's drill sergeant, who testified that the accused was the worst shot he had ever seen and that he could not even aim straight.

Hanged by Tom Pierrepoint and Harry Allen.

September 19th: Eli RICHARDS (45)   Birmingham

A crippled hawker of Weoley Castle, Birmingham, sentenced to death by Mr Justice Stable at Birmingham Assizes on 22 July for the murder of Mrs Jane Turner (64), a hawker.

On 28 March, Richards met Mrs Turner, an alcoholic, and the two began drinking together. Later that night they had an argument at Cotteridge, witnessed by members of the Home Guard, and shortly afterwards screams were heard.

Mrs Turner was found battered to death on a footpath. Beside the body was a walking stick belonging to Richards, and a broken beer bottle. It was alleged that Richards had struck her with the bottle after she had refused his advances.

Richards denied the charge, saying they had parted amiably after he gave her half a crown.

Hanged by Tom Pierrepoint and Stanley Cross.

October 31st: Antonio MANCINI (39)   Pentonville

One night in April 1941 two men called at The Palm Beach Bottle Party club in Soho. There was a scuffle at the door and Mancini, the club manager, promptly barred them.

On 1 May the same men, accompanied by a friend Harry Distleman (36), returned to the club and another fracas erupted during which Distleman received a fatal wound. He died in hospital after claiming Mancini had stabbed him.

Mancini was one of three men charged with being involved in the murder. Two others were convicted of attempted murder, Mancini alone was convicted of murder and sentenced to death by Mr Justice MacNaughton on 4 July.

His first appeal was heard in September and dismissed, as was an appeal before the House of Lords on 16 October.

Finally, almost four months after conviction, Mancini was hanged by Albert Pierrepoint, officiating at his first senior execution, assisted by Steve Wade.

November 12th: Lionel Rupert Nathan WATSON (30)   Pentonville

Watson was a Bakelite moulder of Greenford, Middlesex. He was separated from his wife when in the summer of 1940 he met Phyllis Crocker (28) the mother of an 18-month-old daughter, Eileen. They went through a bigamous marriage and set up home together.

In June 1941 Watson was seen by a neighbour digging his garden. Asked if he was 'digging for victory' he replied that he was burying rubbish. When his 'wife's' disappearance was noted he said she had fled 'the blitz' and gone to Scotland, but when a strange smell began to appear in the garden neighbours called the police to investigate.

Buried beneath the flagstones were the bodies of Phyllis and her daughter. They had been poisoned with cyanide, a poison to which Watson had access at work. He denied the charge but it was shown that he had recently started dating another girl and had drawn all Phyllis's money out of her account.

His defence before Mr Justice Cassels at the Old Bailey on 15-18 September was that he had returned home to find that his 'wife', who had recently told him she was pregnant, had poisoned the baby and committed suicide. He claimed she was fearful of being pregnant after having a very difficult time with Eileen's birth.

The prosecution alleged he had killed them so he could be free to court his new girlfriend whom he showered with gifts, including items belonging to Phyllis.

Hanged by Tom Pierrepoint and Henry Critchell.

December 3rd: John Ernest SMITH (21)   Wandsworth

Smith and Christina Rose Dicksee (24) had been neighbours in London's East End until her family moved to Kent. They were very much in love and planned to marry, but when her father suggested they wait until the war ended, Smith took this as a sign of disapproval.

On 29 October she visited Smith at home. While they were alone together he stabbed her 34 times. Drenched in blood, Smith was stroking her hair and declaring his love for her when the police arrived.

Tried before Mr Justice Hilbery at the Old Bailey on 14 November, his defence was insanity. The prosecution referred to the statement Smith made on arrest in which he claimed to have bought the knife with the intention of killing her, because he was scared she would find someone else.

Hanged by Albert Pierrepoint and Harry Allen.

December 10th: Karel Richard RICHTER (29)   Wandsworth

On 13 May, Sudeten-born Richter was dropped by parachute near London Colney. He carried £500, US$1,000 and a map of East Anglia. Once he removed his flying suit and changed into his civilian clothes he became a spy, and after burying the parachute and money he hid until the following evening.

At 10.15pm he set out on his journey, and almost immediately he was stopped and asked directions by a lorry driver. His surly reply was enough for the driver to report him to a policeman a little up the road. PC Scott cycled after the man and asked to see his papers. Richter was carrying an alien's visa card with an address in London. As one condition of carrying such a card was that the holder had to be at that address by an 11pm curfew, Scott asked him where he had come from and was told he had walked from Dover and that it had taken him two hours. (The journey, by foot would take approx 24 hours). The man spoke with a slight accent and suspecting he was a spy, Scott took Richter into custody.

Richter subsequently found himself before Mr Justice Tucker at the Old Bailey and on 24 October, after a four-day trial held '*in camera*' (in secret so that the enemy would be unaware of his capture) he was sentenced to death.

Hanged by Albert Pierrepoint, in what he later described as his toughest session on the scaffold. Richter's brute strength was enough to break the arm pinion straps and he fought vainly as he was dragged to the scaffold. As the hangman pulled the lever, Richter jumped forward and the noose slipped catching on his nose. Cause of death was a broken neck as planned. Richter is easily identifiable as 'Otto Schmidt' in Pierrepoint's biography.

Assistant executioner Steve Wade recorded in his diary that the struggle lasted 17 minutes and continued over the trap-doors, with Richter continually screaming 'Help me'. Wade noted that he would not have missed this for £50!

December 18th: Patrick KELLY (31)   Dublin

A Riverstown, County Sligo, labourer convicted of the murder of Mary Brehony (39) a spinster of Rossmore, County Sligo.

The woman was strangled and drowned, her body having been dragged across a field and thrown into a river. One of the features of the convicting evidence was the heel impressions detectives found adjacent to the body, which corresponded with those on boots worn by Kelly. Traces of blood were also found on his clothing.

Hanged by Tom Pierrepoint and Albert Pierrepoint.

December 23rd: Thomas William THORPE (61)   Leicester

Mrs Nellie Thorpe (47) worked as a machinist in a Leicester shoe factory. On Monday 14 July, as she walked home from work, she was attacked by her estranged husband. Thorpe, a labourer, first took a running kick at her, then grabbed her by the head and drew a razor across her throat. As she fell dead on the pavement he tried to cut his own throat, but succeeded only in inflicting minor wounds before being immediately arrested.

At his trial before Mr Justice Stable on 29 October it was alleged that Thorpe was desperate to win back his wife after she had left him and found someone else. They had been married 25 years and had three grown children. Prior to the attack he had threatened to take poison hoping she would come back to him, and when she refused he decided to threaten her with the razor. He claimed that the killing was accidental and he never intended to cut her throat.

Hanged by Tom Pierrepoint and Albert Pierrepoint.

1942

Cases where no executioner is recorded are multiple executions, and readers are asked to refer to the entries before or after for details of the hangman.

January 30th: Arthur PEACH (23)   **Birmingham**

Peach, a native of Walsall, joined the South Staffordshire Regiment in December 1939, but less than two years later he was back home, having deserted from his unit in Devon.

On 21 September 1941, two young girls were strolling down a footpath at the 'Cattle Arch', Walsall, when they were shot at by a soldier. Kitty Lyon (18) died instantly from a bullet to the head. Her friend survived a wound to the chest and later identified Peach as the man who had then battered her about the head with the butt of the gun before fleeing with Kitty's handbag.

Witnesses saw the soldier throw something into a nearby brook and a search found a gun identified as a Webley stolen from a store in Devon. Peach was picked up as a deserter on the following day and identified by witnesses as being seen in the area.

At his trial before Mr Justice MacNaughton at Stafford Assizes on 24-26 November, Peach admitted stealing the gun, but claimed that it had since been stolen from him. He also claimed that another deserter had accidentally shot the girls whilst testing the weapon and that he had been identified because he hurried to give assistance following the shooting. He had picked up the handbag and put it under his arm for safe keeping. Once assistance was called for he had fled and had forgotten to give the handbag back!

Hanged by Tom Pierrepoint and Henry Critchell.

Harold Dorian Trevor

March 11th: Harold Dorian TREVOR (62)   **Wandsworth**

An habitual criminal sentenced to death by Mr Justice Asquith at the Old Bailey on 29 January, for the murder of Mrs Theodora Jessie Gledhill (65).

On 14 October 1941, Trevor, who had recently been released from Parkhurst Prison, called in response to an advert placed by the elderly widow of a room to rent at her tower block home in Elsham Road, West Kensington.

As Mrs Gledhill was writing out a receipt, Trevor beat her over the head with a beer bottle then strangled her as she lay on the carpet. He fled taking a small amount of cash he had found while ransacking the flat.

When the body was discovered detectives immediately found two vital clues. Lying on the table was a receipt made out to Dr H D Trevor and also there were fingerprints on the broken bottle. A quick check found that the man they were looking for was indeed Harold Trevor. He was arrested at Rhyl on 18 October and brought back to London.

Trevor, a Yorkshireman, had spent almost the last 40 years in prison on a variety of charges from larceny to fraud. He had no previous record of violence.

Hanged by Albert Pierrepoint and Herbert Morris.

March 25th: David Roger WILLIAMS (33)   Liverpool

An aircraftsman of Crickhowell, Brecon, South Wales, sentenced to death by Mr Justice Oliver at Liverpool Assizes on 4 February, for the murder of Elizabeth Smith (28) of Carnforth.

On 30 November 1941, Williams travelled from his unit in Essex to meet Elizabeth at Morecambe. During a quarrel he was alleged to have knocked her into a stream and then held her head under the water. He then fled, leaving her for dead. Elizabeth was able to summon assistance and she was taken to the local hospital where she developed bronchial pneumonia. Two days later she died.

Williams was questioned and claimed that it was an accident and that they had been standing on a bridge kissing when she fell in. He later stated that he had not meant to kill her, only to try to persuade her not to end the relationship or to go out with a soldier she had just met. The jury gave a strong recommendation for mercy.

Hanged by Tom Pierrepoint and Steve Wade.

April 15th: Cyril JOHNSON (20)   Wandsworth

In November 1941, Miss Maggie Smail (29) met Johnson, a Bolton-born private in the West Yorkshire Regiment, at Ashford Corn Exchange. They became friendly and on 5 February he called at the flat she shared with her sister and after having tea escorted Maggie to a dance. They returned later that night and Johnson spent the night in the spare room.

On the following morning Daisy Smail left to go to work and when she returned she found her sister Maggie strangled in her bed. She had a scarf around her neck and bruises to her face. Johnson was arrested later that day.

He offered a defence of insanity at his trial before Mr Justice Croom-Johnson at the Old Bailey on 20 March, where the prosecution pointed to a letter Johnson had written to his ex-girlfriend. The letter said that Johnson hated all women since he had been jilted and that he had killed Maggie because she had teased him and would not let him get into bed with her.

Hanged by Tom Pierrepoint and Henry Critchell.

April 30th: Frederick James AUSTIN (28)   **Bristol**

On 31 January Austin, a driver with the RAMC, was home on leave and staying with his wife, Lillian Dorothy Pax Austin (22), and their young child in the attic room they rented in Bristol. During the afternoon he came downstairs and said that he had accidentally shot his wife whilst cleaning his gun.

Evidence was heard at his trial, before the Lord Chief Justice at Hampshire Assizes, that they had quarrelled a few days before the shooting after his wife had found a love letter in his kit bag written by a girl he had met near his camp. Forensic evidence also found that the gun could not have gone off as Austin had claimed, since the trajectory of bullets suggested the gun had been fired deliberately. Austin admitted later that he had pointed the gun to frighten his wife during another quarrel, but maintained that it had gone off by accident.

Hanged by Tom Pierrepoint and Harry Kirk.

Harold Hill

May 1st: Harold HILL (26)   **Oxford**

On 19 November 1941, two young schoolgirls, Doreen Hearne (8) and Kathleen Trendle (6), disappeared as they walked home from school at Penn in Buckinghamshire. They were last seen asking a soldier for a ride in his army truck.

Three days later they were found stabbed to death in Rough Wood, a copse at Amersham. There were several clues left at the scene, the most vital being a khaki handkerchief with a laundry number that led police to Hill, a driver in the 86th Regiment.

Hill denied the charge, but the evidence against him was substantial and he was convicted before Mr Justice Humphreys at the Old Bailey on 5 March.

Hanged by Tom Pierrepoint and Albert Pierrepoint.

June 24th: Douglas EDMUNDSON (28)   **Liverpool**

A petty officer stoker of Southport, convicted of the murder of nurse Imeldred Maria Ostliff (28), a childhood friend and frequent companion, who regarded herself as his fiancée despite the fact he regularly dated other women.

At the outbreak of the war, Edmundson joined the Royal Navy stationed at Plymouth and in the autumn of 1941, he was seriously injured when an Italian U-boat torpedoed his ship.

Whilst in hospital in the Midlands, he met Delia Chatterton and on his discharge from hospital they returned to his camp on the south coast and married. Edmundson soon found himself short of money and in January 1942, leaving his wife at the naval camp, he returned to Southport asking Imeldred for a loan. She agreed to meet him and next day her body was found in Victoria Park. Following a short investigation, on 10 February Edmundson was arrested in Birmingham.

Mr Justice Wrottesley presided over his trial at Liverpool Assizes on 20 April. He pleaded not guilty. The prosecution's case was that Edmundson had killed Imeldred after she had refused to give him some money. He later admitted that he had strangled her, but denied it was for the reasons alleged in court. He said that Imeldred had agreed to a meeting and had suggested Victoria Park. She told him she was prepared to lend him some money, but when he told her that it was not only for himself but also for his wife, she suddenly became abusive and refused him the money.

Hanged by Tom Pierrepoint.

June 25th: Gordon Frederick CUMMINS (28)   **Wandsworth**

The 'Black-out Ripper', Cummins, a Yorkshire-born leading aircraftsman and RAF cadet, murdered four women in a few short days during February 1942.

On 9 February schoolteacher Miss Evelyn Margaret Hamilton (42) was found strangled in an air raid shelter at Marylebone. She had been travelling alone through London from her job in Essex to her home in Newcastle. Although a scarf had been tied across her throat and nose, marks on the throat suggested that the killer was left handed. Her handbag, containing £80, was stolen but she was not sexually assaulted.

On the following night, Mrs Evelyn Oatley (35), a prostitute, also known as Nita Ward, was found strangled in her Soho flat. Her naked body had then been mutilated with a tin opener and fingerprints recovered from this again suggested a left handed killer. The prints did not match any on file. The attack was so horrific that it was dubbed the work of another 'Jack the Ripper'.

On 13 February, the naked body of prostitute Margaret Florence Lowe (42), known as Pearl, was found in her flat off Tottenham Court Road. The attack was even more horrific that on the previous victim; the lower part of her body having been subjected to a frenzied attack from a knife and razor.

As detectives were at the scene investigating this murder, news came through of another murder. Mrs Doris Jouannet, also known as Doris Robson (32), the wife of an elderly hotel manager, was found strangled and mutilated in her flat near Paddington.

Gordon Frederick Cummins

A few hours later a young woman was accosted by a man in a Piccadilly public house. As she left he followed her outside, pushed her into a doorway and tried to strangle her. A passer by intervened and the attacker fled leaving his belt and gas mask. The number on the mask was traced to Cummins, stationed at St John's Wood, who was found to be missing a belt from his uniform. When asked to sign a statement after being interviewed, Cummins used his left hand.

Although he claimed an alibi for the times of the murders, by stating he had not left camp, it was found that he had sneaked out after getting someone else to vouch for his presence in camp.

His two-day trial at the Old Bailey before Mr Justice Asquith began on 27 April. He was indicted on just the murder of Evelyn Oatley. It was found that although he was clearly a sexual deviant, Cummins had also committed the murders for gain.

Hanged by Albert Pierrepoint and Harry Kirk.

July 7th: Jose Estelle KEY (34)   **Wandsworth**

A British subject, born in Gibraltar, Key was charged under the Emergency Powers (Defence) Act, with espionage. He was arrested trying to leave Gibraltar on 4 March, heading for central Spain, allegedly to see his brothers who worked in the dockyards. In his possession was information recording the movements of the British forces, warships and aircraft in and around Gibraltar.

As he had been arrested in a British territory, it was decided to take him to London for trial. There had been a lot of sabotage in the area and the intelligence chiefs felt that Key's trial would '*encourager les autres*'.

Sentenced to death by Mr Justice Humphreys at the Old Bailey on 18 May.

July 7th: Alphonse Louis Eugene TIMMERMAN (37)   **Wandsworth**

Timmerman, a Belgian born in Ostend, was arrested as a spy after arriving at Glasgow from Portugal, posing as a Belgian refugee. He told the authorities that when Belgium became occupied by the German forces, he had decided to make his way to England to join the Free Belgian Merchant Navy.

He had previously worked on the Dover to Ostend ferries as a merchant seaman and in 1940 was serving on a Belgian ship when it was sunk by a torpedo. He was picked up by a Spanish vessel and taken to Spain where he was asked to spy for the Germans and agreed.

He denied this saying that when they reached Spain he was detained in a prison. The Belgian consulate arranged for his release and he was sent to Lisbon to await shipment to the United Kingdom as a refugee.

On arriving in England, he was interviewed by a Belgian security officer who found items in his possession that suggested he was a spy. These included cotton wool, Pyramidon powder and orange sticks - items used for secret writing.

At his trial, before Mr Justice Humphreys at the Old Bailey on 20 May, he alleged that these items had been given to him by Spanish Communists, but it was shown that the items could only have been acquired in England.

Hanged alongside **KEY** (above) by Albert Pierrepoint assisted by Steve Wade, Harry Kirk and Henry Critchell.

July 21st: ARTHUR ANDERSON (52)   Wandsworth

Also known as George Achilles Apergis, a former Greek soldier and engineer sentenced to death by the Lord Chief Justice at the Old Bailey on 29 June for the murder of Pauline Barker, his partner of 10 years, at their home in West Hampstead.

At his trial it was alleged that he committed the murder whilst suffering depression brought on by the failure of his garage business in Ireland. Evidence was shown that in recent times they had quarrelled often and he had moved out of the home for a time. On the evening of the murder he had returned to the house and after a quarrel he shot her. He then went to his local pub and confessed to the landlord who called the police. The jury strongly recommended mercy.

Hanged by Albert Pierrepoint and Herbert Morris.

September 2nd: Thomas Joseph WILLIAMS (19)   Belfast

On 5 April, Easter Sunday, an RUC patrol was ambushed by members of an IRA gang, as it patrolled the Kashmir district of Belfast. The police van then gave chase and later stormed a house at Clonard. The first man to approach the house was PC Patrick Murphy, who entered via the back door. He was later found shot dead in the scullery.

Amongst those arrested for his murder was Tom Williams who himself had received three gunshot wounds during the incident. In total six men, all aged between 18 and 21, stood trial before the Lord Chief Justice at Antrim. On 30 July they were all sentenced to death. A woman was also tried separately for the murder but she was convicted of a lesser charge after pleading guilty.

Following large protests five were reprieved. They had been housed in pairs and just four days before the scheduled execution they were brought together to see their solicitor. 'I have good news for you all, with one exception,' he told them. The others bade Williams goodbye and were transferred to another part of the Crumlin Road Gaol.

Hanged by Tom Pierrepoint and Albert Pierrepoint.

1942

September 10th: Harold Oswald MERRY (40)   **Birmingham**

On 30 March the body of Joyce Dixon (27) was found in a pool at Turves Green, Birmingham, close to her house at Northfield. Death was due to strangulation and drowning.

In the summer of the previous year, Merry, a married man with five children, met Joyce when she started work as a typist at the sheet metal works where he was employed. Later that year, following a quarrel with his wife on account of him seeing Joyce, he left home and went to live with a sister in Redditch.

On 20 March, Merry asked Joyce's parents for permission to marry her and after being granted consent they went to stay in London for a few days, returning on 27 March. They didn't know he was already married and only found out while the couple were in London. On their return Joyce's parents made it clear they were now against their plans to marry.

Two days later Joyce was killed and Merry was soon charged with her murder. At his trial before Mr Justice Croom Johnson at Warwickshire Assizes on 17-18 July, it was claimed that Merry had killed her as part of a suicide pact and that he had attempted to hang himself from a light flex in his room. The reason for committing the murder, he told the court, was so they could be together in the next life.

Hanged by Tom Pierrepoint and Henry Critchell.

September 10th: Samuel DASHWOOD (22)   **Pentonville**
George SILVEROSA (23)

On 30 April pawnbroker Leonard Moules (71) was found battered in his shop on Hackney Road, Shoreditch. It was clear that 'Old Moules', as he was known locally, had been attacked during a robbery and from the extent of the wounding it seemed he had been struck repeatedly with the butt of a gun. Evidence suggested two attackers, with one holding the old man upright as the other struck. He died three days later without regaining consciousness.

Over two weeks later, following a tip off, police interviewed two former borstal boys. Silverosa, a machinist from Pitsea, Essex, admitted that he had been present during the robbery, but named Dashwood as the killer. Dashwood, when questioned, blamed Silverosa.

Tried before Mr Justice Wrottesley at the Old Bailey on 17-21 July, both declined to give evidence and although it seemed likely that it was Dashwood who had actually committed the murder, both were convicted.

A few days before the executions were scheduled, Silverosa asked permission to burn some private letters in the prison incinerator. With permission granted, he was escorted to the furnace where he picked up a poker and attacked his guards, injuring them both.

They were hanged side by side by Albert Pierrepoint, assisted by Herbert Morris, Steve Wade and Harry Kirk.

October 6th: Patrick William KINGSTON (38)   **Wandsworth**

Sentenced to death on 14 September by Mr Justice Hallett at the Old Bailey after pleading guilty to the murder of Sheila Margaret Wilson (11) in Lewisham on 15 July.

Sheila went missing from her home after going to buy sweets and when she failed to return a search of the area was made. Her body was found buried under rubble beneath floorboards at a house where Kingston, a disabled stretcher bearer, lodged. She had been raped and strangled. Kingston fled the area but was detained after a nationwide manhunt.

Hanged by Albert Pierrepoint and Herbert Morris.

October 28th: William Ambrose COLLINS (21)   **Durham**

On the morning of Saturday 13 June, the body of Margaret Mary Rice (24), a corporal in the WAAF, was found at Newcastle Town Moor. She had been strangled and battered about the head. On the previous night Margaret had been walking back to her billet after waving off her husband of seven weeks at Newcastle railway station.

Missing from the body were her wedding ring, identity papers, and a number of personal effects. There was a significant clue left beside the body in the form of two pieces of vulcanite, identified as being from the hand grip of a Webley revolver.

A search of the drains in the area found Margaret's property close to houses in Claremont Road. Police asked for anyone in the area on Friday night to come forward and one of those questioned was William Collins, a Merchant Navy apprentice with a previous conviction for theft. When it was found that Collins, who was home on sick leave, lived close to Claremont Road, an officer searched his room and found items of women's underwear and a Webley revolver with pieces of vulcanite missing.

Collins was tried before Mr Justice Cassels at Northumberland Assizes on 26-27 August; it was shown that he had returned to the body after committing the murder in order to steal from her but then discarded the items as he walked back home.

Hanged by Tom Pierrepoint and Albert Pierrepoint.

November 3rd: Duncan Alexander Croall SCOTT-FORD (21) Wandsworth

A merchant seaman born in Plymouth, Scott-Ford came from a respectable family and had joined the Royal Navy when the war broke out. He spent most of his service on trips to and from Lisbon. In 1941 he served six months for embezzlement and on his release he joined the merchant navy.

While in port at Lisbon he was snared by a female 'hostess' who, after getting him drunk, persuaded him to reveal details of the movements of British shipping convoys. He was paid 1,800 escudos (£18) and told to have the information when he next arrived in Lisbon.

On his subsequent return, Scott-Ford found that the girl with whom he had spent time on his last trip no longer wished to see him, and a German agent was waiting for the information. When he showed reluctance to impart it, the sailor was threatened with blackmail, having already accepted the money

Returning to Plymouth, he attempted to obtain information by eavesdropping in local pubs, and what little information he did acquire, including the movements of his own ship, he passed on to the enemy agent. When he then asked for further reward he was laughed at.

He was arrested on 19 August, on his return to England, and admitted to seeing enemy agents in Lisbon and to passing information. In his possession was other information on convoys and their proposed routes.

He was tried at the Old Bailey on 16 November. It was shown that the information imparted by the sailor had led to the destruction of a convoy. Despite the rather sad circumstances, and the remorse shown by the young man, the jury had no option but to return a guilty verdict. He was sentenced to death by Mr Justice Birkett, the first time he had passed such a sentence.

Hanged by Albert Pierrepoint and Harry Kirk.

November 6th: Herbert Heram BOUNDS (45)   **Wandsworth**

Bounds, a hawker from Croydon, suffered badly with his nerves and he and his wife Elizabeth (39) had a violent, unhappy relationship. She treated him badly and in June he accused her of trying to poison him following an argument.

On the morning of Friday 21 August, they had another row during which she picked up a bread knife and threatened to kill him. Bounds then picked up his razor, he claimed in self-defence, and during the struggle Elizabeth received wounds to her neck. She was rushed to hospital but was dead on arrival.

On 16 September, Bounds stood before Mr Justice Hallett at the Old Bailey. It was claimed on his behalf that there was extreme provocation and there was even a suggestion that the wounds may have been self-inflicted. Nevertheless he was convicted, with the jury offering a strong recommendation to mercy.

His appeal failed on 22 October and despite the jury's recommendation he was hanged by Tom Pierrepoint and Henry Critchell. Pierrepoint was later censured by prison officials for his surly behaviour when entering the condemned cell to carry out the execution.

December 31st: Johannes Marius DRONKERS (46)   **Wandsworth**

During the early hours of Monday 18 May, the look-out on a Royal Navy trawler patrolling the North Sea spotted a distress signal coming from a small yacht flying the Dutch flag. Seeing a lone crewman waving frantically, they drew alongside and offered assistance. Helped aboard the gun-boat, he began dancing and hugging his rescuers as the trawler, with the yacht in tow, headed back to the sanctuary of an English port.

Upon landing, the man was handed over to the port authority for questioning. He told them that he was a Dutch refugee who had fled the German forces occupying the Netherlands. He described how he had bribed a fisherman into lending him his fishing boat and how he had slipped out of a small harbour, Helle-voit-Sluis, near Rotterdam on 16 May. When asked what he hoped to do now he said he wanted to serve either the Dutch or British Government as a clerk.

The authorities were not convinced by his story and he was detained on suspicion of being a spy. Under the skilled interrogation at Latchmere House in Richmond, Surrey, Dronkers admitted he was a former postal clerk from Utrecht, sent by the German Secret Service to collect information on the strength of American and Canadian troops stationed in England. He also confessed that he was a former member of the Dutch National Party, who had been trained in all forms of espionage by the Germans for six months.

On 17 November, after a four-day trial before Mr Justice Wrottesley at the Old Bailey, he was sentenced to death. His appeal was dismissed on 14 December.

Hanged by Albert Pierrepoint and Steve Wade.

1943

Cases where no executioner is recorded are multiple executions, and readers are asked to refer to the entries before or after for details of the hangman.

January 26th: Franciscus Johannes WINTER (40)   **Wandsworth**

Born in Antwerp, Belgium, Winter was a steward in the merchant marine service. In July 1942, he contacted the British authorities in Spain, posing as a Belgian refugee, and was given help to reach the United Kingdom.

On 31 July, he arrived by ship at Glasgow. Questioned by immigration officers, he told them he had escaped from Belgium and had made his way across France into Spain where he had been imprisoned. Upon release he had contacted the British consul saying he was eager to offer his services in any capacity to the Allies. In his possession was over £100 in various currencies.

Winter's story was not believed and he was further questioned by Intelligence Officers. Finally he admitted he had been sent by the Germans to report on shipping convoys.

He was tried before Mr Justice Humphreys at the Old Bailey on 4 December, and convicted of espionage.

Hanged by Albert Pierrepoint and Henry Critchell.

Harry Dobkin

January 27th: Harry DOBKIN (49)   **Wandsworth**

In the summer of 1942, workmen clearing a bombed chapel in Lambeth, London, unearthed the remains of a mummified body.

After an examination by pathologist Professor Keith Simpson, it was found that the body was that of a woman and she had been strangled.

Simpson was able to tell detectives that the murder had taken place approximately 18 months before, and after brilliant forensic work, he was able to say that the body was that of Rachel Dobkin, who was aged 45 when she disappeared in April 1941.

Her estranged husband, a Jewish fire-watcher, was contacted and his arrogant behaviour immediately made him a suspect. Dobkin denied knowledge of the chapel where the body was found, but it was known to the police that he had been recently employed there as a fire-watcher.

He was tried before Mr Justice Wrottesley at the Old Bailey on 23 November where it was shown that he had killed his wife after a dispute over maintenance payments.

Hanged by Albert Pierrepoint and Herbert Morris.

February 10th: Ronald ROBERTS (28)   **Liverpool**

Mrs Nellie Pearson (39) was the agent for a mail order catalogue and paid weekly visits to the house in Barrow-in-Furness where Roberts, a nightwatchman, lived. On 5 October, she disappeared, and during the next few days Roberts began to spend money freely, and managed to repay a large number of debts.

Detectives investigating the case called at the house during routine enquiries and after interviewing Roberts about his whereabouts on 5 October they asked to search the house. Mrs Pearson's body was found in one of the bedrooms. She had been battered to death with a hammer. She also had two stab wounds to the neck, found to have been made several hours after death.

At his trial, before Mr Justice Stable at Manchester Assizes on 11 December, the prosecution alleged that Roberts had committed murder and robbery to repay his pressing debts. His defence claimed he was insane.

Hanged by Tom Pierrepoint and Harry Kirk.

March 12th: David COBB (21)   **Shepton Mallett**

In the early hours of 27 December 1942, Cobb, a soldier from Alabama, USA, was serving in the 827th Engineer Battalion (Aviation), stationed at Desborough, Northamptonshire. He was on guard duty when he approached Lieutenant Robert Cobner and complained about the length of time he had been on duty.

Cobner reprimanded the private for carrying his rifle in an improper manner and told him to stand to attention when addressing an officer. Cobb said that as he was confined to barracks for an earlier offence he did not care. Cobner then called for a sergeant to arrest Cobb and when the sergeant approached, the private pulled down his rifle and refused to hand it over. The Lieutenant stepped forward to take it and Cobb shot him in the heart. He died instantly.

He was tried by General Court Martial at Cambridge on 6 January. Cobb said he did not recognise the officer and had refused to hand over the rifle until proper procedure had been followed. He was sentenced to death and the American authorities were allowed to retain most of the traditional formalities of an American execution, except that the actual method had to conform to British practice.

Hanged by Tom Pierrepoint and Albert Pierrepoint.

March 24th: William Henry TURNER (19)   Pentonville

On Saturday 9 January, the body of Mrs Ann Elizabeth Wade (82) was found under a bed in her house at Colchester. She had been strangled. The discovery followed the arrest for theft earlier that day of Private Turner, a native of Stainforth, near Doncaster, who had deserted from his unit. In his possession were items belonging to Mrs Wade, including her identity card.

At Essex Assizes Turner was tried twice for the crime. At the first trial the jury failed to agree on a verdict, at the second, before Mr Justice Asquith, the jury asked whether, if the intention was merely to quieten the victim during the course of a robbery, the charge was still murder?

When directed that it was, they took just 35 minutes to find Turner guilty, adding a strong recommendation for mercy, presumably on account of his age.

Hanged by Tom Pierrepoint and Henry Critchell.

March 31st: Dudley George RAYNOR (26)   Wandsworth

A Burmese sergeant in the Pioneer Corps convicted of the murder of his new bride Josephine (19), a member of the A.T.S.

Raynor, a former horse trainer and survivor of a ship-wreck, married Josephine in September 1942, but less than two months later they had separated. He was heartbroken at the break-up of the marriage and in November he returned to their home in Anerley, South London.

Josephine refused to discuss the separation and continued to polish her shoes as her husband pleaded with her. In a rage he kicked her to death.

He pleaded guilty at his trial before Mr Justice Oliver at the Old Bailey on 12 March. The trial lasted nine minutes.

Hanged by Albert Pierrepoint and Steve Wade.

April 6th: Gordon Horace TRENOWORTH (34)　　　　　　　**Exeter**

On Christmas Eve 1942, the body of Albert James Bateman (61) was found lying behind the counter of his tobacconist shop at Falmouth. When he failed to return home that evening, his wife, fearing the worst, asked a policeman to accompany her back to the shop.

A post-mortem revealed the extent of his injuries. He had been battered about the head with a blunt instrument and had died of asphyxiation - drowning in his own blood. It was also thought that the killer had stamped on the old man's head.

Robbery seemed to have been the motive as over £25 was missing from the till. Found at the scene was a Webley revolver, which had been stolen from a yacht moored at Falmouth Docks in the previous February.

Trenoworth, a casual labourer at Falmouth Docks, was routinely interviewed on the following day. He had been previously interviewed in connection with the theft of the revolver and, as he had worked at the docks at the time of the theft, he had been one of the suspects. An examination of his clothes found traces of blood, and other vital clues, including a recently repaired pound note, sealed his guilt.

He was sentenced to death by Mr Justice Tucker at Exeter Assizes on 16 February after a five-day trial.

Hanged by Tom Pierrepoint and Herbert Morris.

August Sangret

April 29th: August SANGRET (30)　　　　　　　　**Wandsworth**

On 7 October 1942, two soldiers walking on Hankley Common, Godalming, discovered the arm of a de composing body protruding from a mound of earth. The body was identified as Jean Pearl Woolf (19) who lived in a crude wigwam close to an army camp. She had been stabbed with a knife with a distinctive hooked tip, and then battered to death with a heavy branch.

A search of the common found her identity card and a letter that led detectives to Sangret, a French-Canadian part Red Indian soldier. He admitted to knowing the victim and that for a time he had lived with her in the wigwam.

He was asked to hand over his knife, but he claimed to have lost it. A search of property found bloodstains on his uniform. The knife was found on 26 November. It had been hidden inside the waste pipe in the latrine block at the Canadian army camp. It was identified as belonging to Sangret and he was charged with murder.

He was sentenced to death by Mr Justice MacNaughton at Kingston Assizes on 2 March. For the first time, the dead girl's skull had been produced in court to show the nature of the injuries.

Hanged by Albert Pierrrepoint and Henry Critchell.

June 2nd: Bernard KIRWAN (35)   Dublin

In 1936, Bernard Kirwan was convicted of armed robbery and sentenced to seven years imprisonment. During his incarceration, his mother died leaving the family's 70-acre farm in the sole hands of his younger brother Laurence.

In 1941, Kirwan was released from gaol and returned to the farm at Ballinclogan Rahan, near Tullamore. At first there was no trouble; Bernard shared a room with his brother and an employee, and worked on the farm.

In the autumn of 1942 an incident occurred which caused bad feeling between the brothers. They had been out drinking in a local pub when Laurence returned home, conscious of the early start in the morning. Bernard rolled home drunk in the early hours and when he was unable to gain entry he had to break down the door. On the following morning they had a fight and after Bernard stabbed his brother in the arm with a knife, Laurence told him to leave.

On 22 November, Laurence Kirwan (30) disappeared. He had last been seen by a n employee that afternoon. Bernard told the worker that Laurence had gone to Tullamore on business. Police made repeated visits to the farm when rumours spread that the previously penniless Kirwan was spending money freely. Finally, six months after he vanished, the dismembered body of Laurence Kirwan was found trussed up in a sack in a nearby bog.

On 18 January, Kirwan stood trial before Mr Justice Maguire at Dublin. The prosecution alleged he had drugged his brother with sleeping tablets, then hacked him to death. The trial lasted 16 days, with the defence refuting the claim that the body found was in fact Laurence Kirwan.

Hanged by Tom Pierrepoint and Albert Pierrepoint. Bernard Kirwan was confined in Mountjoy Prison at the same time as playwright Brendan Behan, who wrote the play *'The Quare Fellow'* following his release. Bernard Kirwan was *'The Quare Fellow'*.

June 25th: Harold A. SMITH   Shepton Mallet

Smith was a native of West Georgia, serving in the First Tank Destroyer Group based at Chisledon Camp, near Swindon. On New Year's Day 1943, after being paid, he went absent without official leave and travelled to London with a fellow deserter.

After spending a week in London he became short of money and returned to Swindon, only to find his unit had moved on. He hung around the camp until the following day (9 January), when he stole a pistol off a bunk. As he was leaving the barracks he was accosted by Private Harry Jenkins of the 116th Infantry. Fearful that he would be arrested for the theft, Smith shot him with the pistol and fled the camp. He was arrested at a YMCA in London two days later when he was routinely asked to show his papers to detectives.

He was tried by court martial at Bristol on 12 March and sentenced to death by hanging.

Hanged by Tom Pierrepoint and Albert Pierrepoint.

July 10th: Charles Arthur RAYMOND (23)   Wandsworth

On the afternoon of 31 January, the body of Marguerite Beatrix Burge (22), a member of the WAAF, was found behind bushes near Halnaker, Sussex. She had been sexually assaulted before receiving severe head wounds caused by a blunt instrument. She died later that night in hospital.Raymond, a French-Canadian soldier, was charged with the murder after he made a number of suspicious remarks to colleagues. At the Old Bailey, on 14 May, after a five-day trial, he was sentenced to death, through an interpreter, by Mr Justice Lawrence. He maintained throughout that the murder was committed by a fellow soldier, but following his conviction, he confessed he was guilty.

Hanged by Tom Pierrepoint and Steve Wade.

August 3rd: Gerald Elphinstone ROE (41)   Pentonville

On the morning of 17 May a neighbour heard screams coming from a house at New Barnet. Looking through the window, he saw a woman standing at the upstairs bedroom window shrieking for help. A man clad in pyjamas then appeared behind and pulled her from the window. Assuming it was just a family tiff he thought nothing more of it.

A short time later he saw Roe, an Anglo-Indian research chemical engineer, leave the house carrying two suitcases. The cleaner called soon after and found the body of Mrs Elsie Roe (41) lying dead in the kitchen. She had died from shock after being struck about the head with a blunt instrument, her death being accelerated by coal-gas poisoning.

Roe, who was detained in Hampshire later that night, gave no explanation as to why he had killed his wife. They had been married for 15 years and had two children at boarding school.

On 18 June he was sentenced to death by Mr Justice Humphreys at Hertford Assizes. It was the first capital conviction here for 40 years.

Hanged by Albert Pierrepoint and Steve Wade.

August 3rd: William QUAYLE (52)   Birmingham

On 5 May, Vera Clark (8) failed to return home from school at Ladywood, near Birmingham. It was found she had left with a classmate but had volunteered to run an errand for a man witnesses named as William Quayle, a works policeman. Quayle was spoken to by Vera's mother, but denied any knowledge of the girl, saying he had not seen her.

On the following day police called at the house, but Quayle was out. A search of his cellar uncovered Vera's coat. Quayle was spotted by a detective and detained for questioning. A further search found the girl's skipping rope stuffed down the side of his sofa, yet still Quayle denied knowing anything about the girl's disappearance. Finally he confessed and led police to a bombed out cellar at Edgbaston. Vera's naked and bound body was lying under a pile of bricks. She had been raped and strangled.

At his trial, before Mr Justice Wrottesley at Birmingham Assizes on 13 July, Quayle said that he had been drinking heavily since his wife had left him and when Vera returned from running an errand he had a brainstorm. His defence counsel claimed he was insane.

Hanged by Tom Pierrepoint and Alex Riley.

August 12th: William O'SHEA (24)   Dublin

William O'Shea married his wife Maureen in 1940. He earned a living as a rabbit trapper on farm in and around Ballyhane, County Wexford.

Relations between husband and wife had quickly become strained, due in the main to O'Shea's friendship with a young man named Tom White.

The two worked together as rabbit trappers and spent time away from work drinking together.

In February 1943, Maureen gave birth to their first child and told a friend that she thought her husband hoped she would die during childbirth! A few weeks later her house was set alight while she was alone inside, and investigations showed that the fire was deliberate.

On 15 March, O'Shea went for a stroll and later that night he returned home alone in tears claiming someone had shot his wife. Later both O'Shea and his young friend were arrested and charged with murder.

White was found unfit to plead and charges against him were not proceeded with. O'Shea was then tried alone before Mr Justice Overend KC, at Dublin on 8 June. The prosecution's case was built on a confession the accused had made after arrest.

Hanged by Tom Pierrepoint and Albert Pierrepoint.

September 10th: Trevor ELVIN (21)   Leeds

Elvin, a Barnsley glass worker, had been going out his fiancée, Violet Wakefield (20), who worked as a lorry driver's assistant in the land army, for two years. Although they had discussed marriage, his father did not think they were old enough.

On the evening of 4 May, they where seen walking together towards a Barnsley fairground. On the following morning Violet was found beside the dodgem car track. She was rushed to hospital with severe head injuries, and died without regaining consciousness. Found beneath the body was a bloodstained hammer. Elvin fled to Blackpool, where he was traced and under questioning confessed to the murder.

He stood trial before Mr Justice Tucker at Leeds Assizes on 12 July, and pleaded insanity. The prosecution alleged that the motive was jealousy with Elvin wrongly suspecting she was having a relationship with the lorry driver she worked with. They also alleged there was no sign of insanity, claiming that Elvin had told police that he had a hammer in his raincoat pocket, but that he had only meant to frighten her.

Hanged by Tom Pierrepoint and Harry Kirk.

September 24th: Charles Eugene GAUTHIER (25)   Wandsworth

A French-Canadian soldier found guilty at his second trial of the murder of Annette Pepper (30), at Portslade.

With her husband held as a prisoner of war, Mrs Pepper was having a string of affairs with soldiers and had told Gauthier she no longer wished to see him as she wanted to rekindle a previous romance with another Canadian. In a jealous rage he went to her house on 15 March and shot her with his Bren gun.

At his first trial (Lewes Assizes, 12 July) the jury failed to agree on a verdict, but he was later sentenced to death by Mr Justice Oliver on 25 July at the Old Bailey. His appeal failed as did an appeal to the House of Lords, and he was to spend a record 60 days in the condemned cell.

Hanged by Albert Pierrepoint and Alex Riley.

November 19th: Terence CASEY (22)   Wandsworth

On the night of 13 July Mrs Bridget Nora Milton (45) called into a Putney public house to purchase a bottle of stout. As she left she was followed by Casey, a soldier in the RAMC, who was staying with relatives in Fulham whilst on leave. Later that night an air raid warden was alerted by screams coming from a garden and called the police, who arrested Casey as he tried to flee. Bridget Milton had been brutally raped, suffered throat injuries and died of strangulation a short time later.

On 22 September, Casey was sentenced to death at the Old Bailey by Mr Justice Singleton. He appealed on the grounds that he was insane at the time of the murder and that he had no intention to commit the crime. The prosecution referred to a statement made following his arrest, in which Casey admitted that he killed her after she had fought him off as he tried to rape her.

Hanged by Albert Pierrepoint and Henry Critchell.

December 14th: Lee A. DAVIS (18)   Shepton Mallett

On the evening of 28 September, two nurses, Muriel Fawden and June Cynthia Lay (19), were returning from a visit to a cinema at Marlborough, Wilts. As they walked towards the hospital they were approached by an American soldier who asked where they were going. Indicating the hospital ahead, they walked on, only for the soldier to raise his rifle and threaten: 'Stand still or I'll shoot.'

Davis told the women to walk into the adjacent field and when they made an attempt to flee, Davis shot June in the back killing her instantly. He then dragged Muriel into the field where he raped her. Davis then left the women in the field and fled.

The nearest American unit was at Iron Gate Camp. On the following day items of bloodstained clothes and a carbine were found hidden. The serial number on the weapon led to Davis and he was arrested.

At his court martial at Marlborough in October, Davis was identified as the rapist and killer by Nurse Fawden and through forensic evidence from his clothing.

Hanged by Tom Pierrepoint and Alex Riley.

December 15th: Charles William KOOPMAN (22)   Pentonville

Koopman, an aircraftsman of Hanwell, along with his wife and child, shared a room at the house of Mrs Gladys Lavinia Brewer (21) and her daughter Shirley (2), in Ealing. He was hiding at the house after receiving his call up papers because he did not want to join his unit at Bridlington.

On 8 September, after going out drinking with his wife, Koopman returned to the house where he formed the impression that Mrs Brewer wanted them to leave. They had a quarrel during which Koopman hit her with a hammer. She died from massive head injuries. He then battered the child to death with the hammer, and left a note for her husband claiming he had killed her because she was immoral and that he (the husband) would be better off without her.

At his trial before Mr Justice Asquith at the Old Bailey on 27 October, Koopman admitted the attack, but claimed he was insane at the time.

Hanged by Tom Pierrepoint and Steve Wade.

December 22nd: John Joseph DORGAN (46)   Wandsworth

Dorgan shared a flat with his wife Florence Elizabeth Agnes Dorgan (60) at Brighton. He was her second husband and they sublet a room in the flat to a waiter named Fife.

On the afternoon of 30 July, Fife left to go to work. Dorgan, who had been drinking heavily since losing his job four days earlier, had left a short time earlier and when Fife returned home from work he found Mrs Dorgan under a bed with a tie tied tightly around her neck.

Dorgan was arrested the following day and confessed to strangling his wife. He said that on the days leading up to the murder he had sold items belonging to his wife and told friends that she had gone to Scotland.

His defence, at his trial before Mr Justice Charles at Sussex Assizes on 1 December, alleged that Dorgan, a former soldier, was insane and had been in hospital three times suffering from shell shock.

Hanged by Tom Pierrepoint and Henry Critchell.

December 29th: Thomas JAMES (26)   Liverpool

On 17 August, the body of Geraldine Sweeney (28) was found in the cellar of a bombed house in Liverpool. She had been strangled and suffered horrific sexual injuries caused by a bottle and a broom handle.

James, a ship's fireman, had confessed to a friend that he had killed her, and the friend's wife subsequently told the police. He was known to be an associate of Geraldine, who, it was contended, was highly promiscuous and worked as a prostitute. James denied having admitted to killing the woman and said that if he was to kill someone he would not strangle them, he would stab them. Up until that time no mention had been made that she had been strangled.

He was sentenced to death at Liverpool Assizes by Mr Justice Wrottesley on 5 November. In his defence it was claimed that James had drunk 22 pints on the day of the murder and could not remember anything. His counsel also suggested that the victim was a sexual pervert and her injuries may have been self-inflicted.

Hanged by Tom Pierrepoint and Herbert Morris.

1944

Cases where no executioner is recorded are multiple executions, and readers are asked to refer to the entries before or after for details of the hangman.

February 2nd: Christos GEORGIOU (38)   **Pentonville**

A Cypriot cook sentenced to death by Mr Justice Hilbery at the Old Bailey on 10 December 1943, for the murder of Savvas Demetriades (43), a fellow Cypriot.

The two men had been friends and business partners whilst living in Cardiff but had fallen out. In April 1943, Georgiou moved to London and found work in a Soho café. On 24 October, Demetriades came to London on business and that night bumped into Georgiou. There was no trouble between the two, but on the following day as Demetriades was walking down Old Compton Street, Soho, Georgiou stabbed him three times in the chest and then fled. Georgiou was arrested on the following day and picked out of an identity parade by witnesses to the attack.

Hanged by Albert Pierrepoint and Herbert Morris.

February 3rd: Mervin Clare McEWEN (35)   **Leeds**

On 3 April 1943, Mark Turner (82), a retired postman, was found with severe head injuries on the sofa at his home in Moorfield St, Halifax.

Clues left at the scene led police to McEwen, a Canadian soldier, who had gone absent without official leave from his unit. He was arrested at his lodgings in Manchester on 23 June, and in his possession were Turner's ration card and identity card which had been altered.

At his trial before Mr Justice Stable at Leeds on 1-2 December 1943, it was shown that McEwen was a deserter living in a hut near Turner, who had befriended him. They went out for a drink together and after they had parted he followed the old man back home, broke in through a window and then beat him to death with a hammer, stealing clothes and food.

Hanged by Tom Pierrepoint and Steve Wade.

February 10th: John H. WATERS (38)   **Shepton Mallet**

In February 1943, Waters, a married man from New Jersey, began a relationship with Doris Staples, a dressmaker who worked in a shop close to where his unit was stationed at Henley-on-Thames, Oxfordshire. Waters served with a model making unit and shared guard duties with British airmen at the camp.

Following a short, intense relationship Doris cooled towards Waters and when he heard she was seeing other soldiers he declared that he would commit suicide. On 14 July, Waters went to the shop where she worked and shot her five times before holing himself up in the shop and having a shoot out with military police. He was finally arrested after tear gas was lobbed into the shop. Doris was found dead and Waters was found slumped in an outside toilet having shot himself through the mouth.

1944

Although the bullet had smashed his mouth, palate and jaw, coming to rest close to the brain and causing blindness in one eye, Waters was deemed fit to stand trial at a court martial held at Watford on 29 November 1943. Besides the murder charge he was also accused of leaving his post and wilfully maiming himself contrary to the 96th Article of War.

Hanged by Tom Pierrepoint and Alex Riley.

March 16th: Oswald John JOB (58)   **Pentonville**

Oswald or Oscar Job was born in London on 4 July 1885, of German parents. Although there are conflicting reports as to his actual name and place of birth, all sources agree Job was educated at a public school and moved to Paris in 1911.

Following the invasion of France in 1940, as the holder of a British passport, he was interned by the Germans at St Denis Camp. At some point he was approached by the Germans and agreed to offer his services as a spy. Regarded as someone who would not arouse suspicion, he was sent to England to report on bomb damage and state of morale.

Posing as an escapee from a Paris POW camp, Job arrived at the British Embassy in Madrid and although embassy officials were a little sceptical about his story, one official had been to the same school and he was allowed to return to England. He was granted assistance and rented a room in Bayswater from where he sent his reports back. He sent them in coded invisible writing, written between the lines on what appeared to be innocent letters to former friends at St Denis.

He aroused suspicion by the sheer volume of letters sent to and from the St Denis camp. Investigations learned that some of the people credited with writing to Job from the camp had written no such letters. Also, when word came back from a double agent that someone was operating from a Bayswater address, officers from Special Branch raided his flat.

Nothing untoward was found at first until an officer asked Job why he had such a large bunch of keys for a one room flat. On 1 November 1943, Job was taken to Scotland Yard where his keys were found to be hollowed out and concealing chemicals for secret writing.

His three-day trial ran until 26 January before Mr Justice Stable at the Old Bailey, and although he admitted agreeing with the Germans to act as a spy he said he had only done so to escape from France. He could not, however, explain why he had continued to act as a spy once he arrived in London.

Hanged by Albert Pierrepoint and Harry Kirk. Of all the spies captured in Great Britain during the war, Oswald Job was at liberty the longest.

March 16th: Ernest Charles DIGBY (35)   Bristol

A sergeant in the Royal Artillery, Digby was a married man, stationed at Milborne Port, near Yeovil, Somerset. In the autumn of 1943 he took lodgings near the camp, telling the landlady his wife would be joining him from London.

On 11 October Mrs Olga Davy Hill (29), his heavily pregnant 'wife', joined him. It was clear to the landlady that the couple had not made any plans for the impending birth.

Ten days later the child, named Dawn, was born, but by this time Digby had been transferred to Witney in Oxfordshire where he worked as an instructor. The landlady was told that on 12 November Digby would return on leave and make arrangements for the child to be cared for by Olga's mother.

A day or so later the couple left the lodgings, carrying the baby and supposedly heading for London. Later that night they returned, carrying two suitcases and saying the baby was being cared for. The landlady was suspicious, however, and alerted the police. The couple were arrested and later Digby confessed that he had battered the child before burying it in woods at Eynsham Hall, near to his camp at Witney.

Tried before Mr Justice Singleton at Taunton Assizes on 1 March, it was alleged that he had killed the baby in Yeovil and transported it to Witney in a suitcase for burial. They were jointly charged but only Digby was convicted, his 'wife' being acquitted and discharged.

Hanged by Tom Pierrepoint and Steve Wade. Digby claimed after conviction that he killed another child in a similar incident in the previous year. He told police he had buried it in a wood in Kent but efforts to locate the body failed.

April 13th: Sydney James DELASALLE (39)   Durham

In January, Chingford-born Delasalle was in his room at an RAF camp in the north of England when an inspection took place, headed by Flight Sergeant Ronald John Murphy (23). Delasalle, a leading aircraftsman, was warned about the state of his room whereupon he began to complain about his rations and other matters. Murphy told him that the rations were not his responsibility and ordered him to tidy his room. Delasalle then asked the sergeant outside for a fight and as a result was confined to barracks for 14 days for insolence.

On 4 February, soon after his release and whilst still enraged at the punishment he had recently served, he approached Murphy who was queuing with colleagues for tea at a NAAFI van. Shouting for the other men to get out of the way, Delasalle pointed his gun at Murphy and fired.

Tried at Leeds before Mr Justice Hallett on 22 March; the prosecution claimed he had fired two shots from 50 yards, killing Murphy and wounding four other airmen. When overpowered, Delasalle claimed that Murphy had asked for it. His defence pleaded insanity.

Hanged by Tom Pierrepoint.

John C Leatherberry

May 16th: John C. LEATHERBERRY (21)   **Shepton Mallet**

On the night of 8 December 1943, taxi driver Henry Claude Hailstone (28), a bachelor who lived in Colchester, was found dead beside his cab at Birch near Colchester. He had told his landlady on the previous night that he had a job for that night driving two coloured American soldiers to their nearby camps.

Examination of the body found that he had been attacked from behind and struck with three heavy blows to the head, although death had been caused by strangulation. It was also clear that Hailstone had been killed elsewhere and then driven to where he was found. Also, the way the vehicle was parked, on the wrong side of the road, suggested his killer might be an American.

Investigations among the 5,000 or so American soldiers stationed nearby led police to interview Private George Fowler, stationed with the 356th Engineer General Service Regiment at Birch. He admitted going absent without official leave on 5 December along with a fellow soldier from his unit, John Leatherberry. Fowler said it was his friend who suggested robbing the taxi driver on the way to camp, and that after the driver stopped the car so Fowler could relieve himself, Leatherberry strangled him.

Leatherberry denied being with Fowler on the night of the murder, but when police found bloodstains on his uniform he too was charged. At their court martial, held at Ipswich on 19 January, the only direct evidence against the two men came from Fowler's testimony. Both were convicted; Leatherberry, deemed the wilful perpetrator in the murder, was sentenced to death, Fowler was sentenced to life imprisonment.

Hanged by Tom Pierrepoint and Albert Pierrepoint.

May 26th: Wiley HARRIS Junior (26)   Shepton Mallet

Privates Wiley Harris and Robert Fils were stationed with the 626th Ordnance Ammunition Corps in Belfast. On 6 March they were out drinking when they were approached by Harry Coogan, who asked Harris if he wanted a woman. Harris said he did and Coogan pointed to a girl standing across the street. They agreed a fee and Coogan told them he knew a place to which they could go.

They approached an air-raid shelter and after Harris handed over the money, Coogan said he would keep guard. No sooner had Harris and the woman entered the shelter than Coogan shouted that the police were coming. Harris and the woman emerged from the shelter and, seeing it was a false alarm, Harris told her to go back inside. Saying she was now scared of being arrested, the woman refused. Coogan also refused to hand back the money.

A quarrel then ensued, whereupon the woman dropped the money on the floor and, as Harris went to pick it up, Coogan punched him in the face. Harris then pulled out a jack-knife and stabbed the Irishman 17 times.

At his court martial his defence asked for a lesser verdict of voluntary manslaughter, but due to the number of blows struck and the ferocity of the attack he was convicted of murder.

Hanged by Tom Pierrepoint and Alex Riley.

June 6th: Ernest James Harman KEMP (20)   Wandsworth

On the morning of 14 February, the body of Iris Miriam Deeley (21), a leading aircraftswoman in the WAAF, was found strangled with a scarf on an allotment on Foxhole Road, Eltham.

Kemp, a gunner in the Royal Artillery and a former bank clerk, of Eltham, was picked up on the following day on a charge of desertion and wearing false decorations on his tunic. He aroused suspicion and a search of his belongings revealed clothing coupons belonging to the dead woman's fiancé that had been stolen from her handbag.

Convicted at the Old Bailey on 18 April before Mr Justice Cassels.

Hanged by Albert Pierrepoint and Herbert Morris on D-Day.

June 23rd: Pierre Richard Charles NEUKERMANS (27)   Pentonville

Born in Waarbecke, Belgium, on 1 May 1916, Neukermans was sent to Britain by the German Secret Service to get information on military matters and conditions. He was a former regular officer invalided out in 1938. When Belgium was occupied in 1940 he tried to escape to France, but being unable to do so had returned to Brussels, where he was approached by the Germans and consented to being trained in sabotage, wireless transmission and all other forms of espionage.

Suitably trained, he was deposited at the Spanish border from where he made his way to Lisbon posing as a loyal Belgian subject. His story, that he had been given aid in crossing France by two men, being accepted as plausible, he flew into England on 16 July 1943, where being unfit to serve he found work as a clerk in the Belgian Government offices.

Following information received by the Secret Service on 2 February 1944 he was thoroughly questioned again and this time confessed that he was acting as a spy. Neukermans had written numerous letters in invisible ink to an address in a neutral country informing the Germans of the strength and location of Belgian troops in England, and on the departure times of convoys sailing to the Belgian Congo.

His arrest was kept secret and his three-day trial before Mr Justice MacNaughton at the Old Bailey at the end of April was held 'in camera' (in secret).

Hanged by Albert Pierrepoint and Alex Riley.

July 12th: John Gordon DAVIDSON (19)   Liverpool

On the morning of 20 March, the body of Gladys May Appleton (27) was found in the garden of the headquarters of the Fire Service at St Helens. She had been savagely assaulted, her clothing had been torn and she had been strangled with her own scarf.

Investigations in the area led detectives to believe the killer may be a young Scottish soldier seen in the area at the time of the murder. A description was issued, but due to the sheer number of soldiers in the area the investigation progressed slowly.

On 31 March, Davidson, a native of Grangemouth, Stirlingshire, was arrested for being absent without official leave and when it was found that his description matched that of the wanted murderer he was questioned by Scotland Yard detectives. He immediately broke down and confessed.

At his trial before Mr Justice Hilbery at Manchester on 2 May, it was claimed that Davidson had spent the evening of 19 March drinking heavily with comrades in a number of pubs. He had left them and gone to find a woman. He had approached Gladys as she walked home from spending the evening with her fiancé and tried to kiss her. When she resisted his advances he lost control and in a drunken rage strangled and sexually assaulted her.

Despite the savage nature of the crime the jury added a strong recommendation for mercy after returning a guilty verdict.

Hanged by Tom Pierrepoint.

July 12th: Joseph Jan VANHOVE (27)   Pentonville

Born on 27 May 1917, Vanhove had spent the early part of the war working on the black market in his native Belgium, fleeing when he became wanted by the police for his illegal activities. He made contact with a friend whom he knew to be working for the Germans, and through this acquaintance he was asked by the German Secret Service to spy on French and Belgian workmen at airfields in Northern France, and report if any were working for the resistance.

In the summer of 1942, he received further training including code breaking and secret writing. His first mission to enter enemy territory ended in failure and for his next assignment he was sent to Sweden and told to report details of shipping, movements and activity in dockyards, and information on the planned invasion. Reaching Sweden, he left the ship and contacted the British authorities asking to be allowed to join the allied forces.

Although the authorities suspected he might be a spy, Vanhove was however allowed to enter Britain at Leuchars, Fife on 11 February 1944, only to be immediately arrested. Found in his possession were materials that suggested he was a spy. Tried at the Old Bailey on 23-24 May, he was the 16th and last spy captured during the war.

Hanged by Albert Pierrepoint and Steve Wade.

July 26th: James GALBRAITH (26)   Manchester

On 8 April, the body of James William Percey (48) was found in the cabin of his ship moored in Salford Docks, Manchester. He had been battered to death with an axe and robbed of his recently collected pay packet. In the cabin was a set of fingerprints on a tumbler believed to have been used by the killer, presumably the same man in whose company Percey was seen returning to the ship.

Investigations led police to Galbraith, a petty criminal from Moss Side who was employed on a retainer at the docks waiting to find work on one of the ships. In his possession was money traced as being issued to the murdered man; his fingerprints matched those found in the cabin and bloodstains on clothes recovered from his home matched Percey.

Faced with a wealth of evidence against him, his three-day trial before Mr Justice Hilberry at the end of May was little more than a formality.

Hanged by Tom Pierrepoint and Harry Kirk.

August 8th: William Alfred COWLE (31)   Leicester

A painter convicted of the murder of Nora Emily Payne (32) in Leicester on 18 May.

Nora Payne worked as a receptionist for a petrol company and met Cowle when he was employed to do some work at her offices three years earlier. Cowle made repeated advances to her which she in turn repeatedly refused as, although he lived alone, he was still legally married.

Finally, on 18 May, enraged that she would have nothing to do with him, Cowle stabbed her to death.

Sentenced to death by Mr Justice Singleton at Nottingham Assizes on 26 June, his defence had been guilty but insane.

August 8th: William George Frederick MEFFEN (52)   Leicester

A rubber worker convicted of the murder of his step-daughter, Winifred Ellen Stanley (38), at Chaddesden.

Meffen became enraged when a workmate began courting his step-daughter. He repeatedly tried to end the relationship, although no reason was put forward, other than that he was being overly protective of his family. One night in February, Winifred stayed out all night and when she returned she found Meffen had sat up all night in tears. He confronted the workmate who denied anything untoward had taken place, but a few days later, on 29 February, while the family were dressing for breakfast, Meffen followed Winifred into the bathroom and cut her throat with a razor. He then left the house and surrendered to a policeman.

In his pocket was a letter stating that he intending to kill Winifred and this formed the basis of the prosecution's claim of premeditated murder at his trial before Mr Justice Singleton on 19 June.

Hanged alongside **COWLE**, in the first double execution at Leicester for 41 years, by Tom Pierrepoint, assisted by Albert Pierrepoint, Alex Riley and Harry Kirk.

August 11th: Eliga BRINSON (25)   Shepton Mallet
Willie SMITH (21)

On the evening of 4 March, Dorothy Holmes left a dance hall at Bishop's Cleeve, Gloucestershire, in the company of Private Edward Hefferman, her American soldier boyfriend. They were followed outside by Brinson and Smith, two soldiers serving with the 49090th Quartermaster Service Company.

As Dorothy and her boyfriend kissed goodnight, they were attacked by the two men. Hefferman was hit in the face with a bottle as Dorothy was dragged into woods. He ran to get help, but by the time he returned both men had taken it in turns to rape the terrified woman.

Evidence soon led police to the two men and they were court martialled at Cheltenham on 28-29 April, accused of rape.

Hanged by Tom Pierrepoint and Albert Pierrepoint, they were the first men to be executed solely for rape in this country for close on 100 years.

October 12th: Madison THOMAS   Shepton Mallet

Mrs Beatrice Maud Reynolds was widowed during the last war and lived with her invalided brother at Gunnislake, Cornwall.

Late on the evening of 26 July, she left a local British Legion meeting and was walking home when she was approached by a black soldier who asked to walk her home. Afraid of being pestered by him, she told him to go home and stopped to talk to a neighbour as he walked off into the distance.

As Mrs Reynolds walked down a deserted road, the soldier reappeared and after a short struggle, dragged her through a hedge and viciously raped her at knife point. Before leaving he pulled out a gun and threatened to shoot her if she tried to run.

On the following day the company of Whitchurch Down Camp were lined up on an identity parade where Thomas, a private in the 964th Quartermaster Service Corps, was picked out by the neighbour as the attacker. Forensic tests found bloodstains on his trousers, which were different from Thomas's blood and matched that of Mrs Reynolds.

Convicted at a Plymouth court martial on 21 August of 'forcibly and feloniously having, against her will, carnal knowledge of Beatrice Maud Reynolds'.

Hanged by Tom Pierrepoint and Albert Pierrepoint.

December 1st: Charles KERINS (26)   Dublin

A native of Caherina, Tralee, sentenced to death by the Special Criminal Court on 9 October for the murder of Detective Sergeant Denis O'Brien at Ballyboden, Rathfarnham, County Dublin on 9 September 1942.

O'Brien was ambushed by a gang of men wearing trench-coats and dark glasses and carrying Tommy Guns and pistols as he left his home to report on duty at Dublin Castle. He was shot at several times as he started the engine in his car. He returned fire and tried to run back to his house, where he received a fatal bullet wound to the back of the head.

Kerins was a member of the IRA and at his trial refused to recognise the court, put forward any defence or make any statement. The court heard that Kerins was one of several persons alleged to have carried out the killing, but the only one brought to trial.

Hanged by Tom and Albert Pierrepoint.

1945

Cases where no executioner is recorded are multiple executions, and readers are asked to refer to the entries before or after for details of the hangman.

January 8th: Ernest Lee CLARK   **Shepton Mallet**
            Augustine M. GUERRA (20)

On the evening of 22 August 1944, Betty Green (15) disappeared as she cycled to her home at Ashford, Kent. The following morning her body was found on a cricket field. She had been raped and strangled. Her father had been drinking in a bar close to where Betty was attacked and remembered two American airmen, one black, one white, leaving the bar and heading in the direction of the cricket field.

At an identification parade made up of American servicemen stationed in the area, Mr Green picked out Corporal Clark and Private Guerra of the 306th Fighter Control Squadron as the two men he had seen. Examination of their clothing found traces of blood and hairs that matched those of the dead girl.

Faced with the evidence, both confessed to being with the girl on the night she died but pleaded guilty of rape only, saying they thought she was still alive when they left her.

Both were convicted at their court martial at Ashford Town Hall on 22 September. Corporal Clark was convicted of murder, Private Guerra of aiding and abetting the crime.

Hanged by Tom Pierrepoint and Albert Pierrepoint.

January 9th: Horace Beresford GORDON (29)   **Wandsworth**

On the early evening of 7 September, Mrs Dorothy Mary Hillman (18), left her in-laws' home in Bramley, Surrey, to walk her dog. She was heavily pregnant at the time and was heading to a nearby public house to buy some cigarettes.

She was later found with multiple stab wounds in a nearby orchard. She was taken to Guildford hospital where she later gave birth to a stillborn baby. She was able to make a statement about her attacker. She had told police that a black soldier, serving in the Royal Canadian Ordnance Corps, had approached her as she walked the dog and tried to interfere with her. She refused his advances and he attacked her with a knife. Several other witnesses came forward to identify Jamaican-born Gordon as the man seen cycling in the area shortly before the attack. When questioned he was found to have bloodstains on his uniform.

Gordon said that he had been cycling past when Mrs Hillman waved him down and told him she had been attacked. He said he would go to get help, but took the wrong turning and got lost. 15 days after the attack she died from blood poisoning and Gordon was charged with murder.

Sentenced to death by Mr Justice Humphreys at Surrey Assizes on

1 December 1944. His execution was due on 3 January, but postponed after the Canadian Government pleaded that the man had a previous good character. After considering the appeal it was decided that the law must take its course.

Hanged by Albert Pierrepoint and Steve Wade.

January 30th: Andrew BROWN (26)   **Wandsworth**

69-year-old Amelia Elizabeth Ann Knowles kept a small antique shop at Arundel, Sussex. She lived alone and it was rumoured that she kept large amounts of money on the premises. She was also known amongst antique dealers for her large collection of gold watches, another fact that was common knowledge to local people.

On 18 September, the shop was broken into and 'Millie', as she was known locally, was found battered to death on the following morning. The killer had broken her jaw in three places and then smashed her ribs by repeatedly jumping on the body.

As only cash had been stolen, police believed that the killer was not aware of the watch collection and this led them to suspect a stranger to the area. Enquiries were focused on the nearby air-base after a witness mentioned seeing an airman standing outside the shop on the evening of 18 September. She had heard another airman call him Paddy and this led police to Belfast-born Andrew Brown who, shortly after the murder, had been seen paying for cinema seats from a thick wad of ten shilling notes.

Under questioning Brown admitted being at the shop on the night but denied murder. He pleaded manslaughter at his trial but medical evidence was offered that showed the injuries were too severe to have been accidentally inflicted. The jury took just 11 minutes to find him guilty of murder. Sentenced to death by Mr Justice Humphreys at Sussex Assizes on 7 December 1944.

Hanged by Albert Pierrepoint and Steve Wade.

January 31st: Arthur THOMPSON (34)   **Leeds**

On 21 September 1944 a neighbour, disturbed by the sound of a dog barking, found the body of Mrs Jane Coulson (69), the licensee of a Bradford public house. She had been strangled with her own stocking. The killer had cut his hand breaking a window to gain entrance, presumably to

117

commit robbery, as the old lady's purse was empty and some jewellery was missing.

Thompson, a lance corporal in the General Service Corps, had been reported absent without official leave on the night of the murder, 20 September 1944. A regular in the pub, he was a known persistent thief with scores of convictions in his native Merseyside. He was arrested near Morecambe trying to sell stolen jewellery and taken back to Bradford where he was charged with murder. During the journey he managed to stash some of the stolen jewels beneath a carpet in the police car.

Tried before Mr Justice Oliver at Leeds on 6 December 1944; it was alleged he had carried out the robbery whilst drunk and short of money, and that he had strangled the landlady when she disturbed him.

Hanged by Tom Pierrepoint and Herbert Morris.

March 8th: Karl Gustav HULTEN (23)   Pentonville

Hulten, a Swedish-American paratrooper, had already deserted from his unit when he met Elizabeth Marina Jones (18), also known as Georgina Grayson, in a London café in the autumn of 1944. Jones had left her native Wales to seek her fortune in the big city but had ended up working as a stripper. They teamed up together, he fantasising about being a gangster and she his moll. By night they cruised around in a stolen army truck attacking and robbing people in the black-out.

On 7 October they hailed a taxi driven by George Heath (34) and after reaching their destination Hulten shot Heath dead, whilst Jones rifled his pockets, stealing a small amount of money, a pen and cigarette case. They then drove to Staines, Middlesex, and hid the body in a ditch before driving off in the taxi.

Hulten was arrested three days later, still in possession of the stolen taxi cab, and that day Jones was also taken into custody. She made a statement to the effect that Hulten had bullied her into helping him commit the murder. Upon hearing this, Hulten claimed that it was she who was the instigator and had kept egging him on to do something 'exciting'.

Although Hulten was an American serviceman it was decided to break with precedent and allow him to be tried by a British court. On 16 January they stood trial together at the Old Bailey before Mr Justice Charles. During the six-day trial her defence continued to plead that it was Hulten alone who was guilty of murder, but the trial ended with them both being convicted.

Appeals to have the sentences reduced to manslaughter failed. Elizabeth Jones was reprieved, on account of her age, two days before she was due to go the gallows, apparently much to the anger of Winston Churchill.

Hulten was hanged by Albert Pierrepoint and Henry Critchell.

March 13th: Arthur HEYS (37)   Norwich

Heys was a leading aircraftsman stationed near Beccles in Suffolk, a married man with a young family back at home in Colne, Lancashire. On the night of 8 November 1944 he attended a dance with some fellow airmen. Heys returned alone to the camp drunk and when he tried to enter the women's quarters he was sent away by the duty corporal. He then staggered back to his own billet.

Next morning the body of Winifred Mary Evans (27) was found in a ditch close to the camp. She had been brutally raped and suffocated. The duty corporal told police about the drunken airman she had seen on the previous night and at a pay parade on the following day she identified Heys.

He denied being out that night, saying he was in his quarters, but his alibi could not be supported and scratches on his hands led to him being arrested on suspicion. Held in custody, he wrote an anonymous letter to his commanding officer, pretending that it was from the killer. The note was traced back to Heys and, as he had made the mistake of revealing too much about the crime, the note as good as sealed his fate. He was convicted at Bury St Edmunds before Mr Justice MacNaughton on 25 January.

Hanged by Tom Pierrepoint and Steve Wade.

March 17th: Robert L. PEARSON   Shepton Mallet
Cubia JONES

On the evening of 3 December 1944, heavily pregnant Mrs Joyce Brown left her home in Chard, Somerset. She was followed by two soldiers, who caught up with her, forced into a nearby orchard and raped her at knife point.

At a search of the nearby army camps Corporal Pearson and Private Jones, both members of the 1698th Engineers, had muddy and soiled trousers and were identified as the rapists.

On 16 December they were court martialled at Chard and both claimed that the woman had consented to have sex with them. This was in contrast to the beating she had taken and her extremely distressed condition following the assault.

Hanged by Tom Pierrepoint and Herbert Morris.

March 19th: James Herbert LEHMAN (45)   **Dublin**

Although Montreal-born Lehman was discharged from the American Army in 1917 on medical grounds and despite living on a disability pension in the following years, in 1939 when war broke out he volunteered for the Canadian Army and was posted to Aldershot in 1940.

Soon after his arrival in Britain he met and later married his wife Margaret and in 1943, with a young family, they came to Ireland. Lehman by this time had been invalided out of the army with back problems.

Mrs Lehman died of cyanide poisoning on 19 March 1944. She was heavily pregnant at the time. Lehman, during her pregnancy, had been having a series of relationships with other women and shortly after the death of his wife he was arrested on suspicion of murder.

At his trial, held before Mr Justice Maguire at Dublin in October, his defence was that his wife had committed suicide. Lehman also claimed to have no recollection of events from around the time of his wife's death until he found himself at Mountjoy Gaol awaiting trial.

Hanged by Albert Pierrepoint and an Irish assistant named S Johnstone.

April 7th: William HARRISON   **Shepton Mallet**

Private Harrison served with the US airforce stationed near Stewartstown, County Tyrone, Northern Ireland. During the autumn of 1944 he became friendly with the Wylie family who lived close to his camp.

On 25 September whilst visiting the house he asked if he could take Patricia Wylie (7), the daughter, to help him buy some drinks from a local store. During the trip to the shop, he took the young girl into a field where he sexually assaulted and strangled her.

Hanged by Tom Pierrepoint and Herbert Morris.

May 8th: George Edward SMITH (28)   **Shepton Mallet**

Sir Eric Teichmann was a retired former diplomat living at Homingham Hall, Norfolk. On 3 December, 1944, he heard shots being fired in his extensive grounds and went to investigate. When he failed to return home a search was made and he was found shot through the head in the thick undergrowth. The fatal shots had been fired from a .30 carbine.

The nearby army camp was sealed off and a search made of property and weapons. Police were tipped off that Private George Smith, of the 784th Bomb Squadron, and another airman, Private Wojtacha, had gone hunting in the woods near Homingham Hall.

Wojtacha was interviewed and said that they had done a little shooting when Teichmann had challenged them. Smith had then turned and coldly shot the man dead. Smith was questioned and as evidence linked him conclusively to the murder, he made a full confession.

At his court martial held in the camp chapel on 8 January, Smith retracted his confession and, despite evidence that he had a low mentality and suffered from insanity, he was convicted of murder at what had been his sixth court martial since being enlisted.

Hanged by Tom Pierrepoint and Herbert Morris.

June 15th: Aniceto MARTINEZ (24)   **Shepton Mallet**

In the early hours of 6 August 1944, Mrs Agnes Cope (75), was awoken by the sound of a man climbing the stairs of her house in Rugeley, Staffordshire. She told him that she had no money in the house but he replied: 'I don't want money... it be a woman I want'. She was then raped in her bed.

When the frail old lady staggered to the police station she told police she thought her attacker was an American. Investigations at a local camp found that the only American absent on the previous night during a midnight bed check was Private Martinez.

Martinez, an Hispanic, admitted the crime but claimed that he had been drunk and had entered the house thinking it was a brothel. Convicted at a court martial held at Lichfield on 21 February.

Hanged by Tom Pierrepoint and Albert Pierrepoint.

September 5th: Howard Joseph GROSSLEY (37)   **Cardiff**

Grossley was a Canadian soldier who had arrived in Wales in 1941. Despite having a wife in his homeland he met Lily Griffiths, some eight years his junior, from Cwmamman, near Abedare. They began to live together as man and wife and in 1943 she gave birth to a son.

In the spring of 1945, with the war in Europe showing signs of coming to an end, Grossley had to face up to the fact that he would soon be sent back home. This disturbed him very much and finally he decided that rather than face the decision of choosing between his wife back in Canada, who had dutifully written to him every week, and staying with his new family in Wales, he would commit suicide.

On 12 March, he met up with Lily at Porthcawl and told her his plans. He then pulled out his gun and turned it on himself. Lily made a frantic attempt to stop him and in doing so was shot in the stomach. Help arrived and Lily confirmed Grossley's story to the police as she was taken to Bridgend hospital. Four days later she died and Grossley, despite the deathbed testimony, was charged with murder.

Tried before by Mr Justice Singleton at Swansea Assizes on 12 July. The defence claimed it was an accident and at worst a case of manslaughter, but ballistics experts who examined the weapon claimed this was not possible.

Hanged by Tom Pierrepoint and Steve Wade.

September 7th: Thomas Eric RICHARDSON (27)   **Leeds**

In the early hours of Sunday morning, 29 April, the body of Dr David Dewar (41) was found in the driveway at his home in Leeds. He had been battered about the head with a sharp weapon, presumably as he was opening the garage door.

Investigations soon discovered that the doctor had been having an affair with a woman named Laura, the wife of a soldier serving overseas. It was also found that Dewar was not her only lover and that for some time she had been having a clandestine relationship with Richardson, a local engineer.

When questioned, Richardson confessed that he had killed the doctor with an axe which he had subsequently thrown in a river.

Tried before Mr Justice Hallett at Leeds in July, Richardson admitted that he killed Dewar through jealousy. The jury, returning a guilty verdict, added a strong recommendation to mercy.

Hanged by Tom Pierrepoint and Herbert Morris.

October 6th: Joachim GOLTZ (20)   **Pentonville**
Heinz BRUELING (21)
Josef MERTENS (21)
Kurt ZUEHLSDORFF (20)
Erich Pallme KOENIG (20)

Sergeant Major Wolfgang Rosterg (35) was made a prisoner of war in September 1944 after surrendering his arms. Although he had fought in the German Army Rosterg was not a Nazi, he had enlisted purely to fight for his country. He was sent to a camp near Devizes where, due to his high standard of education, he become the camp interpreter.

Unlike Rosterg a large number of prisoners were fanatical Nazis and in the winter of 1944 they planned a mass breakout. Word of the plan reached the British guards and the ringleaders were quickly removed to the high security Comrie Camp in Perthshire, Scotland. For some reason never explained Rosterg was also taken to Comrie and, although word of the planned escape had not come from him, he was immediately suspected, tried by kangaroo court and sentenced to death. In the early hours of 23 December, he was mercilessly beaten and kicked before being hanged in the hut latrine.

The five listed above all took an active part in the murder. Under the guidance of Koenig, Zuelsdorff put the rope around the man's neck and hanged him. The others all beat Rosterg before he died. They were convicted at a military court in London, which sat for two weeks in July.

Hanged in five single executions by Albert Pierrepoint assisted by Steve Wade and Harry Allen who was participating in his first execution since being reinstated as a hangman. Koenig, the last to go to the gallows, shouted 'Long live the Fatherland' as the rope was placed around his neck.

October 31st: Ronald Bertram MAURI (32)   Wandsworth

Vera Guest (18) was engaged to an American soldier when she met Mauri, a lorry driver, in their home town of Nottingham. He was already married with a four-year-old child, but Vera became infatuated with him and they began a relationship.

In the summer of 1945, Mauri got into trouble over the theft of some cigarettes and taking Vera with him he fled to Hillingdon, London, where his sister lived. On 11 July, Vera was found strangled with a ligature in a bedroom at the house. Mauri fled the area and after a cross country chase he was arrested in Monmouth, following a shootout with police during which he was shot in the head.

Evidence was shown that Mauri had written a letter to his former employer after strangling Vera, claiming that he planned to kill six more people before he committed suicide. Convicted before Mr Justice Tucker at the Old Bailey on 20 September.

Hanged by Albert Pierrepoint and Harry Kirk.

November 16th: Arnim KUEHNE (21)   Pentonville
Emil SCHMITTENDORF (31)

On 24 March, German prisoners of war at a camp on the outskirts of Sheffield were furious that a tunnel they had long been working on was uncovered just days from completion. Suspecting an informer, they looked round for a likely suspect and opted for Gerhardt Rettig (25) who had been seen in the vicinity of the tunnel chatting to British guards. Unlike many of the prisoners, Rettig was not a Nazi and when the guards learned of the threats made to Rettig it was decided to ship him and a comrade out to another camp. Before this could be arranged a baying mob attacked Rettig and kicked him to death.

Four men were identified as ringleaders and taken for trial at Kensington by military court martial on 7-13 August. Two of the accused, deemed not to be as actively involved in the attack, were acquitted, two were sentenced to death by hanging.

Hanged by Albert Pierrepoint and Alex Riley.

John Amery

December 19th: John AMERY (33)   **Wandsworth**

Harrow-educated Amery was the son of Leopold Amery, who was Secretary of State for India and a leading figure in Churchill's wartime cabinet. John Amery left England in 1935 and worked as a would-be film producer in Spain and other parts of Europe. In 1940, while living in France, he was caught up in the invasion. He approached the head of the 'English Service' in Germany and offered to broadcast propaganda messages.

He was also alleged to have made regular visits to prisoner of war camps in France trying to persuade captured soldiers to change sides. He was arrested in northern Italy in April 1945.

He was charged with treason at the Old Bailey on 28 November, before Mr Justice Humphreys. Amery tried to claim he had taken Spanish nationality and there were discussions as to whether he should stand trial for treason. Hearing that there would have to be a lengthy enquiry Amery decided to spare his family further embarrassment by pleading guilty. His trial lasted just eight minutes.

Hanged by Albert Pierrepoint and Harry Critchell. Amery told the hangman as he was led to the gallows: 'I've always wanted to meet you, Mr Pierrepoint. But not, of course, under these circumstances!'

1945

December 21st: John Riley YOUNG (40)   Pentonville

On the night of 6 June, Eva Lucas returned to her home in Leigh-on-Sea, Essex, and found her parents battered to death. Her father Frederick (52) had died from severe head injuries that had fractured his skull and lacerated his brain. Her mother, Cissie (52) had similar injuries and died in hospital a short time later.

Neighbours reported a stranger in the area on the morning of the murder, and he had even asked someone where the Lucas family lived. On the following day, Young, a builder from Ilford, tried to commit suicide by first cutting his wrists, then trying to gas himself. The police were called and it was learned that Young had had business dealings with the murdered man.

It was found that Young had tried to con Lucas, who was involved in a number of shady deals, out of a large amount of money to buy some dodgy gold coins. It seems that Young had visited Lucas and told him that he had conned him and during the quarrel that ensued Young picked up a chair and attacked Lucas.

Insanity was his defence when he appeared at Essex Assizes on 9 November before Mr Justice Lewis.

Hanged at 8am by Albert Pierrepoint, assisted by Herbert Morris and Steve Wade.

December 21st: James McNICOL (27)   Pentonville

Sergeant McNicol, a native of Motherwell, had fought at Dunkirk and Burma and had just been demobbed from the army when he got into a quarrel over a woman with a Sergeant Cox. They had been celebrating VJ Day at a gun site on the Thorpe Bay camp in Essex where they were stationed and the quarrel came after a lot of drink had been consumed.

That same day, 16 August, after another row, McNicol fired two shots through a window into a billet hut at the camp, killing Sergeant Donald Alfred Richard Kirkaldie (28), a married man with one child, from Essex, and wounding Cox.

Convicted before Mr Justice Lewis at Essex Assizes on 13 November. Over 20,00 people signed a petition for a reprieve organised by his brother-in-law, who claimed that as McNicol had been very drunk (he had consumed over 15 pints of beer) at the time, he should only have been charged with manslaughter.

Hanged at 9.30am by Albert Pierrepoint, assisted by Herbert Morris and Steve Wade.

December 29th: Robert BLAINE (24)   Wandsworth

Captain John Alex Ritchie of the Canadian Army was in London on leave. On the night of 14 September he dined with friends then made his way back across Soho to the YMCA, where he was staying. Two patrolling policemen turned down a quiet street and passed two soldiers on the opposite side. Moments later they came across Ritchie lying in a pool of blood.

The officers gave chase and managed to arrest one of the soldiers, who gave his name as Robert Blaine. He was also known as Reginald Douglas Johnson and had a string of convictions for theft. He was arrested and claimed that the other soldier had killed the Captain by hitting him with a brick before turning out his pockets and robbing him.

Despite his blaming his mystery accomplice, items belonging to the murdered man were found in Blaine's tunic. He pleaded not guilty to murder but admitted he had helped to rifle Ritchie's pockets after his accomplice had hit the captain with a brick. Convicted after a four-day trial at the Old Bailey, before Mr Justice Humphreys on 16 November. The 'other man' was never traced.

Hanged by Albert Pierrepoint and Harry Kirk.

1946

Cases where no executioner is recorded are multiple executions, and readers are asked to refer to the entries before or after for details of the hangman.

William Joyce

January 3rd: William JOYCE (40)   **Wandsworth**

Born in New York of Irish-American parents, Joyce found lasting notoriety when he earned the nick-name 'Lord Haw-Haw' for his 'Germany Calling…' radio broadcasts during the war.

Raised in Ireland, in 1922 his family moved to England, where he was educated at a London university. In 1933 he joined the British Union of Fascists and secured a British passport by falsely claiming to have been born in Galway. In 1937, after being expelled from Oswald Mosely's Fascist party, Joyce started his own British Nazi party and shortly before the war broke out he fled to Germany.

Between September 1939 and April 1945, Joyce broadcast from Hamburg a stream of anti-British messages and falsehoods designed to undermine morale on the home front. He was wounded and captured by British troops as he tried to flee Germany via the Danish border, trapped by his instantly recognisable voice.

At his three-day trial, held at the Old Bailey on 17-19 September before Mr Justice Tucker, his defence was that as he was born in America, Joyce could not be a traitor as he was not a British subject. Two of the three counts on which he was to have been tried were dismissed, but he was convicted because of the passport he had lied to obtain. As the British passport he held did not expire until July 1940, technically, from the moment war was declared until his British passport expired - a period of some nine months - he was a British citizen. Therefore, as he had been working for the enemy during this time, he had been committing treason and for this he was convicted.

Hanged by Albert Pierrepoint and Alex Riley.

1946

January 4th: Theodore John William SCHURCH (27) **Pentonville**

A private in the Royal Army Service Corps, Schurch was a former member of the British Union of Fascists, born in London of Swiss parents, who joined the British Army in 1936.

He was court martialled at Chelsea in September on nine charges of treachery and one of desertion with intent to join the enemy. It was alleged that whilst serving in Tobruk he volunteered to join a front line unit in order to desert. Schurch was taken prisoner and asked his Italian guards to put him in touch with intelligence officers.

He told them he was a Swiss subject and that although born in London his father had registered him as Swiss. He then gave them information he had gathered from British prisoners of war in Italy. Found guilty on all 10 charges, his defence claimed he was a poor uneducated fool.

Hanged by Albert Pierrepoint and Alex Riley, he became the last person executed for treachery.

January 8th: William BATTY (27) **Leeds**

A Bradford labourer convicted of the murder of Samuel Hammond Grey (33), a Bradford soldier, who was shot dead on his own doorstep on 14 August 1945 three days after returning from Burma.

Batty had built up a relationship with Mrs Nellie Grey, although whether they had been having an affair was not made clear. In early August she received a telegram from her husband telling her he was demobbed and due home on the following day. When Batty heard of this he said he would speak to Grey, and tell him to stay away from Nellie or he would shoot him.

With Grey back home he wrote a letter to Nellie asking her to run away with him. Not only did she refuse his request, but she also showed it to her husband and claimed that Batty had been making unwanted advances to her.

On the night of the murder Batty called at the house and fired a single shot into Grey's stomach with a Luger pistol. He then fled, leaving Grey dead on the floor. Police arrested Batty at his mother's house a short time later.

He claimed at his trial before Mr Justice Lynskey at Leeds on 29-30 November that after he had gone to the house to discuss the situation, Grey had pulled out a gun, which had gone off accidentally during a struggle. This was refuted by witnesses who saw him toying with a gun outside the house prior to the murder.

Hanged by Tom Pierrepoint and Harry Allen.

January 31st: Michael NIESCIOR (29) **Wandsworth**

Niescior, also known as Michael Morior, was invalided out of the Polish navy and found work as a chef at Brighton. He met a Mrs Elphick at a dance and they subsequently lived together at Portslade, whilst her husband

129

was away at war. In August 1945, Charles Elphick returned home unexpectedly and found his wife and Niescior together. There was a fierce quarrel, the upshot being that Mrs Elphick and Niescior left the house and took lodgings together.

A short time later, after a quarrel with her lover, Mrs Elphick returned to her husband and family, and soon after the reconciliation they went on a short family holiday. Returning home, she found a letter written by Niescior asking her to return to him. Damage had also been done to the house, which the Pole was suspected of committing.

Shortly before midnight on 22 October, Niescior called at the Elphick house carrying a large carving knife. He knocked on the glass door and when Elphick saw he was carrying a knife he went to get a weapon for his own protection. In the meantime, Mrs Elphick came downstairs and opened the door. Her husband rushed behind her to stop Niescior entering and as he did so he was stabbed in the chest.

Convicted before Mr Justice Wrottesley at Lewes Assizes on 11 December.

Hanged by Albert Pierrepoint and Steve Wade.

February 8th: John LYON (21)   Glasgow

Convicted before Lord Mackay at Glasgow High Court, on 15 December 1945, of the murder of John Thomas Brady (19), a Royal Navy sailor who had recently been demobbed.

On the night of 20 October 1945, Lyon was one of a crowd of eight youths who went into Argyle Street, Glasgow, looking for members of a rival gang. They set upon one youth who managed to outrun them before attacking Brady, an innocent bystander, unconnected to any gang, who was stabbed to death with a bayonet and a wood chisel. During the ferocious attack he received 40 stab wounds.

Five of the gang were arrested but only four brought to trial. Three were found guilty and sentenced to death, one being liable for the death penalty because his 18th birthday had fallen on the fifth and final day of the trial. This youth and another man were later reprieved.

Lyon became the first man to be executed at Barlinnie Prison when he was hanged by Thomas Pierrepoint.

March 5th: Charles Edward PRESCOTT (23)   Durham

Prescott, a marine of Biglands, near Wigton, had been going out with Belle Young (18) when in October 1945 she told him she wanted to break up the relationship, but to stay friends. A short time later at a dance-hall he saw her with another man and threatened that he would kill them both.

On 17 November, he approached Belle's home at Cummock Bank Farm, Waverton, where he saw five people silhouetted against the firelight. They were looking through some photographs when Prescott fired a gun through the window, fatally wounding Sarah Jean Young (19), Belle's sister.

The prosecution at his trial, before Mr Justice Lynskey at Carlisle Assizes on 17 January, claimed it was a deliberate case of murder except that he had shot the wrong person. Prescott claimed he had not meant to fire the gun, but it had gone off accidentally when he was startled by a horse. He could not explain why he had been carrying a loaded gun.

Hanged by Tom Pierrepoint.

March 19th: Arthur CLEGG (42)   **Wandsworth**

A Brixton engineer, sentenced to death by Mr Justice Croom-Johnson at the Old Bailey on 8 February for the murder by drowning of his daughter's 11-day-old illegitimate child, Jill Clegg.

Unmarried Joan Clegg (20) fell pregnant in the spring of 1945 and her father went to great lengths to conceal the fact from almost everyone, including his own wife. It has been rumoured that he himself was the baby's father, but Joan Clegg later claimed that the father was a soldier called Bob!

On 6 November 1945, the baby's body was found washed up on the shore of the Thames at East Greenwich. A piece of tape with the words 'Baby Clegg' fastened to the child's arm led police to Clegg, who said that on 30 October he had taken the child in for adoption and whilst entering the offices had met a couple hoping to adopt. They had come to an agreement with him and taken the child away. There was no evidence to suggest Clegg was telling the truth.

Hanged by Albert Pierrepoint and Herbert Morris.

March 26th: Arthur CHARLES (34)   **Durham**

Charles, a South African seaman, had lived in England for five years and for a period of time lived with a Mrs Hannah Burns at South Shields, as man and wife. Towards the end of the war they parted and John Duplessis (35), a shipmate and fellow black South African, later moved in with her. The two men remained friends and in September 1945, they signed up for a ship together.

On 28 November, they returned to South Shields where Duplessis spent the night with Mrs Burns. Charles, it seemed, had grown jealous of this arrangement and on the following night he called at the house where there was a quarrel. Charles then fired six shots at Duplessis as he lay in bed. Five of the bullets hit Duplessis, causing him massive injuries from which he died in hospital on 31 December.

Tried before Mr Justice Oliver at Durham Assizes on 14 February, Charles denied the charges and claimed it was a case of mistaken identity.

Hanged by Steve Wade, carrying out his first engagement as chief executioner, assisted by Harry Allen.

April 2nd: Marion GRONDKOWSKI (33)   Wandsworth
Henryk MALINOWSKI (25)

The body of Reuben Martirosoff (39) was discovered in the back of a saloon car on 1 November 1945 at Notting Hill Gate. He had been shot through the head at close range and his pockets emptied. Better known in the underworld as 'Russian Robert', he was an Armenian-born general dealer, and the second person to be killed in similar circumstances in the area. Detectives hunting the killer of Frank Everitt a fortnight earlier noticed many similarities in the two murders and believed they had been killed by the same person or persons.

It was learned that on the night of his murder Martirosoff had arranged a meeting with Malinowski, a deserter from the Polish navy, and soon both he and Grondkowski, another Polish deserter, were brought in for questioning. In their possession were Martirosoff's lighter and his wallet.

The police soon had an overwhelming case against them and this was borne out when both men then tried to blame the other for the murder, during their trial at the Old Bailey on 11-13 February, before Mr Justice Croom-Johnson.

They were hanged separately by Albert Pierrepoint, assisted by Alex Riley and Harry Kirk. Although detectives were convinced that both men had murdered Frank Everitt, and there was strong evidence to suggest they had, neither would admit to the crime despite last-minute pleas to confess before they went to the gallows.

Marion Grondkowski & Henryk Malinowski

April 6th: Patrick CARRAHER (39)   **Glasgow**

A hard-man and habitual criminal, Carraher was sentenced to death at his third murder trial.

In 1938, the 'fiend of the Gorbals', as he was known, was convicted of the culpable homicide of a man who had tried to break up an argument involving Carraher. For his trouble Carraher whipped out a knife and slit his throat. He was jailed for three years.

Upon his release he continued to earn his living from theft and housebreaking, often resorting to violence. In 1943, he was sent to prison again for attempted murder after attacking a man with a razor. Again he served a little under three years and in the autumn of 1945, he was released again.

On 23 November, upon hearing his brother-in-law was involved in a street fight, Carraher rushed to help. Watching the fight was John Gordon (39), a former prisoner of war, recently demobbed after serving Seaforth Highlanders for over twenty years. Without waiting to ask questions, Carraher assumed Gordon was connected with the 'enemy' and stabbed him in the neck with a carving knife.

Gordon died in hospital from the wound, which had penetrated four inches into his neck. Carraher was asleep in bed when detectives came for him in the early hours and although he denied the attack, some of his former associates in crime testified against him.

As a result 'Carry' Carraher again stood trial for murder. His defence was that the knife he carried had a blade of less than three inches and could therefore not have caused the fatal wound. This was dismissed when medical evidence showed that with force Carraher's knife could easily have penetrated to the depth of the wound. On 2 March, he was finally convicted of murder before Lord Russell.

Hanged by Tom Pierrepoint.

April 9th: Harold BERRY (30)   **Manchester**

Bernard Phillips (37), a Manchester money-lender, disappeared after leaving his office on the afternoon of 3 January. He had left in the company of a client who wanted to borrow a large sum of money. Three days later, he was found stabbed to death in a culvert at Winsford, Cheshire.

A knife found beside the body led police to Harold Berry, the watchman at a local factory. Berry was having an affair with one of the women at the factory and they had gone off to spend a weekend in London. He was arrested on his return and subsequently stood trial before Mr Justice Stable at Chester on 11-14 February.

It was claimed that Berry had pretended to be a wealthy farmer seeking a loan and, having lured Phillips into a quiet road, had stabbed him to death and stolen £50. He had then frivolously spent the money on himself and his girlfriend in the 'West End'.

Hanged by Tom Pierrepoint.

April 24th: Martin Patrick COFFEY (23)　　　　　　　　**Manchester**

On 26 November 1945, Coffey entered a pawnshop in Hulme, Manchester, and pointing a gun at the proprietor Henry Dutton (72), demanded all the money in the shop. Dutton unlocked the safe, which contained over £2,000, but as Coffey reached for the money, the old man blew a police whistle. Coffey fired the gun, hitting him in the wrist. Undeterred, Dutton continued to blow on the whistle, and in a panic Coffey shot him twice in the chest before fleeing without the money.

Convicted before Mr Justice Morris at Manchester Assizes on 12 March, Coffey had been arrested after boasting about the crime to some friends. A witness then picked him out as the man seen running from the shop after hearing the whistle.

Hanged by Tom Pierrepoint.

May 28th: Leonard HOLMES (32)　　　　　　　　**Lincoln**

Holmes, a lorry driver, lived happily together with his wife Peggy Agnes (29), at Walesby, Nottinghamshire. In 1943, whilst serving in the army at Huddersfield, he began an affair with a local woman, who agreed to live with him if he left his wife.

On 19 November 1945, Holmes went to Huddersfield and told the woman that his wife had left him, but on his return home he was arrested after his wife's body had been found in their house. She had been beaten about the head with a blunt instrument and then strangled.

Convicted at Nottingham Assizes before Mr Justice Charles on 28 February. It was suggested at the trial that he had attacked his wife after accusing her of being unfaithful to him. This followed an evening in a local public house when she was being, in his words, 'too friendly' with a number of soldiers in the bar. On their return home they quarrelled and he admitted he struck her with a hammer after she admitted she had been unfaithful.

Despite his own infidelity, Holmes lodged an appeal on the grounds of provocation, through his wife's behaviour in having an affair whilst he was serving in the army. The appeal was dismissed and a further appeal was then made to the House of Lords. The verdict of the appeal was the same: that unfaithfulness is not an excuse for murder.

Hanged by Tom Pierrepoint, carrying out his last execution in an English prison.

July 17th: Thomas HENDREN (31)　　　　　　　　**Liverpool**

Liverpool police had had 'Bobby's Gentleman's Manicure Saloon' in the city centre under observation, believing it to be used for immoral purposes. On 20 May, while two officers were spying on the shop, a man entered and soon after a scream was heard.

Hendren was spoken to as he left the building, but not held. He disappeared down the street and when the officers tried to enter they found the door locked. Eventually it was opened and the body of Ella Valentine

Staunton (41) was found. She had been stabbed through the heart, attacked with a box opener and strangled with a light flex.

Hendren, a ship's baker from Birkenhead and former client of Mrs Staunton's, was arrested in Salford four days later. Tried before Mr Justice Oliver at Liverpool Assizes on 27 June, his defence was insanity.

Hanged by Albert Pierrepoint and Herbert Morris.

August 7th: Walter CLAYTON (22)   Liverpool

The body of Joyce Jacques (22) was found on the beach at Bare, Morecambe, on the evening of 12 April. She had been strangled with her own silk scarf. From papers in her handbag left beside the body they discovered her name and address, and a search of her room found letters written by a soldier with whom she had recently started an affair.

Clayton, a soldier from Clitheroe, was arrested at his in-laws' and confessed that he had killed her as he was jealous that she still flirted with other men.

He pleaded guilty at his trial before Mr Justice Stable at Manchester on 16 July. The whole proceedings lasted less than three minutes.

Hanged by Albert Pierrepoint and Steve Wade.

August 10th: John CALDWELL (20)   Glasgow

On 26 March, a couple returning to their Glasgow home saw they had an intruder. They asked their neighbour James Straiton (61), a retired detective, to accompany them to the house. Noticing the back window open, the man climbed through and opened the front door for his neighbour to enter.

Inside were two youths who made good their escape by shooting James Straiton in the stomach. He died from his injuries before help could arrive. From evidence left at the house police suspected the killer may have been the same man who had broken into a number of houses in the area recently and in one case had left fingerprints.

A check on these prints led police to Caldwell who, along with his father, was arrested. Caldwell senior was a fence who sold on the goods his son and his younger accomplice stole.

Tried before Lord Mackay at Glasgow High Court on 23 June, Caldwell was condemned to death; his accomplice in the murder, a 15-year-old youth, was detained at His Majesty's Pleasure, whilst his father and girlfriend were convicted of receiving stolen goods.

Hanged by Tom Pierrepoint, carrying out his last execution. Albert Pierrepoint has been credited with carrying out this and the two previous executions at Barlinnie Gaol. However, when copies of his diaries were consulted, there was no mention of any of these three executions.

September 6th: Sydney John SMITH (24)   Wandsworth

On 3 March, the body of John Whatman (73), a wealthy horse and cattle dealer, was found shot dead at his home at Hollington, near Hastings. The house had also been ransacked.

Smith, a labourer from Markyate, Hertford, had been in the area visiting relatives at the time of the murder and investigations in his home town traced a five pound note stolen from the house at Hastings. He had also been trying to sell items of jewellery in a number of pubs and when arrested he was in possession of items bearing the name of John Whatman.

Convicted at Sussex Assizes on 18 July, before Mr Justice Singleton.

Hanged by Albert Pierrepoint, assisted by Henry Critchell and Harry Allen.

September 6th: David Baillie MASON (39)   Wandsworth

A milling machine operator of Wallington, Surrey, sentenced to death by Mr Justice Cassels at the Old Bailey on 25 July, for the murder of his wife, Dorothy (37), by strangling on 29 May.

In his defence it was claimed that Mason had attacked his wife after he returned home to find that she had suffocated and killed their three-year-old son.

Hanged by Albert Pierrepoint, assisted by Henry Critchell and Harry Allen. **SMITH**, above, was hanged at 9am, Mason followed him to the gallows at 10.15am. Allen noted that Mason's execution was very poor and the hangmen were very grateful for the work done by the 'screws'.

October 16th: Neville George Clevely HEATH (29)   Pentonville

On the afternoon of 21 June, the body of film extra Margery Aimee Brownwell Gardner (32) was found in a hotel room at Notting Hill, London. She had been bound at the ankles, bitten, whipped and then savagely mutilated. The cause of death was asphyxiation. The room had been booked to a Mr and Mrs N.G.C. Heath with an address in Hampshire.

Although police now suspected the killer may be Heath, a former airforce officer with a long criminal past, they neglected to release his photograph to the press, fearing it may prejudice the case when it came to court. A few days after the murder, detectives received a letter from Heath saying that he had loaned Margery the key to his room so she could 'entertain a friend'.

In the meantime Heath, now posing as Group Captain Rupert Brooke, had travelled down to Bournemouth where on 3 July, he met Doreen Marshall (21), a former Wren, who was at the seaside recovering from an illness. They had dinner at her hotel and departed together. When Miss Marshall failed to return to her hotel the police were informed. 'Brooke' offered to help and visited the police where he was recognised as Heath and

Neville George Clevely Heath

detained. On 8 July, Doreen's body was found in some bushes. She had been sexually assaulted, mutilated and her throat cut.Heath's three-day trial opened before Mr Justice Morris at the Old Bailey on 24 September. Faced with the brutal nature of the crimes, his counsel offered a defence of insanity. The jury took less than an hour to convict him.

Hanged by Albert Pierrepoint and Harry Kirk, Heath was alleged to have asked for a whiskey before being led to the gallows, adding: 'in the circumstances, you might make that a double!'

November 1st: Arthur Robert BOYCE (45)　　　　　　**Pentonville**

On 14 June the body of Elizabeth McLindon (41) was found in Belgravia House, the wartime home of the King of Greece, where she worked as a housekeeper. She had been shot through the head as she was making a telephone call. Beside the body was a discarded .32 shell. She had been dead for six days.

Detectives learned that she had been engaged to Boyce, a painter and decorator from Brighton. Boyce had served a prison sentence for bigamy and when questioned told police he had planned to marry Elizabeth on 16 July. Although police were suspicious, a search of the property did not find the murder weapon. They took possession of his diary and address book and this led them to a friend named Rowland in North Wales.

The friend was in due course questioned and told police that he had shared lodgings with Boyce in the previous year and that he believed Boyce had stolen his .32 pistol. Rowland still had a cartridge which matched the one found at the scene and proved that this same gun had killed Miss McLindon and Boyce was convicted on this evidence before Mr Justice Morris at the Old Bailey on 19 September.

Hanged by Albert Pierrepoint and Henry Critchell.

November 13th: Frank Joseph FREIYER (26)   **Wandsworth**

A Plumstead telephone engineer convicted of the murder of Joyce Brierley (19), his girlfriend, whose body was found in an air-raid shelter at Maryon Park, Charlton, on 20 September. She had been strangled.

Freiyer confessed to the police that he had killed her. At his trial before Mr Justice Stable at the Old Bailey on 25 October, the only motive the Crown could suggest for the murder was that he had grown tired of her. The jury took just a few minutes to find him guilty and he refused to appeal.

Hanged by Albert Pierrepoint and Harry Kirk.

November 19th: Arthur RUSHTON (31)   **Liverpool**

A Birkenhead labourer, Rushton had become engaged to Catherine Rene Cooper (18) even though he was already married. He had left his wife after the war because of her infidelity, but was unable to raise the money for a divorce.

On 2 September, after being told by her parents to cool their relationship until he was divorced, Rushton stabbed Catherine with a German dagger which he had given her as a gift and which she had just returned. Sentenced to death by Mr Justice Lynskey at Chester Assizes on 31 October. He also refused to appeal against conviction.

Hanged by Albert Pierrepoint and Henry Critchell.

December 10th: John Fleming McCready MATHIESON (23)   **Pentonville**

A sailor on the HMS Victory, Mathieson was arrested in a London cafe for being drunk and disorderly on the night of 20 July and held in police custody at Holloway. On the following morning the body of a former music hall artiste, Mrs Mona Victoria Vanderstay (46), was found strangled in St Luke's churchyard, Holloway. During investigations detectives spoke to all those placed in custody on the night of the 20 July and amongst items taken from Mathieson was Mrs Vanderstay's ID card and clothing coupons.

At his trial before Mr Justice Stable at the Old Bailey on 19-23 October, his defence was that he was insane and he had committed the murder whilst drunk and in the same state of consciousness as a sleepwalker.

Hanged by Albert Pierrepoint and Harry Allen.

1947

Cases where no executioner is recorded are multiple executions, and readers are asked to refer to the entries before or after for details of the hangman.

1947

January 3rd: Stanley SHEMINANT (28)   Liverpool

Private Harry Berrisford (20) disappeared on 17 May 1946, after taking leave from his regiment in Lincolnshire and returning to see his mother at their home on Cromwell Street, Hanley. Lodging at the house were Sheminant, an out of work bus driver, and his girlfriend.

On 19 July, after becoming suspicious about her son's disappearance, Mrs Berrisford entered the lodger's room and found the remains of her son buried under the floorboards.

Tried at Stafford Assizes on 29 November, it was claimed that the two men had quarrelled after Berrisford returned home and discovered Sheminant had pawned a number of items belonging to him. Sheminant, fearful of being charged with theft, had then beaten him to death with a hammer. He pleaded self-defence.

Dismissing his appeal on 19 December, Lord Goddard said it was a cruel and wicked murder and robbery of a young soldier home on leave.

Hanged by Steve Wade and Harry Allen.

January 30th: Albert SABIN (21)   Leeds

On the afternoon of 21 September 1946, Dr Neil McLeod (52), a Leeds based psychiatrist, and one of the leading mental health specialists in the North of England, was seen reluctantly giving a soldier a lift in his car. Later that afternoon his body was found in a disused colliery outside Leeds, close to a prisoner of war camp at Tangley Hall. He had been shot dead.

Birmingham-born Sabin, a guard at the camp, was routinely questioned and admitted that he had killed the doctor but claimed it was an accident.

His defence, at Leeds Assizes before Mr Justice Henn-Collins on 5-6 December, claimed that McLeod had made improper advances to him and the gun was accidentally discharged during a struggle in the doctor's car. The prosecution alleged that Sabin had been trying to blackmail the doctor and that after shooting him he had stolen £20.

Hanged by Steve Wade and Harry Kirk.

February 27th: Walter Graham ROWLAND (38)   Manchester

On 20 October, 1946, the body of a Manchester prostitute, Olive Balchin (40), was found on a bomb site in the city centre. She had been beaten to death with a cobbler's hammer.

Rowland was identified as buying the hammer, and witnesses saw him in the company of the woman on the previous night. When questioned he said that he suspected she had infected him with venereal disease, but denied murdering her.

His five-day trial before Mr Justice Sellars ended on 16 December and, although he strongly denied the crime, the evidence against him was strong and he was convicted.

140

1947

Walter Graham Rowland

On 22 January, five days before his appeal was due to be heard, David Ware, a prisoner in Liverpool's Walton Gaol, confessed that he was the real killer. He gave an account of what had happened, but his version was ignored when it was found that nothing he had revealed had not already been reported in the newspapers. Ware later retracted the confession and Rowland's appeal was unsuccessful.

Rowland was hanged by Albert Pierrepoint and Henry Critchell. It was the second time Pierrepoint had been engaged to execute Rowland. In 1934, he had been sentenced to death for the murder of his two-year-old daughter. Pierrepoint and his uncle were engaged for the execution which was later commuted. Rowland served 6 years and was released in 1940 after volunteering to join the army.

The case has a strange footnote. In 1951, David Ware was convicted of the attempted murder of a woman whom he attacked with a hammer. He committed suicide in Broadmoor in 1954.

March 18th: Harold HAGGER (45)   **Wandsworth**

Dagmar Peters (also known as Petrzywalski) (47), left her home in Kingsdown, Kent, on the morning of 31 October 1946, intending to hitch hike to visit her sister-in-law in London. Later that day her body was found beside the A20 at Wrotham Hill. She had been strangled. The motive for the murder was unclear: she was not sexually assaulted and as she carried no money robbery was discounted.

Amongst the few items the killer had taken was a yellow string bag which was found floating in a mill stream. The source of the stream was near a factory where a consignment of bricks had been delivered. The delivery driver was interviewed and gave his name as Sydney Sinclair.

He later admitted his real name was Hagger and it was found that he had a long list of convictions, including one for assaulting a woman. He initially denied any knowledge of the murder, but later admitted that he had given her a lift and that he had killed her by accident after catching her trying to steal his wallet.

Sentenced to death at Kent Assizes on 28 February by Mr Justice Byrne. He declined an appeal.

Hanged by Albert Pierrepoint and Harry Kirk.

March 26th: Frederick William REYNOLDS (39)   Pentonville

A book-maker sentenced to death at the Old Bailey on 7 February for the murder of Mrs Beatrice Greenberg (40) in Highbury, north London.

Reynolds and Mrs Greenberg were both married but had been having an affair for almost 20 years. It was customary for him to call at her flat after a night at the pub. He would whistle or sing as he approached and if her husband was away she would let him in. On 17 December 1946, he called at the flat as usual and during a quarrel shot her dead.

At his trial he alleged that it was an accident and that he had been drunk at the time.

Hanged by Albert Pierrepoint and Harry Kirk.

March 31st: Joseph McMANUS (41)   Dublin

Late on the night of 5 October 1946, Alice Gerrard (26) was found shot dead in the bed she shared with her six-month-old baby. Although she was married, her husband was not the father of the child and rumour in her home town of Donaghmore, County Meath, was rife that the father was McManus, a labourer who had been having an affair with the young woman.

Forensic evidence found that the shot had been fired from outside the house through a small hole in a window, and police noticed footprints outside from which they made casts. They matched those of McManus and his guilt was further sealed when tiny fragments of glass from the window matched ones found at his own house.

At the end of January he was sentenced to death, after a trial lasting over two weeks, by Mr Justice Overend. He had pleaded insanity and his trial had twice been postponed to hear medical evidence regarding this issue. The jury added a strong recommendation to mercy, but nevertheless his appeal a few weeks later was dismissed. It was stated that by firing through the closed window at a 'blind' target he could easily have killed both the mother and child, and this seemed to weigh against him.

Hanged by Albert Pierrepoint and S. Johnstone.

April 15th: David John WILLIAMS (26)   Wandsworth

On 6 February, Margaret Williams (26) was accosted on the street in Merton, London, by her estranged husband who pleaded with her to return home with him. When she refused he pulled out a hammer and struck her on the head. As she slumped to the pavement he repeatedly hit her until he thought she was dead. He then covered her in his coat. He was arrested at once, Margaret was rushed to hospital where she died soon after admittance.

Sentenced to death by Mr Justice Byrne at Surrey Assizes, Kingston upon Thames, on 7 March, his defence was insanity.

Hanged by Albert Pierrepoint and Harry Kirk.

June 20th: Eric Charles BRIGGS (40)   Leeds

The hardest task for detectives investigating the murder of Gertrude Briggs (49) at Leeds was deciding which of the two suspects, who both confessed to the crime, was telling the truth.

In the early hours of 10 February, Mrs Briggs left her job as a kitchen maid at a Leeds hotel. Moments later she was found stabbed to death on a deserted street. She had received close on fifty stab wounds, half of them to her neck. It was the second brutal attack on a woman in the city: a week earlier Mrs Elizabeth Donoghue received a fractured skull and severe cuts to her hands and face after a late night assault.

Briggs, a weaver, was arrested almost at once when police noticed bloodstains on his hands when they reported his wife's murder. He initially denied the murder but on the following night he confessed he had killed her with a hacksaw blade.

Two days later Dennis Wood, a soldier from Leeds, was arrested in Sheffield after confessing to the police that he had attacked both Mrs Donoghue and Mrs Briggs. He was charged with the attempted murder of Mrs Donoghue, but not with the murder of Mrs Briggs.

Eric Briggs, upon hearing of the confession, retracted the statements he had made and he kept up the denial of his wife's murder when he appeared before Mr Justice Pritchard on 8 May.

Briggs, by his own mouth, had given an accurate account of how his wife had met her death. Wood, when he took the stand, claimed he had stabbed her with his bayonet. Medical evidence refuted this. The jury took less than an hour to convict Briggs. On the following day Wood was convicted of attempted murder and ordered to be detained at His Majesty's Pleasure.

Briggs was hanged by Steve Wade and Harry Kirk.

August 14th: William SMEDLEY (38)   Leeds

The body of Edith Simmonite (29), a Sheffield prostitute, was found on a city centre bomb site on 9 March. She had a scarf tightly knotted around her neck. Witnesses told police they had seen her in the company of two men from a local hostel, one of whom was a miner named William Smedley. Both men made statements to the police; Smedley said they had both parted company with Edith at the same time and left her on a street corner; the other man said that he had left Smedley talking to her.

Further questioned, Smedley then said he had been chatting to Edith when they were approached by an Irishman with whom Edith went off to do business. Smedley said that he had since spoken to the Irishman who had confessed he had committed the murder.

Sentenced to death by Mr Justice Pritchard at Leeds Assizes on 22 July, it was suggested that Smedley, a former customer of the prostitute, had two motives for killing her. Firstly that she had robbed him of some money during a previous liaison, and secondly that on the night of her death, he had had sex with her after which she revealed that she had venereal desease. In a rage he had strangled her.

Hanged by Steve Wade and Harry Kirk.

August 21st: John Edward GARTSIDE (24)   Leeds

Friends were shocked to find that Percy Baker (44) and his wife Alice (42) had broken up after a quarrel in May 1946, and furniture from their house at Standedge, near Huddersfield, was being taken into storage.

The removal man showed them a receipt signed by Baker which was suspected of being a forgery. The police were informed and investigations led them to John Gartside, a former airman, who had rented a shop for which some items belonging to the Bakers were destined. When arrested he was driving their car.

At his trial before Mr Justice Pritchard at Leeds Assizes on 30 July, it was alleged that Gartside had shot the couple and buried them on the moors. He had then tried to off-load their belongings for financial gain.

His defence pleaded that the killings were an accident. Gartside claimed he arrived at their house during a quarrel between Mr and Mrs Baker and as Gartside tried to intervene Baker accidentally shot his wife. As the two men then struggled with the gun Percy Baker received fatal but accidental gunshot wounds.

He made no appeal after sentence of death was passed.

Hanged by Steve Wade and Henry Critchell.

John Edward Gartside

September 19th: Christopher James GERAGHTY (20)   Pentonville
Charles Henry JENKINS (23)

On 29 April, Alec de Antiquis (36) was shot dead as he tried to prevent three armed robbers from fleeing a West End jewellery shop. The men had raided the shop and as they fled Antiquis tried to prevent their escape by swinging his motorcycle in their path. He was shot in the head by one of the gang who escaped in the busy traffic.

A witness came forward who saw two masked men enter a building on Tottenham Court Road, and a search yielded a raincoat that was traced to Jenkins, who had a long criminal record. Two friends of Jenkins, Chris Geraghty and Terence Rolt, were also picked up. Under questioning Geraghty implicated Rolt in the murder and he in turn implicated Jenkins.

Sentenced to death by Mr Justice Hallett at the Old Bailey on 28 July. Their conviction and subsequent execution led to the disbanding of many criminal gangs, with a large number of discarded weapons being handed in to police.

Hanged by Albert Pierrepoint assisted by Henry Critchell and Harry Allen.

December 30th: Eugenius JURKIEWICZ (34)   Bristol

On the night of 12 September, Jurkiewicz, after finishing supper and drinking only a moderate amount, decided he wanted female company. Failing to find a woman near his base at the Tohsi Army Camp, he travelled into Middlezoy, Somerset where he spent the rest of the evening at The George Inn. He had been chatting to the landlady Mrs Emily Bowers (76), and she had even given him a peck on the cheek goodnight as she locked up.

In a drunken state the Polish sergeant returned to the secluded public house at the dead of night, broke into the inn and viciously raped and murdered the old lady. She died from sheer exhaustion trying to fight off her attacker.

Sentenced to death on 15 November by Lord Chief Justice Goddard at Bristol Assizes.

Hanged by Albert Pierrepoint and Harry Allen.

1948

Cases where no executioner is recorded are multiple executions, and readers are asked to refer to the entries before or after for details of the hangman.

January 7th: George Henry WHELPTON (31)   **Leeds**

The bodies of Mrs Alison Parkin (48) and two of her children, Joyce (23) and Maurice (15) were found dead in their home at Doncaster on 9 October 1947.   They had been strangled and then subjected to horrific sexual mutilation.

Whelpton, a Doncaster bus driver, was arrested on the following day and confessed that he had killed Mrs Parkin, a widow, during a jealous quarrel when she intimated that her previous boyfriend had treated her better. He had then killed the two children when they stumbled across the body of their mother.

Despite Whelpton's having suffered mentally during the war, and the horrific nature of the killing, his plea of insanity was surprisingly rejected at his Leeds Assizes trial before Mr Justice Morris on 19 December.

Hanged by Steve Wade and Harry Kirk.

George Henry Whelpton

February 3rd: Evan Haydn EVANS (22)   **Cardiff**

Late on the night of 12 October 1947, Mrs Rachel Allen (76), a washerwoman from Wattstown, in the Rhondda Valley, was found dead in an alley close to her house. She had a sustained a fractured skull from being thrown to the ground, savagely kicked and then raped as she lay dying.

Evans, a local collier, was interviewed at the home he shared with his parents, after Scotland Yard detectives asked local police if they had any suspects; it was learned he had been seen drinking with the woman earlier that night. Witnesses in the pub said Evans was wearing a brown suit and had quarrelled with Mrs Allen.

He later confessed that he had kicked the woman in the dark alley after she had insulted him, but he did not think he had killed her. He also denied owning a brown suit, but it was eventually found hidden inside the sofa in his home.

Sentenced to death by Mr Justice Byrne at Cardiff Assizes on 15 December 1947.

Hanged by Albert Pierrepoint and Harry Kirk.

February 6th: Stanislaw MYSZKA (23)   **Perth**

Catherine McIntyre (47) lived with her husband and three children in an isolated cottage overlooking Loch Tay, Tayside. On 26 September 1947 she had been alone in the house all day; when she failed to turn up as planned at a friend's house they went to investigate. Her son was at the house, expecting his mother to return and let him in, and being now concerned, he forced entry into the house and found her dead in his room. She was bound and gagged and had suffered terrible cuts and bruises to her head and throat. Missing from the house were her gold wedding ring and £90 in cash.

Myszka, a Polish deserter, who lived nearby in a Polish camp, was suspected. The bruises had been caused by the butt of a gun recovered in a field, which police believed the Pole had stolen from a house earlier that year while working there. There was also a bloodstained shaving razor which had been used to cut the victim's throat. Traces of stubble attached were the same as whiskers on Myszka's face.

The suspect was arrested on 2 October and when searched, the stolen wedding ring was found hidden in his shoe. In the face of such damning evidence the jury at his trial, before Lord Sorn on 9 January, needed less than 20 minutes to find him guilty.

Hanged by Albert Pierrepoint and Steve Wade.

February 19th: Walter John CROSS (21)   **Pentonville**

Neighbours heard screams and groans coming from a house at Barking on the night of 14 November 1947. A man was seen leaving and when they went to investigate, they found the body of Percy Busby (55), a crippled watchmaker. He had been strangled and his empty wallet was found beside the body.

Cross, a Dagenham lorry driver, was identified as the man leaving the house. At his trial before Mr Justice Cassels at the Old Bailey on 14-16 January, it was alleged that he had gone to the house with a friend on the pretence that his friend wanted a watch repaired. The plan was that the friend would leave the door ajar as he left and Cross would enter and steal the money from the wallet. His defence, that Busby was alive when Cross left the house and perhaps someone else had then committed the murder, was rejected.

Hanged by Albert Pierrepoint and Harry Allen.

For a period between 14 April and 6 June, following a bill introduced to the House of Commons, the death penalty was suspended and all persons sentenced to death during this period were automatically reprieved. Although it was proposed to suspend the death penalty for a five-year period, following a vote in the House of Lords the bill was thrown out and executions were again sanctioned.

November 18th: Stanley Joseph CLARKE (34)   Norwich

A pig breeder from Great Yarmouth who pleaded guilty to the murder of Florence May Bentley (32), a chambermaid, who was found stabbed to death at a Yarmouth boarding house on 16 June.

When questioned, Clarke told police he knew nothing about the attack, believing she had only been wounded. When they told him it was a murder investigation, Clarke confessed.

His trial, before Mr Justice Cassels at Norfolk Assizes on 20 October, lasted less than five minutes.

Hanged by Albert Pierrepoint and Harry Kirk.

November 19th: Peter GRIFFITHS (22)   Liverpool

In the early hours of 14 May, a nurse at Queen's Park Hospital, Blackburn, noticed a cot was empty. The missing child, June Ann Devaney (3), was later found in the hospital grounds. She had been raped and beaten to death.

The killer left a vital clue in a fingerprint on a bottle in the ward and the entire male population of Blackburn - over 46,000 - were fingerprinted. Griffiths, a former soldier, was number 46253, and on 12 August officers checking his prints found a match.

Peter Griffiths

He was arrested outside his home on Birley Street, Blackburn. **(See Volume One, 1876, August 14th William FISH)**. After initial denials he confessed that whilst drunk he had snatched the child from her cot, assaulted her and then murdered her by repeatedly bashing her head against a wall. Convicted before Mr Justice Oliver at Lancashire Assizes on 18 October. His failed defence had been insanity. He made no appeal.

Hanged by Albert Pierrepoint and Harry Allen.

November 24th: William M GAMBON (28) **Dublin**

Convicted of the murder of James Long (39) who, in August, was battered to death with an iron bar in the back room of a Dublin tenement house occupied by Gambon.

When police went to the house they found the door had been

padlocked and had to force it open. Long's body was on the bed, the pillow saturated with blood, and an iron bar was found in the room.

At his trial at Dublin Assizes, it was alleged that Long had gone to work in England and sent letters to Gambon enclosing sums of money. Long returned to Dublin on 21 August, and went with Gambon to the back room of the tenement. Gambon's wife was staying with a friend. According to Gambon, Long got into bed and started playing pontoon with him. Long then started to call him names and insulted his wife. As Long tried to get out of bed he caught Gambon by the throat. Gambon saw an iron bar near the washstand. He said he did not remember striking Long.

After the murder he got someone to fix a padlock onto the door and went off intending to go to see his wife at Cabra. Next day he gave himself up to police telling them he had committed murder.

Hanged by Albert Pierrepoint. It was the only time, certainly at an execution in Great Britain and Ireland, that Pierrepoint did not have an assistant with him.

December 2nd: George RUSSELL (45)   Oxford

Mrs Minnie Freeman Lee (89) lived alone in her large 11-bedroom mansion in Maidenhead. On 1 June, the milkman noticed that the previous day's supplies were still on the step and called the police.

Forcing entry, officers noticed a large trunk and inside was the woman's body. She was bound and had head injuries, although cause of death was suffocation through being enclosed in the trunk.

From fingerprints found at the scene, Russell, a small-time housebreaker, habitual criminal and vagrant Irishman, was questioned. Although he admitted calling at the house looking for work he denied the crime. Under cross-examination he said, 'Did I murder a woman for something she was supposed to have, but had not?' Those last three words suggested he had therefore looked for money, and were enough to convict him.

Sentenced to death by Mr Justice Hallett after a four-day trial at Berkshire Assizes on 16 October.

Hanged by Albert Pierrepoint and Steve Wade.

December 9th: Clifford Godfrey WILLS (31)   Cardiff

An electrician from Pontnewydd, South Wales, sentenced to death by Mr Justice Hallett at Monmouth Assizes on 19 November, for the murder of Mrs Sylvina May Parry (32).

Clifford Godfrey Wills

They had been having an affair for some time when, on 8 June, Wills called at her house while her husband was at work. After having sex with her he stabbed her to death. Her husband found the body later that night under a bed in the spare room.

Neighbours told the police the name of a man seen entering the house on the day of the crime and Wills was arrested at home, moments after taking an overdose of pills. He was rushed to hospital for a stomach pump, then charged with the murder. He continually denied the crime but, although no motive was established, he was nevertheless convicted

Hanged by Steve Wade and Henry Critchell. This was the last time Critchell assisted at an execution, as he was listed as having been dismissed on a Government document issued soon after this execution.

December 30th: Arthur George OSBORNE (28)   Leeds

Despite his age, Ernest Hargreaves Westwood (70) still worked full time in a Halifax factory and supplemented his income by working several evenings as a debt collector.

On the morning of 25 September, he was found severely battered at his home in Southowram. He died in hospital later that day. From fingerprints found at the scene, police launched a manhunt for Osborne, originally from Bognor Regis, but missing from his lodgings in Halifax.

Although already married, it was learned that Osborne planned to marry a woman in Chichester. He fled the area by rail after learning that police were looking for him, but was arrested when the train was stopped at Sutton.

He duly confessed to stabbing Westwood with a screwdriver but claimed he had had been provoked after the old man had attacked him. He pleaded guilty to manslaughter at his trial before Mr Justice Slade at Leeds on 1 December. The jury, following the judge's suggestion that provocation was not enough to warrant a manslaughter verdict, returned a verdict of guilty of murder. They made a strong recommendation to mercy.

Osborne was hanged on his 28th birthday by Steve Wade and Harry Allen.

1949

Cases where no executioner is recorded are multiple executions, and readers are asked to refer to the entries before or after for details of the hangman.

January 12th: Margaret ALLEN (43)   **Manchester**

In the early hours of Sunday, 29 August 1948, the body of Mrs Nancy Ellen Chadwick (68) was found lying in the road in Rawtenstall, Lancashire. Initial reports that she had been the victim of a hit and run driver were dismissed when it was found that she had been battered to death with a hammer. Maggie Allen, a neighbour, was routinely interviewed and when detectives noticed bloodstains on her kitchen walls, she readily confessed.

Tried before Mr Justice Sellers at Manchester Assizes on 8 December. The prosecution alleged that she had committed the murder for gain: the victim was reputedly wealthy and often carried large sums of money. The motive being that Allen had been forced to give up work and as she was short of money, she had attacked and robbed her friend.

Margaret Allen

The defence focused on her insanity. Allen dressed in men's clothing and liked to be known as Bill. She had confessed that she had killed Mrs Chadwick because she was in one of her funny moods. There was no appeal against conviction and a petition in her home town, asking for clemency, received only a handful of signatures.

Hanged by Albert Pierrepoint and Harry Kirk, she allegedly kicked her last breakfast over, saying that she did not want it and no-one else was going to enjoy it. Denied her last request of being hanged in men's clothing: she met her fate wearing a prison frock.

January 27th: George SEMINI (26)   Liverpool

Joseph Gibbons (22) and three friends had travelled to Staffordshire in the summer of 1948 to work as labourers at Stafford gas works. On 8 October, having finished their contract, three of the men went out for a drink in Newcastle-under-Lyme where, during a disturbance, Gibbons was stabbed to death.

Before Mr Justice Hallett at Staffordshire Assizes on 29-30 November, it was alleged that Semini, a Maltese miner, had stabbed Gibbons after Gibbons and his friends had made an insulting remark about Semini's girlfriend.

Hanged by Albert Pierrepoint and Harry Allen. Prior to his execution, Semini received a letter from Gibbons's mother saying she had forgiven him and hoped he would be reprieved.

March 22nd: Kenneth STRICKSON (21)   Lincoln

Sentenced to death by Mr Justice Lynskey at Nottinghamshire Assizes on 2 March, for the murder of Mrs Irene May Phillips (56).

On 19 November 1948, Mrs Phillips, a matron at Sherwood Borstal, was found sexually assaulted and severely beaten in the chapel. She died in hospital from horrific head injuries.

Strickson offered a defence of insanity and it was claimed he had carried out the attack during a 'brainstorm'. It was claimed that his father had suffered from insanity and that Strickson had been traumatised when his mother ran off with another man. As a result he had been cared for by his grandparents and later lived in an orphanage.

The prosecution claimed that Strickson had told a fellow inmate that he fancied his chances with the matron and was going to 'try it on' with her. Asked what he would do if she rebuked him, Stickson was alleged to have said he would cosh her. This showed that the crime was premeditated.

Hanged by Albert Pierrepoint and Harry Kirk. He was the last person to be hanged for the murder of a serving prison officer.

March 29th: James FARRELL (19)   Birmingham

On the morning of 20 November, 1948, the body of Joan Mary Marney (14), was found in bushes at Sutton Park, near Birmingham. She had been strangled. Joan had been reported missing on the previous evening after a visit to the cinema with schoolfriends, who told police that Joan had been seated next to a young fair-haired soldier who got chatting with her and offered to walk her home.

A few hours later Farrell walked into a Birmingham police station and said that he was a deserter from his unit and wanted to give himself up. He said that he was from Kingstanding and had absconded from the Royal Army Service Corps. Suspecting Farrell might be involved in the murder, the police detained him for further questioning and eventually he confessed.

At his trial before Mr Justice Lynskey at Warwick Assizes on 10 March, it was claimed that he taken Joan to the park believing that she was 17 years old. He had then become angry when she refused to kiss him and pushed her to the ground. She then said that she would report him to the police because she was under age and he had molested her. Frightened of the consequences, Farrell had then strangled her with his hands. His defence pleaded he was insane.

Hanged by Albert Pierrepoint and Harry Kirk. Syd Dernley and Herbert Allen were present as trainee observers.

April 21st: Harry LEWIS (21)   Pentonville

In the early hours of 26 December 1948, Harry Saul Michaelson (50) was found suffering from severe head wounds in his basement flat at Marylebone, London. Although conscious he could not explain who was responsible for his injuries, and on the following day he died during surgery in hospital. He had fractured ribs and a fractured skull.

Police investigating the mysterious death found a bloodstained fingerprint on a metal chair. The print belonged to Lewis, a well known thief, and on 18 January he was arrested and charged with murder.

Tried before the Lord Chief Justice at the Old Bailey on 7 March; it was claimed that Lewis had broken into the flat after seeing an open window. As the man lay asleep in bed Lewis stole his wallet, but as he was preparing to leave, the man woke up and called out. In a panic Lewis claimed he picked up the chair and hit him twice.

His defence claimed that Michaelson's death was due to the operation and not the attack, and therefore pleaded guilty of manslaughter.

Hanged by Albert Pierrepoint and Harry Allen.

June 2nd: Dennis NEVILLE (22)   Leeds

On the morning of Sunday 20 February, the body of Marian Poskitt (21) was found strangled and battered in a cricket field at Dewsbury.

She had been seen in a local dance-hall with Neville on the previous evening and when questioned he first denied any knowledge of the crime, but later confessed.

At Leeds Assizes before Mr Justice Finnemore on 10 May, it was alleged that he had killed her after she had told him that she was pregnant by another man, but would say that he was the father if he did not marry her. His defence offered a plea of insanity and claimed that Neville had been discharged from the army suffering from anxiety and psycho-neurosis.

Hanged by Steve Wade and Harry Allen.

June 21st: Bernard Alfred Peter COOPER (49)   Pentonville

The body of Mary Elizabeth Cooper (38) was found under a bed at home in Shepherd's Bush on 1 April. She had been strangled with one of her own stockings.

Cooper, her husband, was arrested five days later and confessed that he strangled her during a quarrel over him having sex with their 14-year-old daughter. He had previously admitted doing so and the daughter had, at one time, had an abortion.

Convicted at the Old Bailey, before Mr Justice Hallett on 5 May. It was alleged that Cooper had asked in the past to be castrated, after confessing to having sex with his young daughter. He had claimed to have stopped this relationship; the accusations that he had started it again had caused him to lose his temper and strangle his wife.

Hanged by Albert Pierrepoint and Harry Kirk.

July 28th: Sydney Archibald Frederick CHAMBERLAIN (32)   Winchester

A lorry driver convicted at Exeter Assizes, before Mr Justice Jones on 17 June, of the murder of Doreen Primrose Messenger (15) at Chudleigh.

Chamberlain, a married man, had been having an affair with Doreen, until both their families found out and they were told to stop the relationship. They did so for a short time and then secretly started again.

On 19 February, whilst they were in his car, he strangled her, claiming that she had asked him to kill her and that her death was part of a suicide pact upon which they had agreed because they were upset at having to break off their affair.

The prosecution claimed that Chamberlain, having become tired of Doreen and with the strain of keeping the relationship a secret, had deliberately murdered her. His defence claimed that he was insane and had a mental age of 11. The judge told the jury, in summing up, that having a low mental age is not the same as being insane and he was duly convicted.

Hanged by Albert Pierrepoint and Harry Allen.

August 4th: Rex Harvey JONES (21)   Swansea

A collier of Duffryn Rhondda Colliery, sentenced to death at Swansea Assizes by Mr Justice Croom-Johnson on 12 July, for the murder of his girlfriend Beatrice May 'Peggy' Watts (20), of Abercregan.

Her body was found on a mountainside plantation near Port Talbot on 6 June. Jones had met her at a bus stop, after he had spent the night drinking over seven pints of beer and she had been to a dance. They left the bus and walked down a dark road towards their homes where he strangled her after they had sex. He then confessed to the police and led them to the body.

At his trial the Judge directed the jury that the charge should be murder or nothing. He also told them to ignore his previous good character and to 'steel your hearts against good character and steel your hearts in order to see that justice is done, not merely to the individual, but for the good of all citizens.' Returning a guilty verdict, the jury strongly recommended him to mercy.

August 4th: Robert Thomas MACKINTOSH (21)   Swansea

On the morning of Saturday 4 June, the body of Beryl Beechey (16) was found on a railway embankment at Port Talbot. She had been strangled.

Beryl had called at the home of Mackintosh, a steel-worker from Aberavon, on an errand while his parents were out. Evidence suggested she had been strangled with a cord at the house and later dumped on the embankment.

His trial was held on the same day as **Rex JONES** (above) and it was alleged by his counsel that Mackintosh was of previous good character until 'the devil of lust' had taken possession of him. Defence also claimed that he had been suffering blackouts following his army service in Egypt and Palestine.

Hanged alongside **Rex JONES** in a double execution carried out by Albert Pierrepoint assisted by Harry Kirk and George Dickinson.

August 10th: John George HAIGH (39)   Wandsworth

On 18 February, a wealthy widow, Mrs Olive Henrietta Helen Olivia Robarts Durand Deacon (69), went missing after arranging a business meeting with a fellow guest at a Kensington hotel. When a friend became anxious about her whereabouts, Haigh, the guest whom Mrs Durand Deacon had agreed to accompany to his factory at Crawley, offered to accompany her to the police station, where his glib manner aroused the suspicions of a female officer on duty.

A check found that Haigh had a long criminal record and when detectives visited the factory - in reality a small storeroom - they found evidence to suggest Mrs Durand Deacon had been murdered. Haigh then confessed that he had shot her and dissolved her body in acid. He then admitted to killing eight other people.

The two-day trial of 'The Acid Bath Murderer', as it became known, opened at Lewes Assizes on 18 July before Mr Justice Humphreys. Haigh's defence was insanity and he was made out to be a vampire killer who drank the blood of his victims. The prosecution claimed simply that Haigh had killed all his victims purely for financial reasons and was nothing more than a ruthless killer.

Hanged by Albert Pierrepoint and Harry Kirk. Kirk was not the original choice as assistant but stepped in at short notice when Dickinson tendered his resignation.

John George Haigh

August 16th: William John DAVIES (30)   Wandsworth

An Eastbourne waiter convicted of the murder of waitress Mrs Lucy Watson (37) with whom he had lived for four years.

Mrs Watson died on 23 March, 15 days after Davies had stabbed her at the cafe where they worked following a quarrel in which she accused him of being unfaithful.

Sentenced to death by Mr Justice Humphries at the Old Bailey on 14 July; his appeal was dismissed on 28 July.

Hanged by Albert Pierrepoint and Harry Kirk.

September 28th: William Claude Hodson JONES (31)   Pentonville

In the summer of 1949, Jones was serving a six-year sentence at Dartmoor Gaol after being convicted of housebreaking and other offences.
He made repeated requests to be transferred to a prison in the north of England so he could be near his family and after his last request was rejected, he asked a warder for a pencil and paper and made out a written confession to a murder.

Jones confessed that while stationed at Rotenburg, Germany, on 22 June 1945 he had shot dead a German woman, Waltraut Lehmann (24). Jones said he had met her while on leave and during a conversation they agreed that he would give her some chocolate in exchange for sex. When she later asked him for the chocolate he told he had none and offered her cigarettes instead. She called him a 'filthy English pig' and he told her that if she called him that again he would shoot her. 'Shoot then pig.' she called out and Jones claimed he then shot her in the back and stole her ring, which he traded with another soldier.

Jones was questioned during the murder investigation in Germany but was never under suspicion and the case remained unsolved until his confession. Detectives went back to Germany and found that Jones's confession was genuine. On 5 September, one week after his confession, he stood before Mr Justice Streatfeild at the Old Bailey. The trial lasted three days, and Jones offered a defence of insanity that was rejected.

Three weeks later, the man who preferred death to Dartmoor was hanged by Albert Pierrepoint and Harry Allen.

December 14th: Benjamin ROBERTS (23)   Durham

On Sunday evening, 14 August, Lillian Vickers (21) left home to go the pictures in Darlington with a girl friend. She caught the last bus and was escorted to her home in Chilton Buildings, a prosperous mining village between Ferryhill and Darlington, by a male friend.

Shortly after midnight she was found dead on an allotment 50 yards from her home. Beside her was Roberts, a single man, suffering from self-inflicted wounds from a shotgun lying close by.

Roberts recovered from his injuries and stood trial before Mr Justice Oliver at Durham Assizes on 2 November. It was revealed that Roberts was very fond of Lillian, but his feelings were not reciprocated and she preferred the company of his friend, Alan Neale, the man who had escorted her home on 14 August.

On the night of the tragedy, Lillian and Alan had called at Roberts' house as they walked towards her home. After stopping for a few minutes they continued on. It was alleged that, driven by jealousy, Roberts loaded the gun he used for shooting rabbits, followed the couple and shot Lillian and then himself. The whole of the prosecution's evidence came from a testimony by Alan Neale.

December 14th: John WILSON (26)   Durham

A coal cutter of Murton Colliery who strangled Lily Nightingale (25), a seaman's wife, in a field in Cold Hesledon on the night of 13-14 August.

Wilson had been drinking with the woman and it was alleged that, after leaving a public house together, they had gone to the field where she was found next morning. Lily had been battered, sexually assaulted and strangled with her own scarf. Detectives noted that she seemed to have been attacked by a wild animal.

When arrested Wilson, who had immediately confessed to his father, said he had strangled her after he suggested making love and she asked him for 10 shillings.

Sentenced to death by Mr Justice Oliver on the same day as **Roberts** (above).

Hanged in a double execution alongside **Ben ROBERTS** by Steve Wade, assisted by Harry Kirk with Syd Dernley and Herbert Allen, both participating in their first executions.

December 30th: Ernest Soper COUZINS (43)   Wandsworth

An assistant caretaker at Canterbury Technical College, sentenced to death on 19 November at Kent Assizes by Mr Justice Croom-Johnson, for the murder of Victor Desmond Elias (30), an insurance agent.

On 3 August, the body of Elias was found in the basement of a Canterbury office block by his mother-in-law Mrs Mabel Rose, with whom he and his wife lived. He had been shot in the head and body, stabbed in the chest and his throat had been cut. When the police arrived they found Couzins, who had worked at this office block tending the boiler, lying on a floor in an office. He had deep gashes in his neck and left arm and at first it appeared he was dead.

Couzins, a married man with four children, had been having an affair with Mrs Rose until earlier that year, when there had been some unpleasantness between Couzins, Mrs Rose and Elias, as Couzins was alleged to owe Mrs Rose some money which he was unable to pay back. He was resentful that Elias had taken over from him in working at the office block.

When Couzins, a former Regimental Sergeant Major in the Royal Army Service Corps., appeared in the dock, the self-inflicted neck wound was clearly visible and affected his speech to the extent he was barely able to be heard giving evidence. He collapsed as sentence of death was passed.

Hanged by Albert Pierrepoint and Harry Allen who gave him a drop of 7 feet 8 inches. The resulting drop ripped open Couzins' neck wound and the execution was described as being 'very messy'.

1950

Cases where no executioner is recorded are multiple executions, and readers are asked to refer to the entries before or after for details of the hangman.

January 6th: Daniel RAVEN (23)   **Pentonville**

On the night of 10 October 1949, a Russian Jewish couple, Leopold Goodman (49) and his wife Esther (47) were found dead in their home at Edgware. The heavy aluminium base of a television aerial had been used to batter the couple: Goodman had over 14 wounds to the head, his wife seven. Robbery was discounted as a motive when a large amount of money was found at the house.

Earlier that evening, the couple had been visiting their daughter Marie in hospital after she had recently given birth to their first grandchild. Also present was their son-in-law Raven, a dapper Jewish advertising agent. Police telephoned Raven after the discovery of the bodies and when he arrived he was wearing a clean shirt and tie and a different suit to the one he had on an hour earlier. Police went to Raven's house and in the boiler was the partly burned suit, containing bloodstains of the rare 'AB' type, the same as Leopold Goodman.

Daniel Raven   Timothy John Evans

At his trial before Mr Justice Cassels at the Old Bailey on 22 November, Raven maintained his innocence and his counsel suggested that the killer was a business rival of Goodman's. He also said that the male victim was a police informer and suggested this may have been the motive for the killer.

Under examination Raven admitted that he was at the house later than he had first claimed and stated that he had got blood on his clothing when he tried to revive the couple after finding them dead.

Hanged by Albert Pierrepoint and Harry Kirk. Marie Raven changed her name by deed poll four days before her husband was executed for a murder where no clear motive was ever established.

1950

March 8th: James Frank RIVETT (21)   **Norwich**

Sentenced to death by Mr Justice Stable at Norfolk Assizes on 27 January, for the murder of Christine Ruth Cudden (17).

On the night of 5 November 1949, Rivett, a builder's labourer from Beccles, Suffolk, called on a friend and admitted that he had killed his girlfriend. He was advised to go to the police station where he made the same statement and led police to a bicycle shed where Christine's body was found. She had been strangled.

Beside the body were Rivett's shotgun and cartridges which he said he had brought to shoot himself after killing Christine. He said the motive was that he was distraught that her father wanted the couple to break up and he could not bear the thought of her with someone else. He pleaded insanity at his trial and tried to offer a guilty plea. The judge refused to allow it to be entered.

Hanged by Albert Pierrepoint and Herbert Allen.

March 9th: Timothy John EVANS (25)   **Pentonville**

On the afternoon of 30 November 1949, Evans, an illiterate Welsh-born lorry driver living at 10 Rillington Place, Notting Hill, London, walked into Merthyr Vale police station and confessed that he had disposed of his wife in London. He then made a number of contrary statements about what had happened, saying at various times that he had killed his wife Beryl (20) and their one-year-old baby, Geraldine.

On 3 December their bodies were discovered in a wash house at Rillington Place. They had been strangled. Evans said that Beryl was pregnant and that a tenant at the house, John Christie, had offered to perform an abortion. Christie later told him that Beryl had died during the operation and that if he told the police then Evans would also be blamed for her death. Poorly educated, Evans said he had taken the advice of Christie, a former policeman, and even allowed him to find a home for Geraldine.

Tried just for the murder of his daughter, he appeared before Mr Justice Lewis at the Old Bailey on 11-13 January. Evans stuck to the story that Christie had killed his wife and child. Christie was the chief witness for the prosecution. Faced with the numerous and varied accounts Evans had given, the prosecution showed him to be a liar and on the third day of his trial he was convicted. Christie burst into tears as sentence of death was passed.

Hanged by Albert Pierrepoint and Syd Dernley.

In the light of the Christie case (see **1953, July 15th**), an inquiry was held in 1966 and found that although it was likely that Evans had murdered his wife, he probably did not strangle his daughter. As he had only been charged with the murder of Geraldine, technically there had been a miscarriage of justice and Evans became the first of a number of executed murderers to be formally pardoned.

167

George Kelly

March 28th: George KELLY (27)   **Liverpool**

On 19 March 1949, Leonard Thomas (39) and John Bernard Catterall (25), the manager and assistant manager of the Cameo Cinema at Wavertree, Liverpool, were shot dead during a bungled robbery.

Police investigations drew a blank until a tip-off, over six months later, suggested that the wanted men were two local small-time criminals, George Kelly and Charles Connolly (26).   Kelly was said to be the man who had robbed the cinema and shot the two men, whilst Connolly supposedly kept watch outside.

They were tried together before Mr Justice Oliver at Liverpool Assizes in January.   Kelly was defended by Miss Rose Heilbron, the first time that a woman led for the defence in a murder case. She was able to cast enough doubt on the prosecution's case that the jury failed to reach a verdict and a retrial was ordered.

Mr Justice Cassels presided when Kelly and Connolly were tried separately in February. Although Kelly maintained he did not know the co-accused, this was not believed and when Connolly was persuaded to plead guilty to robbery, the fact that Kelly was deemed in league with him persuaded the jury of his guilt and he was convicted.

Hanged by Albert Pierrepoint and Harry Allen.

In June 2003, the Court of Criminal Appeal overturned the verdict stating that the conviction was unsafe. The court heard evidence that a man had made a confession to the police which was withheld at the original trials.

1950

March 29th: Piotr MAKSIMOWSKI (33)   **Birmingham**

Maksimowski was a Polish refugee who lived on a camp near Beaconsfield, Buckinghamshire. He began courting Dilys Campbell of Slough, who told him she was a widow. Later she confessed that her husband was alive and they still lived together.

On 31 December 1949, Maksimowski called at his local police station. Showing them his wrists were cut and bleeding, he said that he had killed a woman in the woods. Dilys's body was found there, covered in a blanket and with both her wrists cut.

Questioned by detectives Maksimowski said that they had agreed on a suicide pact because she could not face living a lie, and he could not stand knowing she still lived with her husband. He claimed that he had lost his nerve after cutting her wrists and had called the police in the hope that Dilys could get medical attention.

At his trial, before Mr Justice Croom-Johnson at Warwick Assizes on 10 March, he pleaded not guilty on the grounds of insanity. It was shown that Maksimowski's claim to have gone straight for help after cutting Dilys's wrists was false and that she had been dead for at least four hours when a doctor reached the scene.

Once sentence of death had been passed on him, Maksimowski, speaking through an interpreter, asked if he could be shot instead of hanged. The judge told him he had no power to deal with the matter as it had passed out of his hands. There was no appeal but he made a failed attempt to commit suicide by breaking a window in his cell and trying to cut his wrists on the broken glass.

Hanged by Albert Pierrepoint and Syd Dernley.

Walter Sharpe

March 30th: Walter SHARPE (20)   **Leeds**

Along with Gordon Lannen (17), Sharpe entered a Leeds jewellery shop on 16 November 1949. They demanded money and when the owner Abraham Harry Levine (52) refused and put up a fight, he was hit over the head and then shot in the stomach. He later died from his wounds.

The two youths were arrested in Southport two days later and Lannen immediately confessed that he had struck Levine over the head with the butt of his gun during a struggle, but that Sharpe had shot him.

Tried before Mr Justice Streatfeild at Leeds Assizes on 10 March, in his defence Sharpe, who was described as a 'young gangster' influenced by violent movies, claimed that he was unaware the gun had gone off and that Lannen had panicked when Levine put up such a struggle. Lannen, due to his age, was ordered to be detained at His Majesty's Pleasure.

Hanged by Steve Wade and Harry Allen. In 1950 the film The Blue Lamp was produced by Ealing Films. Along with the Cameo Cinema Murder (see **1950, March 28th**) & the Antiques Murder (see **1947, September 19th**), the murder of Abraham Levine had clearly been the inspiration behind the film. Amongst the montage of newspaper clips shown at the start of the film are ones relating to this case.

April 19th: Albert Edward JENKINS (37)   Swansea

Jenkins was a strict, hard working and thrifty man who lived with his wife and family on a tenanted farm at Haverfordwest, Pembrokeshire.

Despite his parsimony, Jenkins was in financial trouble, owing money on both his rent and payments for his tractor. He had asked to buy the farm but the asking price of £1,000 was too much, and so in October 1949, with his financial problems getting more and more pressing, he made a plan to murder his landlord William Henry Llewellyn (52).

Llewellyn lived in nearby Rosemarket, and on 10 October he accepted an invitation to come to the farm to discuss a possible sale. Jenkins had sent his family away, forged the rent book and dug a grave in a clay pit before the landlord arrived. He then battered him to death with a piece of iron, wrapped the body in a tarpaulin and buried it in the pre-dug grave.

The alarm was raised when Llewellyn's wife reported her husband missing. Questioned by police Jenkins admitted that the landlord had called to see him, and that after Jenkins had paid £1,050 for the farm and back rent, he had left. Searching the surrounding area, a sharp-eyed detective noticed that some of the ground had been recently tended. He dug down and found the missing man.

Tried before Mr Justice Byrne at Haverfordwest on 27 February, the evidence against Jenkins was overwhelming and on the third day of the trial he was convicted.

Hanged by Albert Pierrepoint and Harry Kirk.

July 7th: Zbigniew GOWER (23)   Winchester
Roman REDEL (23)

Gower and Redel both arrived in Bristol from their native Poland at the end of the war. On 13 March, being out of work and short of money, they decided to rob a bank. On the night before, to get up courage, they drank so much that on the morning of the planned robbery, they were so drunk that they had to abandon plans to steal a motorcycle and travelled to the bank by bus.

The robbery and subsequent attempted escape were farcical. Gower held the staff at gunpoint whilst his companion vaulted the counter. In a panic Redel snatched just a small amount of cash and a pile of paying-in slips. Fleeing the bank, they boarded a bus, chased by the bank guard who shouted for the driver to stop. They managed to escape from the bus by pointing the gun at anyone who tried to stop them. A chase then ensued during which Redel shot dead Robert Taylor (30) after he had tried to make a citizen's arrest.

Sentenced to death by Mr Justice Oliver on 23 May. Gower, who was some way ahead of Redel during the chase, was given a strong recommendation to mercy.

Hanged by Albert Pierrepoint, assisted by Harry Kirk, Syd Dernley and Herbert Allen.

July 11th: George Finlay BROWN (23)   Durham

A labourer sentenced to death by Mr Justice Morris at Newcastle Assizes on 31 May, for the murder of Mrs Mary Victoria Longhurst (23).

Mrs Longhurst was separated from her husband and lived with her four-year-old child on King Street, North Shields. In the early hours of 11 March she was found strangled at her lodgings. Brown was identified by fellow tenants as being at the house on the night of the murder. He claimed an alibi by saying he was with a prostitute, but efforts to find her failed.

Hanged by Albert Pierrepoint, officiating for the only time at Durham Gaol, and Harry Kirk.

July 13th: Ronald Douglas ATWELL (24)   Bristol

On the evening of 14 April, Atwell, a gas-works labourer, spotted Lily Palmer (26) as she walked along a street in Bridgwater. They had met briefly when he had sat next to her in a local cinema, and after chatting they agreed to go for a drink together. They were seen together by a farmer who recognised Atwell.

The following morning, that same farmer found the body of Lily Palmer in one of his fields. She had been raped and strangled. He told the police the victim had been with Atwell the previous night and when Atwell was questioned he admitted being with Lily, but said that she had left him and walked home with another man.

At his trial before Mr Justice Oliver at Wells Assizes on 30 May, it was revealed that Atwell had later confessed that he had walked home with Lily, who was classed as a mental defective awaiting a bed in a local asylum, and they had began t o kiss in the fields. He stopped short of making love to her after she told him she had recently been with another man. She then began to curse and insult him - causing him to lose his temper. He then strangled and kicked her to death.

Hanged by Albert Pierrepoint and Syd Dernley.

July 13th: John WALKER (48)   Durham

A labourer sentenced to death at York Assizes by Mr Justice Croom-Johnson on 22 June for the murder of Francis Henry Wilson (47) at Brompton, near Northallerton.

John Walker had met Gladys Wilson in 1944. In 1947, following his demob from the army, he moved in with Gladys and her husband Francis as a lodger. Theirs was an unusual relationship, for soon Wilson and Walker swapped roles and Walker began to share a bed with Gladys, with the consent of her husband, who slept in the spare room.

Wilson was violent to his wife, but less so when Walker was around. On 29 April, there was an argument between Wilson and his wife over some money. That evening she went out, leaving the two men alone in the house. Wilson made a remark to the effect that next time he was alone with Gladys he would give her a good hiding. Walker, who was just five foot tall, took an axe from the scullery and struck Wilson six times on the head, killing him instantly. He then hid the body.

The following morning he woke Gladys, confessed what he had done and fled. He was arrested in Bishop Auckland the following day. Wilson had allegedly been having an affair with Walker's wife.

Hanged by Steve Wade and Harry Kirk.

August 16th: Albert PRICE (32)   Wandsworth

A painter and decorator from Bognor, sentenced to death at the Old Bailey on 12 July for the murder of his wife Gladys and their two children.

At the trial, before Mr Justice Parker, he pleaded guilty but insane. It was alleged that Price had suffered a breakdown following years of financial troubles and he 'snapped' after being given notice of eviction from his home. With nowhere to go and no money, he suffocated the children as they slept, before battering his wife with an axe. He claimed he had intended to commit suicide but lacked the courage to go through with it.

The jury, finding him guilty as charged, added a strong recommendation for mercy. His appeal before the Lord Chief Justice, and Justices Byrne and Donovan, was dismissed on 31 July.

Hanged by Albert Pierrepoint and Harry Allen.

1950

October 30th: Paul Christopher HARRIS (28)   Glasgow

On Friday evening, 7 July, Paul Harris was drinking in a Glasgow public house with his brother Claude (30) and two friends. There was a disagreement over a woman and a fracas broke out . The four left the pub and later called at the tenement house in the Tradeston district where a further fight broke out. During the brawl a member of the Harris gang smashed a bottle against a wall and struck the weapon into the face and neck of Martin Dunleavy (37).

His wounds were so serious that a constable was detailed to stay by his bedside and get whatever information the wounded man could relate. 'I know the bastards,' he told the constable, 'but I'm not telling you. I'll get them myself!' He died from massive haemorrhage of his wounds in the early hours of the morning.

Subsequently three men found themselves before Lord Thomson at Glasgow High Court in September. They pleaded self-defence and their four-day trial ended with sentence of death passed upon brothers Paul and Claude Milford Harris. The third accused was found not guilty and discharged.

The brothers were known throughout the Govan district as 'the inseparable Harrises' and were allowed to share the same condemned cell. Their appeal was unsuccessful as was a petition to the Secretary of State for Scotland signed by some 7,000 people.

As execution day neared, lawyers for the brothers were visited by their local MP who intimated that if one or the other were to confess that he had struck the fatal blow, then the other might come under consideration for clemency. With less than 48 hours before the execution was scheduled, Paul spoke to the Governor and confessed that it was his hand that had wielded the broken bottle and that his brother Claude was not directly responsible.

Claude Harris was given a respite of one week while further investigations were made into the death cell confession. At Claude's request he was allowed to remain with his brother until midnight on Sunday 29 October.

Hanged by Albert Pierrepoint and Steve Wade. A week later it was announced that Claude Harris had been granted a reprieve and his sentence commuted to life imprisonment.

November 14th: Patrick George TURNAGE (31)   Durham

On the afternoon of 30 July, the body of Mrs Julia Beesley (78), a prostitute, was found at Billingham Wharf, Teesside. She had been strangled and dumped in bushes close to where the SS Absalon was moored.

Turnage, an African sailor, was recognised by fellow shipmates as having been seen in the company of the old woman heading towards his ship and he was arrested just a few hours before the ship was due to set sail. Questioned by detectives, Turnage admitted that he had killed the woman after she pestered him with sexual suggestions, claiming it was an accident.

173

Evidence from witnesses gave a different account of what had happened and he was duly charged with murder.

Turnage was adamant that he wanted to plead guilty at Durham Assizes, before Mr Justice Hallett on 24 October, even though both counsels agreed that a manslaughter verdict was the the likely outcome. Turnage said he preferred execution to 15 years in gaol.

Hanged by Steve Wade and Syd Dernley.

November 23rd: Norman GOLDTHORPE (40)   Norwich

On 12 August, Emma Elizabeth Howe (66), a prostitute from Yarmouth, was found strangled at her home. A neighbour identified Goldthorpe as the man seen leaving the house in the early hours and he was arrested the following afternoon.

Tried before Mr Justice Hilbery at Norfolk Assizes on 25 October, it was stated that Goldthorpe had gone looking for a prostitute after being jilted by his girlfriend who had gone back to see her husband in Yorkshire. His failed defence was that he was insane.

Hanged by Harry Kirk and Syd Dernley. It was Kirk's first engagement as chief executioner. It was alleged that in his haste to carry out the job, he did not take sufficient care in placing the noose and as a result the white cap got caught up and the noose failed to operate properly. Although Goldthorpe died almost at once the incident was noted and Kirk was never again called to participate at an execution.

November 28th: James Henry CORBITT (37)   Manchester

On Sunday morning, 20 August, the body of Eliza Wood (36) was found strangled in a hotel room at Ashton-under-Lyne. Written on her forehead was the word 'whore'. Her sometime boyfriend, Corbitt, a toolmaker, was soon charged with the murder.

He was tried before Mr Justice Lynskey at Liverpool Assizes on 6 November. He pleaded insanity but the Crown pointed to a diary in which Corbitt had made a number of entries detailing how he had planned at various times to kill Eliza and how fate had intervened on more than one occasion.

His defence also referred to the diary but claimed it supported their view that he was insane.

Hanged by Albert Pierrepoint and Herbert Allen. Corbitt was a regular customer at Pierrepoint's public house and the two were well acquainted, referring to each other as 'Tish and Tosh'.

December 14th: Edward Isaac WOODFIELD (49)　　　　　**Bristol**

A Bristol labourer sentenced to death by Mr Justice Devlin at Bristol Assizes on 23 November, for the murder of Mrs Ethel Melinda Worth (65).

Mrs Worth, a shopkeeper, was found battered with a bottle and strangled in Horfield, Bristol on 20 September. Woodfield's sister lived next door to the shop, which stood in the shadows of Horfield Gaol, and he had been seen in the area at the time of the murder. When questioned about his movements he said he had been at the labour exchange, but when told he had been seen near the shop he broke down and confessed.

The prosecution at the trial admitted they had been unable to find any motive for the attack, whilst the defence was based on insanity. Woodfield was described as being mild-mannered and timid; he had borrowed money from the shopkeeper twice before and it was alleged that he may have killed her after she had refused to lend him money

When asked if he had anything to say before sentence of death was passed he said, 'God knows best, sir.'

Hanged by Albert Pierrepoint and Herbert Allen.

James Ronald Robertson

December 16th: James Ronald ROBERTSON (33)　　　　　**Glasgow**

Shortly after midnight, 29 July, the body of Catherine McCluskey (40), an unmarried mother of two, was found lying in the road in Glasgow. At first glance it appeared that she had been the victim of a hit-and-run, but on closer examination it was found that she had been deliberately run over and that the driver, upon knocking the woman down, had then reversed the car over the victim before speeding off.

Investigations into the background of Miss McCluskey revealed that she had been having an affair with Robertson, a Glasgow policeman, who was married with two young children. Robertson, who was alleged to be the father of her children, was interviewed by CID officers at work, but denied any knowledge of the murder.

At his six-day trial before Lord Keith at Glasgow High Court in November, it was alleged that Robertson had gone absent from duty earlier on the night of the murder, telling a colleague he had a date. He had returned looking dishevelled and claimed the exhaust had fallen off his car. The car he was driving at the time was stolen, as were a number of log books found in his room.

Robertson admitted that he had accidentally knocked Catherine down after she had jumped out of the car following a quarrel. He claimed that as he reversed back up the road to speak to her, she fell under the wheels. Realising his predicament, he had panicked and left the body in the road hoping that it would appear to be an accident.

Hanged by Albert Pierrepoint and Steve Wade.

December 19th: Nicholas Persoulious CROSBY (22)   Manchester

On Sunday morning, 9 July, a caretaker checking on premises at Holbeck, Leeds, found the body of Ruth Massey (19), a seamstress, on spare ground close to the canteen. She was half-naked and her throat had been cut.

Medical investigations indicated that she had had sex, a used condom found nearby suggesting with her consent, before being violently ssaulted and having her throat cut. She died from haemorrhaging of the wound.

Ruth had last been seen in the company of Crosby, a gypsy, by her sister as they left a Leeds public house the previous evening. Crosby was charged with murder on the following day.

He was tried before Mr Justice Finnemore at Leeds Assizes on 27-29 November. He denied the charges and gave varying accounts of what had happened; amongst them that she had gone off with another man after they had parted. He also told one friend that he had walked her home, and another that they had parted and as he walked away he heard a scream.

His defence was based on the fact that Crosby was drunk when he left the pub and had no recollection of events from then on. They also pleaded insanity.

Hanged by Albert Pierrepoint and Syd Dernley. Crosby would normally have been hanged at Leeds, but as the execution suite at Armley Gaol was being modernised, Crosby was the first of three people convicted during this period to be sent over the Pennines for execution. Two trainee observers, Robert Leslie Stewart and Harry Smith, were also in attendance.

1951

Cases where no executioner is recorded are multiple executions, and readers are asked to refer to the entries before or after for details of the hangman.

January 4th: Frank GRIFFIN (40)   **Shrewsbury**

The body of Mrs Jane Edge (74), landlady of a public house at Ketley, Shropshire, was found by her son when he returned home from work on the afternoon of 6 September 1950. She had been battered about the head and the killer had attempted strangulation, although cause of death was heart failure.

During investigations amongst the local workforce, Griffin, a Bolton-born steelworker, was questioned at his lodgings and following statements he made, police kept a watch on his movements. On 10 September, Griffin was again questioned. He was very drunk at the time and after confessing to the murder he collapsed in a drunken stupor.

He pleaded not guilty when he appeared before Mr Justice Cassels at Shropshire Assizes on 19 November. There was strong evidence, notwithstanding the confession, that suggested Griffin was the guilty man. His defence offered a plea of manslaughter due to the accused being too drunk to form the necessary intent. After a three-day trial the jury needed less than one hour to return a guilty verdict.

Hanged by Albert Pierrepoint and Herbert Morris. Morris had re-applied to join the list, although it seems this was the only execution in which he participated during his second spell as a hangman.

January 26th: Nenad KOVASEVIC (29)   **Manchester**

On 9 October 1950, the battered body of a man was found in a track-side hut near Rossendale. He was identified as Radomir Djorovic (26), a Yugoslavian refugee who lived in Blackburn. Police soon learned that Kovasevic, another Yugoslavian refugee, had disappeared from his lodging and he was arrested at Cannock on the following day.

At the trial before Mr Justice Jones at Manchester Assizes on 7 December, it was shown that the two men had quarrelled as they made their way across the moors. As the rain began to fall they took shelter in the hut, where they began to talk about the war. Djorovic teased his friend when he began to cry as he told how his family had been killed by the Germans and, to add further insult, he told Kovasevic that he had sided with the Germans. In a rage, Kovasevic picked up an axe that lay on the floor of the hut and struck his friend over the head.

Any chance the accused may have had of getting the jury to accept a lesser charge, on the grounds of provocation, was lost when it was reported that after killing his fellow countryman he had stolen some personal items which he had then sold.

Hanged by Albert Pierrepoint and Herbert Allen. Last-minute pleas for clemency by the King of Yugoslavia failed to prevent the law taking its course.

April 3rd: William Arthur WATKINS (49)   Birmingham

A Birmingham enameller sentenced to death for the murder of his unnamed baby, who was drowned in a bath.

His defence, at the trial before Mr Justice Finnemore at Birmingham Assizes on 16 March, was that the child's death was an accident and that it had slipped out of his hands into the bath tub.

The prosecution claimed that Watkins and the woman he lived with had not planned for the child, had failed to notify anyone when it died and had killed it to be rid of the unwanted burden of responsibility.

Hanged by Albert Pierrepoint and Harry Allen.

April 25th: Joseph BROWN (30)   Wandsworth
Edward Charles SMITH (30)

On 11 January police at Chertsey, Surrey, received a telephone call from Frederick Gosling (71), a shopkeeper, who told them that two men had made an attempt to steal from his shop. After checking that all was now well, the constable left. The next morning 'Old Gossy', as the old man was known locally, was found dead inside the shop. He had been tied to the bed and beaten and had died from suffocation caused by an old duster being forced into his mouth.

Following a tip off police arrested Frederick Brown (27), a labourer and petty thief who told detectives that it was not him who had committed the murder, but his brother Joe. Both Fred and Joe Brown were arrested for the murder but Fred, determined to clear himself of any charges, passed the blame onto Smith, a lorry-driver who had been persuaded by Joe Brown to carry out the robbery.

At the trial before Mr Justice Parker, at Surrey Assizes on 5 March, it was a straightforward battle between Fred Brown, who admitted making the aborted first robbery at the shop in the afternoon, but strenuously denied any part in the latter and fatal robbery, and the two accused, who tried to pass the blame and claim that it was Fred Brown and not they who should be in the dock.

Hanged by Albert Pierrepoint, assisted by Harry Allen, Syd Dernley and Herbert Allen.

April 26th: James VIRRELS (55)   Wandsworth

A labourer of Worthing, Virrels was having a relationship with his widowed landlady, Mrs Alice Kate Roberts (40). On 29 January, her son came home from work and found Mrs Roberts lying in the scullery. She had been stabbed and battered with an axe.

Tried before Mr Justice Parker at Sussex Assizes on 12 March, it was alleged that they had quarrelled because she repeatedly made jam sandwiches for him to take for lunch at work. During the quarrel, Virrels said that she had picked up a dagger and tried to stab him. He managed to wrestle the weapon from her and used it to stab her. He then picked up an axe and inflicted wounds that proved fatal. Virrels immediately went to his brother's house where he confessed to the crime.

Hanged by Albert Pierrepoint and Syd Dernley.

May 8th: James INGLIS (30)   Manchester

Alice Morgan (50) was a prostitute who worked in the area around the docks at Hull. On 1 February, she was battered and strangled in her home. Her body was discovered two days later and police suspected that the killer was Inglis, a Scotsman, who they wished to interview for a similarly brutal - but not fatal - attack on his landlady on the previous day.

Inglis was arrested after a massive manhunt and admitted that he had killed Alice Morgan. He said after he had spent the day drinking with her, and spending money on her, he asked her for sex and she named a price. . Angry, as he had by then spent all his money and she refused to have sex without payment, he attacked her in a drunken rage.

He was sentenced to death by Mr Justice Gorman at Yorkshire Assizes on 17 April.

Hanged by Albert Pierrepoint and Syd Dernley.

May 9th: William Edward SHAUGHNESSY (48)   Winchester

Sentenced to death on 13 March, by Mr Justice Byrne at Hampshire Assizes, for the seemingly motiveless murder of his wife Marie Alexine (46). He was also suspected of murdering his daughter Joyce (20), but only one count was brought to trial.

On 19 December 1950, he strangled his wife with a stocking and hid her body beneath the stairs at their home in Portsmouth. The following day he strangled his daughter before taking the rest of his children to London. On 21 December his 16-year-old son returned to the house alone and discovered the bodies.

Shaughnessy, who was arrested two days later, denied the killings.

Hanged by Albert Pierrepoint and Harry Allen.

June 12th: John DAND (32)   Manchester

A former soldier, Dand had left his native Scotland and lived in York with his wife. He had become friendly with a neighbour, Walter Wyld, (72), a former Rugby league footballer who also ran a very small-time loan business.

On 27 January, Wyld was stabbed to death at his home and from letters found at the house, Dand was questioned about the murder. He denied any knowledge of it and offered an alibi which was found to be unsubstantiable.

While interviewed at York police station, he allegedly made a full confession to Scotland Yard detectives and he was charged with the murder. When he appeared before Mr Justice Gorman at Leeds Assizes in April, Dand's counsel denied that the accused had confessed and claimed the police had framed him. Police evidence linking him to the murder, however, was strong, and he was convicted.

Hanged by Albert Pierrepoint and Harry Allen.

John Dand

July 3rd: Jack WRIGHT (30)   **Manchester**

Wright, a miner from Tyldesley, near Manchester, had been courting Mona Mather (28) during the summer of 1950, but they had drifted apart following a minor quarrel.

On 7 April, they met by chance in a public house. They spent the rest of the evening at a fairground. The next morning, Mona was found dead on wasteland near a colliery at Little Hulton, Bolton. She had been sexually assaulted and strangled. Wright was identified as the man seen walking her home and he was picked up at a Manchester railway station.

He was tried before Mr Justice Oliver at Liverpool Assizes on 12 June, where a defence of insanity was put forward. It was alleged that Wright had made a number of assaults on females, but in each case the victim had refused to come forward.

Hanged by Albert Pierrepoint and Harry Smith, participating at his first execution.

July 19th: Dennis Albert MOORE (23)   Norwich

On 4 February, the body of Eileen Cullen (21) was found in a cow shed at Catton, Norwich, two weeks before she was due to be married. She had been strangled.

Moore, her fiancé, who led police to the body, told them that they had been shopping for her wedding dress after a visit to a doctor to check that Eileen's pregnancy was progressing well. After returning home from shopping they went for a walk, during which she refused to have sex with him until after the baby was born and they quarrelled. In a rage, he attacked her.

Moore was sentenced to death by Mr Justice Parker at Norfolk Assizes on 2 June.

July 19th: Alfred George REYNOLDS (24)   Norwich

Sentenced to death by Mr Justice Parker at Norfolk Assizes on 4 June, for the murder of his fiancée.

Reynolds, a labourer from Dereham, had been courting Ellen Ludkin (19) and when she fell pregnant he proposed marriage. Her father, however, was adamant that there would be no wedding.

Reynolds said that, frustrated at being unable to wed, they had made a suicide pact and had gone to a cycle shed. He was about to shoot himself when she begged him to shoot her first. Having done that he then failed to carry out his side of the agreement, telling police that she had begged him to help her commit suicide and when he refused she had turned the gun on herself.

At the trial it was proven that from the distance the gun was fired there was no way Ellen could have shot herself.

Hanged alongside **MOORE** (above) by Albert Pierrepoint, assisted by Harry Allen, Syd Dernley and Robert Stewart.

September 15th: Robert Dobie SMITH (30)   Edinburgh

On 22 May, police at Dumfries were alerted that a gunman was prowling the city threatening to shoot the first policeman he saw. Three officers went out in a patrol car to find the man and when they did so they were shot at; two were injured, but Sergeant William Gibson (44), was fatally wounded. Smith, a Dumfries electrician and former sailor, was arrested at the scene.

Tried before Lord Mackay in July, the defence offered a plea of insanity and pointed to two recent key events that had triggered the insanity. The first being a quarrel Smith had had with a girlfriend following a trip into Glasgow where she purchased a book on crime to which he objected. They parted after the quarrel. Soon after, Smith was distraught to hear that a young lad who lived close by him had died in a tragic accident. On the following day he forced his brother to write a note in which he boasted that he would kill a policeman.

Hanged by Albert Pierrepoint and Steve Wade.

October 24th: John O'CONNER (29)　　　　　　**Pentonville**

The body of Mrs Eugenie Le Maire (84) was found stabbed and partially strangled at her home in Kensington on 11 August. A recluse, the old woman had not left the house in 20 years. Her lodger, O'Conner, a labourer, who gave himself up to the police.

At his Old Bailey trial before Mr Justice Barry on 2 October, he said that he had felt an urge to destroy his victim, who often used to invite him into her room for drinks. During one of these friendly chats, O'Conner had suddenly attacked his landlady, ripped at her clothes and attempted to strangle her, before picking up a knife and stabbing her in the chest.

He had then stolen some jewellery and fled, staying with a friend across town for one night before confessing to his crime.

Hanged by Albert Pierrepoint and Herbert Allen.

December 11th: Herbert Leonard MILLS (19)　　　　　　**Lincoln**

On 9 August, Mills telephoned the News of the World newspaper in London, claiming that he had discovered the body of a woman in Nottingham who had been strangled. He said that he had yet to inform the police and offered them an exclusive story if they paid him £250.

Mills, an unemployed clerk, was calling from a call-box and while a reporter kept him talking, another called the police who hurried to the scene and questioned Mills.

He led them to an orchard at Sherwood Vale where they found the body of Mrs Mabel Tattershaw (48) who had disappeared from her home six days earlier. From her injuries it appeared that she had been battered to death. Mills was treated as a witness and because police could establish no link between him and the victim he was allowed to leave custody after being questioned.

A few days later his account of the discovery was published in the newspaper along with his photograph. When police re-read through his account they picked up on the fact that Mills had mentioned strangulation, although this only came to light at the inquest and was impossible to tell from the state of the body when discovered. Also he claimed that the victim's face was white when he found her when, after six days of decomposition, this was not the case.

Re-questioned by newspaper reporters, Mills admitted that he had in fact found the body a few days before when the face had been white. Convinced that Mills was the real killer, the police invited him to make further statements until he caught himself out and on 24 August, he confessed to the murder.

Described at his trial before Mr Justice Byrne, at Nottingham Assizes on 21-22 November, as a desperately lonely boy, cruel, boastful and vain, who wrote bad poetry, Mills was alleged to have met his victim when she sat next to him in a cinema.

At this point he was obsessed with committing the perfect murder and after luring her to the orchard he had killed her. He then became frustrated that his crime had not been discovered, wishing to gloat over the police's failure to solve it. The prosecution alleged that the main reason for the murder was exhibitionism.

Hanged by Albert Pierrepoint and Herbert Allen. It was alleged that Pierrepoint may have made a rare blunder at this execution, for it took over 20 minutes for Mills's heart to stop beating after his hanging. It was also the last time Herbert Allen assisted at an execution.

Herbert Leonard Mills

1952

Cases where no executioner is recorded are multiple executions, and readers are asked to refer to the entries before or after for details of the hangman.

January 1st: Horace CARTER (30)   **Birmingham**

On 1 August 1951, Carter, a labourer, lured Sheila Attwood (11), who lived on the same street in Kingstanding, Birmingham, into his house after promising her some sweets. He then took her upstairs and raped her. Frightened that she would report him to the police, Carter strangled her and when darkness fell, he carried her body outside and dumped it in the corporation yard behind his own back garden.

A neighbour discovered the body the next day and Carter was arrested when he confessed during a routine interview. He told police: 'I knelt on her arms and smothered her with a pillow.'

Sentenced to death on 12 December, 1951, at Birmingham Assizes by Mr Justice Cassels, his defence of insanity was rejected.

Hanged by Albert Pierrepoint and Syd Dernley.

January 15th: Alfred BRADLEY (24)   **Manchester**

A Macclesfield labourer convicted at Manchester Assizes of the murder of George Camp (58), a nightwatchman from Wythenshawe, Manchester.

It was alleged that on 12 August 1951, Bradley beat the older man to death with a plank in his hut after Camp told him he was going to tell Bradley's parents about their homosexual relationship. Bradley was charged with the crime whilst on remand in Strangeways Gaol on a lesser charge, when he asked to see the Governor saying he wished to confess to a murder.

At his first trial, before Mr Justice Lynskey on 24 November 1951, he hurled the Bible at the Judge whilst taking the oath and as a result the trial was postponed to allow Bradley to be examined by doctors. A week later, before a new judge, Mr Justice Stable, he was sentenced to death.

Hanged by Albert Pierrepoint and Robert Stewart. The Prison Governor later recalled that Bradley was so calm on the morning of the execution that: 'Anyone would think he was going to the pictures instead of the scaffold.'

February 6th: Alfred MOORE (36)   **Leeds**

A poultry farmer of Kirkheaton, Huddersfield, who, on the night of 15 July 1951, was alleged to have shot dead Detective Inspector Duncan Fraser (46) and Constable Arthur Jagger (44) as they were organising a police cordon around his farm.

Moore was suspected of carrying out a series of burglaries in the area and the police were attempting to catch him as he returned home with some stolen property. He was arrested inside his farmhouse in the early hours when police saw smoke coming from his chimney.

Alfred Moore

His alibi that he was in the house throughout the night was not believed and he was charged with the murder of Inspector Fraser after PC Jagger, on his deathbed in a local hospital, identified him as the gunman.

At his trial before Mr Justice Pearson at Leeds Assizes on 13 December 1951, Moore protested his innocence and claimed the police had arrested the wrong man.

Hanged by Steve Wade and Harry Allen.

February 26th: Herbert Roy HARRIS (24)   **Manchester**

A silk worker of Flint, North Wales, convicted of the murder of his wife Eileen (22) who was found battered about the head on a railway bridge in Flint on 8 December 1951. Harris was arrested in London where he had fled after the murder.

Herbert Roy Harris and Eileen Harris.

At his trial before Mr Justice Oliver at Flint Assizes, Harris claimed he was very much in love with his wife and that despite frequent quarrels they always made up later. At the time of the murder they were living apart but planning to move in together when they could get a council house.

On the night of the murder they had argued after Eileen went to the cinema without him. They met up later and whilst walking in a quiet road he picked up a large stone and threw it at her. The pathologist who examined the body said that her skull was fractured in 10 places and the wounds seemed to have been made by a man in a frenzy. Sentenced to death on 5 February; the jury added a strong recommendation for mercy.

Hanged by Albert Pierrepoint and Robert Stewart.

March 21st: Takir ALI (39)   **Durham**

Evelyn McDonald (25) was living with a Bengali sailor named Ullah at South Shields, but when he went back to sea she began seeing Ali, a cousin of the absent sailor. Ali lavished gifts and money on her and when he in turn went off to sea, he fully expected Evelyn to be waiting for him when he returned. In November 1951, when Ali returned to the north east, he found that she had moved back in with Ullah.

On 20 November Ali met up with Evelyn and her friends in a public house and during a quarrel he pulled out his flick knife and stabbed her three times. He then walked to the police station and surrendered.

At his trial before Mr Justice Hallett at Durham Assizes on 1 February, it was suggested that she had used Ali whilst her boyfriend was at sea and allowed him to spend all his money on her. The judge stated, 'The position could be described as one in which the woman had got his money and fooled him.'

Hanged by Steve Wade and Harry Smith.

James Smith

April 12th: James SMITH (21)   **Glasgow**

A labourer, known to his friends as Spider, convicted at Glasgow on 27 February, after a two-day trial, of the murder of Martin Joseph Malone (35) who he stabbed to death at the Ancient Order of Hibernians' Dance Hall, Glasgow.

Malone had gone to assist a friend who was being attacked by Smith. As Malone lay bleeding to death on the dance floor many of the 200-strong crowd carried on dancing around the body. Police had to stop the band playing so that assistance could be given.

Smith claimed at his trial he had acted in self-defence, but was found guilty. He lodged an appeal on the grounds that the prosecution had failed to reveal at the trial that, during a search made of the dance hall for the murder weapon, the police had discovered more than one knife.

Hanged by Albert Pierrepoint and Steve Wade. Smith celebrated his 21st birthday in the death cell

Alfred Burns   Edward Francis Devlin

April 25th: Alfred BURNS (21)   **Liverpool**
Edward Francis DEVLIN (22)

Mrs Beatrice Rimmer of Cranborne Road, Liverpool, had been a recluse for a number of years, since the death of her husband. This had led to local rumours of her having large amounts of money and her property being broken into a number of times.

She was last seen alive on the night of Sunday 19 August 1951, by one of her neighbours, as she returned from her son's house. On the following evening her son called and found her lying in a pool of blood on the hall floor. She had been attacked by two different weapons, suggesting two killers. In October, Burns and Devlin, two petty criminals, were arrested in Manchester, following the testimony of a soldier held in Walton Prison, Liverpool, on a charge of desertion.

On 19 February, before Mr Justice Finnemore at Liverpool Assizes, the 10-day trial began. Their defence was that they could not have been in Liverpool on the night of the murder as they were in Manchester with a third person, carrying out a robbery in a factory. This was destroyed in court when the other man who had been arrested for this offence admitted that the robbery was on 18 August.

Hanged by Albert Pierrepoint, assisted by Syd Dernley, Robert Stewart and Harry Smith.

May 7th: Ajit SINGH (27)   **Cardiff**

In March 1951 Singh, a Pakistani-born painter, met Joan Marion Thomas (27), a widow of two years, at Maesteg market, Bridgend. They began seeing each other on a regular basis, with Joan even taking him home to meet her parents. When they began to talk of marriage her parents became alarmed and begged her to stop seeing him.

Fascinated by his tales of India, Joan began to meet Singh in secret for a while until November when, tired with the relationship, she ended it. Singh was distraught, stating that if he could not have her then no one else would. He began to pester her continually, resulting in police warning him to leave her alone. On 30 December, whilst she was on her way with a friend to visit her sister in hospital, Singh shot and killed Joan.

His defence of insanity failed and on 20 March he was sentenced to death at Cardiff Assize Court before Mr Justice Byrne after a two-day trial.

Hanged by Albert Pierrepoint and Harry Allen. It is Sikh custom for a body to be cremated after death, and when it was announced that Singh would be buried in the confines of the prison in line with tradition, representatives from the Indian High Commission in London appealed to the Home Office for special dispensation.

The appeal was accepted and after the inquest Singh's body was removed to a local crematorium for cremation. The Home Office would not, however, allow the ashes to be handed back to relatives, and later that day they were buried within the precincts of Cardiff prison.

May 27th: Backary MAUNEH (25)   **Pentonville**

Besides working for British Rail at Euston Station, Gambian Joseph Aaku (28) was also a drug dealer living in lodgings at Camden Town, London. On 4 January he was found stabbed to death in his room, moments after neighbours had heard a scream and seen a black man flee the scene.

Aaku had been punched in the face so hard that his teeth were loosened but death had been caused by a stab wound to the neck, which had been struck with such force that it had severed the spinal column. Bloodstains found at the scene included both group 'A' and group 'O'. Aaku had group 'A', which suggested the killer may also have received cuts during the attack.

Mauneh, who also worked at Euston Station, was questioned four days later and it was noticed that his hand was bruised and cut. He told police he had been mugged and his story was accepted until a witness came forward who had purchased a watch from Mauneh shortly after the murder. The watch had belonged to Aaku and ten days after the murder, Mauneh was questioned again and charged with murder.

At his Old Bailey trial before Mr Justice Gorman on 25-27 March, Mauneh swore that all of the prosecution's 40 witnesses were lying. When the black cap was placed upon the head of Mr Justice Gorman prior to passing the death sentence, Mauneh shouted out, 'In the name of God, take that black cap off and abide by the word of God: Thou shalt not kill.'

Hanged by Albert Pierrepoint and Harry Smith. Aaku's diary, recovered from his flat following his murder, listed numerous drug suppliers and pushers, enabling detectives to make scores of arrests.

May 29th: Peter Gallagher DEVENEY (42)   Glasgow

An unemployed Glasgow labourer convicted of the murder of his wife, Jeannie (37), the mother of his five children. Following a quarrel she had been strangled with a tie and then beaten about the head with a hammer.

He pleaded insanity at his three-day trial on 8 May. The defence called a doctor who had treated him while he was in the army to testify that in 1942 Deveney had been diagnosed as a psychopath and discharged.

Hanged by Albert Pierrepoint and Steve Wade.

July 8th: Harry HUXLEY (42)   Shrewsbury

Huxley worked as a labourer on an industrial estate at Farndon, on the Welsh border near Wrexham. Also working there was Charles 'Harry' Royce, with whose wife Ada (32) Huxley was very friendly. Suspecting they were having an affair, Royce confronted Huxley, warning him not to call on his wife while she was alone.

By the winter of 1951, Ada Royce had grown tired of Huxley's attentions, even though he was allegedly the father of her youngest child. On Christmas Day, they met by chance in a public house in nearby Holt, and later that evening Ada and a friend refused to join Huxley in a drink. That same afternoon Huxley had asked a farmer friend to lend him a gun to shoot pheasant. Lending the gun, the farmer warned that the right hammer was faulty and the slightest touch could set it off.

On 29 December, they met in again in Holt where they argued over her refusal to drink with him on Christmas Day. He then followed Ada and her friend outside and during a quarrel shot her in the chest, killing her instantly. He then turned the gun on himself.

His defence before Mr Justice Croom-Johnson, on 29 May at Ruthin Assizes, was that the gun went off accidentally due to it being faulty

Hanged by Albert Pierrepoint and Harry Allen.

July 15th: Thomas EAMES (31)   Bristol

A labourer from West Hoe, Plymouth, sentenced to death by Mr Justice Lynskey at Devon Assizes on 23 June for the murder of Muriel Bent (26).

Eames had married his first wife before the war and although they split up in 1940, they remained legally wed. In 1947 he was charged with bigamously marrying Muriel Bent and served a short prison sentence. They reunited on his release and had a child.

In early 1952 Muriel had left Eames and taken up with a new lover. Eames saw them together on 26 February and asked her if she would call at the house to collect her mail. On the following morning he took a knife to work and sharpened it with a file. When Muriel called at the house that night she told Eames she planned to marry her new boyfriend and as she went to kiss him goodbye he stabbed her twice in the back.

Hanged by Albert Pierrepoint and Robert Stewart; Eames did not go quietly to the gallows, having to be dragged fighting and kicking as he struggled all the way to the drop.

July 22nd: Frank BURGESS (21)   Wandsworth

Johanna 'Joan' Hallahan (23) was a stunningly attractive woman who had only been employed at the Elgin Court Hotel, Croydon, for a matter of weeks. On 21 April, she failed to report for duty. As she was living at the hotel, the manager let himself into her room with a pass key and found her strangled. The gas meter had been forced open and money stolen.

Another employee had also failed to report for duty. When the manager entered the room of Burgess, a hotel porter, there was no sign of him, just an empty forced gas meter and a letter to his probation officer confessing to the murder.

Following his arrest he made a statement to police, 'I asked Joan if I could borrow some money, she seemed angry with me for asking, but she owed it to me. I do not know what happened, but the next thing she was dead.'

His defence before Mr Justice Streatfeild, at Surrey Assizes on 30 June, was insanity, his counsel stating Burgess had been born in a mental hospital and until recently he had regularly been in a mental hospital.

Hanged by Albert Pierrepoint and Syd Dernley.

August 12th: Oliver George BUTLER (24)   Oxford

Although married, Butler had a girlfriend, Rose Margaret Meadows (23) whom he told he planned to marry when he was divorced. Butler's wife had heard about the relationship and told her husband that she would not give him a divorce. When Rose heard this she told Butler she wanted to end the relationship. On 19 May while walking through the woods near Hanwell, Oxon, Butler strangled her and then alerted a railway signalman who called the police.

At Stafford Assizes before Mr Justice Hallett on 4 July it was alleged that Rose had dared him to put his hands round her throat and when she laughed at his attempt he applied more pressure till she went limp in his arms. Realising he had killed her he immediately tried to contact the police.

Hanged by Albert Pierrepoint and Harry Smith. Shortly before her death Rose Meadows had visited a fortune teller who seemingly had told her she would be murdered in the not too distant future!

September 3rd: Mahmood Hussain MATTAN (29)   Cardiff

A Somali sailor sentenced to death by Mr Justice Ormerod on 24 July at Glamorgan Assizes for the murder of Mrs Lily Volpert (41), a Jewish shopkeeper in the docklands area of Cardiff.

On 6 March, Mrs Volpert had been working in her outfitters' shop when a man entered. During a struggle her throat was cut and over £100 was stolen from the till.

Her family put up a large reward for information and shortly after a witness claimed to have seen a man matching Mattan's description outside the shop prior to the murder. He was arrested and traces of blood matching the murdered woman were found on his shoes. Described by his own counsel as a semi-civilised savage, Mattan was convicted on circumstantial evidence and mainly on the testimony of a fellow Somalian.

Hanged by Albert Pierrepoint and Robert Stewart.

Mahmood Hussain Mattan was granted a posthumous pardon in February 1998. The witness who had identified Mattan at the scene of the crime had also identified another Somalian, Tehar Gass, as being at the shop near the time of the murder. When interviewed by detectives Gass admitted this, but this evidence was withheld from the defence counsel.

September 5th: John Howard GODAR (31)   Pentonville

Maureen Jones Cox (20) had been engaged to Godar, a film cameraman, for almost a year before she discovered he had an ex-wife and a young child. This news caused her to cool the relationship and she began to date another man.

On 6 June, she was travelling in a taxi with Godar at Uxbridge; she told him she had arranged to meet her new boyfriend that evening and in a rage he stabbed her almost 50 times with a stiletto.

At his two-day trial before Mr Justice Barry at the Old Bailey on 7-8 July his defence was insanity. It was also shown that in 1944 he had been court martialled for cowardice, and from this time had also suffered a disease of the mind.

Hanged by Albert Pierrepoint and Robert Stewart.

September 30th: Raymond Jack CULL (25)   Pentonville

Cull, a Middlesex labourer, had been married to his wife Jean Frances (19) for less than three months when she left because of frequent rows and went back to live with her father and younger sister at Northolt. As she left the house Cull threatened to kill her if she did not return. He wrote begging her to return and said he could not live without her. She replied by saying she did not wish to return as she no longer loved him.

On 29 June, Cull went to her father's house armed with a bayonet. As he entered through the bedroom window Jean began to scream. Hearing his daughter scream, her father ran to her room and found her lying on the floor dead from stab wounds. Cull fled the scene but was soon arrested.

At his Old Bailey trial on 11-12 September, before Mr Justice Donovan, he claimed it was an accident and Jean had fallen on the bayonet.

September 30th: Dennis George MULDOWNEY (41)   Pentonville

Mrs Christine Glanville OBE, (37) also known as Krystyna Skarbek, was a Polish countess and former secret agent, who held the George

Medal and Croix de Guerre for heroism during the war. On 15 June she was stabbed to death by Muldowney in the foyer of a Kensington hotel.

Muldowney, a porter at the Reform Club, Pall Mall, was immediately detained and claimed that he had killed her out of jealousy after she had ended their relationship. He told the police that he was going to poison himself and that he wanted to hang.

Tried at the Old Bailey before Mr Justice Donovan on 11 September, he insisted on pleading guilty. Evidence was heard from friends of the victim who claimed there was no proof that they had even been acquaintances, least of all lovers.

Hanged alongside **CULL** (see above) by Albert Pierrepoint assisted by Robert Stewart and Harry Smith.

October 9th: Peter Cyril JOHNSON (24)   Pentonville

On 28 June, Johnson, a Brixton-based Caribbean market trader, got into a quarrel with his close friend and fellow trader Charles Mead (24) of Bethnal Green. The quarrel ended when Johnson picked up a heavy jagged piece of concrete and battered Mead about the head with it, killing him instantly.

Tried before Mr Justice Donovan at the Old Bailey on 17-18 September; his counsel pleaded manslaughter as he was acting in self-defence. Attempting to demonstrate how he had carried out the attack as he described in court, Johnson was unable to show he had acted as he claimed. It was alleged that the two men had been having a homosexual relationship, and that Johnson was jealous of Mead's wife.

Hanged by Albert Pierrepoint and Harry Allen.

October 23rd: Donald Neil SIMON (32)   Shrewsbury

Simon was a former Canadian soldier working as a machinist and living in Slough. He met his wife Eunice while stationed in England and when he was posted back home she accompanied her husband. She soon became homesick and they returned to live in Slough where he found work as a machinist.

Eunice Simon was now aged 27 and in the nine years since her marriage she had grown tired of Simon's drinking to the extent that she had left home and gone to live with her mother. She had also been enjoying the company of Victor Brades (27), her partner at a local dance club before her domestic upheaval, who now became a close friend.

On 21 June, as Brades walked Eunice home following a night in a local pub, they were attacked by Simon who shot them both. Brades was hit four times and died at once, Eunice was struck twice and died on the following day from her wounds.

Sentenced to death by Mr Justice Jones at Birmingham Assizes on 31 July, Simon's plea of insanity was based on the fact he was a heavy drinker who had recently suffered a nervous breakdown, which resulted in him spending two months in a mental hospital.

Hanged by Albert Pierrepoint and Syd Dernley.

December 12th: Eric NORTHCLIFFE (30)   Lincoln

An ex-RAF sergeant of Warsop, convicted before Mr Justice Hallett at Nottingham Assizes on 20 November, of the murder of his wife Kathleen (23).

On 25 June, following a domestic quarrel, he stabbed her 12 times with a sheath knife before making a weak attempt to cut his wrists. Both were taken to hospital where she died.

A psychiatrist called by the defence claimed that he suffered from amnesia and melancholia and was probably unaware of committing any crime.

Hanged by Albert Pierrepoint and Robert Stewart.

December 17th: John Kenneth LIVESEY (23)   Wandsworth

A miller of Blackheath Hill, South East London, convicted of the murder of his mother-in-law, Stephanie Marie Small (49).

Livesey and his wife shared a house with her parents but relations were strained and on several occasions Livesey and his wife were asked to move out and find their own home.

On 26 July as Livesey and Stephanie were alone in the house together they began to quarrel. It ended with her being found dead in a pool of blood. She had been stabbed 24 times. Livesey was soon arrested and denied the killing.

He maintained his innocence throughout the Old Bailey trial before Mr Justice Hilbery on 24 October.

Hanged by Albert Pierrepoint and Syd Dernley.

December 23rd: Leslie Terrence GREEN (29)   Birmingham

On 16 July, the body of Mrs Alice Wiltshaw (62), was discovered by her husband at their mansion at Barlaston, Staffordshire. She had been battered to death and beside the body were the remains of a broken vase and a heavy metal poker. Jewellery, including rings and a brooch, along with a wallet and a purse had been stolen.

A check on past employees at the house was able to eliminate them all from the enquiries except for Green, a former chauffeur who had been dismissed in May. Green had a string of previous convictions for theft and had disappeared, finally surrendering to police after wanted notices

Leslie Terrence Green

appeared in the press. His alibi for the day of the murder did not stand up and items of stolen jewellery were recovered from a house in Leeds which he had visited after the murder.

Tried before Mr Justice Stable at Staffordshire Assizes on 3-5 December, the jury took just 28 minutes to find Green guilty. He made no appeal.

Hanged by Albert Pierrepoint and Syd Dernley. It was Dernley's last job as an assistant.

December 24th: Herbert APPLEBY (20)   **Durham**

In the early hours of Sunday 21 September, a taxi driver called at a police station near Middlesbrough and told the sergeant he had a young man in his taxi, claiming to have stabbed a man. The passenger gave his name as Appleby and admitted stabbing John David Thomas (29) whom he accused of stealing his girl.

Appleby, a sling loader at the local docks, had been attending a wedding with his girlfriend Dolly and, following the departure of the bride and groom, the party continued in a guest's house. Appleby had been drinking all day and was very drunk. While he was in the kitchen, Thomas, the bridegroom's step-brother, sat beside Dolly on the sofa and put his arm round her waist.

Appleby saw this as he entered the room and left for home, returning soon after holding a carving knife. The couple were still on the sofa when he returned. He approached Thomas and stabbed him in the chest. He fled the house and got a friend to call a taxi to take him to the police.

Tried before Mr Justice Cassels at Leeds Assizes on 4-5 December, his defence of insanity was rejected.

Hanged by Steve Wade and Harry Allen.

1953

Cases where no executioner is recorded are multiple executions, and readers are asked to refer to the entries before or after for details of the hangman.

January 2nd: James John ALCOTT (29)   Wandsworth

On the evening of 22 August 1952, a porter at Ash Vale Railway Station near Aldershot became concerned that something was amiss. Forcing entry into the booking office, he found the body of clerk George Charles Dean (27). He had been stabbed 20 times with a sheath knife. Missing from the office were cash and bonds worth over £160. Alcott, a railway fireman from Eltham, London, was traced to an Aldershot boarding house where following arrest he made a full confession.

He was tried at Surrey Assizes on 19 November. A defence of insanity was rejected and after Mr Justice Finnemore had passed sentence of death it was revealed that he had been convicted of the murder of a German nightwatchman in 1949 whilst serving in the army. He had been sentenced to death after a court martial, but the conviction was later quashed on a technicality and he was released.

Hanged by Albert Pierrepoint and Harry Smith.

January 26th: George Francis SHAW (25)   Glasgow

Shaw, an Irishman, and accomplice George Dunn (22) were convicted of the murder and robbery of an old recluse, Michael Connelly (78) at a derelict farm building in Lanark on 17 August 1952. Mr Connelly had been beaten, kicked, and struck all over his body and head with an iron bar. Both men had been seen in the area, working casually as labourers and sleeping rough.

Tried before Lord Justice Carmont at Glasgow High Court, Shaw protested his innocence, whilst Dunn, who had a mental age of eight, pleaded insanity. The seven-day trial ended on 9 December. Shaw was found guilty of murder and sentenced to death, whilst Dunn was ordered to be detained as a mental defective in Carstairs, the Scottish equivalent of Broadmoor.

Hanged by Albert Pierrepoint and Steve Wade. Shaw claimed he was not the actual killer and had no idea his accomplice would attack his victim.

January 28th: Derek William BENTLEY (19)   Wandsworth

Convicted of the murder of PC Sydney Miles (38), who was shot dead during a robbery at a Croydon warehouse on 2 November 1952. Bentley and Christopher Craig (16) had gone to the building intending to steal but were thwarted when the police were called.

Bentley was soon taken into custody, and was under arrest. Although Craig shot the officer, Bentley was alleged to have shouted, 'Let him have it', (see **1940, July 11th: APPLEBY and OSTLER**).

Tried before Lord Chief Justice Goddard at the Old Bailey on 9-11 December; the judge seemed unfairly biased in favour of   the

Derek William Bentley

prosecution and whilst there was no doubt that Craig was guilty of the murder of the police officer, he was too young to hang. Bentley was deemed to be equally guilty of the murder – although his counsel strenuously denied this was the case. He was found guilty, with the jury adding a strong recommendation for mercy. Despite widespread public appeal no reprieve was forthcoming.

Hanged by Albert Pierrepoint and Harry Allen.

On 30 July 1998, the conviction was quashed at the Court of Appeal.

February 24th: Miles William GIFFARD (26)   **Bristol**

Charles Giffard (62) was the senior partner in a firm of Cornwall solicitors, and hoped his son would follow him into the profession. Miles Giffard, however, despite being a talented sportsman who had represented Cornwall at cricket, had been expelled from public school and showed no interest in following his father, preferring to idle away his time in London, living on an allowance paid by his parents.

In late 1952, Giffard became infatuated with a girl he met in London. His parents disapproved and told him to end the relationship, hinting that the allowance might stop if he disobeyed them. Giffard was unwilling to do so and, on 4 November, wrote to the girl telling her that the only solution to the problem would be to kill his parents.

On 7 November he returned to the family home at St Austell, where he waited in the garage for his father to return home. He then battered him unconscious with an iron pipe before entering the kitchen where he battered his mother Elizabeth (56). He then telephoned his girlfriend in London and told her he would be returning to London. Discovering that both his parents were still alive, he placed them one at a time in a wheelbarrow and tipped them over the edge of a cliff where they were discovered next morning. Giffard was arrested in London the following day. He had already confessed to his girlfriend that he killed his parents and had sold some of his mother's jewellery.

He pleaded insanity at his three-day trial before Mr Justice Oliver at Bodmin on 4-6 February. Evidence was shown that he had been receiving psychiatric care in the past, but the jury preferred to believe the prosecution's case of murder for financial gain.

Hanged by Albert Pierrepoint and Harry Smith.

May 19th: John Lawrence TODD (20)   Liverpool

Police discovered the body of Hugh George Walker (82), proprietor of an antique shop known locally as 'The Olde Curiosity Shop' on Warbreck Moor, Liverpool, on the afternoon of 15 January, after neighbours had reported that something seemed amiss. He had been battered to death with an axe, receiving 32 blows to the head and upper body.

Walker's sister was able to give police a detailed description of the clock repairer she had seen with her brother in the shop on several occasions shortly before the murder. Newspaper articles describing the wanted man caught the attention of a young girl from Bootle whose boyfriend fitted the wanted man exactly. She contacted the police who interviewed Todd, an unemployed labourer of Walton.

At his trial before Mr Justice Cassels at Liverpool Assizes on 8-9 April, the case against him was strong. Todd made a number of statements before admitting he had been a regular visitor to the shop where he repaired several clocks. His clothing contained bloodstains from the same blood group as the victim which he claimed were made when the old man fell against him and burst his nose.

Hanged by Albert Pierrepoint and John Broadbent, assisting for the first time at an execution.

July 15th: John Reginald Halliday CHRISTIE (55)   Pentonville

10 Rillington Place, Notting Hill, had come to the attention of the police in the autumn of 1949 when tenant **Timothy EVANS** (see **1950, March 9th**) was charged with the murder of his wife and child. Evans went to the scaffold blaming his landlord Christie for the murders.

By March 1953 Christie had moved out of Rillington Place and the new owner soon discovered a body hidden behind a false wall in the kitchen. A subsequent police search unearthed five further bodies. Ruth Fuerst (21)

John Reginald Halliday Christie

and Muriel Eady (31) were discovered in the garden; Kathleen Maloney (26), Rita Nelson (25) and Hectorina Maclennan (25) in the kitchen and Christie's wife Ethel (55) beneath the living room floor. All had been strangled and with the exception of his wife all had had sexual intercourse around the time of death.

Christie was arrested in Putney a week later and immediately confessed. He was tried before Mr Justice Finnemore at the Old Bailey on 22-25 June. He offered a plea of insanity, but this was rejected and whilst he claimed he could not be certain if he had killed Beryl Evans in 1949, he was adamant that he had not strangled the young child.

Hanged by Albert Pierrepoint and Harry Smith.

July 30th: Philip HENRY (25)   Leeds

The body of Flora Jane Gilligan (76) was found naked outside her home in York on the morning of 10 March. It appeared she had fallen from an upstairs window but medical evidence found she had been raped, then beaten and strangled before being thrown from the window.

A fingerprint discovered at the scene matched that belonging to Henry, a soldier stationed at nearby Strensall. He denied the murder but had no alibi for the previous night and splinters of wood found on his clothing matched the wood from the window frame at the house.

Henry was tried before Mr Justice Jones at York Assizes on 16-18 June; the trial was memorable in that the jury asked the judge if they could visit the scene of the crime before returning a verdict. They were escorted to the house and on returning to court needed just a few minutes to find Henry guilty of murder. He had been due to be posted overseas just days after he was arrested.

Hanged by Albert Pierrepoint and Royston Rickard. It was Rickard's first execution as an assistant and, interestingly, it was the only time that Albert Pierrepoint officiated as either assistant or chief executioner at Leeds prison.

Louisa May Merrifield

September 18th: Louisa May MERRIFIELD (46)   Manchester

On 12 March, Louisa Merrifield and her third husband Alfred took up positions as live-in housekeeper-companions to the twice-widowed Mrs Sarah Ann Ricketts (79) in Blackpool. Within the month Mrs Ricketts had changed her will in favour of the Merrifields.

By early April, Louisa Merrifield was telling friends she had been left a bungalow by an elderly widow and when Mrs Ricketts died on 14 April, one of the Merrifields' friends contacted the police. A post-mortem revealed that Mrs Ricketts had died as a result of phosphorus poisoning and both Merrifields were charged with her murder.

Despite no trace of poison being found at the house and conflicting medical evidence that suggested cause of death was liver failure, Louisa was sentenced to death by Mr Justice Glyn-Jones at Manchester Assizes on 30 July after an 11-day trial. The jury failed to reach a verdict on Alfred Merrifield and he was released. He later inherited a half share in the bungalow and appeared in seaside shows for several years until his death in 1962.

Hanged by Albert Pierrepoint and Robert Stewart.

October 20th: John Owen GREENWAY (27)   **Bristol**

Greenway, a Welsh-born machine operator, shared a room at a Swindon guest-house with another Welshman. The two men slept in the same double bed and became lovers. In May, Greenway's lover left the house and returned to Wales. He left a note saying that he had left the house because the food was awful and if Greenway wanted to get in touch he should contact relatives.

On the night of 2 June, Greenway returned to his lodgings. He was upset at being unable to track down his friend and showed the letter to his landlady, Mrs Beatrice Ann Court (62). She denied it was her fault he had left and during a quarrel Greenway picked up an axe and battered her to death. He also attacked her husband who had tried to intervene.

Against the wishes of his counsel he pleaded guilty before Mr Justice Parker, thus leaving them unable to offer a defence of insanity, and was convicted at Wiltshire Assizes on 2 October.

Hanged by Albert Pierrepoint and Harry Allen.

Joseph Christopher Reynolds

November 17th: Joseph Christopher REYNOLDS (31)   **Leicester**

Janet Mary Warner (12) was waylaid and strangled with a silk stocking and a tie as she walked her dog along a canal towpath in Blaby, Leicestershire, on 22 May. Her screams attracted the attention of two boys out playing, who alerted the police.

Reynolds, an Irish labourer who had served a prison sentence for an attack on a woman in South Wales several years earlier, was known to the police as a potential suspect and when they went to question him they found he had disappeared. He was detained two days later.

He pleaded guilty at his trial before Mr Justice Pilcher at Leicester Assizes on 26 October. He told the court he was very sorry and deserved the extreme penalty. He had also told officers that the reason for committing the crime was that he wanted to die and reasoned that if he were convicted of murder he would be executed.

Hanged by Albert Pierrepoint and Robert Stewart.

December 17th: Stanislaw JURAS (43)   Manchester

A Polish mill worker of Halifax sentenced to death by Mr Justice Stable at Leeds Assizes on 26 November for the murder of his landlady, Mrs Irena Wagner (29), who was found raped and strangled in Juras's room at her guest-house.

She and her husband had rented rooms to many of the Polish immigrants working in the area. Mrs Wagner's husband had left Halifax to visit friends, leaving his wife and several lodgers at the house, one of whom was Juras. On 16 September, Juras killed her claiming that he was in love with her and wanted her all to himself; her husband told the court she did not like Juras and was scared of him.

Hanged by Albert Pierrepoint and Royston Rickard.

December 18th: John Francis WILKINSON (24)   Wandsworth

Wilkinson, a furnace man, had been lodging with the Schreiber family in Balham, London, since June. On the night of 15 August, he got drunk in his bedroom. He had been reading a number of 'magazines' one of which, '*Bedside Clubman*', contained pictures of masochism and torture.

Breaking off a chair leg, he wrapped it in a towel and went down into the kitchen where the landlady's daughter Miriam Susan Gray (5) slept. He shone a torch into her face and when she awoke beat her to death with the chair leg. He then made a failed attempt to have sex with her before fleeing the house. He was arrested on the following morning and confessed to the crime.

Tried before Mr Justice Hilbery at the Old Bailey on 2-3 November, his defence was based on insanity. Evidence was shown of a history of family insanity, but although doctors claimed he was suffering from a psychotic personality, he was not classed as insane by the MacNaughten rules, used to gauge whether the accused is insane by law.

Hanged by Steve Wade and Royston Rickard.

December 22nd: Alfred Charles WHITEWAY (22)   Wandsworth

Two teenage girls, Barbara Songhurst (16) and Christine Reed (18), were attacked as they cycled on a tow-path at Teddington on 31 May. They were both battered unconscious before being raped and stabbed to death.

Both were then thrown into the river Thames. Barbara's body was found the next day, Christine's was not found for five days.

Almost a month later, Whiteway, a builder's labourer of Teddington, was arrested following sexual assaults on two women in Surrey. Although married, he and his wife lived with their respective parents whilst waiting to be housed. Taken in for questioning, he denied murdering the two girls, but traces of blood found on his shoes matched that of one of the girls. A few days later, the police car Whiteway had been taken to the station in was being cleaned and an axe was discovered hidden in the back. It was proved to be the weapon used to batter the two girls.

At his trial, before by Mr Justice Hilbery on 2 November at the Old Bailey, the prosecution based its case around a confession Whiteway was alleged to have made following his arrest. He claimed to have planned to rape just one of the girls when he spied her cycling alone down the tow-path. As he attacked her he was shocked to hear the other girl, whom he had not spotted, screaming for help. He chased after her and realising that he knew her, was scared she would identify him. He had no choice but to kill them both if he wanted to avoid arrest. He pleaded not guilty at his trial and denied he had made any confession.

Hanged by Albert Pierrepoint and John Broadbent.

Alfred Charles Whiteway

December 23rd: George James NEWLANDS (21)   **Pentonville**

Newlands had become friendly with Henry Tandy (65) and his wife Honor (59) whilst serving in the army. He was a frequent visitor to their bungalow in Orsett, Essex. On 30 May, now working as a metal toy maker, Newlands left his home in Walthamstow and travelled to Orsett. Welcomed into the house, he soon pulled out a hammer and battered the old couple before stealing £8. Henry Tandy died from his injuries, his wife later recovered.

Tried before Mr Justice Streatfeild at Chelmsford Assizes on 13 November, it was alleged that Newlands had committed the crime when he needed money for a new suit. He got the idea for the robbery after watching a 'cosh-boy' film at the cinema.

Hanged by Albert Pierrepoint and Harry Allen.

1954

Cases where no executioner is recorded are multiple executions, and readers are asked to refer to the entries before or after for details of the hangman.

January 5th: Robert William MOORE (27)   Leeds

A Harrogate car dealer sentenced to death by Mr Justice Stable at Leeds Assizes on 25 November 1953, for the murder of Edward Watson (28), a rival car dealer.

Watson had disappeared from his home on 31 May. He had planned to meet up with Moore, who on the previous day had arranged to take Watson to view a car. Moore was questioned following the disappearance and following a further visit by police, he made an attempt to gas himself by placing his head in an oven.

Following his arrest, he confessed that he had lured Watson to a plantation at Fewston where he had shot him five times at close range and buried him. Moore claimed the motive for the murder was revenge after being cheated on a car deal. He was sold a faulty car by Watson, and lost money on it when Watson bought it back from him for a lot less than Moore had first paid.

Hanged by Steve Wade and Harry Smith.

January 8th: Czeslaw KOWALSKI (32)   Manchester

For two days every week Doris Douglas (29) lived with Kowalski, a Polish refugee. The rest of the week, she lived and worked as a housekeeper to an elderly man at Quarry Hill, Leeds. Kowalski was initially unaware where she was when she was not at their home and when he found out he became jealous and accused her of having an affair. She denied the accusations.

On 6 October 1953, they were out drinking when they got into a quarrel. Doris returned to Quarry Hill where a short time later Kowalski turned up. Refused entry, he forced open the door and in front of witnesses attacked Doris with his feet and fists before stabbing her in the head with a scout knife.

Tried before Mr Justice Stable at Leeds Assizes on 15-17 December 1953, his defence was that he was too drunk to have formed the necessary intention to commit murder. He was the seventh man sentenced to death at the Leeds Winter Assizes and due to a shortage of condemned cells at Leeds prison, Kowalski, like **JURAS (1953, December 17th)** was transferred across the Pennines for execution.

Hanged by Albert Pierrepoint and John Broadbent. In an attempt to cheat the hangman Kowalski had attempted to bleed to death by scraping off the skin of his penis with his fingernails, and his last days in the death cell were reportedly spent in tremendous agony.

January 26th: Desmond Donald HOOPER (27)   **Shrewsbury**

On 21 July 1953, Elizabeth 'Betty' Selina Smith (12) disappeared after a visit to her friend and neighbour Keith Hooper (7), in Atcham, Shropshire. Her mother called to the house at around midnight and learned that Betty had left to go home at 10.40pm. Hooper's father Desmond, a gardener and keen pigeon fancier, had left the house a short time later to see about some pigeons which had not returned to their coop at a nearby farm.

A search was made and her body was found less than two miles away, down a ventilation shaft at a disused part of the Shropshire Union Canal near Shrewsbury. She had been strangled with a tie, kicked repeatedly in the stomach and thrown down the 40-foot shaft where she drowned in the shallow stagnant water. A jacket recovered from the mouth of the shaft was identified as belonging to Desmond Hooper.

Tried before Mr Justice Cassels at Shrewsbury Assizes on 23-27 November; the evidence against Hooper was mainly circumstantial, based around the jacket and that no one could offer him an alibi for the night of the murder. No motive was suggested and Hooper maintained his innocence to the last.

Hanged by Albert Pierrepoint and Robert Stewart.

January 27th: William LUBINA (42)   **Leeds**

A Polish miner sentenced to death by Mr Justice Stable at Leeds Assizes on 27 November, for the murder of his German-born landlady Mrs Charlotte Ball at Barnsley.

Lubina was one of a number of lodgers at the house and had been living there for several years, during which time he fell in love with Mrs Ball. In mid-June 1953, Lubina and Mrs Ball quarrelled and she kicked and punched him. He refused to strike back and several days later he told her that he was going to find new lodgings.

On 25 June, Lubina again quarrelled with her. Her husband and a fellow lodger returned to the house just as Charlotte began to scream as Lubina attacked her. Lubina fled to an adjacent room where he smashed a mirror and tried to cut his throat with the glass. Mrs Ball died from multiple stab wounds to the chest.

Lubina claimed that the murder was not premeditated and that he had only struck her after she had attacked him, but a witness testified that he had seen Lubina sharpening the knife used to commit the crime earlier that same day at work.

Hanged by Steve Wade and Harry Allen.

April 14th: James Reginald DOOHAN (24)   Wandsworth

On 9 February, Doohan walked into a police station at Queenborough, Isle of Sheppey, Kent, and confessed that he had shot a man on nearby Rushden Marshes. He led the police to the body of Herbert Victor Ketley (40), the step-father of his girlfriend, and told how he had lured him to the marshes and shot him in the neck.

At his trial before Mr Justice Sellars at Maidstone on 22-23 March, it was alleged that Doohan believed that Ketley was behind the his girlfriend's refusal to accept his marriage proposal, although this was found not to have been the case. His defence counsel claimed he had been diagnosed as a schizophrenic whilst in the army, but medical experts called by the Crown could find no evidence of insanity.

Hanged by Albert Pierrepoint and Harry Allen.

April 20th: Michael MANNING (25)   Dublin

A carter of Limerick, convicted before Mr Justice Murnaghan at Dublin on 17 February of the rape and murder of Catherine Elizabeth Cooper (65), a nursing sister at Barrington Hospital, Limerick, on 18 November 1953.

Manning waylaid Mrs Cooper as she walked down a quiet lane near Castleroy and dragged her into a nearby field where he raped and beat her, forcing grass into her mouth to stop her screaming. Death was due to suffocation caused by the grass.

He confessed to the crime and his defence was manslaughter as Manning was shown to have been very drunk on the night of the murder.

Hanged at Mountjoy Gaol by Albert Pierrepoint and Robert Stewart. Michael Manning was the last man hanged in the Irish Republic.

April 22nd: Albert George HALL (48)   Leeds

Mary Hackett (6) disappeared while playing outside her home in Halifax on 12 August 1953. Amongst the first to be questioned was Hall, the newly appointed caretaker at the Park Congregational Church, a matter of yards from where Mary had been seen playing. After a 16-day search, during which time the grounds of the church were once again searched, Scotland Yard were called in.

Hall was revisited and aroused suspicion by his over-friendly manner and by the fact that two tins of paint without lids, which Hall claimed to have lost, were standing in a corner of the crypt. A fourth search of the crypt was made, aided by industrial lighting and heavy equipment. This time the search unearthed the body of Mary in a shallow grave. She had been beaten to death and her skull smashed. There was no sign of a sexual assault.

Although Hall was the prime suspect there was no evidence to connect him to the murder. Kept under police surveillance, he was followed to a nearby mental hospital, where he kept an appointment with a doctor to whom he revealed details of the murder known only to police and the killer.

Sentenced to death by Mr Justice Pearson at Leeds Assizes on 12 March, his plea of insanity being rejected. No motive for the crime was ever established.

Hanged by Steve Wade and Harry Smith.

Albert George Hall

April 23rd: John LYNCH (43)   **Edinburgh**

On Friday 11 December 1953, Lesley Jean Nisbett, also known as Sinclair (4), and Margaret Curran, also known as Johnson (3), were reported missing from their homes in an Edinburgh tenement block. A search of the area found the bodies in a lavatory in the block; they had been badly beaten and assaulted. Death was due to suffocation.

Dublin-born Lynch lived in an apartment across the corridor from where the bodies were discovered. As the search took place he watched and was noticeably drunk. His manner attracted attention and when questioned he confessed. He was charged with murder when traces of blood and vomit found on his shirt linked him to the crime.

Sentenced to death at Edinburgh by Lord Justice Clerk Thompson on 26 March after a five-day trial.

Hanged by Albert Pierrepoint and Robert Stewart.

April 28th: Thomas Ronald Lewis HARRIES (24) **Swansea**

Farmer John Harries (63) and his wife Pheobe Mary (54) were last seen alive following a visit to a harvest festival service at a church close to their farm near St Clears, Carmarthanshire, on 16 October 1953.

The reason for their disappearance was explained away by a nephew, 'Ronnie', who said he had driven them to a local railway station where they had caught a train to London for a secret holiday.

Foul play being suspected, Scotland Yard were called in, and investigations led police to believe that Harries had killed his aunt and uncle after they had refused to lend him money. A forged cheque was found made out to Ronnie Harries and friends of the missing couple told police they did not believe the elderly couple would go away without informing them.

Detectives leading the hunt suspected that Harries had buried the bodies in kale fields close to his own farm at nearby Cadno. Thread was tied over entrances leading into the fields and a disturbance made to make Harries think the fields had been searched. On the following day Harries went to check and in doing so broke the thread and led police to a spot in the fields where they found the bodies buried in a shallow grave. They had been battered to death.

Sentenced to death by Mr Justice Havers at Carmarthen on 16 March after an eight-day trial.

Hanged by Albert Pierrepoint and Robert Stewart.

Thomas Ronald Lewis Harries

June 17th: Kenneth GILBERT (21) **Pentonville**
Ian Arthur GRANT (24)

George Frederick Smart (55) worked as a porter at a Kensington hotel. On 9 March his body was found in the basement of the hotel. He had been battered about the head, then bound and gagged as he lay unconscious on the floor. Death had been due to suffocation caused by the gag.

Missing from the hotel stores were a small amount of cash and a large quantity of cigarettes. The following day, Grant, a porter at a nearby hotel, told a friend that he and Gilbert had killed the porter and stashed the cigarettes in a left luggage locker at Victoria Station. The friend contacted the police who soon had both men in custody.

At the trial before Mr Justice Glyn-Jones at the Old Bailey on 10-12 May, it was described how Gilbert, a former employee at the hotel, had led Grant onto the property via the coal cellar where they were disturbed by Smart. Both men admitted striking the victim before he was tied up.

Hanged together by Albert Pierrepoint, assisted by Harry Smith, Royston Rickard and John Broadbent. It was the last double execution carried out in Great Britain.

June 22nd: Milton TAYLOR (23)   Liverpool

Taylor and Marie Bradshaw (25) had been living together as man and wife in lodgings at Crewe, moving there from Bury after Marie's husband had discovered they were having an affair.

On the evening of 20 February, her husband called at the house to ask if she would come back with him. By this time Marie was now pregnant with Taylor's child, although it seems this relationship was not always a happy one. She asked both men for time to think. There had also been a quarrel and the outcome was that the landlady, learning the true relationship between the couple, told them to leave the lodgings that night.

As her husband returned to Bury to await his wife's possible return, Marie and Taylor took refuge in a hut at Worleston. On the following morning, Taylor confessed to a friend that he had strangled Marie and surrendered to the police. She had been strangled with a tie.

At the trial before Mr Justice Byrne on 5 June at Chester Assizes, evidence was shown that Taylor was a ex-borstal boy with a mental age of 11. It was also shown that he suffered inflammation of the brain following an operation during his childhood. His defence of insanity failed and the jury took just 35 minutes to find him guilty.

Hanged by Albert Pierrepoint and Robert Stewart.

June 23rd: George Alexander ROBERTSON (40)   Edinburgh

Sentenced to death by Lord Thompson at Edinburgh High Court on 2 June, for the murder of his ex-wife, Mrs Elizabeth Greig (39) and their son George Alexander (18) at their flat on the Royal Mile, Edinburgh.

The couple had separated before Robertson came back to live with his family. On 28 February his ex-wife and son were found stabbed to death. He pleaded insanity at his trial.

Hanged by Albert Pierrepoint and Harry Allen.

August 11th: William Sanchez de Pina HEPPER (62)   Wandsworth

Hepper was a Spanish-born artist living in Chelsea, London, with a studio flat in Hove, Sussex.   In late January, Margaret Rose Louise Spevick (11), a school friend of his youngest daughter, injured her arm in a fall.   Hepper suggested to her mother that she accompany him for a short break to help her recovery and Mrs Spevick readily agreed.   Hepper had also told her that he had the services of a nurse at the sea view flat.

On 3 February, Hepper and Margaret caught a train to Sussex.   She sent postcards home and it was agreed that Hepper would meet Mrs Spevick at Brighton Station on 7 February, who would then accompany her daughter back home.

When no-one was there to meet Mrs Spevick at the station she had to return to London to get the address as, having no worries about Hepper being genuine, she had not troubled to ask the actual address of the studio.   Returning with the address, she got the caretaker to let her in and found Margaret's body on a bed beside a half painted portrait.   She was naked and had been raped and strangled.

A hunt for Hepper led police to Spain, where he was finally reported to police by relatives shocked at the horrific nature of the crime.   As a Spanish national he applied to fight the extradition, but as he had fought on the opposing (and losing) side in the civil war, his request was ignored.

At his four-day trial before Mr Justice Jones at Lewes on 19-22 July, his defence was based on insanity and amnesia.   Hepper was known to have suffered horrific head injuries in a car crash whilst working as a translator for the BBC in 1946, and he insisted throughout the trial that he had no knowledge of committing murder.

Hanged by Albert Pierrepoint and Royston Rickard.

William Sanchez de Pina Hepper

August 12th: Harold FOWLER (21)   **Lincoln**

Kenneth Joseph George Mulligan (28) had split up with his wife after he discovered she was having an affair with Fowler, an engineering labourer. She moved out of the marital home and later set up house with Fowler in Nottingham. She had given birth to a son by Fowler, but despite this Mulligan still made efforts to get his wife back.

After several failed attempts to get her to return, Mulligan became resigned to it and on 19 May called to see her to ask for his wedding certificate back. As he made to leave, he turned to his wife and called her a fool, pushing her back and causing her to bang her head on a wall. Fowler, who had been present at the meeting, rushed over and during a struggle, Mulligan collapsed and died from a stab wound to the chest.

At his trial before Mr Justice Sellars at Nottingham Assizes on 24-25 June, Fowler claimed that it was an accident, but was convicted after the prosecution showed that the knife's sheath was in the living room, which suggested that the weapon had deliberately been wielded. Also, the depth of the fatal wound suggested considerable force had been used.

Hanged by Albert Pierrepoint and Harry Allen.

September 1st: Edward REID (24)   **Leeds**

On the night of 3 April, the body of Arthur White (60) was found in the yard of his lodging house in Bradford. From the state of his injuries it appeared he had fallen from the upper bedroom window. Police called to the scene interviewed White's room mate Reid, who aroused suspicions by his dishevelled appearance and bruised hand. The room also showed signs of a disturbance. Witnesses claimed that Reid and White had been quarrelling earlier that evening.

Tried before Mr Justice Donovan at Leeds Assizes on 5-6 June. No real motive was established although Reid had been drinking that night and was known to have a fierce temper.

Hanged by Steve Wade and Harry Smith.

September 1st: Rupert Geoffrey WELLS (53)   **Wandsworth**

On the afternoon of 10 May, Wells confessed to the landlord of his local pub that he had killed his girlfriend at their home at Kingston-upon-Thames. Police were called and found the body of Nellie Officer (46) lying in an armchair. She had been strangled the previous day.

Tried before Mr Justice Jones on 26-28 July, Wells's defence was based on the fact that he had been unaware of his actions due to mixing a vast quantity of alcohol and a prescribed sedative. Prosecution counsel showed that the deceased had been worried about Wells's drinking and had confided to a friend that she feared he might do her harm.

Hanged by Albert Pierrepoint and Robert Stewart.

December 15th: Styllou Pantopiou CHRISTOFI (53)   Holloway

Sentenced to death by Mr Justice Devlin at the Old Bailey, for the murder of her German-born daughter-in-law Hella Christofi (36) whom she battered to death at her home in Hampstead.

Mrs Christofi had left her native Cyprus to live with her son, daughter-in-law and their three children, in the summer of 1953. The two women did not got along from the start and after several months of unhappiness, Hella told her husband that his mother must leave the house.

On 29 July, shortly after her son had told her she must prepare to leave the house, a neighbour saw Mrs Christofi starting a fire in the back yard and in the early hours of the following morning, she rushed out into the street asking for help. A passer by followed her into the house and found the body of Hella in the yard.

Police investigations found that Hella had been strangled and then battered about the head with a heavy ash plate. Paraffin was then poured onto her body. Mrs Christofi claimed it had been an accident.

Hanged by Albert Pierrepoint and Harry Allen. Almost 30 years earlier, Mrs Christofi had stood trial for the murder of her mother-in-law by ramming a burning torch down her throat. On this occasion she was found not guilty.

Styllou Pantopiou CHRISTOFI

1955

Cases where no executioner is recorded are multiple executions, and readers are asked to refer to the entries before or after for details of the hangman.

March 29th: William Arthur SALT (45)   Liverpool

On 16 December 1954, Salt, a labourer, called at a school in Hanley, Staffordshire, to collect Dennis John Shenton (6), the son of his fiancée. He was well known to the school and told the teacher he was taking the child to visit elderly relatives. Later that afternoon the boy's mother called to collect Dennis and was shocked to learn he had left with Salt.

Salt arrived home alone at 6pm saying that he had taken Dennis to stop with a relative in Runcorn. When it was suggested they go to collect him Salt agreed, but vanished on the way to the railway station. Next morning he confessed he had killed the child by drowning him in a canal at nearby Trentham.

Tried at Staffordshire Assizes on 8-9 March, Salt admitted the crime, saying, 'He got on my nerves so I drowned him.' Summing up, Mr Justice Devlin told the jury that there was a good deal of evidence to show that Salt was suffering from 'anxiety neurosis' when he committed the crime.

Hanged by Steve Wade and Harry Smith.

April 14th: Sydney Joseph CLARKE (32)   Wandsworth

A Kennington labourer sentenced to death by Mr Justice Pilcher at the Old Bailey on 23 March for the murder of prostitute Rose Elizabeth Fairhurst (45) who was found strangled on a bomb site at Southwark, London on 9 February.

Clarke had been seen propositioning the victim in a public house on the night before her body was found. Blood found at the scene was from a rare blood group that matched Clarke's and a receipt for a lodging also found beside the body was traced to the accused.

He later confessed saying that after he had agreed to pay her for sex they made for the bomb site where she refused to lie down on an old mattress. They quarrelled and Clarke claimed that he 'went mad'.

Hanged by Albert Pierrepoint and Robert Stewart.

May 4th: Winston SHAW (39)   Leeds

An unemployed radio engineer of Shipley, West Riding, sentenced to death on 17 March at Leeds Assizes by Mr Justice Pearce for the murder of Mrs Jean Tate (24), the mother of his two children.

Their relationship had broken up in the summer of 1954, when after the intervention of Social Services she fled with the children to a temporary 'safe' flat in a residential block at Knaresborough Hospital.

In February, Shaw learned of her whereabouts and tried to persuade her to return to live with him. He called at the flat on the afternoon of 3 February, where he was escorted away by the police. Later that night she was found battered and stabbed.

Shaw was visited on the following day and confessed he had killed her but said that it was accidental. He said that after returning to the flat he found an intruder and during the struggle he may have accidentally struck Mrs Tate. He could offer no explanation as to why she had received six blows from an axe and had been stabbed 25 times. He told the court he did not know why he had done it and offered no defence.

Hanged by Steve Wade and Harry Smith.

May 22nd: James ROBINSON (27)   **Lincoln**

A labourer from Skegby, Nottinghamshire, convicted of the murder of an elderly widow, Mrs Mary Dodsley (83), who was strangled and sexually assaulted at her home on 15 December 1954.

Robinson had an alibi for the alleged time of the murder but was one of almost 70 local men asked to give a 'palm print' as one had been left on a window frame at the house. Palm prints are as individual as fingerprints and Robinson's matched the one from the scene.

Convicted before Mr Justice Jones at Birmingham Assizes on 25-29 March; the jury returned a guilty verdict adding that they believed that death was unintentional and had been caused during an attempted rape.

Hanged by Albert Pierrepoint and Harry Allen.

June 21st: Richard GOWLER (43)   **Liverpool**

On the morning of 11 March, Wallasey police received a call that a man had stabbed to death two women. They called at the house at Seacombe and found the body of widow Mrs Mary Boothroyd (53). Beside her was her daughter who had been severely wounded. Both had been stabbed with a marlinespike – a long pointed tool used by dockers.

Gowler, a ship's rigger from Wallasey, was arrested that same morning. He admitted breaking into the house with the intention of killing his estranged girlfriend, but mistakenly murdering her mother.

Tried at Chester Assizes before Mr Justice Sellers on 2 June, his defence claimed that as Mrs Boothroyd was not his intended victim, the charge should be reduced to manslaughter.

Hanged by Albert Pierrepoint and Robert Stewart.

July 12th: Kenneth ROBERTS (24)   **Lincoln**

In the early hours of 11 May, police were called to a house in Scunthorpe where they spoke to Roberts, a warehouseman, with a pregnant wife and two young children. He told them that he had strangled a woman and left the body in a builder's yard at Winterton. A search discovered the body of Mary Georgina Roberts (18) (no relation) at the yard.

At his trial at Nottingham Assizes, before Mr Justice Finnemore on 21-22 June, it was alleged that he had picked up Mary, who worked as a prostitute, as he left a nightclub and that they went to the yard for sex. He then strangled her with his scarf.

Hanged by Steve Wade and Robert Stewart.

July 13th: Ruth ELLIS (28)   Holloway

A former model and club hostess from South Kensington sentenced to death by Mr Justice Havers on 21 June for the murder of her former lover, David Moffat Drummond Blakely (25) whom she shot dead outside a Hampstead public house.

She was the mother of two young children, with failed marriages and a string of lovers, one of whom was alleged to have supplied her with the gun. She shot Blakely, a racing driver from Penn, Buckinghamshire, after he had tried to end their relationship.

At her trial she was asked what her intentions were when she pulled the trigger. She said that she intended to kill Blakely and that sealed her fate. She refused to appeal.

Hanged by Albert Pierrepoint and Royston Rickard. Ruth Ellis gained lasting infamy as the last woman executed in Great Britain.

Ruth Ellis

July 26th: Frederick Arthur CROSS (33)   Birmingham

An unemployed concrete mixer from Great Haywood, Staffordshire. His wife had left him at New Year and taken his two children, leaving Cross so upset that he bought some rat poison, intending to commit suicide. Afraid to take his own life, he changed his mind, deciding that if he was convicted of murder he would be executed.

On 25 February he persuaded Donald Haywood Lainton (28), an insurance salesman from Stockport, who had stopped in a snowstorm to ask directions, to give him a lift. Reaching Willslock, near Uttoxeter, he told Lainton to pull off the road where he then stabbed him to death.

After being arrested he told the police, 'I don't want legal aid and I don't want defending - I want to hang.' He pleaded guilty before Mr Justice Gorman at Birmingham Assizes on 5 July. He smiled when the judge sentenced him to death, but next morning in the condemned cell he declared he wished to live. Appeals for a reprieve failed.

Hanged by Albert Pierrepoint and Robert Stewart. Cross had been relaxed during his stay in the death cell, but on the morning of the execution he offered fierce resistance when his arms came to be pinioned and went to the gallows fighting and screaming.

July 27th: Norman William GREEN (25) Liverpool

On the night of 11 April, Easter Monday, Norman Yates (10) left his home in Lower Ince, Wigan to run an errand. A short time later he was found stabbed to death close to his home. It was the second murder of a young boy in the town following the fatal stabbing of William Harmer (11) nine months earlier.

Witnesses claimed to have seen a blond-haired man in the area and investigations led them to Green, a corn grinder. He initially denied the accusations but later confessed to both murders and took police to his place of work where the murder weapon was located.

At his trial before Mr Justice Oliver at Lancashire Assizes on 5 July, it was alleged that Green was epileptic and there was a history of insanity in his family. Following his arrest, he had claimed he kept getting the urge to kill and that he might kill again. He made no appeal.

Hanged by Albert Pierrepoint and Robert Stewart. It was Albert Pierrepoint's last execution.

August 2nd: Corbett Montague ROBERTS (46) Birmingham

An unemployed Jamaican, of Aston, sentenced to death by Mr Justice Gorman at Birmingham Assizes on 15 July for the murder of his Jamaican-born wife Doris Acquilla Roberts (41).

On the morning of 31 May, Roberts beat her to death with two hammers while she was combing her hair, after she refused to give him some money to take to work. She had dropped her purse down her blouse when he asked her for the cash. There had recently been some money stolen from a member of the family and although Roberts had denied it, his wife believed him guilty.

He pleaded guilty at his trial and said that his life was forfeit. He asked that none of his family benefit from the sale of his property and that it should go to an old people's home.

Hanged by Steve Wade and Harry Allen.

August 9th: Ernest Charles HARDING (42)   Birmingham

Schoolgirl Evelyn Patricia Higgins (10) disappeared after visiting a Coventry hairdressing salon on the afternoon of 8 June. Investigating her disappearance, police spoke to two girls who told them they had been approached by a man driving a black car. He had tried to lure them into the car, but they had refused.

Another witness gave a detailed description of the car which led police to Harding, a bricklayer, who was found inside his car. He had fixed a pipe to the exhaust and was trying to commit suicide. He made a number of conflicting statements; in one he claimed to have no recollection of finding Evelyn inside the car. He then realised she was dead and decided to bury her body. He led police to a wood near Coleshill, Coventry where she was found in a shallow grave. She had been raped and asphyxiated and then stabbed in the throat.

He offered a defence of insanity before by Mr Justice Lynskey at Birmingham on 21 July. It was claimed that Harding had suffered a head injury in 1952, which had caused him to be moody and bad-tempered.

Hanged by Steve Wade and Robert Stewart. Harding was the last man to be hanged for child murder.

August 12th: Alec WILKINSON (21)   Leeds

Wilkinson, a Barnsley miner, had married his wife Maureen in the summer of 1954 but soon found that his mother-in-law Clara Farrell (50), a former prostitute, seemed intent on making his life a misery. She consistently interfered in the relationship, to the extent that his wife had left home on a number of occasions. In the spring of 1955, Maureen was living with her mother, who had taunted Wilkinson that Maureen would rather become a prostitute that return to her husband.

On 30 April, Wilkinson spent the night drinking before calling to see his wife. He was very drunk when he called at the house in the early hours of the following morning. Within moments of his arrival he had punched both women before picking up a bread knife and stabbing Mrs Farrell. He then set fire to the house before confessing to a stranger and was soon arrested.

Tried before Lord Chief Justice at Sheffield Assizes on 22-24 June, he pleaded extreme provocation and self-defence claiming that the woman had wielded a bread knife at him before he stabbed her.

Hanged by Steve Wade and Robert Stewart. As he was led to the gallows Wilkinson quipped, 'At least I know where I'm going and can use a shovel', referring to his occupation as a miner. It was the last execution carried out by Steve Wade.

1956

There were no executions in 1956.

1957

Cases where no executioner is recorded are multiple executions, and readers are asked to refer to the entries before or after for details of the hangman.

July 23rd: John Willson VICKERS (22)   Durham

On Sunday 14 April, Vickers, a labourer, broke into a general store at Carlisle. The proprietress, Miss Jane Duckett (72) was partially deaf, and Vickers, knowing the money was kept in the basement, surmised she would not hear him break in.

Failing to find the money, he emerged from the cellar to see the old lady awoken by the noise. Aware that she recognised him, Vickers struck her, she fell, he kicked her in the face several times and she lay dying. Unable to find the money, he left empty handed. Miss Duckett died shortly afterwards. Vickers, well known to the local police, was quickly arrested and admitted striking her but denied intending to kill.

Tried before Mr Justice Hinchcliffe at Cumberland Assizes on 23 May, the evidence against Vickers was his damning statement that he had gone to the shop to 'rob the woman after hours', that she rushed at him and he struck her 'in a panic'. By admitting this he left himself open to a verdict of capital murder in the course or furtherance of theft under the newly passed Homicide Act (1957).

Hanged by Harry Allen, carrying out his first engagement as chief executioner, and Harry Smith. Under the Homicide Act, notice of execution was no longer placed on the prison gate.

December 4th: Dennis HOWARD (24)   Birmingham

On 17 May, Howard, an unemployed labourer from Smethwick, entered a gents' outfitter's shop in Dudley, with the intention of robbing the till. Once inside he panicked and after picking up a sweater tried to flee the shop. He was stopped by a member of staff, David Keasey (21), who jammed his foot against the door.

Howard then pulled out a gun and ordered Keasey to stand back. A struggle ensued which ended up in the street, in the course of which Keasey was shot dead.

Howard was identified as the gunman and arrested on 24 June. He readily admitted stealing the sweater but claimed that the gun had discharged inadvertently during the struggle. Howard claimed Keasey grabbed the gun and pulled it towards himself, whereupon it went off, accidentally.

Howard's claim that the killing was an accident was repeated when he stood trial for capital murder in the furtherance of theft and by shooting at Worcestershire Assizes on 18 October, before Mr Justice Hinchcliffe.

Hanged by Harry Allen and Royston Rickard.

1958

Cases where no executioner is recorded are multiple executions, and readers are asked to refer to the entries before or after for details of the hangman.

May 6th: Vivian Frederick TEED (24)   **Swansea**

William Williams (73) had been sub-postmaster at Fforestfach, Glamorgan, for 40 years. On Sunday 17 November 1957 an intruder armed with a hammer entered the shop. He was discovered by the old man and struck 27 blows before fleeing empty handed.

Police interviewed workmen who had been employed at the post office a few months earlier and in due course spoke to Teed, who had a history of thefts and assault. A witness also told police that Teed had confided in him that he planned to rob the post office.

Tried before Mr Justice Salmon at Glamorgan Assizes, Swansea, on 18 March, charged with capital murder in the furtherance of theft. Teed having confessed to the crime, his counsel pleaded manslaughter on the grounds of diminished responsibility.

Hanged by Robert Stewart and Harry Robinson. It was Stewart's first time as chief executioner and Robinson was assisting at his first execution.

Peter Thomas Anthony Manuel

July 11th: Peter Thomas Anthony MANUEL (31)   **Glasgow**

Born in New York of English parents, he came to England in his youth and served a number of terms in borstal and approved schools for theft and assaults. In 1945 he was released and went to live in Scotland with his family. In March 1946, he was sent to prison for eight years, convicted of 15 cases of housebreaking and one of rape.

On 2 January 1956 Anne Kneilands (17) was battered to death and sexually assaulted on East Kilbride golf course. Manuel was questioned, but released and even though police believed him guilty, they could not prove anything.

On 17 September, sisters Marion Watt (45) and Margaret Brown (41) and Marion's daughter Vivienne (16) were found shot dead in a house at High Burnside, Lanarkshire. Manuel was again questioned, as was Marion's husband William Watt who had been away on a fishing trip. Watt was charged with the murder of his family and detained.

On 8 December, taxi driver Sidney Dunn (37) was shot dead near Newcastle. On 28 December Isabelle Cooke (17) was reported missing after attending a dance in Lanarkshire. On 1 January 1958, as detectives searched for her, reports came in that a family had been shot dead at nearby Uddington: Peter Smart (45), his wife Doris (40) and son Michael (11). Manuel was interviewed again on 18 January and made a full confession to all the crimes.

Sentenced to death by Lord Cameron at Glasgow High Court on 29 May after being convicted on seven counts of murder. He was not charged with the murder of Anne Kneilands as there was no evidence to link Manuel to the murder other than his own confession which was not admissible under Scottish law. The murder of Sidney Dunn was not proceeded against, but English detectives were waiting to arrest Manuel should he have been acquitted.

Hanged by Harry Allen. According to Scottish newspaper accounts of the execution and official documents held in the Scottish Record Office, the assistant executioner is recorded as Harry's son, Brian Allen.

August 12th: Matthew KAVANAGH (32)   Birmingham

Isaiah Dixon (60) lived in a boarding house at Warwick. Kavanagh, an Irish labourer, had also lodged there for a time until he lost his job and, being unable to pay rent, had to move out.

On 12 April, Kavanagh was out drinking and returned to the boarding house. He met Dixon, who was very drunk, and helped him upstairs to his room. He then strangled Dixon with his own black silk tie, before stealing almost £5. He then travelled into Coventry where he confessed to a café owner who called the police.

Convicted on 3 July before Mr Justice Streatfeild at the Warwickshire Assizes of capital murder in the furtherance of theft. In 1957, Kavanagh had been charged with the non-capital murder of a married woman with whom he had been associating, but the charge was later dropped on medical evidence.

Hanged by Harry Allen and Thomas Cunliffe assisting at his first execution.

September 3rd: Frank STOKES (44)   Durham

On 14 April Mrs Linda Ash (75), a widow, was admitted to hospital with severe head injuries and died on the following day. She had been attacked with a hammer in her home in Gosforth, in Northumberland.

Police wanted to interview a man who replied to an advert for a gardener placed in a corner shop by Mrs Ash. Witnesses gave a description which led them to Stokes, an unemployed hotel porter from Leeds who did gardening jobs.

Arrested on 2 June, Stokes made a statement that on arrival at Mrs Ash's home she let him in and, in her living room, they discussed the hourly rate. Stokes asked for four shillings per hour, but the old lady offered only three shillings and sixpence. He became violent and went to the kitchen, where he picked up a hammer, returned and beat Mrs Ash to death. He said the motive for the killing was not theft, but anger at her offer of employment; he also denied stealing from her house.

Found guilty of capital murder in the furtherance of theft, on 23 July at Yorkshire Assizes, Leeds, before Mr Justice Davies. He entered a plea of guilty to non-capital murder, which was rejected by the prosecution, mainly because when picked up by the police he had Mrs Ash's purse, which contained a number of bank notes. Stokes claimed he had found the purse.

Hanged by Harry Allen and Harry Smith.

December 17th: Brian CHANDLER (20)   Durham

On 8 June Chandler, a Middlesbrough-born private in the Royal Army Medical Corps, went 'absent without leave', from his camp at Catterick, and met up with two teenage girls who had run away from their homes, in Darlington, County Durham. They planned to steal some money and flee to London. One of the girls told him of the widowed Mrs Martha Anne Dodd (83), her former employer who kept large sums of money in her house.

The following day Chandler called at the house asking for work. Invited inside, he followed her into the kitchen where he struck her 19 times with a hammer, taking £4 from her handbag and then fleeing. He was arrested next day and claimed that he had called to ask for work and that he had lost his temper after she had offered him gardening work at three shillings an hour.

At the trial on 27-29 October, before Mr Justice Ashworth at Durham Assizes, the defence claimed that Chandler was accompanied by one of the girls and it was she who had killed Mrs Dodd. This conflicted with Chandler's confession to the police, in which he claimed he did not mention the girl being present, in order to protect her.

Convicted of capital murder in the furtherance of theft and hanged by Robert Stewart and Thomas Cunliffe.

1959

Cases where no executioner is recorded are multiple executions, and readers are asked to refer to the entries before or after for details of the hangman.

February 10th: Ernest Raymond JONES (38)   **Leeds**

On the evening of 30 September 1958, Richard Turner (38) manager of the Co-op store at Lepton, Huddersfield, disturbed an intruder when he went to check on the premises. In making good his escape with less than £80 and 30,000 cigarettes, the intruder struck the manager, knocking him down the stairs. He died instantaneously from a fractured skull.

Jones, a well-known criminal, was questioned and denied being involved, giving himself an alibi for the night of the murder. When this was checked out and found to be flawed, he was questioned again and this time admitted striking Turner so that he could flee.

On 10 December, at Yorkshire Assizes in Leeds, before Mr Justice Hinchcliffe, he was found guilty of capital murder. His defence claimed it was not capital, since the killing was not committed in the furtherance of theft, but in the furtherance of escaping, which they deemed a non-capital offence.

Jones's appeal was rejected on 29 January, 1959. Lord Chief Justice Parker said, 'If a burglar is interrupted and if he murders in order to get away, it is still murder in the course of theft.' 'Course' being the crucial word.

Hanged by Harry Allen and Harry Smith. It was Harry Smith's last execution.

Ernest Raymond Jones

April 28th: Joseph CHRIMES (30)   **Pentonville**

On New Year's Eve 1958, Nora Summerfield (60), a widow, was battered to death with a tyre-lever at her bungalow in Hillingdon in Middlesex. Known locally as the Cider Queen or the Merry Widow, she had been seen alive in a local pub for the festive celebrations.

On 6 January, Chrimes, a stainer from Hayes, and Ronald Pritchard (18), unemployed, were charged with capital murder in the course or furtherance of theft, and non-capital murder respectively. Police had evidence that Chrimes actually killed the old lady, but that Pritchard was present. Pritchard then turned Queen's Evidence for the dropping of the murder charge, claiming they broke into the house, waking Mrs Summerfield before they fled in a panic, stealing a clock, cigarette case, and some spoons.

Tried before Mr Justice Donovan at the Old Bailey on 3-4 March; the jury asked why Pritchard had not been charged with murder too. The judge explained that for Pritchard to have stood trial for non-capital murder, the evidence would have to be that he knew Chrimes intended to kill or cause grievous bodily harm to Nora Summerfield, before the attack on her began, or that he urged Chrimes in his attack. As Pritchard was now testifying for the Crown, he could not be party to a murder. Under the Homicide Act it was only capital murder when a person actually killed the victim, or actually inflicted grievous bodily harm on them.

Hanged by Harry Allen and Royston Rickard.

Pritchard pleaded guilty to breaking and entering and larceny and was sent to borstal. He had two previous convictions. Pritchard's life was spared by the Homicide Act (1957). Prior to its passing, the prosecution did not have to show who dealt the fatal blow or even that violence was contemplated if the accomplice remained with the killer and the crime continued, which it did in this case.

Ronald Henry Marwood

May 8th: Ronald Henry MARWOOD (25)   **Pentonville**

On Sunday night 14 December 1958, PC Ray Summers (23) was stabbed fatally in the back with a frogman's knife as he attempted to break up a gang-fight outside a nightclub in Holloway, London.

Marwood, a scaffolder from Islington, was celebrating his first wedding anniversary and was very drunk, when he and his friends became involved in a full scale gang fight, involving the police and 20 young men armed with knives, bottles and knuckle-dusters. Marwood said he heard the police telling the men to disperse, when he struck at PC Summers, intending to push him away. He said he did not have a knife in his hand.

Marwood was questioned, but released. In January, police let it be known that they wished to interview Marwood who was by now in hiding. On 27 January, he surrendered and confessed, 'I did stab that copper that night...'.

Tried before Mr Justice Gorman at the Old Bailey on 17-19 March, he denied making the statement, claiming the police, '.... had put things down.' Marwood's defence was that apart from the incriminating statement, there was no other evidence to connect Marwood with the killing or even the fight, and certainly not the knife.

Hanged by Harry Allen and Harry Robinson.

Michael George Tatum

May 14th: Michael George TATUM (24)   **Winchester**

On 16 January, an intruder broke into the house of Charles Barrett (85), a retired cavalry officer, in Southampton and struck him three times with a Zulu knobkerrie. His wallet was stolen. Barrett died of a fractured skull on the following day.

On 18 January, unemployed cinema projectionist Tatum (24), husband of Barrett's housekeeper, was charged with capital murder in the furtherance of theft.

Convicted at Hampshire Assizes before Mr Justice Cassels on 23 March. Tatum did not deny killing the old man, but claimed an accomplice actually struck him. His defence was manslaughter, on the grounds of diminished responsibility.

Hanged by Robert Stewart and Thomas Cunliffe.

August 14th: Bernard Hugh WALDEN (33)   **Leeds**

Shot dead Joyce Moran (21) and her boyfriend Neil Saxton (20) at Rotherham Technical College, where Walden, crippled with polio, was a lecturer. Joyce had spent a short holiday with Walden, where he had proposed marriage. She refused his offer.

On 7 April, Walden shot her six times then sought out Saxton and shot him once. When arrested, in Reading on 30 April, he had three guns on his person, several more in the boot of his car, and more were found at his lodgings in Rotherham.

Sentenced to death by Mr Justice Paull at Yorkshire Assizes on 2 July, Walden claimed he intended to kill Miss Moran, but wanted to 'paralyse Saxton from the waist down'. He showed no remorse whatsoever for the killings.

Hanged by Harry Allen and Thomas Cunliffe. Cunliffe failed to strap the prisoner's legs correctly on the drop and as a result he was never called upon again to participate in any executions.

Bernard Hugh Walden

October 9th: Francis Joseph HUCHET (33)   **Jersey**

On 4 April, two children playing found the body of John Perree (45), a road-labourer, buried on the sand dunes by Jersey's airport at St Brelade. He had been shot in the head and had last been seen on 30 March, drinking with his friend Francis Huchet, a labourer on a sewage farm.

At his trial before Mr Justice Harrison at St Helier on 7-10 September, it was alleged that Huchet had lured Perree to the dunes to rob him after Perree had showed him a large of amount of money during a darts match.

Hanged by Harry Allen and Royston Rickard.

Guenther Fritz Erwin Podola

November 5th: Guenther Fritz Erwin PODOLA (30)   Wandsworth

On 3 July a flat in Kensington, west London, belonging to an American model was burgled. Jewellery and furs had been stolen. A couple of days later she received a phone-call from a man attempting to blackmail her and she contacted the police. The phone was tapped and on 13 July, when he called back, she kept him talking whilst the call was traced to a call-box in South Kensington.

Podola, a German-born petty criminal, was arrested by DS Ray Purdy (43) and a colleague. A scuffle broke out, Podola broke free and fled to a nearby block of flats where he was re-arrested. He then drew a gun, shot Purdy through the heart and fled, leaving fingerprints at the scene. On 16 July, he was arrested in a Kensington hotel where he received a crashing blow to the head as the door burst open.

At a 'pre-trial' at the Old Bailey before Mr Justice Davies in September, the defence contended Podola was suffering from amnesia so could not be tried. They had not discussed a 'defence' with Podola, since he could not remember anything following the blow to the head. Remanded in Brixton prison, doctors could not agree whether he was faking. At the end of the first pre-trial trial in English legal history, it was decided Podola should stand trial for his life.

On 24 September, the murder trial began. All references to Podola's memory were not permitted. All Podola said was, 'I cannot put forward a defence... I cannot remember this crime.' On the following day, the jury retired for only half an hour to find Podola guilty.

Hanged by Harry Allen and Royston Rickard.

1960

Cases where no executioner is recorded are multiple executions, and readers are asked to refer to the entries before or after for details of the hangman.

September 1st: John Louis CONSTANTINE (22)   **Lincoln**

A Nottingham box-maker and petty criminal charged with the capital murder of Mrs Lily Parry (75) who was battered to death with a crowbar, in her bedroom over her shop on 22 April, after she had interrupted a burglary. Some money and personal property were stolen.

At his trial before Mr Justice Ashworth at Birmingham Assizes on 18-22 July Constantine claimed he had an accomplice in the robbery and it was this man who, armed with a crowbar, had gone upstairs and committed the assault. The other man, whom he described as a workmate, was able to satisfy police as to his innocence whilst evidence against Constantine was substantial. An appeal on the grounds that the Judge's summing-up was unfair was dismissed on 15 August.

Hanged by Harry Allen and Royston Rickard. Two trainee hangmen, Samuel Plant and John Underhill, witnessed the execution

November 10th: Francis Robert FORSYTH (18)   **Wandsworth**

A road labourer who, along with **Norman James HARRIS** (23) (see below) and two other men, was sentenced to death by Mr Justice Winn at the Old Bailey on 26 September, for the capital murder of Alan Jee (23).

After a heavy drinking session the four men decided to 'jump someone' and waited on a secluded path at Hounslow for a suitable victim to pass. Jee, an engineer, who had just bid goodnight to his fiancée, came along the deserted track and was punched in the face by one of the men. He fell to the ground and Harris rifled his pockets in an attempt to find his wallet, as the others held him down. Harris stopped when he saw blood on his hands and ran away, leaving the 10 shillings the victim was carrying still in his pocket. 'Flossie' Forsyth stood over the stricken man and repeatedly kicked him about the head with his 'winkle-picker' shoes, in order to 'keep him quiet'.

Jee died in hospital from his injuries two days later. Forsyth bragged to a girlfriend that he had been in a fight and when this became known to the police he was taken into custody. The others were soon rounded up and taken to Hounslow police station. Harris, who was questioned first, denied any involvement in the assault but under questioning he admitted that he had held down the victim whilst Forsyth and one of the others had attacked him.

Evidence was produced to suggest one of the gang was only involved in a minor role and that he was standing away from the victim, acting as a lookout; he was convicted of non-capital murder and given life imprisonment. Another of the gang, being under 18, was ordered to be detained at Her Majesty's Pleasure. Forsyth, who had claimed at an earlier court appearance that they would only get 'about five years', and Harris, both of whom had a number of minor convictions, were convicted of capital murder in the course or furtherance of theft and sentenced to death.

Hanged by Harry Allen and Royston Rickard. An inmate who was released on the morning of the execution claimed Forsyth could be heard crying 'I don't want to die.'

November 10th: Norman James HARRIS (23)   **Pentonville**

Hanged by Robert Stewart and Harry Robinson for his part in the Hounslow Footpath Murder. (see above)

December 22nd: Anthony Joseph MILLER (19)   **Glasgow**

Convicted before Lord Wheatley at Glasgow High Court on 16 November of the capital murder of John Cremin (54), a Dundee shopkeeper who was in Glasgow for a football match. Cremin, who was homosexual, was beaten and robbed in the city's Queen's Park recreation ground on 6 April. His death was due to a fractured skull caused by being struck with a plank of wood.

Miller was accompanied on the assault by a 17-year-old accomplice who was found guilty of murder (non-capital) and sentenced to be detained during Her Majesty's Pleasure. It was alleged that the accomplice would lure homosexual men to a secluded area of the park, where Miller would carry out vicious muggings and assaults. Miller was arrested after the other man had been arrested for another offence and during questioning confessed to the Queen's Park Murder.

Hanged by Harry Allen and Robert Stewart.

1961

Cases where no executioner is recorded are multiple executions, and readers are asked to refer to the entries before or after for details of the hangman.

January 27th: Wasyl GNYPIUK (34)   **Lincoln**

An unemployed Ukrainian Pole, convicted before Mr Justice Havers at Nottinghamshire Assizes on 22 November 1960, of the capital murder in the course or furtherance of theft of Mrs Louisa Surgey (64) in her home at Worksop, Nottinghamshire, on 21 July. She had been strangled and her head had been cut off. The body had been found in a shallow grave, 60 yards from her house.

Gnypiuk, a former lodger of Mrs Surgey, who had originally owned the house before selling it to her, admitted to having stolen two handbags containing £250 and £350 respectively, claiming he knew the old lady lived alone and kept large amounts of money in the house.

His defence was that he claimed he awoke from a nightmare and strangled Mrs Surgey whilst half asleep. He then chopped her head off in a panic and hid the body in a local wood. The head was found in a paper bag just over a mile away, along with one of the handbags.

Hanged by Harry Allen and John Underhill, assisting at his first execution.

February 9th: George RILEY (21)   **Shrewsbury**

On the night of 7 October 1960 Riley, a butcher's assistant and son of a local school-teacher, went out drinking with friends in Shrewsbury, Shropshire. He later went to a dance where he got involved in several fights, including one to which the local police were summoned. Very drunk, he was helped home at 1.30 a.m. The following morning the body of his neighbour, Mrs Adeline Smith (62) was discovered in her bedroom, battered to death.

Riley, with previous convictions for violence and one for attempted murder, was an immediate suspect and later that day, following police questioning, he had written a full 'confession' to capital murder in the course or furtherance of theft.

Tried at Stafford Assizes on 9-12 December 1960, before Mr Justice Barry. There was no evidence linking Riley to the crime other than his 'confession' which was alleged to contain the lines 'She was alive when I left her. I wanted some money. I can't remember everything. I was drunk.'

Hanged by Harry Allen and Samuel Plant, assisting at his first execution. Whether or not Riley committed murder is still debated today and allegedly there are still many people in Shrewsbury who claim to know the true identity of the killer of Mrs Smith.

March 29th: Jack DAY (30)   **Bedford**

On the morning of 25 August, the body of Keith Godfrey Arthur (25), a machine-operator who also bought and sold second-hand cars, was found on a farm in Dunstable, Bedfordshire. Enquiries led police to the house of

1961

George Riley

Jack Day, a car salesman. A young babysitter had seen him shoot a man who had been at the house with Day's wife, on the previous evening.

At his trial before Mr Justice Streatfeild at Bedfordshire Assizes on 18-20 January, it was alleged that Day, who owned a .38 revolver and 177 antique firearms, possessed a jealous temper. Arthur often boasted of his 'conquests' and a witness told police Day had told him he would shoot anyone who had an affair with his wife. Day was alleged to have shot Arthur after catching him with his wife. Day claimed the gun went off accidentally.

Hanged by Harry Allen and Harry Robinson.

May 26th: Victor John TERRY (20)   **Wandsworth**

On 10 November 1960 unemployed Terry, from Hounslow, and a 17-year-old accomplice went into Lloyd's Bank at Durrington, near Worthing, Sussex and during the course of a robbery shot dead guard Henry Pull (61). They fled with an attaché case containing £1,372. Waiting outside were two accomplices, one of whom was Terry's 18-year-old girlfriend. Later that morning the car was found abandoned in Worthing, with a single-barrel shotgun inside.

Two of the gang were quickly picked up after trying to pay for a short taxi ride with a 10-shilling note. Terry, with previous convictions for robbery with violence, and his girlfriend were arrested in Glasgow two days later. Terry was charged with capital murder, his girlfriend as an accessory after the fact to capital murder. The other two were charged with non-capital murder.

Tried at Sussex Assizes in Lewes from 20-28 March, before Mr Justice Stable. Terry's defence was twofold: that the shooting was accidental and also that he was suffering from a form of insanity. The 17-year-old accomplice was sentenced to be detained at Her Majesty's Pleasure, the accomplice who had waited in the car was sentenced to life imprisonment, while Terry's girlfriend, who had also waited in the car, was surprisingly given only a suspended sentence.

Hanged by Harry Allen and Samuel Plant. Terry had been a school friend and neighbour of '**Flossie FORSYTH**' (see **1960, November 10th**) and had carried out the murder minutes after hearing in a radio broadcast that his friend had been hanged at Wandsworth. An article in the Today magazine, by a fellow-prisoner released later in the day, said the deathly silence of the prison was broken by Terry's screaming, and by the boom as the trapdoor opened.

June 29th: Zsiga PANKOTAI (31)   **Leeds**

In December 1960, market trader Eli Myers (50), also known as Jack Marsh, was part of a syndicate that won a modest sum of money on the football pools. News of the win made all the local papers and on 24 February, he was found dead at his home in Leeds. He had cuts to his hands and bruises to his face and his van was missing from outside the house. The van and its contents of clothes were discovered abandoned on the outskirts of Leeds and a jacket discarded at the scene led police to Pankotai, a Hungarian miner.

Tried before Mr Justice Ashworth at Leeds Assizes on 24-26 April; it was clearly proved that Pankotai had been at the house at the time Myers was killed. In his defence it was claimed that cause of death was due to heart failure, caused when Myers tried to fend off Pankotai who had broken into the house looking for something to steal after reading about the pools win.

Hanged by Harry Allen and Harry Robinson.

1961

Victor John Terry

July 6th: Edwin Albert Arthur BUSH (21)   **Pentonville**

On 3 March, shop assistant Mrs Elsie May Batten (43) was found dead in an antique shop on Charing Cross Road, London. One antique dagger protruded from her chest, another from her neck. Other shop assistants in the area remembered a coloured man who had asked about the price of a 'dress-sword'. Police issued an Identikit picture that appeared on television and in all the national and local London newspapers. Five days later Bush was picked up in Soho and taken into custody where he was picked out of an identity parade by several shop assistants.

At his trial before Mr Justice Stevenson at the Old Bailey on 12-13 May it was alleged that he made a statement to the police that he had visited the shop in order to steal the sword. Bush's defence had been to admit manslaughter on the grounds of provocation, claiming in court that Mrs Batten had said: 'You niggers are all the same, you come in here and never buy anything.'

Hanged by Harry Allen and John Underhill. Bush was the first murderer to be arrested through the use of the Identikit system, which had been developed by the Los Angeles police department in 1959. It was first tested by Scotland Yard in that year, though not officially used until 1961.

Edwin Albert Arthur Bush

July 25th: Samuel McCLAUGHLIN (40)   **Belfast**
McClaughlin had left Northern Ireland and was living in Derby when he travelled back to County Antrim, after his estranged wife Nellie (32) took out maintenance proceedings against him. On 17 October 1960, they were seen together in a public house and McClaughlin asked her to come back to Derby with him where he had found a job in a foundry. The following day, during a quarrel at her cottage at Cloughmill, he battered her with a broom handle and strangled her with a silk stocking.

At his first trial at the Winter Assizes the jury failed to agree on a verdict, so the trial was rescheduled to the Antrim Spring Assizes. His plea of insanity, due to the amount of drink he had consumed prior to the murder, was rejected.

Hanged by Harry Allen and Royston Rickard. Northern Ireland had not adopted the Homicide Act of 1957, so although McClaughlin would have been convicted of non-capital murder in England and sentenced to life imprisonment, in Northern Ireland he received the mandatory death sentence for murder.

September 7th: Hendryk NEIMASZ (49)   Wandsworth

On the morning of 13 May, the bodies of Alice Buxton (38) and Herbert Buxton (35) were discovered at their home in Addington in Kent. They lived together as man and wife, but were not legally married. Herbert had been shot dead while Alice had been battered to death with the butt of a shotgun.

Evidence at the house led police to Neimasz, a Polish refugee with whom Alice had been having an affair. The murder weapon was found at Neimasz's home and witnesses testified to seeing him close to the house shortly before the murder.

Sentenced to death by Mr Justice Pilcher on 20 July at Sussex Assizes, for the capital murder of Herbert Buxton and non-capital murder of Alice.

Hanged by Harry Allen and Samuel Plant.

December 20th: Robert Andrew McGLADDERY (26)   Belfast

On 18 January, the naked, mutilated body of Pearl Gamble (19) was discovered in a desolate spot in County Armagh, near Newry. She had been battered and stabbed and evidence indicated the motive of the killing was sexual. The direct cause of death was strangulation.

Pearl had last been seen at a dance in Newry the previous night and amongst those interviewed was McGladdery, an unemployed labourer from nearby Damolly.

He was a distant cousin of Pearl's and had been seen dancing with her. Asked about the clothes he wore that night, McGladdery claimed he had worn a dark blue suit, his only one, yet several witnesses said he had on a light blue suit. He was also now sporting scratches on his face which he did not have on the previous night. His bloodstained clothing was later found hidden. Hairs matching those of Pearl Gamble were attached.

The week-long trial was held at the Down Assizes, Downpatrick, before Lord Justice Curran. On 16 October McGladdery was found guilty and sentenced to death. He had maintained he was innocent of the crime with such conviction that strenuous yet unsuccessful efforts were made for a reprieve.

1961

Hanged by Harry Allen and Samuel Plant.   On the eve of his execution McGladdery made a full and detailed confession.

1962

Cases where no executioner is recorded are multiple executions, and readers are asked to refer to the entries before or after for details of the hangman.

April 4th: James HANRATTY (25)   **Bedford**

Sentenced to death by Mr Justice Gorman at Bedfordshire Assizes on 17 February, after a 19-day trial, at the time the longest murder trial in English legal history, for the capital murder of Michael Gregsten (36) on the A6 at Deadman's Hill, near Ampthill, Bedfordshire.

On the night of 22 August 1961, Gregsten and his girlfriend Valerie Storie (23) were disturbed as they were courting in his car. Gregsten was made to drive for several hours then he was shot dead. Miss Storie was then raped and shot several times as she lay on the ground. She was left paralysed for the rest of her life.

Hanratty was pulled in after his description matched that of the wanted man and was picked out of an identity parade by Miss Storie. He presented himself badly in court, changing his alibi halfway through proceedings.

Hanged by Harry Allen and Royston Rickard. Widespread campaigning to clear Hanratty's name began immediately, many believing a miscarriage of justice was done to James Hanratty, and that without Valerie Storie's evidence, he would not have been found guilty. DNA Tests carried out in May 2002 however suggested that Hanratty was 'without doubt' the killer.

James Hanratty

November 20th: Oswald Augustus GREY (20) Birmingham

On the early evening of 3 June, Thomas Bates (47) was found shot dead behind the counter at his newsagent's shop in Edgbaston, Birmingham. He had been killed by a single shot from a revolver left beside the body. The weapon was traced to Grey, an unemployed baker, who lived locally. He admitted possessing the murder weapon but denied shooting Mr Bates. In a statement to the police Grey gave five different stories as to who had the gun at the time of the killing.

Convicted before Mr Justice Paull at Warwickshire Assizes in Birmingham, on 12 October, of capital murder, by shooting, in the furtherance of theft. Grey was alleged to have been desperate for money, having been on National Assistance for a year.

Hanged by Harry Allen and Samuel Plant. Grey spent the six weeks in the condemned cell limbo dancing and hand-jiving, reputedly oblivious and indifferent to his fate.

November 28th: James SMITH (26) Manchester

On the afternoon of 4 May, Mrs Isabella Cross (57) was murdered in her corner-shop in Miles Plating, Manchester. The motive for the killing was theft, and five large bottles of mineral water had been used to batter Mrs Cross to death. A fingerprint was found in the room at the rear of the premises through which the killer had made his escape.. Forensic experts also reconstructed the five bottles, from the thousands of shattered fragments, so that they could identify the fingerprints on them.

Enquiries led detectives to Edinburgh-born Smith, who lived in a soon to be demolished area of Beswick, Manchester. Although his fingerprints matched those in the house, evidence of contact with the mineral bottles was crucial to show he had killed Mrs Cross. Tiny fragment of the glass were found down the side of Smith's sofa.

On 18 October, the jury at Liverpool Crown Court needed just 20 minutes before declaring him guilty of capital murder in the course or furtherance of theft and he was sentenced to death by Mr Justice Stable.

Hanged by Harry Allen and John Underhill. Between the sentence of death and the execution, Smith's brown hair turned pure white.

1963

Cases where no executioner is recorded are multiple executions, and readers are asked to refer to the entries before or after for details of the hangman.

August 15th: Henry John BURNETT (21)   Aberdeen

Burnett had begun an affair with Margaret Guyan when they were employed together at an Aberdeen factory. With her husband away at sea she moved in with Burnett and a short time later she wrote to her husband asking for a divorce.

On 31 May, Thomas Guyan (27) returned to shore and sought out Margaret. She agreed to his plans for reconciliation and returned to the house she shared with Burnett to collect the two children and her belongings. There followed a fight between Margaret and Burnett during which she received minor stab wounds from the knife she picked up in self-defence, as she fought off his attempts to strangle her.

Later that afternoon, Burnett called at the Guyan house and blasted Guyan in the face with a shotgun, killing him instantly. He then snatched Margaret and dragged her outside, where he commandeered a car. They drove for a while until they were spotted by a patrol car. With Margaret promising to stand by him if he gave himself up, Burnett surrendered and was charged with wilful murder.

Sentenced to death by Lord Wheatley at Aberdeen on 25 July, his insanity-based defence being rejected. The jury needed just 25 minutes to find him guilty by majority verdict.

Hanged by Harry Allen and Samuel Plant. The previous hanging at Aberdeen had taken place 106 years earlier, but the gallows at Craiginches prison were the most modern in Great Britain, having been newly built and installed just 12 months earlier.

December 17th: Russell PASCOE (23)   Bristol

William Rowe (64) had been a First World War deserter. Conscripted in 1917, he fled one week later, was soon captured, but once again managed to escape. For 35 years he hid on his parents farm in the Cornish fishing village of Porthleven, then latterly at 'Nanjarrow' near the village of Constantine, seven miles from Falmouth. Neighbours were told he had been killed in France.

Following her coronation in 1953, Queen Elizabeth II granted a pardon to all deserters. Although Rowe was now free he rarely left the farm, having become a hermit and recluse whose only pleasure was studying Esperanto. It was rumoured locally that he was a wealthy man and there had been a robbery at 'Nanjarrow' in 1961.

On 15 August 1963, his body was discovered at the farm. He had severe head injuries, his throat had been cut, and he had five stab wounds in the chest, two in the neck, and one across an ear. Robbery was the apparent motive as the whole farmhouse had been turned over and following initial investigations, police believed £3,000 had been stolen.

Russell Pascoe

The following day, Pascoe was stopped at a police roadblock. He gave his address as a caravan near Truro, which he shared with his teenage wife and young child, along with **Dennis John WHITTY** and two teenage girls. He told police he was in Constantine to visit his parents and that he knew the deceased, having worked at 'Nanjarrow' three years earlier.

Believing that the killer was probably a local man who knew of the supposed wealth of the victim, police visited the caravan and interviewed Whitty and the three girls. Having taken them to Falmouth for questioning, police soon learned that the two men had left Truro on Pascoe's motorcycle on the night of 14 August, returning late in an excited and agitated state.

Whitty eventually confessed that they had called at the house at 11pm, pretending to be helicopter pilots who had crashed nearby and wanted to use a phone. Pascoe had then hit Rowe with an iron bar. Their search failed to find any large sums of money and they fled with just £4.

At Cornwall Assizes, Bodmin, before Mr Justice Thesinger, it became clear that Whitty was the leader who had planned the attack, caused the fatal wounds and threatened the others if they 'grassed'. Despite both counsel trying to put the onus on the other, they were deemed equally guilty and on 3 November, after a five-day trial, both were convicted of capital murder in the furtherance of theft.

Pascoe was hanged by Harry Allen and Royston Rickard. The £3,000 which the police originally believed stolen was later discovered hidden in a safe in the cow-shed, with another large sum of money. Also hidden in the farmyard was a glass jar stuffed with bank notes. The police discovered this haul, by following instructions left in a diary, penned in Esperanto.

Dennis John Whitty

December 17th: Dennis John WHITTY (22)   **Winchester**

Hanged by Robert Stewart and Harry Robinson for the murder of William Rowe (see above).

1964

Cases where no executioner is recorded are multiple executions, and readers are asked to refer to the entries before or after for details of the hangman.

August 13th: Peter Anthony ALLEN (21)   **Liverpool**

In the early hours of 7 April, John Alan West (55) was found dead in his home at Seaton, on the outskirts of Workington, Cumberland. He had been battered and stabbed. A raincoat was found at the house containing a medal with the inscription G.O. Evans 1961 and a piece of paper with a Liverpool address. Allen and Evans, two Preston-based dairy workers, were soon arrested and blamed each other for the murder.

Their seven-day trial was held before Mr Justice Ashworth on 1 July. It was revealed that Evans had once worked with John West and had travelled to see him to ask for a loan. Taking along Allen and Allen's wife and children, they drove to Seaton where it was alleged that Evans may have tried to blackmail West into giving him money. It was also alleged that the old man may have been homosexual and that Evans had agreed to have sex with him for money before they killed him.

It was also alleged that police had told Allen that his wife was having an affair with Evans, who had been living as a lodger at the house. As a result, the two men had to be kept apart in the dock.

Hanged by Robert Stewart and Harry Robinson. Along with her two children, Allen's wife visited her husband for the very last time on the day prior to the execution. The decision of the Home Secretary not to order a reprieve was already known. As the visit came to an end, Allen went berserk, throwing himself against the bullet-proof glass and breaking his wrist in the process. Stewart noted in his diary that Allen ' ...smashed his head against a wall during his last visit and broke a finger. As I was strapping his wrist in the morning, he shouted, 'Jesus.' That was it. Not another word.'

Peter Anthony Allen

> **AII Communications**
> to be addressed to
> **G. L. D. LIGHTFOOT**
> **UNDER SHERIFF**
>
> TEL. NOS. 22922-3
> Your Ref.:
> My Ref.: GLSL

> **UNDER SHERIFF'S OFFICE**
> **21 CASTLE STREET**
> **CARLISLE**

Dear Sir,   14th July 1964

<u>re: 11115 Peter Anthony Allen</u>

  The above is a prisoner at H. M. Prison, Liverpool, who was sentenced to death on 7th July for Capital Murder.

  By reason of the fact that the offence took place in Cumberland the High Sheriff of this County is charged with the duty of making arrangements to carry out the sentence.

  The prisoner has made an application for leave to Appeal which application, I understand, will be heard on Monday 20th July next.

  In the event of the sentence being carried out I shall be glad if you will let me know if you will undertake the duties. In view of the application for leave to Appeal, no date has yet been fixed.

  I enclose a stamped addressed envelope for your reply.

R. L. Stewart, Esq., Yours faithfully,
2 Birchenlea Street,
CHADDERTON,
Lancs.

August 13th: Gwynne Owen EVANS (24)   Manchester

  Real name John Robson Walby, hanged by Harry Allen and Royston Rickard for the murder of John Alan West (see above).

Gwynne Owen Evans

Postscript:

On 16 October 1964, after 13 years of continuous Tory government, the Labour Party was elected with a working majority of five. The staunch abolitionist Sidney Silverman, M.P., assured by the new Labour administration that there would never be another hanging under a Labour government, launched his final Murder (Abolition Of The Death Penalty) Bill. The bill passed its first reading on 21 December, and the new Home Secretary, Frank Soskice, 'let it be known' publicly, through the media, that all capital murderers would be reprieved.

The bill became law on 9 November 1965 when Royal Assent was given to the act. Between October 1964 and this date, 15 men convicted of capital murder, and formally sentenced to death, were formally reprieved.

Victim Index

This is a cumulative index, encompassing
Volumes I, II and III of the Hangman's Record.

Erroneous dates of hangings, and names of victims,
executioners and people hanged, have been corrected in the
relevant indexes. For easy reference, updated entries include
the information as originally given, *shown in italics.*

The Victim Index includes some names which were not
available when Volumes 1 and 2 were published. These
names also appear *in italics.*

* = given name unknown

Victim Index

Aaku, Joseph
1952, May 27th: Backary MAUNEH

Abbey, William
1928, August 10th: Norman ELLIOTT

Abrahams, John
1869, November 15th: Joseph WELSH

Adams, Caroline
1880, July 27th: Thomas BERRY

Addington, Margaret
1871, July 31st: Richard ADDINGTON

Addison, Martha Jane
1874, January 5th: Charles DAWSON

Addison, Mary
1891, December 22nd: John William
JOHNSON

Addnall, Dorothy
1934, January 3rd: Roy GREGORY

Aimes, Peter
1921, March 14th: Patrick MORAN &
Thomas WHELAN

Aitken, Isabella
1931, July 31st: Thomas DORNAN

Aitken, Margaret
1931, July 31st: Thomas DORNAN

Allchin, Esther
1897, February 9th: Robert HAYMAN

Allcock, Emma
1896, December 23rd: Joseph ALLCOCK

Allen, Agnes
1904, July 26th: Thomas GUNNING

Allen, Arthur John
1940, August 8th: George Edward
ROBERTS

Allen, Hannah
1878, April 1st: Henry ROWLES

Allen, Henry
1887, February 17th: Edward
PRITCHARD

Allen, Jane
1902, December 22nd: William James
BOLTON

Allen, Mary Ann
1894, July 31st: William CROSSLEY

Allen, Mary Ann
1905, November 7th: William George
BUTLER

Allen, Rachel
1948, February 3rd: Evan Haydn EVANS

Alston, Elizabeth
1883, November 26th: Thomas RILEY

Amos, Gilbert Caleb
1925, March 31st: William Frederick
BRESSINGTON

Anderson, Alice
1915, August 17th: George MARSHALL

Anderson, Elizabeth
1875, December 22nd: John William
ANDERSON

Anderson, Mary
1883, February 19th: James ANDERSON

Anderson, William
1941, July 31st: Edward Walker
ANDERSON

Andrews, Wiliam Thomas
1931, January 3rd: Victor Edward BETTS

Angel, Miriam
1887, August 22nd: Israel LIPSKI

Ansell, Caroline
1899, July 19th: Mary Ann ANSELL

Ansell, Elsie
1940, February 7th: Peter BARNES &
James RICHARDS

Anstree, Edward
1880, November 29th: Thomas
WHEELER
1880, November 26th

Appleton, Doris
1921, August 16th: Lester HAMILTON

Appleton, Gladys May
1944, July 12th: John Gordon
DAVIDSON

Arbuckle, Agnes
1928, January 24th: James McKAY

Archer, Cissie
1909, August 10th: Julius WAMMER

Armstrong, Katie
1922, May 31st: Herbert Rouse
ARMSTRONG

Armstrong, Rosa
1924, December 17th: Arthur SIMS

Arthur, Keith Godfrey
1961, March 29th: Jack DAY

Ash, Linda
1958, September 3rd: Frank STOKES

Askins, Mary
1885, December 8th: George THOMAS
1885, December 9th

Atkins, Esther
1903, December 16th: William BROWN
& Thomas COWDREY

Atkins, Maud
1922, April 7th: Percy James ATKINS

Atkins, Muriel
1938, November 1st: George BRAIN

Attwood, Sheila
1952, January 1st: Horace CARTER

Austin, Lillian Dorothy Pax
1942, April 30th: Frederick James
AUSTIN

Austwick, PC Alfred
1886, November 29th: James MURPHY

Ayers, Herbert William
1931, August 5th: Oliver NEWMAN
& William SHELLEY

Baggalley, G T
1921, March 14th: Patrick MORAN &
Thomas WHELAN

Bagnal, Edith
1881, February 22nd: James WILLIAMS

Baguley, Ada
1936, April 16th: Dorothea Nancy
WADDINGHAM

Baguley, Louisa
1936, April 16th: Dorothea Nancy
WADDINGHAM

Bailey, Kate
1921, March 2nd: George Arthur
BAILEY

Baillif, Victor
1901, July 9th: Valeri GIOVANNI

Bains, Ellen
1886, February 9th: John BAINS

Baker, Albert Edward
1938, March 8th: Walter SMITH

Bakewell, Fred
1895, August 20th: Thomas BOND

Balchin, Olive
1947, February 27th: Walter Graham
ROWLAND

Baldey, David
1869, January 18th: Martin Henry
VINALL

Baldwin, Elizabeth
1906, August 9th: Thomas Acomb
MOUNCER

Baldwin, PC James
1898, November 15th: John RYAN

Ball, Charlotte
1954, January 27th: William LUBINA

Ballard, Catherine
1905, April 26th: Albert BRIDGEMAN

Ballard, Phillip
1888, March 20th: James JONES &
Alfred SCANDRETT

Ballington, Ann Ellen
1908, July 28th: Fred BALLINGTON

Bannister, *
1877, April 2nd: James BANNISTER

Bar, Khauman Jung
1926, November 22nd: Hashan
SAMANDA
1926, November 2nd: SAMANDER

Barber, Maria
1878, February 11th: James CAFFYN

Bardsley, Daniel
1913, December 17th: Ernest Edwin
KELLY

Barker, Pauline
1942, July 21st: Arthur ANDERSON

Barker, Samuel
1904, December 28th: Arthur JEFFRIES

Barnes, Alice
1893, January 3rd: Cross DUCKWORTH

Barnes, Emily
1909, July 20th: William HAMPTON

Barr, *
1876, May 31st: Thomas BARR

Barrett, Charles
1959, May 14th: Michael George
TATUM

Barrett, Nana
1915, August 11th: Frank STEELE

Barrett, PC Thomas George
1886, November 30th: James BANTON
James BARTON

Barrow, Eliza
1912, April 18th: Frederick Henry
SEDDON

Bartlett, Elizabeth
1888, November 13th: Leir Richard
BARTLETT

Bateman, Albert James
1943, April 6th: Gordon Horace
TRENOWORTH

Bates, Thomas
1962, October 12th: Oswald Augustus
GREY

Batten, Elsie May
1961, July 6th: Edwin Albert Arthur
BUSH

Baxter, Beatrice Delia
1939, June 7th: Ralph SMITH

Beck, Elizabeth
1907, August 13th: Richard Clifford
BRINKLEY

Beck, Richard
1907, August 13th: Richard Clifford
BRINKLEY

Bedford, Joseph
1934, May 4th: Frederick William
PARKER & Albert PROBERT

Beeby, Martha Jane
1913, November 4th: Frederick
SEEKINGS

Beesley, Julia
1950, November 14th: Patrick George
TURNAGE

Beetmore, Jane
1888, December 18th: William
WADDELL

Bell, Mary Elizabeth
1899, July 25th: Edward BELL

Bellamy, Emma
1875, January 4th: James CRANWELL

Benjamin, Elizabeth
1922, February 21st: William
HARKNESS

Bennett, Kitty Constance
1937, December 7th: Ernest John MOSS

Bennett, Mary
1901, March 21st: Herbert John
BENNETT

Bent, Muriel
1952, July 15th: Thomas EAMES

Bentley, Florence
1948, November 18th: Stanley Joseph
CLARKE

Bernard, Frederick
1877, January 2nd: Isaac MARKS

Berridge, William
1888, May 22nd: James William
RICHARDSON

Berrisford, Harry
1947, January 3rd: Stanley SHEMINANT

Berry, Edith
1887, March 14th: Elizabeth BERRY

Berryman, Jean
1908, August 20th: John BERRYMAN

Berryman, William
1908, August 20th: John BERRYMAN

Best, Captain George Edward & crew
1876, August 25th: Christos Emanuel
BAUMBOS

Betham, Alice
1912, July 23rd: Arthur BIRKETT

Betts, William
1897, December 16th: William BETTS

Bidwell, Henry
1877, November 20th: Henry MARSH

Biggadyke, Richard
1868, December 28th: Priscilla
BIGGADYKE

Bird, Captain John Dent
1874, November 16th: Thomas SMITH

Bird, William
1901, January 11th: Timothy CADOGEN

Birds, Julian
1913, August 14th: Hugh McCLAREN

Black, Anne
1922, March 24th: Edward Ernest BLACK

Blakely, David Moffat Drummond
1955, July 13th: Ruth ELLIS

Blewitt, Mary Ann
1900, August 28th: Charles Oliver BLEWITT

Bloxham, Ann
1887, February 14th: Thomas BLOXHAM

Blundell, John
1876, August 14th: Richard THOMPSON

Bly, Edward
1870, August 15th: Thomas RADCLIFFE

Bonati, Minnie
1927, August 12th: John ROBINSON

Boot, Elizabeth
1896, August 5th: William PUGH

Boothroyd, Mary
1955, June 21st: Richard GOWLER

Boss, Ann
1870, August 1st: Walter MILLAR

Boughen, Alice
1875, March 29th: Richard COATES

Bouldrey, Margaret
1908, December 8th: William BOULDREY

Bounds, Elizabeth
1942, November 6th: Herbert Heram BOUNDS

Bousfield, Elizabeth
1924, December 9th: William George SMITH

Bovell, Mary Jane
1889, January 1st: Thomas CLEWES

Bowen, Mary
1902, March 18th: Richard WIGLEY

Bowes, Isabella
1900, December 12th: John BOWES

Bowser, Susan
1897, July 27th: Joseph BOWSER

Boyd, William
1869, December 13th: Frederick HINSON

Boyle, Anne
1893, January 6th: John BOYLE

Brades, Victor
1952, October 23rd: Donald Neil SIMON

Bradfield, Amelia
1914, March 12th: James HONEYANDS

Bradfield, Christina
1914, February 26th: George BALL

Bradshaw, Emma
1891, August 19th: Robert BRADSHAW

Bradshaw, Marie
1954, June 22nd: Milton TAYLOR

Brady, John Thomas
1946, February 8th: John LYON

Breaks, Kitty
1920, April 13th: Frederick Rothwell HOLT

Brehaney, Michael
1880, January 16th: Martin McHUGO

Brehony, Mary
1941, December 18th: Patrick KELLY

Brennan, Lizzie
1901, March 7th: John TOOLE

Brett, Margaret
1889, December 31st: Frederick BRETT

Brewer, Dorothy
1933, July 25th: Frederick MORSE

Brewer, Gladys Levinia
1943, December 15th: Charles William KOOPMAN

Brewer, Shirley
1943, December 15th: Charles William KOOPMAN

Brewster, Alice Emily
1911, October 17th: Francisco Carlos GODHINO

Bridge, Mary Ann
1876, April 4th: Thomas FORDRED

Brierley, Joyce
1946, November 13th: Frank Joseph
FREIYER

Briggs, Gertrude
1947, June 20th: Eric Charles BRIGGS

Britland, Elizabeth Hannah
1886, August 9th: Mary Ann
BRITLAND

Britland, Thomas
1886, August 9th: Mary Ann
BRITLAND

Briton, John
1883, November 6th: Henry POWELL

Brooks, Beatrice
1928, June 28th: Walter BROOKS

Brooks, Paymaster Sergeant John
1878, November 12th: Patrick John
BYRNE

Brosnan, Thomas
1924, March 13th: Jeremiah GAFFNEY

Brown, Fanny
1897, January 5th: Henry BROWN

Brown, Elizabeth
1902, December 16th: William BROWN

Brown, Joyce
1945, March 17th: Cubia JONES &
Robert L PEARSON

Brown, Michael Swinton
1909, July 6th: Alexander
EDMUNSTONE

Brown, Thomas
1883, January 23rd: James BARRETT
& Sylvester POFF

Bryant, Frederick John
1936, July 15th: Charlotte BRYANT

Bulmer, Elizabeth
1889, January 1st: Charles BULMER

Bundy, Mabel Maud
1939, October 25th: Stanley Ernest
BOON & Arthur John SMITH

Bunting, Elizabeth
1885, August 17th: Thomas BOULTON

Burdey, Phillip
1874, December 28th: Hugh DALEY

Burge, Marguerite Beatrix
1943, July 10th: Charles Arthur
RAYMOND

Burgen, Effie
1895, December 3rd: Arthur
COVINGTON

Burke, Harry
1883, May 14th: Joseph BRADY
1883, May 18th: Daniel CURLEY
1883, May 28th: Michael FAGAN
1883, June 2nd: Thomas CAFFREY
1883, June 9th: Timothy KELLY

Burndt, Conrad
1899, January 3rd: John SCHNEIDER

Burnham, Alice
1915, August 13th: George Joseph
SMITH

Burrett, Ada
1900, October 3rd: William BURRETT

Burton, Andrew
1913, July 22nd: John Vickers AMOS

Burton, Elizabeth
1883, August 6th: James BURTON

Burton, Mary
1898, August 3rd: Thomas JONES

Burton, Rosilla Patience
1922, December 19th: William RIDER

Bury, Ellen
1889, April 24th: William Henry BURY

Busby, Percy
1948, February 19th: Walter John
CROSS

Butler, Florence
1916, August 16th: William Alan
BUTLER

Butler, Kate
1913, February 25th: George CUNLIFFE

Butler, Unity Anne
1907, November 5th: William George
Charles AUSTIN

Buxton, Alice
1961, September 7th: Hendryk NEIMASZ

Buxton, Herbert
1961, September 7th: Hendryk NEIMASZ

Byrne, Alice
1885, January 20th: Thomas PARRY
*Burns, ***

Byrne, PC Joseph
1886, February 8th: James BAKER,
James MARTIN & Anthony Ben
RUDGE

Cable, Jim
1893, August 10th: Charles SQUIRES

Calder, Jane
1898, March 14th: John HERDMAN
1898, March 12th

Caldwell, Eliza
1881, August 15th: Thomas BROWN

Caldwell, Eliza Augustine
1938, March 20th: Charles James
CALDWELL

Calladine, Albert
1923, August 8th: Albert BURROWS

Calladine, Elsie
1923, August 8th: Albert BURROWS

Calladine, Hannah
1923, August 8th: Albert BURROWS

Callan, Mary
1928, August 29th: Gerard TOAL

Cameron, Elsie
1925, April 22nd: John Norman
Holmes THORNE

Camp, George
1952, January 15th: Alfred BRADLEY

Campbell, Dilys
1950, March 29th: Piotr
MAKSIMOWSKI

Campbell, John
1877, August 21st: Patrick McGOVERN

Campbell, Walter
1889, March 11th: Jessie King

Campion, *
1904, April 14th: James CAMPION

Caplan, Freda
1920, January 6th: David CAPLAN

Caplan, Herman
1920, January 6th: David CAPLAN

Caplan, Maurice
1920, January 6th: David CAPLAN

Carey, James
1883, December 17th: Patrick
O'DONNELL

Carlam, Samuel
1883, May 8th: Patrick CAREY

Carter, Rhoda Ann
1893, December 5th: John CARTER

Carter, Clara
1912, December 10th: William Henry
BEAL

Cartledge, Helen
1929, April 4th: George Henry
CARTLEDGE

Cassidy, Mary
1884, August 19th: Peter CASSIDY

Cassidy, Rosemary Ann
1880, February 17th: William CASSIDY

Castle, Elizabeth
1932, April 28th: Thomas RILEY

Catterall, John Bernard
1950, March 28th: George KELLY

Cavendish, Lord Frederick
1883, May 14th: Joseph BRADY
1883, May 18th: Daniel CURLEY
1883, May 28th: Michael FAGAN
1883, June 2nd: Thomas CAFFREY
1883, June 9th: Timothy KELLY

Chadwick, Nancy Ellen
1949, January 12th: Margaret ALLEN

Chamberlain, Lilian Maud
1937, November 18th: John Thomas
ROGERS

Chambers, Emily
1902, December 4th: William
CHAMBERS

Chantrelle, Elizabeth
1878, May 31st: Eugene Marie
CHANTRELLE

Charlton, Lillian Jane
1907, August 7th: Charles
PATERSON

Charlton, Sarah
1875, December 23rd: Richard
CHARLTON

Cheeseman, Charlotte
1902, May 6th: George WOOLFE

Cheshire, Alice
1923, April 5th: Bernard POMROY

Chetwynd, Eliza (& mother Eliza & un-named daughter)
1902, December 30th: George PLACE

Chipperfield, Maria
1896, February 25th: Alfred CHIPPERFIELD

Chisholm, Margaret Jane
1904, August 2nd: George BREEZE

Chivers, Sarah
1911, June 20th: Arthur GARROD

Christie, Ethel
1953, July 15th: John Reginald Halliday CHRISTIE

Christofi, Hella
1954, December 15th: Styllou Pantopiou CHRISTOFI

Churchill, Samuel
1879, May 26th: Catherine CHURCHILL

Clark, Vera
1943, August 3rd: William QUAYLE

Clarke, Edward
1907, March 26th: Joseph JONES

Clarke, Frances
1926, March 16th: William Henry THORPE

Clarke, James
1926, December 9th: Henry McCABE

Clarke, John
1923, December 28th: John William EASTWOOD

Clarkson, Ruth
1937, February 4th: Max Mayer HASLAM

Clasby, Mary
1902, April 23rd: Thomas KEELEY

Claydon, Louisa
1901, December 13th: Alick CLAYDON

Clegg, Jill
1946, March 19th: Arthur CLEGG

Clifford, Florence
1894, January 2nd: William HARRIS

Clifford, Maud
1914, August 11th: Percy Evelyn CLIFFORD

Clover, Alice
1905, December 20th: Samuel CURTIS

Clover, Matilda
1892, November 15th: Thomas CREAM

Coates, Emily
1902, December 9th: Thomas FAIRCLOUGH-BARROW

Cobner, Robert
1943, March 12th: David COBB

Cock, Nicholas
1879, February 25th: Charles Frederick PEACE

Coe, John
1880, May 11th: John Henry WOOD

Cole, PC George
1884, October 6th: Thomas Henry ORROCK

Coleman, Stephen
1882, January 30th: Charles GERRISH
1882, January 31st

Collier, Kate
1937, August 12th: Horace William BRUNT

Collins, John
1910, February 22nd: Joseph WREN
1910, February 23rd

Collinson, Amy
1913, April 23rd: Walter William SYKES

Collinson, Amy
1928, April 10th: George Frederick Walter HAYWARD

Connelly, Michael
1953, January 26th: George Francis SHAW

Connely, Mary
1892, December 22nd: Thomas EDWARDS

Connor, Elizabeth
1893, January 18th: William McKEOWN

Convery, Catherine
1916, December 20th: Joseph DEANS

Coogan, Harry
1944, May 26th: Wiley HARRIS

Cook, Annie Farrow
1940, April 24th: William Charles
COWELL

Cook, Elsie
1928, December 11th: Trevor EDWARDS

Cooper, Catherine
1946, November 19th: Arthur
RUSHTON

Cooper, Catherine Elizabeth
1954, April 20th: Michael MANNING

Cooper, Mary Elizabeth
1949, June 21st: Bernard Alfred Peter
COOPER

Cope, Agnes
1945, June 15th: Aniceto MARTINEZ

Corbett, Ethel
1931, August 12th: William John
CORBETT

Cornish, Alice (Miss)
1919, July 10th: Henry PERRY

Cornish, Alice (Mrs)
1919, July 10th: Henry PERRY

Cornish, Marie
1919, July 10th: Henry PERRY

Cornish, Walter
1919, July 10th: Henry PERRY

Correll, Anne
1910, March 1st: George Henry PERRY

Corrigan, Mary
1874, January 5th: Thomas CORRIGAN

Cotterill, Annie
1913, December 31st: George Frederick
LAW

Cotton, Hannah
1898, December 21st: John COTTON

Cotton, Joanna
1875, April 19th: William TOBIN

Coulbeck, Annie
1920, March 10th: William WRIGHT

Coulson, Jane
1945, January 31st: Arthur THOMPSON

Coulson, Jane Ellen
1910, August 9th: John Roper COULSON

Coulson, Thomas
1910, August 9th: John Roper COULSON

Court, Beatrice Ann
1953, October 20th: John Owen
GREENWAY

Cox, Elizabeth
1917, December 19th: Thomas COX

Cox, Bernard
1893, September 2nd: James REILLY

Cox, Mark
1883, May 21st: Joseph WEDLAKE

Cox, Maureen Jones
1952, September 5th: John Howard
GODAR

Crabtree, Mary Illingworth
1926, April 13th: George SHARPES

Crawford, James
1915, December 1st: Young HILL

Crawley, Joseph
1892, March 17th: Frederick
EGGLESTON

Crawley, Joseph
1892, March 17th: Charles RAYNOR

Crawley, Patrick
1889, April 8th: Peter STAFFORD

Cree, William Ronald
1923, October 30th: Phillip MURRAY

Cremin, John
1960, December 22nd: Anthony
Joseph MILLER

Crippen, Belle
1910, November 23rd: Hawley Harvey
CRIPPEN

Crocker, Eileen
1941, November 12th: Lionel Rupert
Nathan WATSON

Crocker, Phyllis
1941, November 12th: Lionel Rupert
Nathan WATSON

Cronin, Thomas
1886, January 12th: John CRONIN

Cross, Laura
1888, January 10th: Phillip Henry
Eustace CROSS

Cross, Catherine
1894, March 27th: Walter SMITH

Cross, Isabella
1962, November 28th: James SMITH

Crossland, Ellen
1919, July 22nd: John CROSSLAND

Crossman, Maria
1892, March 22nd: Joseph WILSON

Crouch, William
1876, August 1st: James PARRIS

Crozier, Ann
1899, December 5th: Samuel CROZIER

Cruise, Tom
1882, December 4th: Bernard
MULLARKEY

Cudden, Christine Ruth
1950, March 8th: James Frank RIVETT

Cudworth, Eliza
1892, August 18th: Moses CUDWORTH

Cull, Jean Frances
1952, September 30th: Raymond Jack
CULL

Cullen, Eileen
1951, July 19th: Dennis Albert MOORE

Cullen, Sarah
1925, August 11th: James MAKIN

Curran, Margaret
1954, April 23rd: John LYNCH

Dainton, Hannah
1891, December 15th: Henry DAINTON

Dalby, John
1904, December 20th: Edmund HALL

Daly, Dennis
1889, August 7th: Lawrence Maurice
HICKEY

Daly, John
1903, January 7th: Joseph TAYLOR
1903, January 9th: Mary DALY

Daniels, Eliza
1880, November 22nd: William Joseph
DISTON
1880, November 27th

Darby, Elizabeth (& child)
1903, March 3rd: Edgar EDWARDS

Darby, John
1903, March 3rd: Edgar EDWARDS

Darwell, Jane
1920, December 30th: Edwin
SOWERBY

Davies, *
1890, August 26th: Frederick DAVIES

Davies, Emma Jane
1889, March 13th: Samuel RYLANDS

Davies, Nancy Anne
1913, February 4th: Eric James
SEDGEWICK

Davies, PC James
1885, May 25th: Moses SHRIMPTON

Davies, Richard
1890, April 8th: Richard DAVIES

Davies, Thomas
1888, March 13th: David REES

Davies, Walter
1890, April 15th: William Matthew
CHADWICK

Davis, Mary
1894, November 29th: Thomas
RICHARDS

Davis, Wilhelmina Vermadell
1937, July 27th: Philip Edward Percy
DAVIS

Dawes, John
1900, December 4th: Joseph HOLDEN

De Grave, Francois
1890, August 27th: Francois MONTEAU

Deacon, Amelia
1876, April 24th: Edward DEACON

Dean, George Charles
1953, January 2nd James John ALCOTT

Death, Maria
1869, December 13th: Frederick HINSON

Deeley, Iris Miriam
1944, June 6th: Ernest James Harman
KEMP

Deggan, Hubert Sydney
1935, April 2nd: Leonard Albert
BRIGSTOCK

Delaney, Alice
1888, August 10th: Arthur Thomas
DELANEY

Delvin, Elizabeth
1890, September 23rd: Henry
DELVIN

Demetriades, Savvas
1944, February 2nd: Christos
GEORGIOU

Dennehy, Cornelius
1939, January 7th: Dermot SMYTH

Dennis, Catherine
1892, January 5th: James STOCKWELL

Dennis, Florence
1894, December 4th: James Canham
READ

Derrick, Lucy
1879, May 12th: Edwin SMART

Devaney, June Ann
1948, November 19th: Peter GRIFFITHS

Deveney, Jeannie
1952, May 29th: Peter Gallagher
DEVENEY

Devereux, Beatrice
1905, August 15th: Arthur DEVEREUX

Devereux, Evelyn
1905, August 15th: Arthur DEVEREUX

Devereux, Lawrence
1905, August 15th: Arthur DEVEREUX

Dewar, David
1945, September 7th: Thomas Eric
RICHARDSON

Dewberry, Mary
1922, April 11th: Frederick Alexander
KEELING

Dews, Benjamin
1894, August 21st: Alfred DEWS

Dickinson, Anne
1885, November 23rd: John HILL &
John WILLIAMS

Dicksee, Christina Rose
1941, December 3rd: John Ernest
SMITH

Distleman, Harry
1941, October 31st: Antonio MANCINI

Dixon, Eliza
1899, November 21st: George NUNN

Dixon, Isaiah
1958, August 12th: Matthew
KAVANAGH

Dixon, Joseph
1933, June 20th: Richard
HETHERINGTON

Dixon, Joyce
1942, September 10th: Harold Oswald
MERRY

Dixon, Mary
1886, August 9th: Mary Ann BRITLAND

Dixon, Mary Ann
1920, March 23rd: William HALL

Dixon, Mary Ann
1933, June 20th: Richard
HETHERINGTON

Dixon, Robert
1921, June 7th: William MITCHELL

Djorovic, Radomir
1951, January 26th: Nenad KOVASEVIC

Dobkin, Rachel
1943, January 27th: Harry DOBKIN

Dobson, Margaret Jane
1938, May 26th: Robert William
HOOLHOUSE

Docherty, Patrick
1902, December 30th: James
DOCHERTY

Dockerty, Margaret
1876, December 21st: William
FLANAGAN

Dodd, Martha Anne
1958, December 17th: Brian
CHANDLER

Dodds, Mary Jane
1908, August 5th: Matthew John
DODDS

Dodge, Emma Holmes
1893, March 28th: William WILLIAMS

Dodsley, Mary
1955, May 2nd: James ROBINSON

Doggett, Alfred
1910, June 14th: James Henry
HANCOCK

Doherty, Hannah Margaret
1941, January 7th: David DOHERTY

Dollinson, William
1926, November 24th: James McHUGH

Doloughty, John
1882, September 11th: Francis HYNES

Donahoe, Daniel
1872, August 13th: Francis BRADFORD

Donnelly, Mary
1909, February 23rd: Jeremiah
O'CONNOR

Donovan, James
1895, February 9th: John TWISS

Donworth, Ellen
1892, November 15th: Thomas CREAM

Dorgan, Florence Elizabeth Agnes
1943, December 22nd: John Joseph
DORGAN

Douglas, Doris
1954, January 8th: Czeslaw KOWALSKI

Dowdle, Ellen
1899, December 6th: Michael DOWDLE

Doyle, Mary
1919, November 11th: James ADAMS

Drewatt, Inspector Joseph
1877, March 12th: Francis TIDBURY
& Henry TIDBURY

Drinkwater, Winifred
1923, January 3rd: George Frederick
EDISBURY

Duckett, Jane
1957, July 23rd: John Willson
VICKERS

Dudley, Florence
1913, January 29th: Edward HOPWOOD

Dugdale, Richard
1884, November 24th: Kay HOWARTH

Dunleavy, Martin
1950, October 30th: Paul Christopher
HARRIS

Dunn, Ada Elizabeth
1928, January 6th: John Thomas
DUNN

Dunne, Patrick
1870, May 27th: Lawrence SHEILD
& Margaret SHEILD

Dunphy, Eddie
1900, April 10th: Patrick DUNPHY

Dunphy, John
1900, April 10th: Patrick DUNPHY

Duplessis, John
1946, March 26th: Arthur CHARLES

Durand Deacon, Olive Henrietta
Helen Olivia Robarts
1949, August 10th: John George
HAIGH

Durkin, Joseph Harold
1918, March 5th: Verney ASSER

Durkin, Patrick
1905, December 6th: Henry PARKINS

Dutton, Henry
1946, April 24th: Martin Patrick
COFFEY

Dyson, Arthur
1879, February 25th: Charles
Frederick PEACE

Dyson, Elizabeth
1902, August 12th: William LANE

Eady, Muriel
1953, July 15th: John Reginald
Halliday CHRISTIE

Eagle, Jane
1895, November 19th: Richard
WINGROVE
1895, November 13th

Eayres, Sarah Ann
1914, November 10th: John Francis
EAYRES

Eblethrift, Emma
1876, August 29th: John EBLETHRIFT

Eckhart, Harriet Ann
1911, November 15th: Frederick
Henry THOMAS

Edge, Jane
1951, January 4th: Frank GRIFFIN

Edmunds, John
1880, May 10th: William DUMBLETON

Edwards, Rosanna
1872, August 13th: Christopher
EDWARDS
1872, August 12th

Elbrough, Florence
1894, April 4th: Frederick William
FENTON

Eley, Elizabeth
1910, July 14th: Frederick FOREMAN

Elias, Victor Desmond
1949, December 30th: Ernest Soper
COUZINS

Ellington, Elsie May
1940, March 27th: Ernest Edmund
HAMERTON

Ellis, Emma
1896, August 25th: Joseph Robert ELLIS

Ellor, Ada
1920, August 11th: James ELLOR

Elphick, Charles
1946, January 31st: Michael NIESCIOR

Evans, Frank
1905, December 27th: Frederick William
EDGE

Evans, Elizabeth Hannah
1887, November 28th: Enoch WADELY

Evans, Geraldine
1950, March 9th: Timothy John EVANS

Evans, Margaret
1922, April 18th: Edmund Hugh
TONBRIDGE

Evans, Winifred Mary
1945, March 13th: Arthur HEYS

Eves, Adam John
1893, August 16th: John DAVIS

Fairhurst, Rose Elizabeth
1955, April 14th: Sydney Joseph
CLARKE

Fairley, Albert Edward
1941, July 23rd: David Millar
JENNINGS

Faithfull, Angeline
1896, July 21st: Frederick BURDEN

Farmer, Matilda Emily
1904, December 13th: Conrad
DONOVAN & Charles WADE

Farnworth, Naomi
1932, May 18th: Charles James COWLE

Farrel, James
1921, April 26th: Thomas TRAYNOR
1921, April 25th

Farrell, Clara
1955, August 12th: Alec WILKINSON

Farrell, Margaret
1927, December 29th: William O'NEILL

Farrow, Anne
1905, May 23rd: Albert & Alfred
STRATTON

Farrow, Thomas
1905, May 23rd: Albert & Alfred
STRATTON

Fawcett, Esther Emily
1891, August 25th: Edward Henry
FAWCETT

Ferguson, Edward
1875, March 24th: John McDAID

Ferguson, Joseph
1901, December 7th: John MILLER &
John Robert MILLER

Fiddler, Dorothy
1875, August 16th: Mark FIDDLER

Field, Rosina
1937, August 17th: Frederick George
MURPHY

Fife, David
1883, May 23rd: Henry MULLEN &
Martin SCOTT

Firth, Elizabeth
1875, December 21st: William
SMEDLEY

Fishive, Patrick
1891, February 2nd: Bartholomew
SULLIVAN

Fitzgerald, Thomas
1923, November 29th: William DOWNES

Fitzsimmons, James
1888, April 28th: Daniel HAYES &
Daniel MORIARTY
1888, April 29th

Fitzsimmons, Maria
1882, May 16th: Thomas FURY

Flanagan, John
1904, December 22nd: Joseph FEE

Flanagan, Mary
1874, August 31st: Henry FLANAGAN

Fleming, Ellen
1934, January 5th: John FLEMING

Fletcher, Caroline
1911, December 15th: Joseph FLETCHER

Flew, Jane Elizabeth
1893, March 16th: Albert MANNING

Fontaine, Alice
1929, March 12th: Joseph Reginald Victor CLARKE

Fort, Winifred Ellen
1917, April 10th: Alexanda BAKERLIS

Fortune, John
1884, March 31st: William INNES & Robert Flockheart VICKERS

Foster, Alice
1904, July 13th: Samuel ROWLEDGE

Foster, Minnie
1919, July 31st: Thomas FOSTER

Foulson, John
1875, March 30th: John MORGAN

Fox, Charles
1933, December 28th: Stanley HOBDAY

Fox, Rosaline
1930, April 8th: Sydney Harry FOX

Franks, Solomon
1920, January 6th: Hyman PURDOVICH

Fraser, Duncan
1952, February 6th: Alfred MOORE

Freeman, Florence Lily
1909, December 7th: John FREEMAN

Fremd, Louisa
1914, November 4th: Charles FREMD

Friedson, Annette
1932, May 4th: Maurice FREEDMAN

Fuerst, Ruth
1953, July 15th: John Reginald Halliday CHRISTIE

Fullerton, Maggie
1922, August 11th: Elijah POUTNEY
1922, August 17th: Simon McGEOWN

Fullick, Mary Alice Maud
1939, October 10th: Leonard George HUCKER

Furlonger, Thomas
1890, June 10th: Daniel Stewart GORRIE

Gaffrey, James
1873, September 8th: James CONNOR

Galbraith, Mary
1912, December 29th: William Wallace GALBRAITH

Gale, Annie Sarah
1896, June 9th: William SEAMAN

Galley (un-named child)
1903, February 3rd: Amelia SACH & Annie WALTERS

Galloway, Florence
1878, February 4th: George PIGGOTT

Galloway, Samuel
1871, April 24th: Michael CAMPBELL

Gamble, Jane
1906, August 7th: Edward GLYNN

Gamble, Pearl
1961, December 20th: Robert Andrew McGLADDERY

Gann, Louise Berthe
1935, October 30th: Allan James GRIERSON

Gardner, Emily
1872, January 8th: Frederick JONES

Gardner, Lyle
1894, August 17th: John GILMOUR

Gardner, Margery
1946, October 16th: Neville George Clevely HEATH

Gardner, Mary Ann
1891, July 28th: Arthur SPENCER

Garner, Agnes
1894, April 3rd: Philip GARNER

Garret, Alice
1925, August 14th: William John CRONIN

Garret, Maud
1903, December 1st: Bernard WHITE

Gaskin, Elizabeth
1919, August 8th: Henry Thomas
GASKIN

Gayer, Bridget
1911, January 4th: William SCANLAN

Gear, Catherine
1907, November 20th: William
DUDDLES

Geraghty, Catherine
1906, February 27th: John
GRIFFITHS

Gerard, Emilienne
1918, March 2nd: Louis Marie Joseph
VOISON

Gerrard, Alice
1947, March 31st: Joseph McMANUS

Gibbons, Bridget
1892, August 17th: Patrick GIBBONS

Gibbons, Joseph
1949, January 27th: George SEMINI

Gibbs, Susan Ann
1874, August 24th: James Henry GIBBS

Gibson, William
1951, September 15th: Robert Dobie
SMITH

Giffard, Charles
1953, February 24th: Miles William
GIFFARD

Giffard, Elizabeth
1953, February 24th: Miles William
GIFFARD

Gilbert, Henry Colbert
1878, November 25th: Henry GILBERT

Gilbert, Mary
1904, March 29th: Henry JONES

Gill, Alfred
1932, April 28th: John Henry ROBERTS

Gilligan, Flora Jane
1953, July 30th: Philip HENRY

Gillon, Annie
1928, January 31st: James GILLON

Gillow, Arthur
1879, February 4th: Stephen GAMBRILL

Girl, Doris Eugenie
1940, October 31st: Stanley Edward
COLE

Glanville, Christine
1952, September 30th: Dennis George
MULDOWNEY

Glass, William
1873, August 26th: Thomas Hartley
MONTGOMERY

Gledhill, Theodora Jessie
1942, March 11th: Harold Dorian
TREVOR

Goddard, Martha Ann
1896, August 4th: Joseph HIRST

Godwin, Louisa
1874, May 25th: John GODWIN

Gold, Isaac
1881, November 29th: Percy LEFROY

Goodale, Bathsheba
1885, November 30th: Robert GOODALE

Goodman, Esther
1950, January 6th: Daniel RAVEN

Goodman, Leopold
1950, January 6th: Daniel RAVEN

Goodspeed, Ellen Maria
1905, June 20th: Alfred John HEAL

Goodwin, Private Albert
1898, April 5th: Wilfrid F KENNY

Gordon, George
1889, December 24th: William DUKES

Gordon, John
1946, April 6th: Patrick CARRAHER

Goslett, Evelyn
1920, July 27th: Arthur Andrew
GOSLETT

Gosling, Frederick
1951, April 25th: Joseph BROWN &
Edward Charles SMITH

Graham, Margaret Ann
1925, April 15th: Henry GRAHAM

Graham, Lucy
1879, March 24th: James SIMMS

Gray, Miriam Susan
1953, December 18th: John Francis
WILKINSON

Green, Betty
1945, January 8th: Ernest Lee CLARK & Augustine M GUERRA

Green, Emma
1876, December 20th: John GREEN

Green, Lydia
1887, April 18th: Thomas William CURRELL

Greenberg, Beatrice
1947, March 26th: Frederick William REYNOLDS

Gregory, Alice Clara
1916, December 12th: Fred BROOKS

Gregson, Ellen
1870, January 10th: John GREGSON

Gregsten, Michael
1962, April 4th: James HANRATTY

Greig, Alexander
1954, June 23rd: George Alexander ROBERTSON

Greig, Elizabeth
1954, June 23rd: George Alexander ROBERTSON

Grey, Samuel Hammond
1946, January 8th: William BATTY

Gribben, Charles
1914, March 24th: Robert UPTON

Grice, Sarah
1913, July 22nd: John Vickers AMOS

Grierson, Jemima
1923, June 11th: John Henry SAVAGE

Griffiths, Edith
1911, December 12th: Walter MARTYN

Griffiths, Lily
1945, September 5th: Howard Joseph GROSSLEY

Griffiths, QM Sergeant Samuel
1878, November 12th: Patrick John BYRNE

Griffiths, Sarah
1887, August 16th: Thomas Henry BEVAN

Grimshaw, George Stanley
1922, September 5th: William James YELDHAM

Grimstone, Thomas
1923, December 15th: Peter HYNES

Grossmith, Emma
1868, September 8th: Alexander Arthur MACKAY

Groves, John
1902, September 30th: John MacDONALD

Guest, Vera
1945, October 31st: Ronald Bertram MAURI

Gunn, Alexander
1889, March 11th: Jessie King

Gurney, Rose Ann
1911, December 21st: Charles COLEMAN

Gutteridge, George
1928, May 31st: Frederick Guy BROWNE & William KENNEDY

Guyan, Thomas
1963, August 15th: Henry John BURNETT

Hackett, George
1895, August 20th: Thomas BOND

Hackett, Mary
1954, April 22nd: Albert George HALL

Hag, Aminul
1938, June 8th: Jan MAHOMED

Hagan, Mary
1941, April 4th: Samuel MORGAN

Hale, Alice
1875, April 26th: William HALE

Hall, Polly
1881, May 23rd: James HALL

Hall, William
1924, July 30th: Abraham GOLDENBERG

Hallahan, Johanna
1952, July 22nd: Frank BURGESS

Halton, Alice
1877, August 13th: Henry LEIGH

Hamblin, Elizabeth
1884, December 8th: Ernest EWERSTADT

Hamblin, George
1935, March 13th: George Frank HARVEY

Hamilton, Evelyn Margaret
1942, June 25th: Gordon Frederick CUMMINS

Hamilton, Maude
1934, April 6th: Lewis HAMILTON

Hammerton, Frederick
1901, July 30th: Charles WATKINS

Hancock, *
1873, January 7th: Edward HANCOCK

Hancocks, Mary Elizabeth
1905, August 9th: William Alfred HANCOCKS

Hannaford, Clara
1909, March 30th: Edmund Walter ELLIOT

Harbor, Charlotte Alice
1928, November 20th: William Charles BENSON

Hardwick, Martha
1903, November 10th: Charles Jeremiah SLOWE

Harries, John
1954, April 28th: Thomas Ronald Lewis HARRIES

Harries, Phoebe Mary
1954, April 28th: Thomas Ronald Lewis HARRIES

Harris, Hannah
1884, October 6th: Thomas HARRIS
Harris, Ann
1911, July 19th: William Henry PALMER

Harris, Cecelia
1909, July 3rd: John EDMUNDS

Harris, Eileen
1952, February 26th: Herbert Roy HARRIS

Harris, Florence
1888, August 28th: Harry Benjamin JONES

Harrison, Hannah
1890, August 26th: James HARRISON

Harrison, Jane
1907, January 1st: John DAVIES

Harrison, John Joseph
1940, November 26th: William Henry COOPER

Hart, Irene
1937, February 10th: Andrew Anderson BAGLEY

Hartigan, Catherine
1906, November 27th: Edward HARTIGAN

Hastings, Emma
1888, August 28th: George Nathaniel DANIELS

Hatfield, Captain Stanley & crew
1876, May 23rd: Giovanni CACCARIS, Pascaler CALADIS, Matteo CORGALIS & George KADI

Hatton, Annie Elizabeth
1929, February 20th: Frank HOLLINGTON

Haynes, Ellen
1882, August 22nd: Thomas HAYNES

Haywood, Jane
1903, December 15th: William HAYWOOD

Healy, John
1910, May 25th: Thomas William JESSHOPE

Heaney, Mary Anne
1892, January 12th: James HEANEY

Hearne, Doreen
1942, May 1st: Harold HILL

Hearne, Elizabeth Ellen
1913, August 13th: Frank GREENING

Heath, George
1945, March 8th: Karl Gustav HULTEN

Hebdon, Sarah
1902, March 25th: Arthur RICHARDSON

Hemmings, Annie
1893, April 4th: Edward HEMMINGS

Hemstock, Teresa May
1932, April 27th: George Emmanuel MICHAEL

Henderson, Thomas
1910, July 12th: Thomas CRAIG

Henshaw, Hannah
1883, December 3rd: Henry DUTTON

Hepworth, Sophia Jane
1902, July 22nd: William CHURCHER

Herdman, Edward Frederick
1935, May 9th: John Stephenson
BAINBRIDGE

Hewitt, Sarah
1886, June 15th: Edward HEWITT

Hickey, James
1891, July 21st: Franz Joseph MUNCH

Hide, Reginald
1879, August 11th: Annie TOOKE

Higgins, Evelyn Patricia
1955, August 9th: Ernest Charles
HARDING

Higgins, John
1913, October 2nd: Patrick HIGGINS

Higgins, Thomas
1884, March 3rd: Catherine FLANAGAN
& Margaret HIGGINS
1884, March 5th

Higgins, William
1913, October 2nd: Patrick HIGGINS

Hill, Mary Jane
1911, October 17th: Edward HILL

Hill, Olga Davy
1944, March 16th: Ernest Charles DIGBY

Hillman, Dorothy Mary
1945, January 9th: Horace Beresford
GORDON

Hing, Go
1904, May 31st: Pong LUN

Hirst, Jane
1904, August 16th: John Thomas KAY

Hoard, Dudley Henry
1934, November 14th: John Frederick
STOCKWELL

Hodgkins, Martha
1914, March 10th: Josiah DAVIS

Hodgson, Margaret
1917, August 16th: William Thomas
HODGSON

Hodgson, Margaret Alderson
1917, August 16th: William Thomas
HODGSON

Hodgson, Louisa
1875, August 9th: Peter BLANCHARD

Hogan, Hannah (& child)
1879, January 10th: Thomas CUNCEEN

Hogan, Patrick
1923, December 12th: Thomas
DELANEY

Hogg, Phoebe (Miss)
1890, December 23rd: Mary Eleanor
WHEELER

Hogg, Phoebe (Mrs)
1890, December 23rd: Mary Eleanor
WHEELER

Holland, Camille
1903, July 14th: Samuel Herbert
DOUGAL

Holland, Emily
1876, August 14th: William FISH

Hollyer, Henry Arthur
1917, December 18th: William
CAVANAGH

Holmes, Maria
1872, August 12th: Charles HOLMES

Holmes, Annie
1898, June 28th: William HORSFORD

Holmes, Dorothy
1944, August 11th: Eliga BRINSON &
Willie SMITH

Holmes, Elizabeth
1880, November 16th: William
BROWNLESS

Holmes, Irene
1941, February 11th: Clifford HOLMES

Holmes, Peggy Agnes
1946, May 28th: Leonard HOLMES

Holmes-Conway, Bella
1916, March 29th: Reginald HASLAM

Holmyard, William
1929, February 27th: William John
HOLMYARD

Holt, Elizabeth Ann
1890, December 30th: Thomas
McDONALD

Holt, Evelyn Victoria
1931, June 3rd: Alexander
ANASTASSIOU

Hook, Julia
1889, December 31st: William
Thomas HOOK

Horry, Jane
1872, April 1st: William Frederick
HORRY

Horton, Charlotte Lyndsey
1886, February 1st: John HORTON

Horton, Edward
1886, February 1st: John HORTON

Horton, Katherine
1889, August 21st: George HORTON

Houghton, Dorcas
1899, July 18th: Charles MAIDMENT

Howard, Charles
1885, July 13th: Henry ALT

Howard, Jane
1920, June 16th: Frederick William
STOREY

Howe, Emma Elizabeth
1950, November 23rd: Norman
GOLDTHORPE

Howell, Clara
1909, March 12th: Thomas MEADE

Hubbard, Emily Violet
1912, December 18th: Alfred John
LAWRENCE

Huddy, John
1883, January 15th: Patrick HIGGINS
1883, January 17th: Michael FLYNN
& Thomas HIGGINS

Hudson, Elizabeth
1873, August 4th: Benjamin HUDSON
Hudson, Heseltine
1895, August 13th: Robert Heseltine
HUDSON

Hudson, Kate
1895, August 13th: Robert Heseltine
HUDSON

Huelin, Elias
1870, August 1st: Walter MILLAR

Hughes, Catherine
1923, July 24th: William GRIFFITHS

Hughes, Jane Hannah
1903, February 17th: William HUGHES
1903, February 18th

Hughes, Peter
1882, November 28th: Edward
WHEATFALL

Hughes, Sarah
1877, November 23rd: Cadwaller
JONES

Humphries, Susan
1904, August 16th: Samuel HOLDEN

Humphries, Thomas
1920, November 1st: Kevin Gerald
BARRY

Hunter, Priscilla
1914, June 16th: Walter James WHITE

Hussell, Mary
1877, November 19th: William
HUSSELL
Hassell, *
1877, November 19th: William
HASSELL

Hyland, John
1876, August 25th: Thomas CROWE

Ibraim, Ayesha (& daughter)
1920, April 14th: Thomas CALER

Idder, Hadjou
1905, August 1st: Ferat Mahomed
BENALI

Imlach, Alexander
1917, May 16th: Thomas McGUINESS

Imlay, Oliver Gilbert
1918, February 21st: Joseph JONES

Ings, Percival John
1887, May 16th: Henry William YOUNG

Inman, Constance
1932, February 3rd: George Alfred RICE

Insole, Sarah Anne
1887, February 21st: Richard INSOLE

Irwin, Catherine Amelia
1900, August 14th: William James
IRWIN

Jackson, Elizabeth
1874, August 18th: William JACKSON

Jackson, Olive
1921, May 24th: Thomas WILSON

Jacques, Joyce
1946, August 7th: Walter CLAYTON

Jagger, Arthur
1952, February 6th: Alfred MOORE

Jeal, Edith
1892, April 26th: George Henry WOOD

Jee, Alan
1960, November 10th: Francis Robert
FORSYTH & Norman James
HARRIS

Jenkins, Sarah
1874, January 12th: Edwin BAILEY
& Ann BERRY

Jenkins, Harry
1943, June 25th: Harold A SMITH

Jenkins, Mary
1910, December 29th: Henry ISON

Jennings, Eve
1927, December 6th: William Meynell
ROBERTSON

Jennings, Mary
1884, March 3rd: Catherine FLANAGAN
& Margaret HIGGINS
1884, March 5th

Jennings-Edmunds, Mabel
1923, November 1st: Frederick
William Maximillian JESSE

Jiminez, Jose
1884, March 10th: Michael McLEAN

John Kiegoam
1875, August 2nd: Michael
GILLINGHAM

Johnson, Anne Mary
1929, August 7th: James JOHNSON

Johnson, Frances
1915, December 1st: John James
THORNLEY

Johnson, John
1923, October 10th: Susan NEWELL

Johnson, Julia Ann
1917, April 18th: Robert GADSBY

Johnson, Louisa
1893, July 18th: Richard SABEY

Johnson, Sarah Ellen
1931, April 16th: Francis LAND

Jones, Ada
1913, March 19th: Edward Henry
PALMER

Jones, Alfred
1924, August 12th: Jean-Pierre
VAQUIER

Jones, Charlotte
1909, April 14th: Joseph Edwin JONES

Jones, Edward
1875, September 6th: Edward COOPER

Jones, Gwen Ellen
1910, February 15th: William MURPHY

Jones, John
1904, December 21st: Eric LANGE

Jones, Mary Jane
1894, February 13th: George THOMAS

Jones, Selina
1900, March 6th: Ada
CHARD-WILLIAMS

Jones, Winifred
1927, January 5th: William Cornelius
JONES

Jonston, Lily
1923, February 8th: William ROONEY

Jouannet, Doris
1942, June 25th: Gordon Frederick
CUMMINS

Joy, Emily
1889, March 6th: Ebeneezer Samuel
JENKINS

Joyce, Bridget
1882, December 15th: Patrick CASEY,
Miles JOYCE & Patrick JOYCE

Joyce, John
1882, December 15th: Patrick CASEY,
Miles JOYCE & Patrick JOYCE

Joyce, Detective Joseph
1892, August 16th: John George
WENZEL

Joyce, Michael
1882, December 15th: Patrick CASEY,
Miles JOYCE & Patrick JOYCE

Joyce, Peggy (Miss)
1882, December 15th: Patrick CASEY,
Miles JOYCE & Patrick JOYCE

Joyce, Peggy (Mrs)
1882, December 15th: Patrick CASEY, Miles JOYCE & Patrick JOYCE

Judge, Amy
1878, October 8th: Thomas SMITHERS

Judge, Jane
1886, November 16th: Patrick JUDGE

Jung, Hermann
1901, November 19th: Marcel FAUGERON

Jupe, Sarah
1894, December 12th: William ROGERS

Kay, Mary
1896, August 11th: Samuel WILKINSON

Kaye, Alice
1915, December 22nd: Harry THOMPSON

Kaye, Emily Beilby
1924, September 3rd: Patrick Herbert MAHON

Keasey, David
1957, December 4th: Dennis HOWARD

Keegan, Bernard
1898, January 14th: Patrick HESTOR

Keen, Ruby Anne
1937, August 13th: Leslie George STONE

Keenan, Mary Kate
1892, April 4th: James CAMPBELL

Kelly, *
1904, April 15th: John KELLY

Kelly, Annie
1887, August 1st: Alfred SOWERY

Kelly, Bernard
1899, January 10th: Thomas KELLY

Kelly, Minetta May
1924, January 2nd: Matthew Frederick Atkinson NUNN

Kemp, Florence
1885, January 13th: Horace Robert JAY

Kempson, Anne Louise
1931, December 10th: Henry Daniel SEYMOUR

Kemster, Elizabeth
1911, May 24th: Michael COLLINS

Kenealy, Mary
1899, March 28th: George ROBERTSON

Kennedy, Ann
1872, December 30th: Michael KENNEDY

Kennedy, Lucy
1911, December 6th: Michael FAGAN

Kenny, John
1883, December 18th: Joseph POOLE

Kent, Charlotte
1915, December 29th: John William McCARTNEY

Kent, Frederick
1889, April 10th: Thomas ALLEN

Ketley, Herbert Victor
1954, April 14th: James Reginald DOOHAN

Kew, PC John William
1900, August 16th: Charles Benjamin BACKHOUSE

Kewish, John (senior)
1872, August 1st: John KEWISH

Key, Ernest Percival
1939, March 29th: William Thomas BUTLER

Kidd, Mary
1874, December 29th: Robert TAYLOR

Kidd, Robert
1895, December 17th: Elijah WINSTANLEY

King, Mary (& 2 children)
1899, January 13th: Philip KING

Kirby, Emily
1929, January 4th: Charles William CONLIN

Kirby, Minnie Eleanor
1928, January 4th: Bertram KIRBY

Kirby, Thomas
1929, January 4th: Charles William CONLIN

Kirkaldie, Donald Alfred Richard
1945, December 21st: James McNICHOL

Kirwan, Lawrence
1943, June 2nd: Bernard KIRWAN

Kitchling, Florence
1928, April 12th: Frederick LOCK

Kneilands, Anne
1958, July 11th: Peter Thomas
Anthony MANUEL

Knight, Bridget
1893, July 10th: Edward LEIGH

Knight, Frances
1894, December 12th: Cyrus KNIGHT

Knight, Margaret Ellen
1941, September 4th: John SMITH

Knighton, Ada
1927, April 27th: William
KNIGHTON

Knowles, Amelia Elizabeth Ann
1945, January 30th: Andrew BROWN

Kunz, Jacob
1929, April 25th: John COX

Lace, *
1872, August 26th: William LACE

Lacy, Pauline
1900, August 21st: William LACY

Laight, Doris Sabine
1926, February 17th: Herbert BURROWS

Laight, Ernest
1926, February 17th: Herbert BURROWS

Laight, Robert
1926, February 17th: Herbert BURROWS

Lainton, Donald Haywood
1955, July 26th: Frederick Arthur CROSS

Lalcaca, Dr Cowas
1909, August 17th: Madar Dal
DHINGRA

Lambert, Annie
1909, December 14th: Samuel
ATHERLEY

Lambert, Charles William
1932, February 23rd: William Harold
GODDARD

Lambert, John
1909, December 14th: Samuel
ATHERLEY

Lambert, Matilda
1909, December 14th: Samuel
ATHERLEY

Lambert, Samuel
1909, December 14th: Samuel
ATHERLEY

Lane, Harriet
1875, December 21st: Henry
WAINWRIGHT

Langan, Charles
1875, September 6th: William BAKER

Last, Henry
1886, December 13th: George HARMER

Laurence, Nancy
1875, August 12th: Joseph Phillip
LE BRUN
1875, August 11th

Lawlor, Ellen
1899, January 7th: Patrick HOLMES

Lawrence, Bensley Cyrus
1889, January 2nd: Charles DOBELL
& William GOWER

Lawrence, Dorothy
1908, December 30th: Noah Percy
COLLINS

Lax, Elizabeth
1926, January 7th: Lorraine LAX

Lay, June Cynthia
1943, December 14th: Lee A DAVIS

Laycock, Maria (& 4 children)
1884, August 26th: Joseph LAYCOCK

Le Guen, Pierre
1907, February 19th: Thomas CONNAN

Leah, Louise
1926, November 16th: James LEAH

Lee, Minnie Freeman
1948, December 2nd: George RUSSELL

Lee, Sing
1923, January 5th: Lee DOON

Lee, Thomas
1928, August 3rd: George REYNOLDS

Leech, Nelson
1924, May 8th: Michael PRATLEY

Lefley, William
1884, May 26th: Mary LEFLEY

Legg, Margaret
1925, February 24th: William Grover
BIGNELL

Leggett, Sarah Jane
1902, November 12th: Patrick LEGGETT

Lehman, Margaret
1945, March 19th: James Herbert
LEHMAN

Lehmann, Waltraut
1949, September 28th: William Claude
Hobson JONES

Leigh, Christina
1883, February 12th: Abraham THOMAS

LeMaire, Eugenie
1951, October 24th: John O'CONNER

Lever, Harriet
1921, January 7th: George Edmund
Freeman Quentin LEVER

Levine, Abraham Harry
1950, March 30th: Walter SHARPE

Levine, Frances
1933, December 19th: William
BURTOFT

Levy, Jonathan Goodman
1896, June 9th: William SEAMAN

Lewis, Dai
1928, January 27th: Daniel
DRISCOLL & Edward
ROWLANDS

Lewis, May
1896, August 18th: Frank TAYLOR

Lieutand, Maggie Ann
1901, December 10th: John George
THOMPSON

Lindsay, Charlotte
1886, February 1st: John HORTON

Lines, PC William
1875, July 27th: Jeremiah CORKERY

Lingard, Lucy Margaret
1903, March 10th: Samuel Henry SMITH

Linney, Harriet
1936, December 16th: Christopher
JACKSON

Llewellyn, William Henry
1950, April 19th: Albert Edward
JENKINS

Lloyd, *
1897, August 18th: Thomas LLOYD

Loake, Elizabeth
1911, December 28th: George LOAKE

Lofty, Margaret
1915, August 13th: George Joseph
SMITH

Long, James
1948, November 24th: William M
GAMBON

Longhurst, Mary Victoria
1950, July 11th: George Finlay
BROWN

Longshaw, Edith
1934, October 9th: Harry TUFFNEY

Lord, Daniel
1877, August 21st: John GOLDING

Lovell, Sophia
1906, November 13th: Frederick
REYNOLDS

Lowe, Margaret Florence
1942, June 25th: Gordon Frederick
CUMMINS

Lowthian, Dennis
1904, July 12th: John SULLIVAN

Lucas, Cissie
1945, December 21st: John Riley
YOUNG

Lucas, Frederick
1945, December 21st: John Riley
YOUNG

Ludkin, Ellen
1951, July 19th: Alfred George
REYNOLDS

Luen, Maud
1903, July 7th: Charles HOWELL

Lyden, *
1882, September 22nd: Patrick
WALSH

Lyden, Martin
1882, September 22nd: Patrick WALSH

Lynas, Mary
1904, March 29th: James Henry
CLARKSON

Lynch, Bridget
1877, October 15th: John LYNCH

Lynch, Patrick
1873, August 16th: Laurence SMITH
1873, August 20th

Lynch, Sergeant Major Henry
1917, March 21st: Thomas CLINTON

Lyon, Kitty
1942, January 30th: Arthur PEACH

Lyons, Mary Ann
1892, April 19th: Daniel HANDLEY

Mabbots, William
1886, July 26th: William SAMUELS
1886, July 27th

Macauley, Margaret
1928, August 8th: William SMILEY

Macauley, Sarah
1928, August 8th: William SMILEY

Maclennan, Hectorina
1953, July 15th: John Reginald Halliday
CHRISTIE

Maguire, Ellen
1929, November 26th: John MAGUIRE

Major, Arthur
1934, December 19th: Ethel Lillie
MAJOR

Malcolm, Percy John
1882, April 28th: George Henry
LAMSON

Malone, Martin Joseph
1952, April 12th: James SMITH

Maloney, Kathleen
1953, July 15th: John Reginald Halliday
CHRISTIE

Manning, Nicholas
1874, August 31st: Mary WILLIAMS

Marmon, Doris
1896, June 10th: Amelia Elizabeth DYER

Marney, Joan Mary
1949, March 29th: James FARRELL

Marriot, Nellie
1915, August 10th: Walter MARRIOT

Marsh, Alice
1892, November 15th: Thomas CREAM

Marsh, Eliza
1906, December 27th: Walter MARSH

Marsh, Mary Ann
1881, May 17th: Albert MOORE

Marsh, Maud
1903, April 7th: George CHAPMAN

Marshall, Annie
1903, December 22nd: Charles William
ASHTON

Marshall, Doreen
1946, October 16th: Neville George
Clevely HEATH

Marshall, Emmanuel (& family)
1870, August 8th: John OWEN

Marshall, Mary Ann
1894, December 11th: Samuel George
EMERY

Marshall, Sally
1871, April 3rd: William BULL

Marsland, Elizabeth
1902, May 20th: Thomas MARSLAND

Martin, Beatrice Philomena
1925, December 15th: Samuel JOHNSON

Martin, Nicholas
1891, August 20th: John CONWAY

Martirosoff, Reuben
1946, April 2nd: Marion
GRONDKOWSKI & Henryk
MALINOWSKI

Masfen, William
1893, August 15th: John Thomas
HEWITT

Mason, Dorothy
1946, September 6th: David Baillie
MASON

Masset, Manfred
1900, January 9th: Louisa Josephine
MASSET

Massey, Margaret
1920, January 6th: Louis MASSEY

Massey, Ruth
1950, December 19th: Nicholas
Persoulious CROSBY

Mather, Ellen
1879, May 20th: William COOPER

Mather, Mona
1951, July 3rd: Jack WRIGHT

Matthews, Albert
1905, March 29th: Ernest HUTCHINSON

Matthews, Elsie
1896, July 21st: Philip MATTHEWS

Matthews, Mabel Elizabeth
1932, March 9th: George Thomas POPLE

Mayne, Annie
1919, January 7th: Benjamin Hindle
BENSON

Mays, Daisy Dorothy
1927, March 29th: James Frederick
STRATTON

Mays, Thomas
1877, November 20th: Henry MARSH

McCann, James
1930, April 8th: Samuel William
CUSHNAN

McCarthy, Mary
1941, April 23rd: Henry GLEESON

McCaughtrie, Robert
1883, May 23rd: Henry MULLEN &
Martin SCOTT

McClaughlin, Nellie
1961, July 25th: Samuel
McCLAUGHLIN

McCluskey, Catherine
1950, December 16th: James Ronald
ROBERTSON

McConnell, Sarah Ann
1905, April 10th: Harry WALTERS

McDermott, John
1932, December 29th: Patrick
McDERMOTT

McDiarmid, John
1884, March 31st: William INNES &
Robert Flockheart VICKERS

McDonald, Evelyn
1952, March 21st: Takir ALI

McDonald, Helen
1878, October 3rd: William McDONALD

McDonnell, Alice
1926, December 9th: Henry McCABE

McDonnell, Annie
1926, December 9th: Henry McCABE

McDonnell, Joseph
1926, December 9th: Henry McCABE

McDonnell, Peter
1926, December 9th: Henry McCABE

McEntire, Ellen
1881, May 31st: Joseph Patrick
McENTIRE

McGann, Rose
1904, January 5th: Joseph MORAN

McGhee, Caroline
1916, December 19th: James Howarth
HARGREAVES

McGill, Mary
1886, February 22nd: Owen McGILL

McGivern, Bridget
1901, January 11th: William WOODS

McGowan, *
1878, November 19th: James
McGOWAN

McGowan, Henry
1926, December 9th: Henry McCABE

McGraw, James
1908, May 12th: John RAMSBOTTOM

McGuiness, Ann
1879, February 11th: William
McGUINESS

McGuire, Mary
1897, June 7th: George PATERSON

McIntyre, Catherine
1948, February 6th: Stanislaw
MYSZKA

McKenna, Anne
1901, December 3rd: Patrick McKENNA

McKenna, Annie
1877, March 27th: John McKENNA

McKivett, Margaret
1875, April 19th: Alfred Thomas HEAP

McLeod, Neil
1947, January 30th: Albert SABIN

McLindon, Elizabeth
1946, November 1st: Arthur Robert
BOYCE

McShane, Mary
1876, August 21st: Steven McKEOWN

Mead, Charles
1952, October 9th: Peter Cyril JOHNSON

Meadows, Mary Elizabeth
1899, July 11th: Joseph Cornelius
PARKER

Meadows, Rose Margaret
1952, August 12th: Oliver George
BUTLER

Mears, Eliza Jane
1899, October 3rd: Frederick PRESTON

Meek, *
1883, November 13th: Thomas Lyons
DAY

Meek, Hilda
1935, October 29th: Raymond
BOUSQUET

Mellor, Ada
1900, August 16th: Thomas MELLOR

Mellor, Ann
1877, November 21st: Thomas GREY

Mellor, Ann
1881, February 21st: William STANWAY

Mellor, Annie
1900, August 16th: Thomas MELLOR

Mellor, Mary Jane
1892, December 20th: James MELLOR

Meredith, Alfred
1879, February 10th: Enoch WHISTON

Messenger, Doreen Primrose
1949, July 28th: Sydney Archibald
Frederick CHAMBERLAIN

Messenger, Jane
1880, December 13th: William
HERBERT

Messiter, Vivian
1930, April 22nd: William Henry
PODMORE

Metcalfe, William
1879, May 27th: John D'ARCY

Meyrick, Ann
1872, March 18th: Edward ROBERTS

Michaelson, Harry Saul
1949, April 21st: Harry LEWIS

Middleton, Hannah
1902, July 15th: Samuel MIDDLETON

Miles, Albert
1884, February 25th: Charles KITE

Miles, Sydney
1953, January 28th: Derek William
BENTLEY

Miller, James
1880, April 14th: Peter CONWAY

Miller, John
1870, October 4th: George CHALMERS

Miller, John
1875, October 5th: Patrick DOCHERTY

Miller, Mary
1888, May 15th: John Alfred GELL

Millstein, Annie
1912, March 6th: Myer ABRAMOVICH

Millstein, Solomon
1912, March 6th: Myer ABRAMOVICH

Milton, Bridget Nora
1943, November 19th: Terence CASEY

Minahan, Bridget
1885, December 7th: Daniel MINAHAN

Mitchell, William
1894, July 18th: Samuel ELKINS

Mitchell, Winifred Mary
1913, June 24th: William Walter
BURTON

Mohammed, Noorh
1925, September 4th: John KEEN

Mohan, Mary
1883, May 8th: Patrick CAREY

Mooney, Thomas
1875, August 2nd: William McHUGH

Moore, Alfred
1928, June 28th: Walter BROOKS

Moore, Elizabeth
1884, August 26th: James TOBIN
1884, August 24th

Moore, Ellen
1872, December 9th: Augustus ELLIOT

Moore, Fanny Adelaide
1907, April 2nd: Edwin James MOORE

Moore, Isabella
1927, September 2nd: Arthur HARNETT

Moore, Mary Anne
1872, August 13th: Thomas MOORE

Moore, Ruth Elizabeth
1918, December 17th: John William
WALSH

Moran, Joyce
1959, August 14th: Bernard Hugh
WALDEN

Moran, Mary Ellen
1891, May 19th: Alfred William
TURNER

More, Alice Catlove
1913, July 8th: Henry LONGDEN

Morgan, Martha
1896, February 4th: William James
MORGAN

Morgan, Alice
1951, May 8th: James INGLIS

Morgan, Mabel Ann
1913, January 13th: Albert RUMENS

Morgan, Richard
1875, January 4th: John McGRAVE &
Michael MULLEN

Morley, Elizabeth
1895, December 31st: Patrick MORLEY

Morris, Minnie
1912, November 5th: Robert
GALLOWAY

Morrison, Margaret
1900, December 27th: James Joseph
BERGIN

Morton, Frederick
1934, February 6th: Ernest BROWN

Mottram, Mary
1928, January 7th: Samuel CASE

Moulden, Sergeant Enos
1892, July 26th: John GURD

Moules, Leonard
1942, September 10th: Samuel
DASHWOOD & George
SILVEROSA

Mowbray, William (& family)
1873, March 24th: Mary Ann COTTON

Moylan, John
1885, January 16th: Michael DOWNEY

Moyse, Edward
1895, June 4th: William MILLER

Mulholland, Maud
1914, March 25th: Edgar Lewis BINDON

Mulligan, Kenneth Joseph George
1954, August 12th: Harold FOWLER

Mundy, Beatrice
1915, August 13th: George Joseph
SMITH

Munro, Irene
1921, February 4th: Jack Alfred
FIELD & William Thomas GRAY

Murphy, Margaret
1870, July 28th: Andrew CARR

Murphy, Patrick
1942, September 2nd: Thomas Joseph
WILLIAMS

Murphy, Ronald John
1944, April 13th: Sydney James
DELASALLE

Musa, Achmet
1932, January 13th: Edward CULLENS

Mussell, George
1913, July 22nd: John Vickers AMOS

Mussow, Fanny
1881, August 23rd: George DURLING

Nagi, Jane
1923, August 8th: Hassan MUHAMED

Nash, Martha Ann
1886, March 1st: Thomas NASH

Neal, Theresa
1890, March 26th: John NEAL

Nelson, Rita
1953, July 15th: John Reginald Halliday
CHRISTIE

Newell, Isabella
1894, December 10th: John William
NEWELL

Newbury, James
1870, March 28th: William MOBBS

Newing, Grace Ivy
1933, October 11th: Robert James KIRBY

Newitt, John C   Victim Index   Palfrey, Mary M

Newitt, John Cox
1874, March 30th: Thomas
CHAMBERLAIN
1874, March 31st

Newman, Ellen
1903, December 8th: James DUFFY

Newton, John
1883, May 7th: Thomas GARRY

Nicholson, Frances
1913, April 23rd: Walter William
SYKES

Nicholson, Mary Ann
1889, January 8th: George
NICHOLSON

Nield, Thomas
1875, March 30th: John STANTON

Nightingale, Elizabeth
1890, July 29th: George BOWLING

Nightingale, Lily
1949, December 14th: John WILSON

Nightingale, Lucy
1919, October 7th: Frank George
WARREN

Nisbet, John Innes
1910, August 9th: John Alexander
DICKMAN

Nisbett, Lesley Jean
1954, April 23rd: John LYNCH

Norman, Ellen
1885, October 5th: Henry NORMAN

Northcliffe, Kathleen
1952, December 12th: Eric
NORTHCLIFFE

Nott, Bessie
1935. June 25th: Arthur Henry
FRANKLIN

Nugent, John
1901, August 20th: John JOYCE

Nurney, Patrick
1869, March 29th: Michael James
JOHNSON

Nuttall, Amelia
1935, May 30th: John Harris BRIDGE

Oakley, Annie Emma
1892, October 11th: John James
BANBURY

Oakley, Mary
1902, December 4th: William
CHAMBERS

Oatley, Evelyn
1942, June 25th: Gordon Frederick
CUMMINS

O'Brien, Dennis
1944, December 1st: Charles KERINS

O'Connor, Thomas
1921, December 22nd: Edward
O'CONNOR

O'Donnell, Elizabeth
1876, December 11th: Charles
O'DONNELL

O'Dwyer, Sir Michael Francis
1940, July 31st: Udham SINGH

Officer, Nellie
1954, September 1st: Rupert Geoffrey
WELLS

O'Halloran, Patrick
1924, August 1st: Felix McMULLEN

O'Keefe, John
1883, April 30th: Timothy O'KEEFE

Oldham, Sarah Ann
1895, March 26th: Edmund KESTEVEN

O'Leary, Patrick
1925, July 28th: Cornelius O'LEARY

Oliver, Constance Gertrude
1928, January 6th: Sydney Bernard
GOULTER

O'Rourke, Frances
1902, March 18th: Harold APTED

Osbourne, Emma Elizabeth
1877, August 14th: Caleb SMITH

O'Shea, Eliza
1899, November 28th: Charles SCOTT

O'Shea, Maureen
1943, August 12th: William O'SHEA

Ostliff, Imeldred Maria
1942, June 24th: Douglas EDMONDSON

O'Sullivan, Ellen
1931, August 4th: David O'SHEA

Palfrey, Mary May
1925, April 2nd: George William
BARTON

Palmer, Emma
1885, March 17th: Henry KIMBERLEY

Palmer, Lily
1950, July 13th: Ronald Douglas
ATWELL

Pamphilon, Margaret
1902, April 29th: Charles Robert EARL

Pankorski, Boleshar
1933, August 10th: Varnavas Loizi
ANTORKA

Parker, Edith May
1930, June 11th: Albert Edward
MARJERAM

Parker, James Stanley
1886, May 31st: Albert Edward BROWN

Parker, Jane Ann
1938, July 26th: William PARKER

Parker, Lily
1933, December 6th: Ernest Wadge
PARKER

Parkin, Alison
1948, January 7th: George Henry
WHELPTON

Parkin, Joyce
1948, January 7th: George Henry
WHELPTON

Parkin, Maurice
1948, January 7th: George Henry
WHELPTON

Parry, Lily
1960, September 1st: John Louis
CONSTANTINE

Parry, Sylvina May
1948, December 9th: Clifford Godfrey
WILLS

Parton, Eliza
1879, May 28th: Thomas JOHNSON

Partridge, James
1874, January 5th: Edward GOUGH

Pastor, Lizzie
1892, January 12th: Frederick Thomas
STOREY
1891, January 11th

Patchett, Sarah Anne (aka Garner)
1903, July 28th: Leonard PATCHETT

Patrick, Elizabeth Ann
1909, December 8th: Abel ATHERTON

Patterson, John
1908, March 24th: Joseph William
NOBLE

Pavey, Frances Florence
1922, December 13th: George
ROBINSON

Payne, Corporal Robert
1896, July 21st: Samuel Edward SMITH

Payne, Jessie
1933, February 2nd: Jeremiah
HANBURY

Payne, Nora Emily
1944, August 8th: William Alfred
COWLE

Pearce, Nellie
1923, July 4th: Rowland DUCK

Pearcey, Charlotte
1893, July 19th: Amie Holman
MEUNIER

Pearson, Alice
1920, May 11th: Herbert Edward
SALISBURY

Pearson, Nellie
1943, February 10th: Ronald ROBERTS

Pearson, William
1901, March 19th: George Henry
PARKER

Penfold, Sarah Ann
1898, December 13th: Thomas DALEY
1898, December 14th

Penny, Mary Matilda
1913, November 26th: Augustus John
PENNY

Pentecost, Peggy Irene
1939, March 25th: Harry ARMSTRONG

Pepper *
1880, January 5th: Charles SURETY

Pepper, Annette
1943, September 24th: Charles Eugene
GAUTHIER

Pepper, William
1882, May 23rd: Osmond Otto BRAND

Percey, James William
1944, July 26th: James GALBRAITH

Percival, James Irwin
1939, February 8th: John DAYMOND

Perree, John
1959, October 9th: Francis Joseph
HUCHET

Perry, Emma
1923, March 28th: George PERRY

Peters, Dagmar
1947, March 18th: Harold HAGGER

Phillips, Amelia
1874, January 12th: Charles Edward
BUTT

Phillips, Bernard
1946, April 9th: Harold BERRY

Phillips, Irene May
1949, March 22nd: Kenneth STRICKSON

Phillips, Margaret
1911, December 14th: Henry PHILLIPS

Phillips, Mary Jane
1889, January 14th: Arthur McKEOWN

Phillips, Winifred Whittaker
1890, January 7th: Charles Lister
HIGGENBOTHAM

Philp, Rose
1912, October 1st: Sargent PHILP

Pickerill, George
1888, March 28th: William
ARROWSMITH

Pickering, Jane
1892, June 14th: Henry PICKERING

Pickles, Sarah
1897, August 17th: Walter ROBINSON

Pickup, John Kirby
1898, February 22nd: George William
HOWE

Pike, Mary
1904, May 31st: William KIRWAN

Pilkington, Eleanor
1928, January 3rd: Frederick FIELDING

Pinchin, Norman
1924, August 13th: John HORNER

Pionbini, Augusta Violette
1926, July 27th: Johannes Josephus
Cornelius MOMMERS
1926, June 27th

Plommer, William
1925, September 3rd: Wilfred FOWLER
1925, September 4th: Lawrence
FOWLER

Plunkett, Jane
1882, May 22nd: William George
ABIGAIL

Poole, Edith
1900, July 17th: Alfred HIGHFIELD

Poskitt, Marian
1949, June 2nd: Dennis NEVILLE

Prentice, Ivy
1922, December 13th: Frank FOWLER

Prescott, Ida
1920, June 22nd: William Thomas
ALDRED

Preston, Oliver
1931, February 4th: Frederick GILL

Price, Gladys
1950, August 16th : Albert PRICE

Price, Nancy
1902, July 30th: John BEDFORD

Pritchard, Annie
1893, January 10th: Andrew George
McCRAE

Puddipant, William
1892, March 17th: Frederick
EGGLESTON & Charles RAYNOR

Pugsley, Henry
1914, November 10th: Henry
QUARTLEY

Pull, Henry
1961, May 26th: Victor John TERRY

Pullen, James
1934, May 3rd: Reginald Ivor HINKS

Purcell, Emily
1889, December 9th: Benjamin
PURCELL

Purdy, Ray
1959, November 5th: Guenther Fritz &
Erwin PODOLA

Pyle, Thomas
1883, November 19th: Peter BRAY

Quinn, Bernard
1923, April 3rd: Daniel CASSIDY

Quinn, Elizabeth
1919, November 26th: Ambrose QUINN

Quinn, Kate
1887, February 15th: Thomas
LEATHERBARROW

Quinn, Patrick
1884, January 15th: Peter WADE

Quinn, Rebecca
1919, November 26th: Ernest Bernard
SCOTT

Quirke, Patrick
1888, May 7th: James KIRBY

Radcliffe, Annie
1881, November 28th: John Aspinall
SIMPSON

Ramsbottom, Emily
1909, August 3rd: Mark SHAWCROSS

Range, Ellen
1903, December 2nd: Charles Wood
WHITTAKER

Rasch, Sophia Frederika
1894, August 14th: Paul KOEZULA

Rawcliffe, Louisa Ann (& 3 children)
1910, November 15th: Thomas
RAWCLIFFE

Raynor, Josephine
1943, March 31st: Dudley George
RAYNOR

Reaney, Elizabeth
1924, June 18th : William Horsley
WARDELL

Redford, Esther
1902, December 2nd: Henry
McWIGGINS

Redmond, James
1937, June 17th: John HORNICK

Reed, Alice
1928, July 25th: Albert George
ABSALOM

Reed, Christine
1953, December 22nd: Alfred Charles
WHITEWAY

Rees, Mary Ann
1909, May 8th: William Joseph FOY

Reeve, Annie
1915, November 16th: William
Benjamin REEVE

Regan, William
1905, April 25th: John FOSTER

Reid, Minnie
1933, April 7th: Harold COURTNEY

Reilly, Mary
1899, January 13th: Philip KING

Relfe, Emma
1876, December 14th: Robert
BROWNING

Rettig, Gerhardt
1945, November 16th: Arnim
KUEHNE & Emil SCHMITTENDORF

Revell, Hester
1878, July 29th: Charles Joseph REVELL

Reynolds, Beatrice Maud
1944, October 12th: Madison THOMAS

Reynolds, Charles
1895, December 24th: Henry WRIGHT

Reynolds, William Henry
1895, December 24th: Henry WRIGHT

Rice, Margaret Mary
1942, October 28th: William Ambrose
COLLINS

Richards, Edward Charles Ingram
1926, March 2nd: Ignatius Emanuel
Nathanial LINCOLN

Richards, Esther Harriet
1909, July 9th: Walter DAVIS

Richards, Kathleen
1938, July 12th: Alfred Ernest
RICHARDS

Richardson, George
1886, May 31st: James WHELAN

Ricketts, Sarah Ann
1953, September 18th: Louisa May
MERRIFIELD

Rickus, Elizabeth Jane
1905, February 28th: Edward
HARRISON

Riley, Ann
1920, November 30th: James RILEY

Riley, Annie
1931, December 15th: Solomon
STEIN

Rimmer, Beatrice
1952, April 25th: Alfred BURNS &
Edward Francis DEVLIN

Ritchie, John Alex
1945, December 29th: Robert BLAINE

Rix, Frank Edward
1925, August 14th: Arthur Henry
BISHOP

Roadley, Richard Francis
1928, July 27th: William John
MAYNARD

Roberts, Alice Kate
1951, April 26th: James VIRRELS

Roberts, Doris Acquilla
1955, August 2nd: Corbett Montague
ROBERTS

Roberts, Mary Georgina
1955, July 12th: Kenneth ROBERTS

Robertson, Nellie Kathleen
1913, November 27th: Frederick
Albert ROBERTSON

Robinson, Florence
1897, August 17th: Joseph ROBINSON

Robinson, James
1893, December 6th: George MASON

Robinson, Jane Eliza
1881, February 28th: Albert ROBINSON

Rockington, Eliza Frances
1877, November 12th: Thomas
Benjamin PRATT

Rodden, Eliza
1879, December 3rd: Henry
BEDINGFIELD

Roe, Elsie
1943, August 3rd: Gerald Elphinstone
ROE

Rogers, Ellen
1923, December 12th: Thomas
McDONAGH

Rogers, Martha
1887, November 21st: Joseph MORLEY

Rogers, Ruth
1925, April 15th: Thomas Henry
SHELTON

Rogers, Sarah
1877, July 31st: Henry ROGERS

Rogerson, Mary
1936, May 21st: Buck RUXTON

Roker, Ada
1911, January 31st: George NEWTON

Rooney, Mary Ellen
1918, December 17th: William ROONEY

Rose, Isabella
1919, February 19th: Joseph ROSE

Rose, Mary
1896, August 11th: John ROSE

Rose, Sarah
1919, February 19th: Joseph ROSE

Rosterg, Wolfgang
1945, October 6th: Heinz BRUELING
& Joachim GOLTZ & Erich Pallme
KOENIG & Josef MERTENS & Kurt
ZUEHLSDORFF

Rowe, Monica
1937, July 27th: Philip Edward Percy
DAVIS

Rowe, William
1963, December 17th: Russell PASCOE
& Dennis John WHITTY

Royce, Ada
1952, July 8th: Harry HUXLEY

Ruffle, Tony
1938, July 19th: William James GRAVES

Rushby, Harriet
1893, December 19th: Henry RUMBOLD

Rushworth, un-named child
1935, January 1st: Frederick
RUSHWORTH

Russell, Amy
1901, August 13th: Ernest Walter
WICKHAM

Ruxton, Isabella
1936, May 21st: Buck RUXTON

Ryan, John
1871, August 17th: William COLLINS

Ryder, Elizabeth Ann
1913, August 13th: James RYDER

Sandford, William
1875, April 9th: John RUSSELL

Sargent, Annie
1888, August 15th: George SARGENT

Saunders, Dorothy May
1920, November 30th: Cyril Victor
Tennyson SAUNDERS

Saunders, Esther Susannah
1886, February 16th: George
SAUNDERS

Saunders, Maria
1877, April 17th: Frederick Edwin
BAKER

Saxton, Neil
1959, August 14th: Bernard Hugh
WALDEN

Schlitte, Frederick
1909, January 6th: John Esmond
MURPHY

Scollen, Beatrice Barbara
1940, December 24th: Edward SCOLLEN

Scott, Betty
1882, February 13th: Richard
TEMPLETON

Scott, Robert
1898, August 30th: Joseph LEWIS

Scrivener, Henry Ernest
1874, June 29th: Frances STEWART

Seabrook-Evans, Annie
1873, August 4th: Henry EVANS

Senior, Henry
1920, May 26th: Albert James FRASER
& James ROLLINS

Seymour, Mary
1911, May 9th: Thomas SEYMOUR

Sharp, Amanda
1935, July 16th: George HAGUE

Sharp, Percy
1924, April 8th: Francis Wilson
BOOKER

Shaughnessy, Marie Alexine
1951, May 9th: William Edward
SHAUGHNESSY

Shaw, Captain Alexander (& crew)
1903, June 2nd: Gustav RAU &
Willem SCHMIDT

Shaw, Ellen
1884, December 8th: Arthur SHAW

Shee, Hannah
1902, December 12th: Jeremiah
CALLAGHAN

Sheehan, Christine
1886, January 20th: William SHEEHAN

Sheehan, Hannah
1886, January 20th: William SHEEHAN

Sheehan, Thomas
1886, January 20th: William SHEEHAN

Shenton, Dennis John
1955, March 29th: William Arthur SALT

Shenton, George
1920, December 31st: Charles
COLCLOUGH

Shepherd, Ada
1880, December 13th: George PAVEY

Sherrat, Elizabeth
1925, September 3rd: Alfred Davis
BOSTOCK

Sheung, Wai
1928, December 6th: Chung Yi MIAO

Sheward, Martha
1869, April 20th: William SHEWARD

Shiell, William Ralph
1940, July 11th: William APPLEBY &
Vincent OSTLER

Short, Frances
1899, May 3rd: Frederick James
ANDREWS

Short, Harry
1903, May 13th: William George
HUDSON

Shorter, PC Thomas
1877, March 12th: Francis TIDBURY
& Henry TIDBURY

Shrivell, Emma
1892, November 15th: Thomas
CREAM

Shufflebotham, Elizabeth
1901, April 2nd: Joseph Arthur
SHUFFLEBOTHAM

Siddle, Gertrude
1908, August 4th: Thomas SIDDLE

Silk, Mary (aka Fallon)
1905, December 29th: John SILK

Simmons, Inspector Thomas
1885, May 18th: James LEE

Simon, Andrew
1910, December 21st: Noah WOOLF

Simon, Eunice
1952, October 23rd: Donald Neil
SIMON

Simpson, Martha
1904, April 5th: Charles Samuel DYER

Skevington-Coppen, Emma
1874, October 13th: John Walter
COPPEN
Skullen, Arthur
1869, October 11th: William TAYLOR

Sloan, Margaret
1876, May 31st: Thomas BARR

Sloper, Eileen
1876, December 19th: Silas BARLOW

Sloper, Ellen
1876, December 19th: Silas BARLOW

Smail, Maggie
1942, April 15th: Cyril JOHNSON

Small, Stephanie Marie
1952, December 17th: John Kenneth
LIVESEY

Smart, George Frederick
1954, June 17th: Kenneth GILBERT
& Ian Arthur GRANT

Smith, Adeline
1961, February 9th: George RILEY

Smith, Bridget
1891, March 13th: John PURCELL

Smith, Catherine
1926, August 10th: James SMITH

Smith, Christina
1921, April 5th: Frederick QUARMBY

Smith, Elizabeth
1942, March 25th: David Roger
WILLIAMS

Smith, Elizabeth Selina
1954, January 26th: Desmond Donald
HOOPER

Smith, Henry
1896, June 9th: Henry FOWLER &
Albert MILSOM

Smith, Henry
1900, May 22nd: Henry GROVE

Smith, Jane
1878, August 12th: Thomas
CHOLERTON

Smith, John
1926, July 15th: James MYLES

Smith, John Barclay
1908, March 5th: Joseph HUME

Smith, Lucy
1887, May 9th: Charles SMITH

Smith, Lucy
1901, February 19th: Sampson Silas
SALMON

Smith, Martha
1905, December 28th: George SMITH

Smith, Mary Ann
1898, March 22nd: Charles SMITH

Smith, Maud
1893, July 25th: George Samuel COOK

Smith, Rosabella
1912, November 26th: Gilbert Oswald
SMITH

Smith, Rose
1926, March 9th: Henry THOMPSON

Smith, William
1884, May 27th: Joseph LAWSON

Songhurst, Barbara
1953, December 22nd: Alfred Charles
WHITEWAY

Southgate, Elizabeth
1924, November 27th: Frederick
SOUTHGATE

Spellar, Mary Elizabeth
1911, December 19th: George William
PARKER

Spevick, Margaret Rose Louise
1954, August 11th: William Sanchez
de Pina HEPPER

Spicer, Henry
1890, August 22nd: Felix SPICER

Spicer, William
1890, August 22nd: Felix SPICER

Spinks, Mary
1903, April 7th: George CHAPMAN

Spooner, Elizabeth
1914, May 14th: Joseph SPOONER

Springhall, Harry
1886, February 10th: John
THURSTON

Sproull, William
1909, May 20th: Marks REUBENS &
Morris REUBENS

Squires, *
1893, August 10th: Charles SQUIRES

Squires, Clara
1925, November 12th: Hubert George
BLOYE

Standley, Elizabeth Mary
1933, June 8th: Jack Samuel PUTTNAM

Staples, Doris
1944, February 10th: John H WATERS

Starkey, Alice Ruth
1877, July 31st: John Henry STARKEY

Starr, Mary Hannah
1903, December 29th: Henry Bertram
STARR

Staunton, Ella Valentine
1946, July 17th: Thomas HENDREN

Staunton, James
1927, August 3rd: Frederick Stephen
FULLER & James MURPHY

Steele, Isabella
1887, November 14th: William HUNTER

Steers, Walter Charles
1891, December 23rd: Charles
SAUNDERS

Stelfox, Edward
1876, April 25th: Joseph WEBBER

Stephens, Frank
1890, March 11th: Joseph BOSWELL
& Samuel BOSWELL

Stevens, Elizabeth
1894, May 22nd: John LANGFORD

Stewart, Mary
1902, December 16th: Thomas
NICHOLSON

Stills, Rachel
1907, December 13th: George STILLS

Stock, George
1872, August 13th: James TOOTH

Stodhart, Ada
1887, August 22nd: Henry HOBSON

Stone, Ada
1914, July 28th: Herbert BROOKER

Straiton, James
1946, August 10th: John CALDWELL

Sullivan, Abigail
1892, March 1st: James MUIR

Sullivan, Catherine
1916, September 6th: Daniel SULLIVAN

Summerfield, Nora
1959, April 28th: Joseph CHRIMES

Summers, Ray
1959, May 8th: Ronald Henry
MARWOOD

Surgey, Louisa
1961, January 27th: Wasyl GNYPIUK

Sutton, Annie
1887, March 21st: Joseph KING

Sutton, Beatrice Vilna
1936, June 30th: Frederick Herbert
Charles FIELD

Sutton, Henry
1887, March 21st: Joseph KING

Swainson, Edith Anne
1920, April 16th: Miles McHUGH

Swann, William
1903, December 29th: John
GALLAGHER & Emily SWANN

Sweeney, Geraldine
1943, December 29th: Thomas JAMES

Swift, Maria Elizabeth
1892, March 29th: John NOBLE

Swinford, Esther
1903, November 17th: Edward
Richard PALMER

Sykes, Sarah Ann
1925, May 26th: Patrick POWER

Tam, Catherine
1926, March 23rd: Lock Ah TAM

Tam, Cecilia
1926, March 23rd: Lock Ah TAM

Tam, Doris
1926, March 23rd: Lock Ah TAM

Tandy, Henry
1953, December 23rd: George James
NEWLANDS

Tarkenter, Rosetta
1911, December 12th: John Edward
TARKENTER

Tate, Jean
1955, May 4th: Winston SHAW

Tattersall, Rebecca
1905, August 15th: Thomas George
TATTERSALL

Tattershaw, Mabel
1951, December 11th: Herbert Leonard
MILLS

Taylor, Bessie
1903, April 7th: George CHAPMAN

Taylor, Caroline Elizabeth
1882, December 12th: Charles TAYLOR

Taylor, Charlotte
1887, December 6th: Thomas PAYNE

Taylor, Ida
1926, January 5th: John FISHER

Taylor, Maria
1892, August 16th: James TAYLOR

Taylor, Robert
1950, July 7th: Zbigniew GOWER &
Roman REDEL

Teichmann, Eric
1945, May 8th: George Edward SMITH

Terry, Mary
1887, February 22nd: Benjamin TERRY

Thomas, Charles
1910, March 24th: William BUTLER

Thomas, Clara
1916, January 1st: Lee KUN

Thomas, David
1886, March 2nd: David ROBERTS

Thomas, Joan Marion
1952, May 7th: Ajit SINGH

Thomas, John David
1952, December 24th: Herbert APPLEBY

Thomas, Julia
1879, July 29th: Catherine WEBSTER

Thomas, Leonard
1950, March 28th: George KELLY

Thomas, Margaret
1922, March 23rd: William SULLIVAN

Thomas, Marie Beddoe
1926, March 9th: George THOMAS

Thomas, Mary
1910, March 24th: William BUTLER

Thompson, Annie
1909, August 19th: Richard JUSTIN

Thompson, Ellen
1922, May 30th: Hyram THOMPSON

Thompson, Jane
1874, January 5th: William THOMPSON

Thompson, John Richard
1926, August 12th: Charles Edward
FINDEN
1926, August 11th

Thompson, Mary
1910, November 22nd: Henry
THOMPSON

Thompson, Percy
1923, January 9th: Frederick Edward
Francis BYWATERS & Edith Jessie
THOMPSON

Thorpe, Nellie
1941, December 23rd: Thomas
William THORPE

Thrussel, William
1876, April 10th: George HILL

Tickner, Harriet
1895, July 2nd: Henry TICKNER

Tighe, Edward
1918, February 12th: Arthur Harry
Victor DE STAMIR

Tindale, Lily
1917, March 27th: John William
 THOMPSON

Tinsley, Mona
1937, December 30th: Frederick
 NODDER

Tomkins, Thomas
1908, December 15th: Henry Taylor
 PARKER

Tomlinson, Violet
1889, March 11th: Jessie KING

Torr, Margaret Ann
1899, August 9th: Elias TORR

Tracey, Patrick
1880, March 2nd: Hugh BURNS
 & Patrick KEARNS

Trainer, Philip
1869, March 22nd: John McCONVILLE
1869, March 23rd

Treasure, un-named child
1907, August 14th: Rhoda WILLIS

Tregillis, Mary
1883, January 2nd: Louisa Jane TAYLOR

Trendle, Kathleen
1942, May 1st: Harold HILL

Trevett, James
1869, August 12th: Jonah DETHERIDGE

Trickett, Mary
1878, February 12th: James TRICKETT

Tuffin, Caroline
1903, August 11th: William Joseph
 TUFFIN

Tugby, Joseph
1877, November 27th: James
 SATCHELL, John SWIFT & John
 UPTON

Turner, Ellen
1882, August 21st: William TURNER

Turner, Jane
1941, September 19th: Eli RICHARDS

Turner, Mark
1944, February 3rd: Mervin Clare
 McEWEN

Turner, Olive
1928, January 31st: James Joseph
 POWER

Turner, Richard
1958, September 30th: Ernest
 Raymond JONES

Tye, Miriam Jane
1902, August 13th: George HIBBS

Tyrer, Catherine
1893, November 28th: Emanuel HAMER

Upton, Emma
1888, July 17th: Robert UPTON

Vanderstay, Mona Victoria
1946, December 10th: John Fleming
 McCready MATHIESON

Vaughan, Annie
1888, March 27th: George CLARKE

Verelist, Clementine
1918, March 9th: Louis VAN DER
 KERK-HOVE

Vernon, Sarah Alice
1879, August 26th: John RALPH

Vickers, Lillian
1949, December 14th: Benjamin
 ROBERTS

Volpert, Lily
1952, September 3rd: Mahmood
 Hussain MATTAN

Wade, Ann Elizabeth
1943, March 24th: William Henry
 TURNER

Wade, George
1873, March 24th: Mary Ann COTTON

Wadge, Henry
1878, August 15th: Selina WADGE

Wagner, Irena
1953, December 17th: Stanislaw JURAS

Waine, Joseph
1873, January 13th: John HAYES &
 Hugh SLANE

Wakefield, Violet
1943, September 10th: Trevor ELVIN

Walber, Margaret
1894, April 2nd: Margaret
 WALBER

Wales, Isabella
1928, August 13th: Allen WALES

Wales, John
1876, July 26th:John WILLIAMS

Walker, Henrietta
1887, November 15th: Joseph WALKER

Walker, Henry
1877, March 26th: William CLARK

Walker, Hugh George
1953, May 19th: John Lawrence TODD

Walker, Mary
1910, January 4th: Joseph HEFFERMAN

Walker, Polly Edith
1926, March 24th: Eugene DEVERE

Walker, Rhoda
1919, January 8th: Percy George
  BARRETT

Walker, Rhoda
1919, January 8th: George Walter
  CARDWELL
George Walter CALDWELL

Wallace, Jane
1908, August 19th: Edward JOHNSTONE

Wallace, Peter
1921, June 7th: Edmund FOLEY &
  Patrick MAHER

Wallace, William John
1878, July 30th: Robert VEST

Walls. Inspector Arthur
1913, January 29th: John WILLIAMS

Walsh, *
1873, August 19th: Edward WALSH

Walsh, Bridget
1874, August 10th: John MacDONALD

Walsh, Edward
1925, August 5th: Michael TALBOT &
  Annie WALSH

Walshe, Edward
1868, August 13th: Thomas WELLS

Walton, Isabella
1902, December 16th: Samuel Thomas
  WALTON

Warburton, Eliza
1908, November 12th: James PHIPPS

Ward, Ada Louise
1899, October 4th: Robert WARD

Ward, Francis
1925, June 10th: Hubert Ernest DALTON

Ward, Hugh John
1869, March 22nd: John DOLAN
1869, March 23rd

Ward, Margaret Florence
1899, October 4th: Robert WARD

Wardlaw, Mary Brown
1875, October 19th: David WARDLAW

Wardle, Emily
1941, March 6th: Henry Lyndo WHITE

Warner, Janet Mary
1953, November 17th: Joseph
  Christopher REYNOLDS

Warren, Gwendoline Annie
1932, November 23rd: Ernest
  HUTCHINSON

Warren, James
1914, November 12th: Arnold WARREN

Washington, Henry
1920, November 1st: Kevin Gerald
  BARRY

Wass, William
1891, August 18th: Thomas SADLER

Waterhouse, Barbara
1891, August 18th: Walter Lewis
  TURNER

Waterhouse, Lily
1926, June 24th: Louie CALVERT

Watkins, un-named child
1951, April 3rd: William Arthur
  WATKINS

Watkins, Alice
1878, November 18th: Joseph GARCIA

Watkins, Charlotte
1878, November 18th: Joseph GARCIA

Watkins, Elizabeth
1878, November 18th: Joseph GARCIA

Watkins, Frederick
1878, November 18th: Joseph GARCIA

Watkins, William
1878, November 18th: Joseph GARCIA

Watson, Albert
1906, December 4th: Richard
  BUCKHAM

Watson, Edward
1954, January 5th: Robert William
 MOORE

Watson, Emma
1906, December 4th: Richard
 BUCKHAM

Watson, James
1875, August 2nd: Elizabeth PEARSON

Watson, Lucy
1949, August 16th: William John
 DAVIES

Watson, William
1875, August 16th: William
 McCULLOUGH

Watt, Sophia
1898, July 12th: James WATT

Watterton, William
1917, March 29th: Leo George
 O'DONNELL

Watts, Beatrice May
1949, August 4th: Rex Harvey JONES

Webb, Alfred
1928, June 6th: Frederick STEWART

Webb, Ralph
1888, August 7th: John JACKSON

Weedey, PC James
1890, December 30th: Robert
 KITCHING

Wells, Florence
1899, November 15th: Thomas
 SKEFFINGTON

Welsh, Mary Jane
1905, November 14th: Pasha LIFFEY
*Walsh, ***

Wendle, Eleanor
1881, November 21st: Alfred GOUGH

West, Emma
1889, December 31st: Robert WEST

West, John Alan
1964, August 13th: Peter Anthony
 ALLEN & Gwynne Owen EVANS

Westwood, Lydia
1920, December 30th: Samuel
 WESTWOOD

Westwood, Ernest Hargreaves
1948, December 30th: Arthur George
 OSBORNE

Wharton, Elizabeth
1873, January 8th: Richard SPENCER

Wharton, Lillian
1913, July 9th: Thomas FLETCHER

Whatman, John
1946, September 6th: Sydney John
 SMITH

White, Amos
1877, April 3rd: John Henry JOHNSON

White, Arthur
1954, September 1st: Edward REID

White, Clara
1883, May 21st: George WHITE

White, Edward
1896, October 6th: James JONES

White, Gilchrist
1923, April 10th: Frederick George
 WOOD

White, Lady Alice
1922, June 7th: Henry Julius JACOBY

White, Leslie
1929, August 7th: Arthur Leslie
 RAVENEY

White, Lydia Wills
1878, April 15th: Vincent Knowles
 WALKER

Whitehead, Mary Ann
1894, November 27th: James Wilshaw
 WHITEHEAD

Whitehead, Matthew
1920, November 1st: Kevin Gerald
 BARRY

Whiteley, Hannah Maria
1909, March 2nd: John HUTCHINSON

Whiteley, Margaret
1876, April 26th: John DALY

Whiteman, Alice Mabel
1925, November 12th: Hubert George
 BLOYE

Whiting, Ellen Margaret
1936, July 14th: George Arthur BRYANT

Whybrow, Harriet Emily
1914, December 23rd: George
ANDERSON

Whye, Alice
1936, August 5th: Wallace JENDEN

Wild, James
1884, November 24th: Harry
Hammond SWINDELLS

Wilkes, Ann
1898, July 19th: William WILKES

Wilkins, Irene
1922, August 19th: Thomas Henry
ALLAWAY

Wilkinson, Eliza
1880, August 16th: John WAKEFIELD

Wilkinson, Elizabeth Horrocks
1925, August 5th: James
WINSTANLEY

Wilkinson, PC William Ariel
1903, July 21st: Thomas PORTER &
Thomas PRESTON
Wilson, PC *

Wilkinson, Tom
1908, December 3rd: John William
ELLWOOD

Willett, Sarah
1900, October 2nd: John PARR

Williams, Alfred
1917, April 17th: William James
ROBINSON

Williams, Elizabeth
1885, August 3rd: Joseph TUCKER

Williams, Hilda
1912, March 19th: John WILLIAMS
1912, March 9th

Williams, Margaret
1902, November 11th: Henry
WILLIAMS

Williams, Margaret
1947, April 15th: David John
WILLIAMS

Williams, William
1958, May 6th: Vivian Frederick
TEED

Williamson, Mary
1922, March 21st: James Hutton
WILLIAMSON

Willis, John
1888, December 11th: Samuel
CROWTHER

Wilson, Anne
1920, May 6th: Thomas Hargreaves
WILSON

Wilson, Francis Henry
1950, July 13th: John WALKER

Wilson, Isabella
1910, November 24th: William BROOME

Wilson, Lily McClaren
1890, March 12th: William ROW

Wilson, Lucy
1907, July 16th: William Edwin SLACK

Wilson, Sheila Margaret
1942, October 6th: Patrick William
KINGSTON

Wilson, Sir Henry
1922, August 10th: Reginald DUNN
& Joseph O'SULLIVAN

Wilson, Susan
1908, December 2nd: James NICHOLLS

Wilton, Sarah
1887, August 29th: William WILTON

Wiltshaw, Alice
1952, December 23rd: Leslie Terrence
GREEN

Wingfield, Margaret
1880, March 22nd: John WINGFIELD

Withey, Jane
1889, April 11th: John WITHEY

Wood, Amelia
1908, March 24th: William LOWMAN

Wood, Eliza
1950, November 28th: James Henry
CORBITT

Wood, Emma
1887, May 30th: Walter WOOD

Wood, Juliet
1896, December 22nd: August CARLSEN

Woodhall, Sarah
1916, March 8th: Frederick HOLMES

Woodhead, Caroline
1878, February 13th: John BROOKS

Woodhouse, Elinor Drinkwater
1926, December 3rd: Charles
HOUGHTON

Woodhouse, Martha Gordon
1926, December 3rd: Charles
HOUGHTON

Woodman, Alice
1903, March 9th: Sydney George
SMITH

Woods, William
1876, March 28th: George HUNTER

Wooldridge, Laura
1896, July 7th: Charles Thomas
WOOLDRIDGE

Woolf, Jean Pearl
1943, April 29th: August SANGRET

Woolfenden, Ivy
1920, May 11th: William
WADDINGTON

Worth, Ethel Melinda
1950, December 14th: Edward Isaac
WOODFIELD

Worthington, Ann
1875, January 4th: William
WORTHINGTON

Worthington, Sybil Emily
1935, July 10th: Walter Osmond
WORTHINGTON

Wright, Alice
1940, September 10th: John WRIGHT

Wright, Alice Ann
1901, December 24th: John
HARRISON

Wright, Sarah
1876, December 19th: James
DALGLEISH

Wu, Zee Ming
1919, December 3rd: Djang Djing SUNG

Wyld, Walter
1951, June 12th: John DAND

Wylie, Patricia
1945, April 7th: William HARRISON

Wyllie, Sir William Curzon
1909, August 17th: Madar Dal
DHINGRA

Wyndham, James
1893, December 21st: Frederick
WYNDHAM

Wyre, James
1888, July 18th: Thomas WYRE

Yap, Young
1909, March 30th: See LEE

Yarnold, Anne
1905, December 5th: William YARNOLD

Yates, Norman
1955, July 27th: Norman William
GREEN

Yeomans, Emily
1935, February 7th: David Maskill
BLAKE

Youell, Jane
1895, June 18th: James CANNING

Young, Sarah Jean
1946, March 5th: Charles Edward
PRESCOTT

Zetoun, Fanny
1920, December 30th: Marks
GOODMARCHER

Method Index

This is a cumulative index, encompassing
Volumes I, II and III of the Hangman's Record.

Erroneous dates of hangings, and names of victims,
executioners and people hanged, have been corrected in the
relevant indexes. For easy reference, updated entries include
the information as originally given, *shown in italics.*

* = given name unknown

Method Index

Abortion
1875, April 19th: Alfred Thomas
　HEAP

Asphyxiation
1932, February 3rd: George Alfred
　RICE
1934, May 3rd: Reginald Ivor HINKS
1946, October 16th: Neville George
　Clevely HEATH

Axe
1869, August 12th: Jonah
　DETHERIDGE
1872, March 18th: Edward ROBERTS
1876, April 24th: Edward DEACON
1878, February 11th: James CAFFYN
1878, November 18th: Joseph GARCIA
1879, July 29th: Catherine WEBSTER
1881, May 23rd: James HALL
1883, May 21st: Joseph WEDLAKE
1888, March 20th: James JONES
1888, March 20th: Alfred SCANDRETT
1888, May 15th: John Alfred GELL
1889, December 9th: Benjamin
　PURCELL
1893, April 4th: Edward HEMMINGS
1893, July 19th: Amie Holman
　MEUNIER
1894, January 2nd: William HARRIS
1894, July 18th: Samuel ELKINS
1894, July 31st: William CROSSLEY
1897, August 18th: Thomas LLOYD
1897, December 16th: William BETTS
1911, June 20th: Arthur GARROD
1916, December 20th: Joseph DEANS
1919, July 10th: Henry PERRY
1923, December 28th: John William
　EASTWOOD
1925, August 14th: Arthur Henry
　BISHOP
1928, January 4th: Bertram KIRBY
1931, August 5th: Oliver NEWMAN
　& William SHELLEY
1933, December 6th: Ernest Wadge
　PARKER
1934, October 9th: Harry TUFFNEY
1941, July 31st: Edward Walker
　ANDERSON
1944, July 26th: James GALBRAITH
1945, September 7th: Thomas Eric
　RICHARDSON
1950, July 13th: John WALKER
1950, August 16th: Albert PRICE
1951, April 26th: James VIRRELS
1953, May 19th: John Lawrence
　TODD
1953, October 20th: John Owen
　GREENWAY
1955, May 4th: Winston SHAW

Beating
1870, August 8th: John OWEN
1871, April 3rd: William BULL
1873, August 4th: Henry EVANS
1874, January 5th: Thomas CORRIGAN
1874, January 5th: Charles DAWSON
1875, March 24th: John McDAID
1875, March 29th: Richard COATES
1876, May 23rd: Giovanni CACCARIS
1876, May 23rd: Pascaler CALADIS
1876, May 23rd: Matteo CORGALIS
1876, May 23rd: George KADI
1876, May 31st: Thomas BARR
1877, March 27th: John McKENNA
1877, April 2nd: James BANNISTER
1877, August 13th: Henry LEIGH
1877, August 21st: John GOLDING
1878, November 25th: Henry GILBERT
1879, January 10th: Thomas CUNCEEN
1879, February 4th: Stephen
　GAMBRILL
1879, May 27th: John D'ARCY
1879, August 25th: James DILLEY
1880, January 5th: Charles SURETY
1880, April 14th: Peter CONWAY
1884, January 15th: Peter WADE
1884, March 10th: Michael McLEAN
1884, May 27th: Joseph LAWSON
1886, February 1st: John HORTON
1886, February 10th: John THURSTON
186, February 22nd: Owen McGILL
1886, December 13th: George HARMER
1887, February 17th: Edward
　PRITCHARD
1887, August 16th: Thomas Henry
　BEVAN
1888, March 13th: David REES
1888, July 17th: Robert UPTON
1888, March 28th: William
　ARROWSMITH
1888, August 7th: John JACKSON
1888, August 10th: Arthur Thomas
　DELANEY
1889, January 14th: Arthur McKEOWN
1889, December 31st: William
　Thomas HOOK
1891, March 13th: John PURCELL
1891, December 23rd: Charles
　SAUNDERS
1892, March 17th: Frederick
　EGGLESTON
1892, March 17th: Charles RAYNOR
1892, April 19th: Daniel HANDLEY
1893, January 6th: John BOYLE
1893, July 25th: George Samuel COOK
1893, August 16th: John DAVIS
1893, December 5th: John CARTER
1894, April 3rd: Philip GARNER
1895, February 9th: John TWISS
1896, June 9th: Henry FOWLER
1896, June 9th: Albert MILSOM

1896, August 5th: William PUGH
1896, August 11th: Samuel WILKINSON
1896, August 18th: Frank TAYLOR
1898, August 3rd: Thomas JONES
1899, January 7th: Patrick HOLMES
1899, January 13th: Philip KING
1899, December 5th: Samuel CROZIER
1902, March 25th: Arthur RICHARDSON
1902, December 2nd: Henry McWIGGINS
1903, August 11th: William Joseph TUFFIN
1903, December 1st: Bernard WHITE
1903, December 16th: William BROWN
1903, December 16th: Thomas COWDREY
1905, December 29th: John SILK
1907, December 13th: George STILLS
1908, December 2nd: James NICHOLLS
1909, March 12th: Thomas MEADE
1909, July 6th: Alexander EDMUNSTONE
1910, March 24th: William BUTLER
1910, July 14th: Frederick FOREMAN
1911, October 17th: Francisco Carlos GODHINO
1911, December 6th: Michael FAGAN
1913, December 17th: Ernest Edwin KELLY
1916, December 19th: James Howarth HARGREAVES
1918, February 21st: Joseph JONES
1917, March 29th: Leo George O'DONNELL
1917, May 16th: Thomas McGUINESS
1918, March 2nd: Louis Marie Joseph VOISON
1919, January 8th: Percy George BARRETT
1919, January 8th: George Walter CARDWELL
George Walter CALDWELL
1919, December 3rd: Djang Djing SUNG
1920, January 6th: Louis MASSEY
1920, May 11th: William WADDINGTON
1920, May 26th: Albert James FRASER
1920, May 26th: James ROLLINS
1920, June 16th: Frederick William STOREY
1921, February 4th: Jack Alfred FIELD
1921, February 4th: William Thomas GRAY
1922, August 19th: Thomas Henry ALLAWAY
1924, June 18th: William Horsley WARDELL
1925, September 3rd: Alfred Davis BOSTOCK

1926, June 24th: Louie CALVERT
1926, December 9th: Henry McCABE
1928, July 27th: William John MAYNARD
1929, January 4th: Charles William CONLIN
1932, March 9th: George Thomas POPLE
1933, June 8th: Jack Samuel PUTTNAM
1933, December 19th: William BURTOFT
1934, January 5th: John FLEMING
1934, May 4th: Frederick William PARKER & Albert PROBERT
1934, November 14th: John Frederick STOCKWELL
1935, May 9th: John Stephenson BAINBRIDGE
1935, October 30th: Allan James GRIERSON
1936, July 14th: George Arthur BRYANT
1937, November 18th: John Thomas ROGERS
1938, July 26th: William PARKER
1939, October 25th: Stanley Ernest BOON & Arthur John SMITH
1940, September 10th: John WRIGHT
1940, November 26th: William Henry COOPER
1942, October 28th: William Ambrose COLLINS
1944, March 16th: Ernest Charles DIGBY
1945, January 30th: Andrew BROWN
1945, October 6th: Heinz BRUELING & Joachim GOLTZ & Erich Pallme KOENIG & Josef MERTENS & Kurt ZUEHLSDORFF
1945, December 21st: John Riley YOUNG
1946, May 28th: Leonard HOLMES
1948, February 3rd: Evan Haydn EVANS
1948, February 6th: Stanislaw MYSZKA
1948, November 19th: Peter GRIFFITHS
1948, December 30th: Arthur George OSBORNE
1949, March 22nd: Kenneth STRICKSON
1949, April 21st: Harry LEWIS
1949, June 2nd: Dennis NEVILLE
1949, December 14th: John WILSON
1950, January 6th: Daniel RAVEN
1950, April 19th: Albert Edward JENKINS
1950, December 14th: Edward Isaac WOODFIELD
1951, January 4th: Frank GRIFFIN
1951, January 26th: Nenad KOVASEVIC
1951, May 8th: James INGLIS
1952, January 15th: Alfred BRADLEY
1952, February 26th: Herbert Roy HARRIS
1952, April 25th: Alfred BURNS & Edward Francis DEVLIN

Beating   Method Index   Blunt instrument

1952, May 29th: Peter Gallagher
DEVENEY
1952, December 23rd: Leslie Terrence
GREEN
1953, January 26th: George Francis
SHAW
1953, February 24th: Miles William
GIFFARD
1953, July 30th: Philip HENRY
1953, December 18th: John Francis
WILKINSON
1953, December 23rd: George James
NEWLANDS
1954, April 22nd: Albert George
HALL
1954, April 28th: Thomas Ronald Lewis
HARRIES
1954, December 15th: Styllou
Pantopiou CHRISTOFI
1955, August 2nd: Corbett Montague
ROBERTS
1957, July 23rd: John Willson
VICKERS
1958, May 6th: Vivian Frederick
TEED
1958, July 11th: Peter Thomas
Anthony MANUEL
1958, September 3rd: Frank STOKES
1958, December 17th: Brian
CHANDLER
1959, April 28th: Joseph CHRIMES
1960, November 10th: Francis Robert
FORSYTH & Norman James
HARRIS
1960, December 22nd: Anthony
Joseph MILLER
1961, February 9th: George RILEY
1961, July 25th: Samuel
McCLAUGHLIN
1964, August 13th: Peter Anthony
ALLEN

Billhook
1876, December 19th: James
DALGLEISH
1879, May 26th: Catherine CHURCHILL
1895, July 2nd: Henry TICKNER

Blunt instrument
1868, September 8th: Alexander
Arthur MACKAY
1870, August 1st: Walter MILLAR
1870, August 15th: Thomas RADCLIFFE
1870, October 4th: George CHALMERS
1871, April 24th: Michael CAMPBELL
1872, August 13th: Christopher
EDWARDS
1872, August 12th
1873, August 4th: Benjamin HUDSON
1873, August 19th: Edward WALSH
1873, August 26th: Thomas Hartley
MONTGOMERY
1874, May 25th: John GODWIN

1874, August 10th: John MacDONALD
1874, December 28th: Hugh DALEY
1875, January 4th: William
WORTHINGTON
1875, April 9th: John RUSSELL
1875, October 5th: Patrick DOCHERTY
1875, October 19th: David WARDLAW
1876, April 10th: George HILL
1876, August 1st: James PARRIS
1876, August 21st: Steven McKEOWN
1876, December 11th: Charles
O'DONNELL
1877, November 20th: Henry MARSH
1877, November 23rd: Cadwaller JONES
1879, August 11th: Annie TOOKE
1880, January 16th: Martin McHUGO
1880, May 11th: John Henry WOOD
1881, May 31st: Joseph Patrick
McENTIRE
1881, August 23rd: George DURLING
1882, December 4th: Bernard
MULLARKEY
1882, December 15th: Patrick CASEY
1882, December 15th: Miles JOYCE
1882, December 15th: Patrick JOYCE
1883, January 15th: Patrick HIGGINS
1883, January 17th: Michael FLYNN
1883, January 17th: Thomas HIGGINS
1883, May 8th: Patrick CAREY
1883, August 6th: James BURTON
1883, November 6th: Henry POWELL
1883, November 19th: Peter BRAY
1883, November 26th: Thomas RILEY
1884, August 19th: Peter CASSIDY
1884, August 26th: James TOBIN
1884, August 24th
1885, August 17th: Thomas BOULTON
1885, November 23rd: John HILL
1885, November 23rd: John WILLIAMS
1885, December 7th: Daniel MINAHAN
1886, January 20th: William SHEEHAN
1886, March 2nd: David ROBERTS
1886, November 30th: James BANTON
James BARTON
1887, February 22nd: Benjamin TERRY
1887, May 9th: Charles SMITH
1888, November 13th: Leir Richard
BARTLETT
1889, March 13th: Samuel RYLANDS
1889, December 24th: William DUKES
1890, April 8th: Richard DAVIES
1890, June 10th: Daniel Stewart GORRIE
1890, July 29th: George BOWLING
1890, August 26th: James HARRISON
1890, September 23rd: Henry DELVIN
1890, December 23rd: Mary Eleanor
WHEELER
1892, August 16th: James TAYLOR
1892, August 18th: Moses
CUDWORTH
1893, September 2nd: James REILLY
1894, December 10th: John William
NEWELL

1896, June 9th: William SEAMAN
1897, January 5th: Henry BROWN
1897, June 7th: George PATERSON
1898, February 22nd: George William HOWE
1898, March 22nd: Charles SMITH
1898, December 13th: Thomas DALEY
1898, December 14th
1898, December 21st: John COTTON
1899, October 3rd: Frederick PRESTON
1900, January 9th: Louisa Josephine MASSET
1900, December 12th: John BOWES
1902, April 23rd: Thomas KEELEY
1902, May 6th: George WOOLFE
1902, July 15th: Samuel MIDDLETON
1902, July 30th: John BEDFORD
1903, March 3rd: Edgar EDWARDS
1903, December 15th: William HAYWOOD
1903, December 29th: John GALLAGHER
1903, December 29th: Emily SWANN
1905, April 10th: Harry WALTERS
1905, April 25th: John FOSTER
1905, April 26th: Albert BRIDGEMAN
1905, May 23rd: Albert STRATTON
1905, August 1st: Ferat Mahomed BENALI
1906, November 27th: Edward HARTIGAN
1907, February 19th: Thomas CONNAN
1907, November 20th: William DUDDLES
1908, March 5th: Joseph HUME
1908, August 20th: John BERRYMAN
1908, December 3rd: John William ELLWOOD
1908, December 15th: Henry Taylor PARKER
1909, July 9th: Walter DAVIS
1909, August 19th: Richard JUSTIN
1910, December 29th: Henry ISON
1911, May 9th: Thomas SEYMOUR
1911, December 15th: Joseph FLETCHER
1912, December 18th: Alfred John LAWRENCE
1914, February 26th: George BALL
1918, February 12th: Arthur Harry Victor DE STAMIR
1919, July 22nd: John CROSSLAND
1920, January 6th: David CAPLAN
1920, August 11th: James ELLOR
1920, November 30th: James RILEY
1922, March 23rd: William SULLIVAN
1922, April 11th: Frederick Alexander KEELING
1922, June 7th: Henry Julius JACOBY
1922, September 5th: William James YELDHAM

1923, January 5th: Lee DOON
1923, December 15th: Peter HYNES
1924, September 3rd: Patrick Herbert MAHON
1925, May 26th: Patrick POWER
1925, June 10th: Hubert Ernest DALTON
1925, September 3rd: Wilfred FOWLER
1925, September 4th: Lawrence FOWLER
1925, November 12th: Hubert George BLOYE
1926, February 17th: Herbert BURROWS
1926, April 13th: George SHARPES
1927, August 3rd: Frederick Stephen FULLER
1927, August 3rd: James MURPHY
1928, April 10th: George Frederick Walter HAYWARD
1928, August 3rd: George REYNOLDS
1929, February 27th: William John HOLMYARD
1929, April 25th: John COX
1930, April 22nd: William Henry PODMORE
1931, February 4th: Frederick GILL
1931, August 4th: David O'SHEA
1931, December 10th: Henry Daniel SEYMOUR
1932, February 23rd: William Harold GODDARD
1932, April 28th: Thomas RILEY
1932, April 28th: John Henry ROBERTS
1934, January 3rd: Roy GREGORY
1935, March 13th: George Frank HARVEY
1936, December 16th: Christopher JACKSON
1937, February 4th: Max Mayer HASLAM
1937, June 17th: John HORNICK
1937, July 27th: Philip Edward Percy DAVIS
1937, December 7th: Ernest John MOSS
1938, June 8th: Jan MAHOMED
1938, November 1st: George BRAIN
1939, February 8th: John DAYMOND
1940, August 8th: George Edward ROBERTS
1941, January 7th: David DOHERTY
1942, September 10th: Samuel DASHWOOD & George SILVEROSA
1943, February 10th: Ronald ROBERTS
1943, March 31st: Dudley George RAYNOR
1943, April 6th: Gordon Horace TRENOWORTH
1943, April 29th: August SANGRET
1943, July 10th: Charles Arthur RAYMOND
1943, August 3rd: Gerald Elphinstone ROE
1943, September 10th: Trevor ELVIN

1943, December 15th: Charles William KOOPMAN
1944, February 3rd: Mervin Clare McEWEN
1945, December 29th: Robert BLAINE
1947, January 3rd: Stanley SHEMINANT
1947, February 27th: Walter Graham ROWLAND
1947, April 15th: David John WILLIAMS
1948, November 24th: William M GAMBON
1949, January 12th: Margaret ALLEN
1952, October 9th: Peter Cyril JOHNSON
1959, May 14th: Michael George TATUM
1960, September 1st: John Louis CONSTANTINE
1961, September 7th: Hendryk NEIMASZ
1962, November 28th: James SMITH

Bomb
1940, February 7th: Peter BARNES & James RICHARDS

Burning
1880, February 17th: William CASSIDY
1885, August 3rd: Joseph TUCKER
1899, January 3rd: John SCHNEIDER
1907, April 2nd: Edwin James MOORE
1930, April 8th: Sydney Harry FOX
1931, March 10th: Alfred Arthur ROUSE
1933, June 20th: Richard HETHERINGTON

Chain
1894, April 2nd: Margaret WALBER
1925, September 3rd: Wilfred FOWLER
1925, September 4th: Lawrence FOWLER

Drowning
1874, June 29th: Frances STEWART
1875, August 2nd: William McHUGH
1878, August 15th: Selina WADGE
1879, August 26th: John RALPH
1881, February 22nd: James WILLIAMS
1882, May 23rd: Osmond Otto BRAND
1882, November 28th: Edward WHEATFALL
1886, March 1st: Thomas NASH
1886, May 31st: James WHELAN
1888, July 18th: Thomas WYRE
1891, December 15th: Henry DAINTON
1896, June 10th: Amelia Elizabeth DYER
1900, August 16th: Thomas MELLOR
1908, November 12th: James PHIPPS
1913, October 2nd: Patrick HIGGINS
1915, August 13th: George Joseph SMITH
1920, July 27th: Arthur Andrew GOSLETT
1924, August 13th: John HORNER

1928, January 31st: James Joseph POWER
1933, July 25th: Frederick MORSE
1941, December 18th: Patrick KELLY
1942, March 25th: David Roger WILLIAMS
1942, September 10th: Harold Oswald MERRY
1946, March 19th: Arthur CLEGG
1951, April 3rd: William Arthur WATKINS
1954, January 26th: Desmond Donald HOOPER
1955, March 29th: William Arthur SALT

Falling
1881, November 29th: Percy LEFROY
1893, November 28th: Emanuel HAMER
1900, December 4th: Joseph HOLDEN
1909, May 8th: William Joseph FOY
1923, October 30th: Phillip MURRAY
1931, January 3rd: Victor Edward BETTS
1954, September 1st: Edward REID
1958, September 30th: Ernest Raymond JONES

Firearms
1868, August 13th: Thomas WELLS
1869, January 18th: Martin Henry VINALL
1869, March 22nd: John McCONVILLE
1869, March 23rd
1869, October 11th: William TAYLOR
1869, December 13th: Frederick HINSON
1870, May 27th: Lawrence SHEILD
1870, May 27th: Margaret SHEILD
1872, April 1st: William Frederick HORRY
1872, December 9th: Augustus ELLIOT
1872, December 30th: Michael KENNEDY
1873, January 8th: Richard SPENCER
1874, January 12th: Charles Edward BUTT
1874, August 31st: Mary WILLIAMS
1874, November 16th: Thomas SMITH
1875, August 12th: Joseph Phillip LE BRUN
1875, August 11th
1875, September 6th: William BAKER
1875, September 6th: Edward COOPER
1875, December 21st: Henry WAINWRIGHT
1875, December 23rd: Richard CHARLTON
1876, March 28th: George HUNTER
1876, April 25th: Joseph WEBBER
1876, May 23rd: Pascaler CALADIS
1876, May 23rd: Matteo CORGALIS
1876, May 23rd: George KADI
1876, July 26th: John WILLIAMS
1876, August 25th: Thomas CROWE
1876, August 29th: John EBLETHRIFT

1876, December 20th: John GREEN
1877, January 2nd: Isaac MARKS
1877, March 12th: Francis TIDBURY
1877, March 12th: Henry TIDBURY
1877, March 26th: William CLARK
1877, April 3rd: John Henry JOHNSON
1878, February 4th: George PIGGOTT
1878, April 1st: Henry ROWLES
1878, October 3rd: William McDONALD
1878, November 12th: Patrick John
  BYRNE
1879, February 10th: Enoch WHISTON
1879, February 25th: Charles Frederick
  PEACE
1880, March 2nd: Hugh BURNS
1880, March 2nd: Patrick KEARNS
1880, November 29th: Thomas
  WHEELER
1880, November 26th
1880, December 13th: William
  HERBERT
1881, November 29th: Percy LEFROY
1882, May 22nd: William George
  ABIGAIL
1882, September 11th: Francis HYNES
1882, September 22nd: Patrick WALSH
1882, December 15th: Patrick CASEY
1882, December 15th: Miles JOYCE
1882, December 15th: Patrick JOYCE
1883, January 15th: Patrick HIGGINS
1883, January 17th: Michael FLYNN
1883, January 17th: Thomas HIGGINS
1883, January 23rd: James BARRETT
1883, January 23rd: Sylvester POFF
1883, February 12th: Abraham THOMAS
1883, April 30th: Timothy O'KEEFE
1883, May 7th: Thomas GARRY
1883, May 23rd: Henry MULLEN
1883, May 23rd: Martin SCOTT
1883, December 17th: Patrick
  O'DONNELL
1883, December 18th: Joseph POOLE
1884, March 31st: William INNES
1884, March 31st: Robert Flockheart
  VICKERS
1884, October 6th: Thomas Henry
  ORROCK
1884, November 24th: Harry Hammond
  SWINDELLS
1885, January 16th: Michael DOWNEY
1885, January 20th: Thomas PARRY
1885, March 17th: Henry KIMBERLEY
1885, May 18th: James LEE
1885, December 8th: George THOMAS
1885, December 9th
1886, February 8th: James BAKER
1886, February 8th: James MARTIN
1886, February 8th: Anthony Ben
  RUDGE
1886, November 16th: Patrick JUDGE
1886, November 29th: James MURPHY
1887, February 21st: Richard INSOLE

1887, April 18th: Thomas William
  CURRELL
1887, August 1st: Alfred SOWERY
1888, April 28th: Daniel HAYES &
  Daniel MORIARTY
1888, April 29th
1888, May 7th: James KIRBY
1888, May 22nd: James William
  RICHARDSON
1888, August 28th: George Nathaniel
  DANIELS
1888, August 28th: Harry Benjamin
  JONES
1889, April 8th: Peter STAFFORD
1889, January 2nd: Charles DOBELL
1889, January 2nd: William GOWER
1890, March 11th: Joseph BOSWELL
1890, March 11th: Samuel BOSWELL
1889, August 7th: Lawrence Maurice
  HICKEY
1890, August 26th: Frederick DAVIES
1890, August 27th: Francois MONTEAU
1890, December 30th: Robert KITCHING
1891, July 21st: Franz Joseph MUNCH
1891, July 28th: Arthur SPENCER
1891, August 25th: Edward Henry
  FAWCETT
1891, December 22nd: John William
  JOHNSON
1892, March 22nd: Joseph WILSON
1892, July 26th: John GURD
1892, August 16th: John George
  WENZEL
1892, October 11th: John James
  BANBURY
1893, March 16th: Albert MANNING
1893, March 28th: William WILLIAMS
1893, August 15th: John Thomas
  HEWITT
1893, December 6th: George MASON
1893, December 19th: Henry
  RUMBOLD
1893, December 21st: Frederick
  WYNDHAM
1894, March 27th: Walter SMITH
1894, April 4th: Frederick William
  FENTON
1894, August 17th: John GILMOUR
1894, December 4th: James Canham
  READ
1894, December 12th: William ROGERS
1895, August 20th: Thomas BOND
1895, December 31st: Patrick MORLEY
1895, December 3rd: Arthur
  COVINGTON
1896, July 21st: Samuel Edward SMITH
1897, July 27th: Joseph BOWSER
1897, August 17th: Joseph ROBINSON
1898, January 14th: Patrick HESTOR
1898, April 5th: Wilfrid F KENNY
1898, August 30th: Joseph LEWIS
1898, July 12th: James WATT
1899, January 10th: Thomas KELLY

1899, July 18th: Charles MAIDMENT
1899, July 11th: Joseph Cornelius PARKER
1899, August 9th: Elias TORR
1900, August 16th: Charles Benjamin BACKHOUSE
1900, October 2nd: John PARR
1900, December 27th: James Joseph BERGIN
1901, January 11th: Timothy CADOGEN
1901, March 19th: George Henry PARKER
1901, July 30th: Charles WATKINS
1901, December 10th: John George THOMPSON
1902, April 29th: Charles Robert EARL
1902, December 4th: William CHAMBERS
1902, December 16th: Samuel Thomas WALTON
1902, December 30th: James DOCHERTY
1902, December 30th: George PLACE
1903, February 17th: William HUGHES
1903, February 18th
1903, May 13th: William George HUDSON
1903, June 2nd: Willem SCHMIDT
1903, July 14th: Samuel Herbert DOUGAL
1903, July 21st: Thomas PORTER
1903, July 21st: Thomas PRESTON
1903, November 17th: Edward Richard PALMER
1903, December 22nd: Charles William ASHTON
1904, May 31st: William KIRWAN
1904, May 31st: Pong LUN
1904, July 13th: Samuel ROWLEDGE
1906, December 4th: Richard BUCKHAM
1908, March 24th: Joseph William NOBLE
1908, May 12th: John RAMSBOTTOM
1909, January 6th: John Esmond MURPHY
1909, March 30th: See LEE
1909, April 14th: Joseph Edwin JONES
1909, July 3rd: John EDMUNDS
1909, August 10th: Julius WAMMER
1909, August 17th: Madar Dal DHINGRA
1909, December 8th: Abel ATHERTON
1910, July 12th: Thomas CRAIG
1910, August 9th: John Alexander DICKMAN
1911, January 4th: William SCANLAN
1913, January 29th: Edward HOPWOOD
1913, January 29th: John WILLIAMS
1913, June 24th: William Walter BURTON
1913, July 9th: Thomas FLETCHER
1913, July 22nd: John Vickers AMOS

1913, August 13th: Frank GREENING
1913, November 26th: Augustus John PENNY
1914, March 12th: James HONEYANDS
1914, March 25th: Edgar Lewis BINDON
1914, June 16th: Walter James WHITE
1914, August 11th: Percy Evelyn CLIFFORD
1914, November 10th: Henry QUARTLEY
1915, November 16th: William Benjamin REEVE
1917, March 21st: Thomas CLINTON
1918, March 5th: Verney ASSER
1920, April 13th: Frederick Rothwell HOLT
1920, May 11th: Herbert Edward SALISBURY
1920, November 1st: Kevin Gerald BARRY
1921, March 14th: Patrick MORAN
1921, March 14th: Thomas WHELAN
1921, April 26th: Thomas TRAYNOR
1921, April 25th
1921, May 24th: Thomas WILSON
1921, June 7th: Edmund FOLEY
1921, June 7th: Patrick MAHER
1921, June 7th: William MITCHELL
1921, August 16th: Lester HAMILTON
1922, August 10th: Reginald DUNN
1922, August 10th: Joseph O'SULLIVAN
1922, December 13th: Frank FOWLER
1922, December 19th: William RIDER
1923, April 3rd: Daniel CASSIDY
1923, August 8th: Hassan MUHAMED
1923, November 29th: William DOWNES
1923, December 12th: Thomas McDONAGH
1924, March 13th: Jeremiah GAFFNEY
1924, May 8th: Michael PRATLEY
1924, July 30th: Abraham GOLDENBERG
1924, August 1st: Felix McMULLEN
1926, February 17th: Herbert BURROWS
1926, March 2nd: Ignatius Emanuel Nathanial LINCOLN
1926, March 23rd: Lock Ah TAM
1926, July 15th: James MYLES
1926, December 3rd: Charles HOUGHTON
1927, January 5th: William Cornelius JONES
1928, May 31st: Frederick Guy BROWNE
1928, May 31st: William KENNEDY
1928, June 6th: Frederick STEWART
1928, June 28th: Walter BROOKS
1928, August 8th: William SMILEY
1930, April 8th: Samuel William CUSHNAN
1931, July 31st: Thomas DORNAN
1932, January 13th: Edward CULLENS

Firearms   Method Index   Kicking

1932, December 29th: Patrick McDERMOTT
1933, August 10th: Varnavas Loizi ANTORKA
1934, February 6th: Ernest BROWN
1935. June 25th: Arthur Henry FRANKLIN
1935, July 10th: Walter Osmond WORTHINGTON
1935, October 29th: Raymond BOUSQUET
1937, August 12th: Horace William BRUNT
1938, March 8th: Walter SMITH
1939, January 7th: Dermot SMYTH
1940, July 11th: William APPLEBY & Vincent OSTLER
1940, July 31st: Udham SINGH
1941, April 23rd: Henry GLEESON
1941, July 23rd: David Millar JENNINGS
1941, September 4th: John SMITH
1942, January 30th: Arthur PEACH
1942, April 30th: Frederick James AUSTIN
1942, July 21st: Arthur ANDERSON
1942, September 2nd: Thomas Joseph WILLIAMS
1943, March 12th: David COBB
1943, June 25th: Harold A SMITH
1943, August 12th: William O'SHEA
1943, September 24th: Charles Eugene GAUTHIER
1943, December 14th: Lee A DAVIS
1944, February 10th: John H WATERS
1944, April 13th: Sydney James DELASALLE
1944, December 1st: Charles KERINS
1945, March 8th: Karl Gustav HULTEN
1945, May 8th: George Edward SMITH
1945, September 5th: Howard Joseph GROSSLEY
1945, December 21st: James McNicol
1946, January 8th: William BATTY
1946, March 5th: Charles Edward PRESCOTT
1946, March 26th: Arthur CHARLES
1946, April 2nd: Marion GRONDKOWSKI & Henryk MALINOWSKI
1946, April 24th: Martin Patrick COFFEY
1946, August 10th: John CALDWELL
1946, September 6th: Sydney John SMITH
1946, November 1st: Arthur Robert BOYCE
1947, January 30th: Albert SABIN
1947, March 26th: Frederick William REYNOLDS
1947, March 31st: Joseph McMANUS
1949, August 10th: John George HAIGH
1949, September 28th: William Claude Hobson JONES

1949, December 14th: Benjamin ROBERTS
1949, December 30th: Ernest Soper COUZINS
1950, March 28th: George KELLY
1950, March 30th: Walter SHARPE
1950, July 7th: Zbigniew GOWER & Roman REDEL
1951, July 19th: Alfred George REYNOLDS
1951, September 15th: Robert Dobie SMITH
1952, February 6th: Alfred MOORE
1952, May 7th: Ajit SINGH
1952, July 8th: Harry HUXLEY
1952, October 23rd: Donald Neil SIMON
1953, January 28th: Derek William BENTLEY
1954, January 5th: Robert William MOORE
1954, April 14th: James Reginald DOOHAN
1955, July 13th: Ruth ELLIS
1957, December 4th: Dennis HOWARD
1959, August 14th: Bernard Hugh WALDEN
1959, October 9th: Francis Joseph HUCHET
1959, November 5th: Guenther Fritz Erwin PODOLA
1961, March 29th: Jack DAY
1961, May 26th: Victor John TERRY
1961, September 7th: Hendryk NEIMASZ
1962, April 4th: James HANRATTY
1962, October 12th: Oswald Augustus GREY
1963, August 15th: Henry John BURNETT

Hanging

1945, October 6th: Heinz BRUELING & Joachim GOLTZ & Erich Pallme KOENIG & Josef MERTENS & Kurt ZUEHLSDORFF

Kicking

1870, January 10th: John GREGSON
1872, August 26th: William LACE
1873, January 13th: John HAYES
1873, January 13th: Hugh SLANE
1875, January 4th: John McGRAVE
1875, January 4th: Michael MULLEN
1876, April 4th: Thomas FORDRED
1876, April 26th: John DALY
1877, November 27th: James SATCHELL
1877, November 27th: John SWIFT
1877, November 27th: John UPTON
1878, February 12th: James TRICKETT
1879, February 11th: William McGUINESS
1882, August 21st: William TURNER
1882, August 22nd: Thomas HAYNES
1883, May 21st: George WHITE

313

Kicking

1886, June 15th: Edward HEWITT
1887, February 15th: Thomas
LEATHERBARROW
1897, February 9th: Robert HAYMAN
1898, March 14th: John HERDMAN
1898, March 12th
1898, July 19th: William WILKES
1890, December 30th: Thomas
McDONALD
1902, December 16th: William BROWN
1903, January 7th: Joseph TAYLOR
1903, January 9th: Mary DALY
1904, April 14th: James CAMPION
1904, April 15th: John KELLY
1904, July 26th: Thomas GUNNING
1916, September 6th: Daniel SULLIVAN
1917, May 16th: Thomas McGUINESS
1922, May 30th: Hyram THOMPSON
1923, February 8th: William ROONEY
1926, November 24th: James McHUGH
1945, November 16th: Arnim KUEHNE
& Emil SCHMITTENDORF

Poisoning

1868, December 28th: Priscilla
BIGGADYKE
1873, March 24th: Mary Ann COTTON
1874, January 12th: Edwin BAILEY
1874, January 12th: Ann BERRY
1875, August 2nd: Elizabeth PEARSON
1876, December 19th: Silas BARLOW
1878, May 31st: Eugene Marie
CHANTRELLE
1879, August 25th: James DILLEY
1882, April 28th: George Henry
LAMSON
1883, January 2nd: Louisa Jane TAYLOR
1884, March 3rd: Catherine FLANAGAN
& Margaret HIGGINS
1884, March 5th
1884, May 26th: Mary LEFLEY
1886, July 26th: William SAMUELS
1886, July 27th
1886, August 9th: Mary Ann BRITLAND
1887, March 14th: Elizabeth BERRY
1887, August 22nd: Israel LIPSKI
1888, January 10th: Phillip Henry Eustace
CROSS
1889, August 21st: George HORTON
1892, November 15th: Thomas CREAM
1894, August 21st: Alfred DEWS
1898, June 28th: William HORSFORD
1899, July 19th: Mary Ann ANSELL
1899, July 25th: Edward BELL
1900, April 10th: Patrick DUNPHY
1903, April 7th: George CHAPMAN
1905, August 15th: Arthur DEVEREUX
1907, August 13th: Richard Clifford
BRINKLEY
1910, November 23rd: Hawley Harvey
CRIPPEN
1912, April 18th: Frederick Henry
SEDDON

1921, March 2nd: George Arthur
BAILEY
1922, March 24th: Edward Ernest
BLACK
1922, May 31st: Herbert Rouse
ARMSTRONG
1924, August 12th: Jean-Pierre
VAQUIER
1934, December 19th: Ethel Lillie
MAJOR
1936, April 16th: Dorothea Nancy
WADDINGHAM
1936, July 15th: Charlotte BRYANT
1941, November 12th: Lionel Rupert
Nathan WATSON
1943, August 3rd: Gerald Elphinstone
ROE
1945, March 19th: James Herbert
LEHMAN
1953, September 18th: Louisa May
MERRIFIELD

Rape (non-fatal)

1944, August 11th: Eliga BRINSON &
Willie SMITH
1944, October 12th: Madison
THOMAS
1945, March 17th: Cubia JONES &
Robert L PEARSON
1945, June 15th: Aniceto MARTINEZ

Run over

1950, December 16th: James Ronald
ROBERTSON

Sharp-edged instrument

1888, March 28th: William
ARROWSMITH
1883, June 9th: Timothy KELLY
1893, August 16th: John DAVIS
1869, April 20th: William SHEWARD
1869, March 23rd: John DOLAN
1869, March 22nd
1869, March 29th: Michael James
JOHNSON
1890, December 23rd: Mary Eleanor
WHEELER
1870, May 27th: Lawrence SHEILD
1870, May 27th: Margaret SHEILD
1870, July 28th: Andrew CARR
1871, July 31st: Richard ADDINGTON
1871, August 17th: William COLLINS
1872, January 8th: Frederick JONES
1872, August 12th: Charles HOLMES
1872, August 13th: Francis BRADFORD
1872, August 13th: James TOOTH
1874, January 5th: William THOMPSON
1874, March 30th: Thomas
CHAMBERLAIN
1874, March 31st
1874, August 18th: William JACKSON
1874, August 24th: James Henry GIBBS
1875, January 4th: James CRANWELL

1875, March 30th: John MORGAN
1875, April 19th: William TOBIN
1875, August 2nd: Michael GILLINGHAM
1875, August 16th: Mark FIDDLER
1875, December 21st: William SMEDLEY
1876, August 14th: William FISH
1876, December 14th: Robert BROWNING
1876, December 21st: William FLANAGAN
1877, April 17th: Frederick Edwin BAKER
1877, August 14th: Caleb SMITH
1877, July 31st: Henry ROGERS
1877, July 31st: John Henry STARKEY
1877, October 15th: John LYNCH
1877, November 21st: Thomas GREY
1878, February 13th: John BROOKS
1878, July 29th: Charles Joseph REVELL
1878, August 12th: Thomas CHOLERTON
1878, November 19th: James McGOWAN
1879, March 24th: James SIMMS
1879, May 12th: Edwin SMART
1879, May 20th: William COOPER
1879, December 3rd: Henry BEDINGFIELD
1880, August 16th: John WAKEFIELD
1880, May 10th: William DUMBLETON
1880, November 16th: William BROWNLESS
1880, November 22nd: William Joseph DISTON
1880, November 27th
1880, December 13th: George PAVEY
1881, May 17th: Albert MOORE
1881, August 15th: Thomas BROWN
1881, November 28th: John Aspinall SIMPSON
1882, February 13th: Richard TEMPLETON
1882, December 12th: Charles TAYLOR
1883, February 19th: James ANDERSON
1883, June 9th: Timothy KELLY
1883, November 13th: Thomas Lyons DAY
1883, December 3rd: Henry DUTTON
1884, August 26th: Joseph LAYCOCK
1884, October 6th: Thomas HARRIS
1884, November 24th: Kay HOWARTH
1885, January 13th: Horace Robert JAY
1885, November 30th: Robert GOODALE
1886, February 1st: John HORTON
1886, February 16th: George SAUNDERS
1886, May 31st: Albert Edward BROWN
1887, February 14th: Thomas BLOXHAM
1887, March 21st: Joseph KING

1887, May 30th: Walter WOOD
1887, August 22nd: Henry HOBSON
1887, August 29th: William WILTON
1887, November 14th: William HUNTER
1887, November 15th: Joseph WALKER
1887, November 21st: Joseph MORLEY
1887, December 6th: Thomas PAYNE
1888, March 27th: George CLARKE
1888, August 15th: George SARGENT
1889, April 10th: Thomas ALLEN
1889, April 11th: John WITHEY
1889, January 1st: Thomas CLEWES
1889, January 8th: George NICHOLSON
1889, December 31st: Frederick BRETT
1889, December 31st: Robert WEST
1890, January 7th: Charles Lister HIGGENBOTHAM
1890, March 12th: William ROW
1890, April 15th: William Matthew CHADWICK
1890, August 22nd: Felix SPICER
1891, August 18th: Walter Lewis TURNER
1891, August 19th: Robert BRADSHAW
1891, August 20th: John CONWAY
1892, January 12th: James HEANEY
1892, March 29th: John NOBLE
1892, June 14th: Henry PICKERING
1892, August 17th: Patrick GIBBONS
1892, December 22nd: Thomas EDWARDS
1893, July 18th: Richard SABEY
1894, February 13th: George THOMAS
1894, November 27th: James Wilshaw WHITEHEAD
1894, December 12th: Cyrus KNIGHT
1895, March 26th: Edmund KESTEVEN
1895, June 18th: James CANNING
1895, November 19th: Richard WINGROVE
1895, November 13th
1895, December 24th: Henry WRIGHT
1896, February 25th: Alfred CHIPPERFIELD
1896, July 7th: Charles Thomas WOOLDRIDGE
1896, July 21st: Frederick BURDEN
1896, August 11th: John ROSE
1896, December 22nd: August CARLSEN
1896, December 23rd: Joseph ALLCOCK
1897, August 17th: Walter ROBINSON
1899, March 28th: George ROBERTSON
1899, October 4th: Robert WARD
1899, November 28th: Charles SCOTT
1899, December 6th: Michael DOWDLE
1899, May 3rd: Frederick James ANDREWS
1900, May 22nd: Henry GROVE
1900, July 17th: Alfred HIGHFIELD
1900, August 21st: William LACY
1900, August 28th: Charles Oliver BLEWITT
1901, January 11th: William WOODS

1901, February 19th: Sampson Silas SALMON
1901, March 7th: John TOOLE
1901, April 2nd: Joseph Arthur SHUFFLEBOTHAM
1901, August 13th: Ernest Walter WICKHAM
1902, March 18th: Richard WIGLEY
1902, May 20th: Thomas MARSLAND
1902, July 15th: Samuel MIDDLETON
1902, July 22nd: William CHURCHER
1902, August 12th: William LANE
1902, November 11th: Henry WILLIAMS
1903, March 9th: Sydney George SMITH
1903, July 7th: Charles HOWELL
1903, December 2nd: Charles Wood WHITTAKER
1904, March 29th: James Henry CLARKSON
1904, March 29th: Henry JONES
1904, April 5th: Charles Samuel DYER
1904, July 12th: John SULLIVAN
1904, August 16th: Samuel HOLDEN
1904, August 16th: John Thomas KAY
1904, December 20th: Edmund HALL
1904, December 22nd: Joseph FEE
1905, February 28th: Edward HARRISON
1905, March 29th: Ernest HUTCHINSON
1905, June 20th: Alfred John HEAL
1905, August 15th: Thomas George TATTERSALL
1905, November 14th: Pasha LIFFEY
1905, December 20th: Samuel CURTIS
1905, December 27th: Frederick William EDGE
1906, November 13th: Frederick REYNOLDS
1906, December 27th: Walter MARSH
1907, January 1st: John DAVIES
1907, March 26th: Joseph JONES
1907, July 16th: William Edwin SLACK
1907, August 7th: Charles PATERSON
1908, March 24th: William LOWMAN
1908, July 28th: Fred BALLINGTON
1908, August 4th: Thomas SIDDLE
1908, August 19th: Edward JOHNSTONE
1908, December 8th: William BOULDREY
1909, February 23rd: Jeremiah O'CONNOR
1909, March 30th: Edmund Walter ELLIOT
1909, December 7th: John FREEMAN
1909, December 14th: Samuel ATHERLEY
1910, January 4th: Joseph HEFFERMAN
1910, February 15th: William MURPHY
1910, February 22nd: Joseph WREN
1910, February 23rd
1910, August 9th: John Roper COULSON
1911, January 31st: George NEWTON
1911, May 24th: Michael COLLINS

1911, June 20th: Arthur GARROD
1911, November 15th: Frederick Henry THOMAS
1911, December 12th: John Edward TARKENTER
1911, December 14th: Henry PHILLIPS
1911, December 19th: George William PARKER
1912, March 19th: John WILLIAMS
1912, March 9th
1912, July 23rd: Arthur BIRKETT
1912, October 1st: Sargent PHILP
1912, November 26th: Gilbert Oswald SMITH
1912, December 10th: William Henry BEAL
1912, December 18th: Alfred John LAWRENCE
1912, December 29th: William Wallace GALBRAITH
1913, February 25th: George CUNLIFFE
1913, March 19th: Edward Henry PALMER
1913, April 23rd: Walter William SYKES
1913, July 8th: Henry LONGDEN
1913, August 13th: James RYDER
1913, November 4th: Frederick SEEKINGS
1914, March 24th: Robert UPTON
1914, May 14th: Joseph SPOONER
1914, July 28th: Herbert BROOKER
1914, November 4th: Charles FREMD
1914, November 10th: John Francis EAYRES
1914, November 12th: Arnold WARREN
1914, December 23rd: George ANDERSON
1915, August 11th: Frank STEELE
1915, August 17th: George MARSHALL
1915, December 1st: Young HILL
1915, December 1st: John James THORNLEY
1915, December 22nd: Harry THOMPSON
1915, December 29th: John William McCARTNEY
1916, March 8th: Frederick HOLMES
1917, March 27th: John William THOMPSON
1917, April 18th: Robert GADSBY
1917, August 16th: William Thomas HODGSON
1917, December 19th: Thomas COX
1919, January 7th: Benjamin Hindle BENSON
1919, February 19th: Joseph ROSE
1919, July 31st: Thomas FOSTER
1919, November 11th: James ADAMS
1919, November 26th: Ambrose QUINN
1919, November 26th: Ernest Bernard SCOTT
1920, March 23rd: William HALL
1920, April 14th: Thomas CALER

1920, April 16th: Miles McHUGH
1920, June 22nd: William Thomas
ALDRED
1920, December 30th: Marks
GOODMARCHER
1920, December 30th: Edwin SOWERBY
1920, December 31st: Charles
COLCLOUGH
1921, January 7th: George Edmund
Freeman Quentin LEVER
1921, April 5th: Frederick QUARMBY
1921, December 22nd: Edward
O'CONNOR
1922, March 21st: James Hutton
WILLIAMSON
1922, August 11th: Elijah POUTNEY
1922, December 13th: George
ROBINSON
1923, January 3rd: George Frederick
EDISBURY
1923, March 28th: George PERRY
1923, April 5th: Bernard POMROY
1923, June 11th: John Henry
SAVAGE
1923, July 4th: Rowland DUCK
1923, July 24th: William GRIFFITHS
1923, December 12th: Thomas
DELANEY
1924, January 2nd: Matthew Frederick
Atkinson NUNN
1924, December 9th: William George
SMITH
1925, February 24th: William Grover
BIGNELL
1925, April 2nd: George William
BARTON
1925, May 26th: Patrick POWER
1925, July 28th: Cornelius O'LEARY
1925, August 5th: Michael TALBOT
1925, August 5th: Annie WALSH
1925, August 11th: James MAKIN
1925, August 14th: William John
CRONIN
1925, September 3rd: Wilfred FOWLER
1925, September 4th: Lawrence
FOWLER
1926, January 5th: John FISHER
1926, January 7th: Lorraine LAX
1926, March 9th: Henry THOMPSON
1926, March 16th: William Henry
THORPE
1926, July 27th: Johannes Josephus
Cornelius MOMMERS
1926, June 27th
1926, November 16th: James LEAH
1927, April 27th: William KNIGHTON
1927, September 2nd: Arthur HARNETT
1927, December 6th: William Meynell
ROBERTSON
1928, April 12th: Frederick LOCK
1928, August 13th: Allen WALES
1928, December 11th: Trevor EDWARDS

1929, April 4th: George Henry
CARTLEDGE
1929, August 7th: James JOHNSON
1929, August 7th: Arthur Leslie
RAVENEY
1929, November 26th: John MAGUIRE
1931, April 16th: Francis LAND
1931, June 3rd: Alexander
ANASTASSIOU
1931, August 12th: William John
CORBETT
1932, May 4th: Maurice FREEDMAN
1933, February 2nd: Jeremiah
HANBURY
1933, April 7th: Harold COURTNEY
1934, April 6th: Lewis HAMILTON
1935, April 2nd: Leonard Albert
BRIGSTOCK
1935, May 9th: John Stephenson
BAINBRIDGE
1935, May 30th: John Harris BRIDGE
1935, July 16th: George HAGUE
1939, June 7th: Ralph SMITH
1940, April 24th: William Charles
COWELL
1941, March 6th: Henry Lyndo WHITE
1941, September 19th: Eli RICHARDS
1941, December 23rd: Thomas William
THORPE
1942, November 6th: Herbert Heram
BOUNDS
1943, June 2nd: Bernard KIRWAN
1946, October 16th: Neville George
Clevely HEATH
1949, December 30th: Ernest Soper
COUZINS
1950, March 29th: Piotr
MAKSIMOWSKI
1950, October 30th: Paul Christopher
HARRIS
1950, December 19th: Nicholas
Persoulious CROSBY
1952, September 3rd: Mahmood
Hussain MATTAN
1963, December 17th: Russell PASCOE
& Dennis John WHITTY

Spy
1915, July 15th: Robert ROSENTHAL
1940, December 10th: Karl Heindrich
MEIR
1940, December 10th: Jose WALDBERG
1940, December 17th: Charles
VAN DER KEIBOOM
1941, July 9th: George Johnson
ARMSTRONG
1941, August 6th: Karl Theo DRUEKE
1941, August 6th: Werner Heindrich
WALTI
1941, December 10th: Karel Richard
RICHTER
1942, July 7th: Jose Estelle KEY

1942, July 7th: Alphonse Louis Eugene TIMMERMAN
1942, November 3rd: Duncan Alexander Croall SCOTT-FORD
1942, December 31st: Johannes Marius DRONKERS
1943, January 26th: Franciscus Johannes WINTER
1944, March 16th: Oswald JOB
1944, June 23rd: Pierre Richard Charles NEUKERMANS
1944, July 12th: Joseph Jan VANHOVE

Stabbing
1869, November 15th: Joseph WELSH
1882, August 22nd: Thomas HAYNES
1890, December 30th: Thomas McDONALD
1898, March 14th: John HERDMAN
1898, March 12th
1870, March 28th: William MOBBS
1881, November 29th: Percy LEFROY
1872, August 1st: John KEWISH
1873, January 7th: Edward HANCOCK
1873, August 16th: Laurence SMITH
1873, August 20th
1873, September 8th: James CONNOR
1874, January 5th: Edward GOUGH
1874, October 13th: John Walter COPPEN
1874, December 29th: Robert TAYLOR
1875, March 30th: John STANTON
1875, April 26th: William HALE
1875, July 27th: Jeremiah CORKERY
1875, August 9th: Peter BLANCHARD
1875, August 16th: William McCULLOUGH
1875, December 22nd: John William ANDERSON
1876, August 14th: Richard THOMPSON
1876, August 25th: Christos Emanuel BAUMBOS
1877, August 21st: Patrick McGOVERN
1877, November 12th: Thomas Benjamin PRATT
1877, November 19th: William HUSSELL
William HASSELL
1878, April 15th: Vincent Knowles WALKER
1878, July 30th: Robert VEST
1878, October 8th: Thomas SMITHERS
1878, November 18th: Joseph GARCIA
1879, May 28th: Thomas JOHNSON
1879, August 25th: Joseph PRISTORIA
1880, March 22nd: John WINGFIELD
1880, July 27th: Thomas BERRY
1881, February 21st: William STANWAY
1881, February 28th: Albert ROBINSON
1882, January 30th: Charles GERRISH
1882, January 31st
1882, May 16th: Thomas FURY

1883, May 14th: Joseph BRADY
1884, February 25th: Charles KITE
1884, December 8th: Ernest EWERSTADT
1885, May 25th: Moses SHRIMPTON
1885, July 13th: Henry ALT
1885, October 5th: Henry NORMAN
1886, February 9th: John BAINS
1887, November 28th: Enoch WADELY
1888, December 11th: Samuel CROWTHER
1888, December 18th: William WADDELL
1889, January 1st: Charles BULMER
1890, March 26th: John NEAL
1891, May 19th: Alfred William TURNER
1891, August 18th: Thomas SADLER
1892, January 5th: James STOCKWELL
1892, January 12th: Frederick Thomas STOREY
1891, January 11th
1892, March 1st: James MUIR
1892, December 20th: James MELLOR
1893, January 18th: William McKEOWN
1893, July 10th: Edward LEIGH
1894, May 22nd: John LANGFORD
1894, December 11th: Samuel George EMERY
1895, June 4th: William MILLER
1895, August 13th: Robert Heseltine HUDSON
1895, December 17th: Elijah WINSTANLEY
1896, February 4th: William James MORGAN
1896, August 25th: Joseph Robert ELLIS
1896, October 6th: James JONES
1898, November 15th: John RYAN
1899, May 3rd: Frederick James ANDREWS
1899, November 15th: Thomas SKEFFINGTON
1899, November 21st: George NUNN
1900, August 14th: William James IRWIN
1900, October 3rd: William BURRETT
1901, July 9th: Valeri GIOVANNI
1901, August 20th: John JOYCE
1901, November 19th: Marcel FAUGERON
1901, December 3rd: Patrick McKENNA
1901, December 7th: John MILLER
1901, December 7th: John Robert MILLER
1901, December 13th: Alick CLAYDON
1902, March 18th: Harold APTED
1902, August 13th: George HIBBS
1902, September 30th: John MacDONALD
1902, November 12th: Patrick LEGGETT

1902, December 9th: Thomas FAIRCLOUGH-BARROW
1902, December 12th: Jeremiah CALLAGHAN
1902, December 22nd: William James BOLTON
1903, March 10th: Samuel Henry SMITH
1903, June 2nd: Gustav RAU
1903, June 2nd: Willem SCHMIDT
1903, November 10th: Charles Jeremiah SLOWE
1903, December 29th: Henry Bertram STARR
1904, January 5th: Joseph MORAN
1904, December 21st: Eric LANGE
1904, December 28th: Arthur JEFFRIES
1905, August 9th: William Alfred HANCOCKS
1905, November 7th: William George BUTLER
1905, December 5th: William YARNOLD
1905, December 6th: Henry PARKINS
1905, December 28th: George SMITH
1906, August 7th: Edward GLYNN
1908, December 30th: Noah Percy COLLINS
1909, January 6th: John Esmond MURPHY
1909, March 2nd: John HUTCHINSON
1909, May 20th: Marks REUBENS
1910, March 1st: George Henry PERRY
1910, May 25th: Thomas William JESSHOPE
1910, June 14th: James Henry HANCOCK
1910, December 21st: Noah WOOLF
1911, December 21st: Charles COLEMAN
1911, December 28th: George LOAKE
1912, March 6th: Myer ABRAMOVICH
1913, February 4th: Eric James SEDGEWICK
1913, August 14th: Hugh McCLAREN
1914, July 28th: Herbert BROOKER
1915, August 10th: Walter MARRIOT
1916, January 1st: Lee KUN
1916, August 16th: William Alan BUTLER
1917, April 10th: Alexanda BAKERLIS
1917, April 17th: William James ROBINSON
1917, December 18th: William CAVANAGH
1918, March 9th: Louis VAN DER KERK-HOVE
1918, December 17th: William ROONEY
1920, January 6th: Hyman PURDOVICH
1920, May 6th: Thomas Hargreaves WILSON
1920, November 30th: Cyril Victor Tennyson SAUNDERS
1920, December 30th: Samuel WESTWOOD

1923, January 9th: Edith Jessie THOMPSON
1923, January 9th: Frederick Edward Francis BYWATERS
1924, April 8th: Francis Wilson BOOKER
1924, November 27th: Frederick SOUTHGATE
1925, April 15th: Henry GRAHAM
1925, April 15th: Thomas Henry SHELTON
1925, September 4th: John KEEN
1925, December 15th: Samuel JOHNSON
1926, March 9th: George THOMAS
1926, August 10th: James SMITH
1926, November 22nd: SAMANDA, Hashan
1926, November 2nd: SAMANDER
1927, March 29th: James Frederick STRATTON
1928, January 3rd: Frederick FIELDING
1928, January 27th: Daniel DRISCOLL & Edward ROWLANDS
1928, January 31st: James GILLON
1928, July 25th: Albert George ABSALOM
1928, August 10th: Norman ELLIOTT
1928, November 20th: William Charles BENSON
1930, June 11th: Albert Edward MARJERAM
1932, April 27th: George Emmanuel MICHAEL
1933, June 8th: Jack Samuel PUTTNAM
1933, December 28th: Stanley HOBDAY
1936, August 5th: Wallace JENDEN
1938, March 20th: Charles James CALDWELL
1938, May 26th: Robert William HOOLHOUSE
1939, March 29th: William Thomas BUTLER
1939, October 10th: Leonard George HUCKER
1940, March 27th: Ernest Edmund HAMERTON
1940, October 31st: Stanley Edward COLE
1940, December 24th: Edward SCOLLEN
1941, February 11th: Clifford HOLMES
1941, October 31st: Antonio MANCINI
1941, December 3rd: John Ernest SMITH
1942, May 1st: Harold HILL
1943, April 29th: August SANGRET
1944, February 2nd: Christos GEORGIOU
1944, May 26th: Wiley HARRIS
1944, August 8th: William Alfred COWLE
1945, January 9th: Horace Beresford GORDON

1946, January 31st: Michael NIESCIOR
1946, February 8th: John LYON
1946, April 6th: Patrick CARRAHER
1946, April 9th: Harold BERRY
1946, July 17th: Thomas HENDREN
1946, November 19th: Arthur RUSHTON
1947, June 20th: Eric Charles BRIGGS
1948, November 18th: Stanley Joseph
CLARKE
1948, December 9th: Clifford Godfrey
WILLS
1948, December 30th: Arthur George
OSBORNE
1949, January 27th: George SEMINI
1949, August 16th: William John
DAVIES
1949, December 30th: Ernest Soper
COUZINS
1951, April 26th: James VIRRELS
1951, June 12th: John DAND
1951, October 24th: John O'CONNER
1952, March 21st: Takir ALI
1952, April 12th: James SMITH
1952, May 27th: Backary MAUNEH
1952, July 15th: Thomas EAMES
1952, September 5th: John Howard
GODAR
1952, September 30th: Raymond Jack
CULL
1952, September 30th: Dennis George
MULDOWNEY
1952, December 12th: Eric
NORTHCLIFFE
1952, December 17th: John Kenneth
LIVESEY
1952, December 24th: Herbert
APPLEBY
1953, January 2nd James John ALCOTT
1953, December 22nd: Alfred Charles
WHITEWAY
1954, January 8th: Czeslaw KOWALSKI
1954, January 27th: William LUBINA
1954, June 23rd: George Alexander
ROBERTSON
1954, August 12th: Harold FOWLER
1955, May 4th: Winston SHAW
1955, June 21st: Richard GOWLER
1955, July 26th: Frederick Arthur CROSS
1955, July 27th: Norman William
GREEN
1955, August 9th: Ernest Charles
HARDING
1955, August 12th: Alec WILKINSON
1959, May 8th: Ronald Henry
MARWOOD
1961, July 6th: Edwin Albert Arthur
BUSH
1963, December 17th: Russell PASCOE
1964, August 13th: Peter Anthony
ALLEN

Starvation
1870, October 11th: Margaret WATERS

1899, January 13th: Philip KING

Strangulation
1870, October 11th: Margaret WATERS
1872, August 13th: Thomas MOORE
1874, August 31st: Henry FLANAGAN
1881, November 21st: Alfred GOUGH
1882, November 13th: William Meager
BARTLETT
1884, December 8th: Arthur SHAW
1886, January 20th: William SHEEHAN
1887, May 16th: Henry William YOUNG
1889, March 6th: Ebeneezer Samuel
JENKINS
1889, April 24th: William Henry BURY
1892, April 4th: James CAMPBELL
1892, April 26th: George Henry WOOD
1894, August 14th: Paul KOEZULA
1896, August 4th: Joseph HIRST
1896, July 21st: Philip MATTHEWS
1870, August 1st: Walter MILLAR
1889, March 11th: Jessie KING
1890, December 23rd: Mary Eleanor
WHEELER
1901, March 21st: Herbert John
BENNETT
1901, December 24th: John HARRISON
1902, December 16th: Thomas
NICHOLSON
1903, July 28th: Leonard PATCHETT
1903, August 11th: William Joseph
TUFFIN
1903, December 8th: James DUFFY
1904, August 2nd: George BREEZE
1906, February 27th: John GRIFFITHS
1906, August 9th: Thomas Acomb
MOUNCER
1907, November 5th: William George
Charles AUSTIN
1908, August 5th: Matthew John DODDS
1909, August 3rd: Mark SHAWCROSS
1910, November 15th: Thomas
RAWCLIFFE
1910, November 22nd: Henry
THOMPSON
1911, July 19th: William Henry PALMER
1911, October 17th: Edward HILL
1911, December 12th: Walter MARTYN
1912, November 5th: Robert
GALLOWAY
1913, November 27th: Frederick
Albert ROBERTSON
1913, December 31st: George Frederick
LAW
1914, March 10th: Josiah DAVIS
1916, March 29th: Reginald HASLAM
1916, December 12th: Fred BROOKS
1918, December 17th: John William
WALSH
1919, August 8th: Henry Thomas
GASKIN
1919, October 7th: Frank George
WARREN

1920, March 10th: William WRIGHT
1922, August 17th: Simon McGEOWN
1923, April 10th: Frederick George WOOD
1923, August 8th: Albert BURROWS
1923, October 10th: Susan NEWELL
1923, November 1st: Frederick William Maximillian JESSE
1924, December 17th: Arthur SIMS
1925, August 5th: James WINSTANLEY
1926, March 24th: Eugene DEVERE
1926, August 12th: Charles Edward FINDEN
1926, August 11th
1927, August 12th: John ROBINSON
1928, January 6th: John Thomas DUNN
1928, January 6th: Sydney Bernard GOULTER
1928, January 7th: Samuel CASE
1928, August 29th: Gerard TOAL
1928, December 6th: Chung Yi MIAO
1929, March 12th: Joseph Reginald Victor CLARKE
1930, April 8th: Sydney Harry FOX
1931, December 15th: Solomon STEIN
1932, February 23rd: William Harold GODDARD
1932, March 9th: George Thomas POPLE
1932, May 18th: Charles James COWLE
1933, June 8th: Jack Samuel PUTTNAM
1933, October 11th: Robert James KIRBY
1935, February 7th: David Maskill BLAKE
1936, May 21st: Buck RUXTON
1936, July 14th: George Arthur BRYANT
1937, February 10th: Andrew Anderson BAGLEY
1937, August 13th: Leslie George STONE
1937, August 17th: Frederick George MURPHY
1937, November 18th: John Thomas ROGERS
1937, December 30th: Frederick NODDER
1938, July 12th: Alfred Ernest RICHARDS
1938, July 19th: William James GRAVES
1938, July 26th: William PARKER
1939, March 25th: Harry ARMSTRONG
1941, April 4th: Samuel MORGAN
1941, December 18th: Patrick KELLY
1942, March 11th: Harold Dorian TREVOR
1942, April 15th: Cyril JOHNSON

1942, June 24th: Douglas EDMONDSON
1942, June 25th: Gordon Frederick CUMMINS
1942, September 10th: Harold Oswald MERRY
1942, October 6th: Patrick William KINGSTON
1942, October 28th: William Ambrose COLLINS
1943, January 27th: Harry DOBKIN
1943, March 24th: William Henry TURNER
1943, August 3rd: William QUAYLE
1943, November 19th: Terence CASEY
1943, December 22nd: John Joseph DORGAN
1943, December 29th: Thomas JAMES
1944, June 6th: Ernest James Harman KEMP
1944, July 12th: John Gordon DAVIDSON
1945, January 31st: Arthur THOMPSON
1945, January 8th: Ernest Lee CLARK & Augustine M GUERRA
1945, April 7th: William HARRISON
1945, October 31st: Ronald Bertram MAURI
1946, May 28th: Leonard HOLMES
1946, July 17th: Thomas HENDREN
1946, August 7th: Walter CLAYTON
1946, September 6th: David Baillie MASON
1946, November 13th: Frank Joseph FREIYER
1946, December 10th: John Fleming McCready MATHIESON
1947, March 18th: Harold HAGGER
1948, January 7th: George Henry WHELPTON
1948, February 19th: Walter John CROSS
1949, March 29th: James FARRELL
1949, June 2nd: Dennis NEVILLE
1949, June 21st: Bernard Alfred Peter COOPER
1949, July 28th: Sydney Archibald Frederick CHAMBERLAIN
1949, August 4th: Rex Harvey JONES
1949, December 14th: John WILSON
1950, March 8th: James Frank RIVETT
1950, March 9th: Timothy John EVANS
1950, July 11th: George Finlay BROWN
1950, July 13th: Ronald Douglas ATWELL
1950, November 14th: Patrick George TURNAGE
1950, November 23rd: Norman GOLDTHORPE
1950, November 28th: James Henry CORBITT
1950, December 14th: Edward Isaac WOODFIELD

1951, May 8th: James INGLIS
1951, May 9th: William Edward
SHAUGHNESSY
1951, July 3rd: Jack WRIGHT
1953, July 15th: John Reginald
Halliday CHRISTIE
1953, July 30th: Philip HENRY
1953, November 17th: Joseph
Christopher REYNOLDS
1953, December 17th: Stanislaw
JURAS
1954, June 22nd: Milton TAYLOR
1954, August 11th: William Sanchez
de Pina HEPPER
1954, September 1st: Rupert Geoffrey
WELLS
1954, December 15th: Styllou
Pantopiou CHRISTOFI
1955, April 14th: Sydney Joseph
CLARKE
1955, May 2nd: James ROBINSON
1955, July 12th: Kenneth ROBERTS
1958, August 12th: Matthew
KAVANAGH
1951, July 19th: Dennis Albert
MOORE
1951, October 24th: John O'CONNER
1951, December 11th: Herbert
Leonard MILLS
1952, January 1st: Horace CARTER
1952, May 29th: Peter Gallagher
DEVENEY
1952, July 22nd: Frank BURGESS
1952, August 12th: Oliver George
BUTLER
1961, January 27th: Wasyl GNYPIUK
1961, July 25th: Samuel
McCLAUGHLIN
1961, December 20th: Robert Andrew
McGLADDERY

Suffocation

1870, October 11th: Margaret
WATERS
1889, March 11th: Jessie KING

1893, January 3rd: Cross
DUCKWORTH
1893, August 10th: Charles SQUIRES

1894, November 29th: Thomas
RICHARDS
1899, January 13th: Philip KING
1900, March 6th: Ada
CHARD-WILLIAMS
1903, February 3rd: Amelia SACH
1903, February 3rd: Annie WALTERS
1904, December 13th: Conrad
DONOVAN
1904, December 13th: Charles WADE
1907, August 14th: Rhoda WILLIS
1907, November 5th: William George
Charles AUSTIN
1909, July 20th: William HAMPTON
1910, November 24th: William
BROOME
1913, January 13th: Albert RUMENS
1922, February 21st: William
HARKNESS
1927, December 29th: William O'NEILL
1929, February 20th: Frank
HOLLINGTON
1932, November 23rd: Ernest
HUTCHINSON
1935, January 1st: Frederick
RUSHWORTH
1936, June 30th: Frederick Herbert
Charles FIELD
1945, March 13th: Arthur HEYS
1948, December 2nd: George RUSSELL
1951, April 25th: Joseph BROWN &
Edward Charles SMITH
1954, April 20th: Michael MANNING
1954, April 23rd: John LYNCH
1954, June 17th: Kenneth GILBERT
& Ian Arthur GRANT

Treason

1916, August 3rd: Roger David
CASEMENT
1921, March 14th: Thomas BRYAN
1921, March 14th: Patrick DOYLE
1921, March 14th: Frank FLOOD
1921, March 14th: Bernard RYAN
1945, December 19th: John AMERY
1946, January 3rd: William JOYCE
1946, January 4th: Theodore John
William SCHURCH

Executioner
Index

This is a cumulative index, encompassing
Volumes I, II and III of the Hangman's Record.

Erroneous dates of hangings, and names of victims,
executioners and people hanged, have been corrected in the
relevant indexes. For easy reference, updated entries include
the information as originally given, *shown in italics.*

* = *given name unknown*

Executioner Index

Allen, Alfred
1932, November 23rd Ernest HUTCHINSON
1936, June 30th Frederick Herbert Charles FIELD
1937, August 17th Frederick George MURPHY

Allen, Alfred (asst)
1930, April 22nd William Henry PODMORE
1931, January 3rd Victor Edward BETTS
1931, December 10th Henry Daniel SEYMOUR
1932, April 28th John Henry ROBERTS
1934, April 6th Lewis HAMILTON
1934, October 9th Harry TUFFNEY
1935, February 7th David Maskill BLAKE
1937, August 13th Leslie George STONE

Allen, Harry
1957, July 23rd John Willson VICKERS
1957, December 4th Dennis HOWARD
1958, July 11th Peter Thomas Anthony MANUEL
1958, August 12th Matthew KAVANAGH
1958, September 3rd Frank STOKES
1958, September 30th Ernest Raymond JONES
1959, April 28th Joseph CHRIMES
1959, May 8th Ronald Henry MARWOOD
1959, August 14th Bernard Hugh WALDEN
1959, October 9th Francis Joseph HUCHET
1959, November 5th Guenther Fritz Erwin PODOLA
1960, September 1st John Louis CONSTANTINE
1960, November 10th Francis Robert FORSYTH & Norman James HARRIS
1960, December 22nd Anthony Joseph MILLER
1961, January 27th Wasyl GNYPIUK
1961, February 9th George RILEY
1961, March 29th Jack DAY
1961, May 26th Victor John TERRY
1961, July 6th Edwin Albert Arthur BUSH
1961, July 25th Samuel McCLAUGHLIN
1961, September 7th Hendryk NEIMASZ
1961, December 20th Robert Andrew McGLADDERY
1962, April 4th James HANRATTY
1962, October 12th Oswald Augustus GREY
1962, November 28th James SMITH

1963, August 15th Henry John BURNETT
1963, December 17th Russell PASCOE
1964, August 13th Gweynne Owen EVANS

Allen, Harry (asst)
1941, February 11th Clifford HOLMES
1941, March 6th Henry Lyndo WHITE
1941, September 4th John SMITH
1941, December 3rd John Ernest SMITH
1945, October 6th Heinz BRUELING & Joachim GOLTZ & Erich Pallme KOENIG & Josef MERTENS & Kurt ZUEHLSDORFF
1946, January 8th William BATTY
1946, March 26th Arthur CHARLES
1946, September 6th David Baillie MASON
1946, September 6th Sydney John SMITH
1946, December 10th John Fleming McCready MATHIESON
1947, January 3rd Stanley SHEMINANT
1948, February 19th Walter John CROSS
1948, November 19th Peter GRIFFITHS
1948, December 30th Arthur George OSBORNE
1949, January 27th George SEMINI
1949, April 21st Harry LEWIS
1949, June 2nd Dennis NEVILLE
1949, July 28th Sydney Archibald Frederick CHAMBERLAIN
1949, September 28th William Claude Hodson JONES
1949, December 30th Ernest Soper COUZINS
1950, March 28th George KELLY
1950, March 30th Walter SHARPE
1950, August 16th Albert PRICE
1951, April 3rd William Arthur WATKINS
1951, April 25th Joseph BROWN & Edward Charles SMITH
1951, May 9th William Edward SHAUGHNESSY
1951, June 12th John DAND
1951, July 19th Dennis Albert MOORE
1951, July 19th Alfred George REYNOLDS
1952, February 6th Alfred MOORE
1952, May 7th Ajit SINGH
1952, July 8th Harry HUXLEY
1952, October 9th Peter Cyril JOHNSON
1952, December 24th Herbert APPLEBY
1953, January 28th Derek William BENTLEY
1953, October 20th John Owen GREENWAY

Allen, Harry (asst)　　Executioner Index　　Baxter, Robert (asst)

Allen, Harry (asst)

1953, December 23rd George James NEWLANDS
1954, January 27th William LUBINA
1954, April 14th James Reginald DOOHAN
1954, June 23rd George Alexander ROBERTSON
1954, August 12th Harold FOWLER
1954, December 15th Styllou Pantopiou CHRISTOFI
1955, May 22nd James ROBINSON
1955, August 2nd Corbett Montague ROBERTS

Allen, Herbert (asst)

1949, December 14th Benjamin ROBERTS
1949, December 14th John WILSON
1950, March 8th James Frank RIVETT
1950, July 7th Zbigniew GOWER & Roman REDEL
1950, November 28th James Henry CORBITT
1950, December 14th Edward Isaac WOODFIELD
1951, January 26th Nenad KOVASEVIC
1951, April 25th Joseph BROWN & Edward Charles SMITH
1951, October 24th John O'CONNER
1951, December 11th Herbert Leonard MILLS

Anderson, Robert

1874, January 12th Edwin BAILEY
1874, January 12th Ann BERRY
1874, January 12th Charles Edward BUTT
1875, January 4th John McGRAVE
1875, January 4th Michael MULLEN
1875, January 4th William WORTHINGTON

Anderson, Robert (asst)

1874, May 25th John GODWIN

Archer, Alfred (asst)

1883, December 17th Patrick O'DONNELL

Askern, Thomas

1868, December 28th Priscilla BIGGADYKE
1874, August 18th William JACKSON
1875, December 21st William SMEDLEY
1876, December 19th James DALGLEISH
1877, April 3rd John Henry JOHNSON

Baxter, Robert

1924, August 12th Jean-Pierre VAQUIER
1925, November 12th Hubert George BLOYE
1926, March 9th George THOMAS

Baxter, Robert (asst)

1926, March 24th Eugene DEVERE
1926, July 27th Johannes Josephus Cornelius MOMMERS
1926, June 27th
1926, November 22nd SAMANDA, Hashan
1926, November 2nd: SAMANDER
1927, March 29th James Frederick STRATTON
1927, August 3rd Frederick Stephen FULLER
1927, August 3rd James MURPHY
1927, August 12th John ROBINSON
1928, January 6th Sydney Bernard GOULTER
1928, January 24th James McKAY
1928, January 27th Daniel DRISCOLL
1928, January 27th Edward ROWLANDS
1928, January 31st James GILLON
1928, April 12th Frederick LOCK
1928, May 31st Frederick Guy BROWNE
1928, June 6th Frederick STEWART
1928, August 3rd George REYNOLDS
1928, August 13th Allen WALES
1928, November 20th William Charles BENSON
1928, December 11th Trevor EDWARDS
1929, February 20th Frank HOLLINGTON
1929, February 27th William John HOLMYARD
1930, April 8th Sydney Harry FOX
1931, June 3rd Alexander ANASTASSIOU
1931, August 5th Oliver NEWMAN & William SHELLEY
1931, August 12th William John CORBETT
1932, February 23rd William Harold GODDARD
1932, May 4th Maurice FREEDMAN
1933, June 8th Jack Samuel PUTTNAM
1933, August 10th Varnavas Loizi ANTORKA
1933, October 11th Robert James KIRBY
1934, October 9th Harry TUFFNEY
1934, November 14th John Frederick STOCKWELL
1935, March 13th George Frank HARVEY
1935, April 2nd Leonard Albert BRIGSTOCK
1935, October 29th Raymond BOUSQUET
1935, October 30th Allan James GRIERSON

Baxter, Robert (asst)

1915, July 15th Robert ROSENTHAL
1915, December 29th John William McCARTNEY
1916, August 3rd Roger David CASEMENT

325

Baxter, Robert (asst) Executioner Index Berry, James

1917, March 29th Leo George O'DONNELL
1917, April 17th William James ROBINSON
1917, April 18th Robert GADSBY
1917, May 16th Thomas McGUINESS
1917, December 18th William CAVANAGH
1919, January 7th Benjamin Hindle BENSON
1919, January 8th Percy George BARRETT
1919, January 8th George Walter CALDWELL
1919, July 22nd John CROSSLAND
1919, November 26th Ambrose QUINN
1920, January 6th: David CAPLAN
1920, January 6th Hyman PURDOVICH
1920, March 23rd William HALL
1920, May 6th Thomas Hargreaves WILSON
1920, May 11th Herbert Edward SALISBURY
1920, May 11th William WADDINGTON
1920, December 30th Marks GOODMARCHER
1921, January 7th George Edmund Freeman Quentin LEVER
1921, February 4th Jack Alfred FIELD
1921, February 4th William Thomas GRAY
1922, April 18th Edmund Hugh TONBRIDGE
1922, August 11th Elijah POUTNEY
1922, December 13th George ROBINSON
1922, December 13th Frank FOWLER
1923, January 9th Edith Jessie THOMPSON
1923, November 1st Frederick William Maximillian JESSE
1924, April 8th Francis Wilson BOOKER
1924, December 9th William George SMITH
1924, December 17th Arthur SIMS
1925, February 24th William Grover BIGNALL
1925, April 2nd George William BARTON
1925, June 10th Hubert Ernest DALTON
1925, August 11th James MAKIN
1925, August 14th Arthur Henry BISHOP & William John CRONIN
1926, April 13th: George SHARPES
1926, August 12th Charles Edward FINDEN
1926, August 11th
1927, January 5th William Cornelius JONES

Berry, James
1884, March 31st William INNES

1884, March 31st Robert Flockheart VICKERS
1884, May 26th Mary LEFLEY
1884, May 27th Joseph LAWSON
1884, August 19th Peter CASSIDY
1884, October 6th Thomas HARRIS
1884, October 6th Thomas Henry ORROCK
1884, November 24th Kay HOWARTH
1884, November 24th Harry Hammond SWINDELLS
1884, December 8th Ernest EWERSTADT
1884, December 8th Arthur SHAW
1885, January 13th Horace Robert JAY
1885, January 16th Michael DOWNEY
1885, January 20th Thomas PARRY
1885, March 17th Henry KIMBERLEY
1885, May 18th James LEE
1885, May 25th Moses SHRIMPTON
1885, July 13th Henry ALT
1885, August 3rd Joseph TUCKER
1885, August 17th Thomas BOULTON
1885, October 5th Henry NORMAN
1885, November 23rd John HILL
1885, November 23rd John WILLIAMS
1885, November 30th Robert GOODALE
1885, December 7th Daniel MINAHAN
1885, December 8th George THOMAS
1885, December 9th
1886, January 12th John CRONIN
1886, January 20th William SHEEHAN
1886, February 1st John HORTON
1886, February 8th James BAKER
1886, February 8th James MARTIN
1886, February 8th Anthony Ben RUDGE
1886, February 9th John BAINS
1886, February 10th John THURSTON
1886, February 16th George SAUNDERS
1886, February 22nd Owen McGILL
1886, March 1st Thomas NASH
1886, March 2nd David ROBERTS
1886, May 31st Albert Edward BROWN
1886, May 31st James WHELAN
1886, June 15th Edward HEWITT
1886, July 26th William SAMUELS
1886, July 27th
1886, August 9th Mary Ann BRITLAND
1886, November 16th Patrick JUDGE
1886, November 29th James MURPHY
1886, November 30th James BANTON
James BARTON
1886, December 13th George HARMER
1887, February 14th Thomas BLOXHAM
1887, February 15th Thomas LEATHERBARROW
1887, February 17th Edward PRITCHARD
1887, February 21st Richard INSOLE
1887, February 22nd: Benjamin TERRY
1887, March 14th Elizabeth BERRY
1887, March 21st Joseph KING

1887, April 18th Thomas William CURRELL
1887, May 9th Charles SMITH
1887, May 16th Henry William YOUNG
1887, May 30th Walter WOOD
1887, August 1st Alfred SOWERY
1887, August 16th Thomas Henry BEVAN
1887, August 22nd Israel LIPSKI
1887, August 29th William WILTON
1887, November 14th William HUNTER
1887, November 15th Joseph WALKER
1887, November 21st Joseph MORLEY
1887, November 28th Enoch WADELY
1887, December 6th Thomas PAYNE
1888, January 10th Phillip Henry Eustace CROSS
1888, March 13th David REES
1888, March 20th James JONES
1888, March 20th Alfred SCANDRETT
1888, March 27th George CLARKE
1888, March 28th William ARROWSMITH
1888, April 28th Daniel HAYES & Daniel MORIARTY
1888, April 29th
1888, May 7th James KIRBY
1888, May 15th John Alfred GELL
1888, July 17th Robert UPTON
1888, July 18th Thomas WYRE
1888, August 7th John JACKSON
1888, August 10th Arthur Thomas DELANEY
1888, August 15th George SARGENT
1888, August 28th George Nathaniel DANIELS
1888, August 28th Harry Benjamin JONES
1888, November 13th Leir Richard BARTLETT
1888, December 11th Samuel CROWTHER
1888, December 18th William WADDELL
1889, January 1st Thomas CLEWES
1889, January 2nd Charles DOBELL
1889, January 2nd William GOWER
1889, January 8th George NICHOLSON
1889, January 14th Arthur McKEOWN
1889, March 6th Ebeneezer Samuel JENKINS
1889, March 11th Jessie KING
1889, March 13th Samuel RYLANDS
1889, April 10th Thomas ALLEN
1889, April 11th John WITHEY
1889, April 8th Peter STAFFORD
1889, April 24th William Henry BURY
1889, August 21st George HORTON
1889, December 9th Benjamin PURCELL
1889, December 24th William DUKES

1889, December 31st William Thomas HOOK
1890, January 7th Charles Lister HIGGENBOTHAM
1890, March 11th Joseph BOSWELL & Samuel BOSWELL
1890, March 12th William ROW
1890, March 26th John NEAL
1890, April 8th Richard DAVIES
1890, April 15th William Matthew CHADWICK
1890, June 10th Daniel Stewart GORRIE
1890, July 29th George BOWLING
1890, August 22nd Felix SPICER
1890, August 26th Frederick DAVIES
1890, August 27th Francois MONTEAU
1890, September 23rd Henry DELVIN
1890, December 23rd Mary Eleanor WHEELER
1890, December 30th Thomas McDONALD
1891, February 2nd Bartholomew SULLIVAN
1891, March 13th John PURCELL
1891, May 19th Alfred William TURNER
1891, July 21st Franz Joseph MUNCH
1891, July 28th Arthur SPENCER
1891, August 18th Thomas SADLER
1891, August 19th Robert BRADSHAW
1891, August 20th John CONWAY
1891, August 25th Edward Henry FAWCETT
1892, January 12th: Frederick Thomas STOREY
1891, January 11th

Billington, James
1884, August 26th Joseph LAYCOCK
1887, August 22nd Henry HOBSON
1888, May 22nd James William RICHARDSON
1889, January 1st Charles BULMER
1889, December 31st Frederick BRETT
1889, December 31st Robert WEST
1890, August 26th James HARRISON
1890, December 30th Robert KITCHING
1891, August 18th Walter Lewis TURNER
1891, December 15th Henry DAINTON
1891, December 22nd John William JOHNSON
1891, December 23rd Charles SAUNDERS
1892, January 5th James STOCKWELL
1892, March 1st James MUIR
1892, March 17th Frederick EGGLESTON
1892, March 17th Charles RAYNOR
1892, March 22nd Joseph WILSON
1892, March 29th John NOBLE
1892, April 26th George Henry WOOD
1892, June 14th Henry PICKERING

1892, July 26th John GURD
1892, August 16th James TAYLOR
1892, August 16th John George
 WENZEL
1892, August 17th Patrick GIBBONS
1892, August 18th Moses CUDWORTH
1892, October 11th John James
 BANBURY
1892, November 15th Thomas CREAM
1892, December 20th James MELLOR
1892, December 22nd Thomas
 EDWARDS
1893, January 3rd Cross DUCKWORTH
1893, January 10th Andrew George
 McCRAE
1893, January 18th William McKEOWN
1893, March 16th Albert MANNING
1893, March 28th William WILLIAMS
1893, April 4th Edward HEMMINGS
1893, July 18th Richard SABEY
1893, July 19th Amie Holman MEUNIER
1893, July 25th George Samuel COOK
1893, August 10th Charles SQUIRES
1893, August 16th John DAVIS
1893, November 28th Emanuel HAMER
1893, December 5th John CARTER
1893, December 6th George MASON
1893, December 19th Henry
 RUMBOLD
1893, December 21st Frederick
 WYNDHAM
1894, January 2nd William HARRIS
1894, February 13th George THOMAS
1894, March 27th Walter SMITH
1894, April 2nd Margaret WALBER
1894, April 3rd Philip GARNER
1894, April 4th Frederick William
 FENTON
1894, May 22nd John LANGFORD
1894, July 18th Samuel ELKINS
1894, July 31st William CROSSLEY
1894, August 14th Paul KOEZULA
1894, August 21st Alfred DEWS
1894, November 27th James Wilshaw
 WHITEHEAD
1894, November 29th Thomas
 RICHARDS
1894, December 4th James Canham
 READ
1894, December 10th John William
 NEWELL
1894, December 11th Samuel George
 EMERY
1894, December 12th Cyrus KNIGHT
1894, December 12th William ROGERS
1895, February 9th John TWISS
1895, March 26th Edmund KESTEVEN
1895, June 4th William MILLER
1895, June 18th James CANNING
1895, July 2nd Henry TICKNER
1895, August 13th Robert Heseltine
 HUDSON

1895, November 19th Richard
 WINGROVE
1895, November 13th
1895, December 3rd Arthur
 COVINGTON
1895, December 17th Elijah
 WINSTANLEY
1895, December 24th Henry WRIGHT
1895, December 31st Patrick MORLEY
1896, February 4th William James
 MORGAN
1896, February 25th Alfred
 CHIPPERFIELD
1896, June 9th Henry FOWLER
1896, June 9th Albert MILSOM
1896, June 9th William SEAMAN
1896, June 10th Amelia Elizabeth
 DYER
1896, July 7th Charles Thomas
 WOOLDRIDGE
1896, July 21st Frederick BURDEN
1896, July 21st Philip MATTHEWS
1896, July 21st Samuel Edward SMITH
1896, August 4th Joseph HIRST
1896, August 5th William PUGH
1896, August 11th John ROSE
1896, August 11th Samuel
 WILKINSON
1896, August 18th Frank TAYLOR
1896, August 25th Joseph Robert ELLIS
1896, October 6th James JONES
1896, December 22nd August CARLSEN
1896, December 23rd Joseph ALLCOCK
1897, January 5th Henry BROWN
1897, February 9th Robert HAYMAN
1897, June 7th George PATERSON
1897, July 27th Joseph BOWSER
1897, August 17th Joseph ROBINSON
1897, August 17th Walter ROBINSON
1897, August 18th Thomas LLOYD
1897, December 16th William BETTS
1898, February 22nd George William
 HOWE
1898, March 14th John HERDMAN
1898, March 12th
1898, March 22nd Charles SMITH
1898, June 28th William HORSFORD
1898, July 12th James WATT
1898, July 19th William WILKES
1898, August 3rd Thomas JONES
1898, August 30th Joseph LEWIS
1898, November 15th John RYAN
1898, December 13th Thomas DALEY
1898, December 14th
1898, December 21st John COTTON
1899, January 3rd John SCHNEIDER
1899, March 28th George ROBERTSON
1899, May 3rd Frederick James
 ANDREWS
1899, July 11th Joseph Cornelius
 PARKER
1899, July 18th Charles MAIDMENT
1899, July 19th Mary Ann ANSELL

1899, August 9th Elias TORR
1899, October 3rd Frederick PRESTON
1899, October 4th Robert WARD
1899, November 15th Thomas
SKEFFINGTON
1899, November 21st George NUNN
1899, November 28th Charles SCOTT
1899, December 5th Samuel CROZIER
1899, December 6th Michael DOWDLE
1900, January 9th Louisa Josephine
MASSET
1900, March 6th Ada
CHARD-WILLIAMS
1900, May 22nd Henry GROVE
1900, July 17th Alfred HIGHFIELD
1900, August 14th William James
IRWIN
1900, August 16th Charles Benjamin
BACKHOUSE
1900, August 16th Thomas MELLOR
1900, August 21st William LACY
1900, August 28th Charles Oliver
BLEWITT
1900, October 2nd John PARR
1900, October 3rd William BURRETT
1900, December 4th Joseph HOLDEN
1900, December 12th John BOWES
1900, December 27th James Joseph
BERGIN
1901, January 11th Timothy CADOGEN
1901, February 19th Sampson Silas
SALMON
1901, March 19th George Henry
PARKER
1901, March 21st Herbert John
BENNETT
1901, April 2nd Joseph Arthur
SHUFFLEBOTHAM
1901, July 9th Valeri GIOVANNI
1901, July 30th Charles WATKINS
1901, August 13th Ernest Walter
WICKHAM
1901, August 20th John JOYCE
1901, November 19th Marcel
FAUGERON
1901, December 3rd Patrick
McKENNA
1901, December 7th John &
John Robert MILLER

Billington, John
1903, December 2nd Charles Wood
WHITTAKER
1903, December 29th Henry Bertram
STARR
1904, March 29th Henry JONES
1904, August 2nd George BREEZE
1904, August 16th John Thomas KAY
1904, December 28th Arthur JEFFRIES
1905, February 28th Edward
HARRISON
1905, March 29th Ernest
HUTCHINSON

1905, April 26th Albert BRIDGEMAN
1905, May 23rd Albert & Alfred
STRATTON
1905, June 20th Alfred John HEAL
1905, August 9th William Alfred
HANCOCKS
1905, August 15th Thomas George
TATTERSALL

Billington, John (asst)
1901, December 10th John George
THOMPSON
1902, March 18th Harold APTED
1902, March 25th Arthur
RICHARDSON
1902, May 20th Thomas MARSLAND
1902, August 12th William LANE
1902, December 4th William
CHAMBERS
1902, December 9th Thomas
FAIRCLOUGH-BARROW
1902, December 12th Jeremiah
CALLAGHAN
1902, December 16th Thomas
NICHOLSON
1902, December 16th Samuel Thomas
WALTON
1902, December 22nd William James
BOLTON
1903, February 3rd Amelia SACH
1903, February 3rd Annie WALTERS
1903, February 17th William HUGHES
1903, February 18th
1903, March 9th Sydney George SMITH
1903, March 10th Samuel Henry SMITH
1903, June 2nd Gustav RAU
1903, June 2nd Willem SCHMIDT
1903, July 28th Leonard PATCHETT
1903, November 10th Charles Jeremiah
SLOWE
1903, November 17th Edward Richard
PALMER
1903, December 8th James DUFFY
1903, December 16th William BROWN
1903, December 16th Thomas
COWDREY
1903, December 22nd Charles William
ASHTON
1904, April 5th Charles Samuel DYER
1904, July 12th John SULLIVAN
1904, July 26th: Thomas GUNNING

Billington, Thomas (asst)
1897, July 27th Joseph BOWSER
1897, August 17th Joseph ROBINSON
1897, August 17th Walter ROBINSON
1897, August 18th Thomas LLOYD
1898, January 14th Patrick HESTOR
1898, February 22nd George William
HOWE
1898, August 3rd Thomas JONES
1898, August 30th Joseph LEWIS
1898, November 15th John RYAN

Billington, Thomas (asst) Executioner Index   Binns, Bartholomew

1898, December 21st John COTTON
1899, March 28th George ROBERTSON
1899, May 3rd Frederick James
ANDREWS
1900, December 27th James Joseph
BERGIN
1901, March 19th George Henry
PARKER
1901, July 30th Charles WATKINS
1901, December 7th John MILLER
& John Robert MILLER
1901, December 10th John George
THOMPSON
1901, December 13th Alick CLAYDON
1903, December 8th James DUFFY

Billington, William
1899, July 25th Edward BELL
1899, December 5th Samuel CROZIER
1901, December 10th John George
THOMPSON
1901, December 13th Alick CLAYDON
1901, December 24th John HARRISON
1902, March 18th Harold APTED
1902, March 25th Arthur
RICHARDSON
1902, April 23rd Thomas KEELEY
1902, April 29th Charles Robert EARL
1902, May 6th George WOOLFE
1902, May 20th Thomas MARSLAND
1902, July 15th Samuel MIDDLETON
1902, July 22nd William CHURCHER
1902, July 30th John BEDFORD
1902, August 12th William LANE
1902, August 13th George HIBBS
1902, September 30th John MacDONALD
1902, November 11th Henry WILLIAMS
1902, November 12th Patrick LEGGETT
1902, December 2nd Henry McWIGGINS
1902, December 4th William
CHAMBERS
1902, December 9th Thomas
FAIRCLOUGH-BARROW
1902, December 12th Jeremiah
CALLAGHAN
1902, December 16th Thomas
NICHOLSON
1902, December 16th Samuel Thomas
WALTON
1902, December 22nd William James
BOLTON
1902, December 30th James
DOCHERTY
1903, January 7th Joseph TAYLOR
1903, January 9th Mary DALY
1903, February 3rd Amelia SACH
1903, February 3rd Annie WALTERS
1903, February 17th William HUGHES
1903, February 18th
1903, March 3rd Edgar EDWARDS
1903, March 10th Samuel Henry SMITH
1903, April 7th George CHAPMAN

1903, May 13th William George
HUDSON
1903, June 2nd Gustav RAU
1903, June 2nd Willem SCHMIDT
1903, July 7th Charles HOWELL
1903, July 14th Samuel Herbert
DOUGAL
1903, July 21st Thomas PORTER
1903, July 21st Thomas PRESTON
1903, July 28th Leonard PATCHETT
1903, November 10th Charles Jeremiah
SLOWE
1903, November 17th Edward Richard
PALMER
1903, December 1st Bernard WHITE
1903, December 8th James DUFFY
1903, December 16th William BROWN
1903, December 16th Thomas
COWDREY
1903, December 22nd Charles William
ASHTON
1903, December 29th John GALLAGHER
1903, December 29th Emily SWANN
1904, January 5th Joseph MORAN
1904, March 9th Sydney George SMITH
1904, March 29th James Henry
CLARKSON
1904, April 5th Charles Samuel DYER
1904, April 14th James CAMPION
1904, April 15th John KELLY
1904, May 31st William KIRWAN
1904, May 31st Pong LUN
1904, July 12th John SULLIVAN
1904, July 13th Samuel ROWLEDGE
1904, July 26th Thomas GUNNING
1904, August 16th Samuel HOLDEN
1904, December 13th Conrad DONOVAN
1904, December 13th Charles WADE
1904, December 20th Edmund HALL
1904, December 21st Eric LANGE
1905, April 25th John FOSTER

Billington, William (asst)
1898, July 12th James WATT
1899, August 9th Elias TORR
1900, August 16th Charles Benjamin
BACKHOUSE
1900, August 16th Thomas MELLOR
1900, August 28th Charles Oliver
BLEWITT
1901, April 2nd Joseph Arthur
SHUFFLEBOTHAM
1901, July 9th Valeri GIOVANNI
1901, August 13th Ernest Walter
WICKHAM
1901, August 20th John JOYCE

Binns, Bartholomew
1883, November 6th Henry POWELL
1883, November 13th Thomas Lyons
DAY
1883, November 19th Peter BRAY
1883, November 26th Thomas RILEY

330

1883, December 3rd Henry DUTTON
1883, December 17th Patrick
  O'DONNELL
1884, January 15th Peter WADE
1884, February 25th Charles KITE
1884, March 3rd Catherine
  FLANAGAN & Margaret HIGGINS
1884, March 5th
1884, March 10th Michael McLEAN

Binns, Bartholomew (asst)
1899, January 10th Thomas KELLY
1901, March 7th John TOOLE

Broadbent, John (asst)
1953, May 19th John Lawrence TODD
1953, December 22nd Alfred Charles
  WHITEWAY
1954, January 8th Czeslaw
  KOWALSKI
1954, June 17th Kenneth GILBERT &
  Ian Arthur GRANT

Brown, George (asst)
1911, December 6th Michael FAGAN
1911, December 12th Walter MARTYN
1911, December 12th John Edward
  TARKENTER
1911, December 15th Joseph FLETCHER
1912, November 5th Robert GALLOWAY
1913, February 4th Eric James
  SEDGEWICK
1913, February 25th George CUNLIFFE
1913, March 19th Edward Henry
  PALMER
1913, June 24th William Walter BURTON
1913, August 13th Frank GREENING
1914, March 25th Edgar Lewis BINDON
1914, November 10th Henry QUARTLEY
1914, December 23rd George
  ANDERSON
1915, August 17th George MARSHALL
1915, December 1st Young HILL
1915, December 1st John James
  THORNLEY
1916, September 6th Daniel SULLIVAN
1916, December 20th Joseph DEANS
1918, February 12th Arthur Harry
  Victor DE STAMIR
1918, March 9th Louis VAN DER
  KERK-HOVE
1919, October 7th Frank George
  WARREN

Calcraft, William
1868, August 13th Thomas WELLS
1868, September 8th Alexander Arthur
  MACKAY
1869, January 18th Martin Henry
  VINALL
1869, March 23rd John DOLAN & John
  McCONVILLE
1869, March 22nd

1869, March 29th Michael James
  JOHNSON
1869, April 20th William SHEWARD
1869, August 12th Jonah DETHERIDGE
1869, October 11th William TAYLOR
1869, November 15th Joseph WELSH
1869, December 13th Frederick HINSON
1870, January 10th John GREGSON
1870, March 28th William MOBBS
1870, August 1st Walter MILLAR
1870, August 8th John OWEN
1870, August 15th Thomas RADCLIFFE
1870, October 4th George CHALMERS
1870, October 11th Margaret WATERS
1871, April 3rd William BULL
1871, April 24th Michael CAMPBELL
1871, July 31st Richard ADDINGTON
1871, August 17th William COLLINS
1872, January 8th Frederick JONES
1872, March 18th Edward ROBERTS
1872, August 1st John KEWISH
1872, August 12th Charles HOLMES
1872, August 13th Francis BRADFORD
1872, August 13th Thomas MOORE
1872, August 13th James TOOTH
1872, August 26th William LACE
1872, December 30th Michael KENNEDY
1872, December 9th Augustus ELLIOT
1873, January 8th Richard SPENCER
1873, January 13th John HAYES
1873, January 13th Hugh SLANE
1873, March 24th Mary Ann COTTON
1873, August 4th Benjamin HUDSON
1873, September 8th James CONNOR
1874, January 5th Thomas CORRIGAN
1874, March 30th Thomas
  CHAMBERLAIN
1874, March 31st
1874, May 25th John GODWIN

Chester, Richard (asst)
1884, March 31st William INNES
1884, March 31st Robert Flockheart
  VICKERS
1884, May 26th Mary LEFLEY
1884, October 6th Thomas Henry
  ORROCK
1884, October 6th Thomas HARRIS
1884, November 24th Kay HOWARTH
1884, November 24th Harry Hammond
  SWINDELLS
1885, January 16th Michael DOWNEY
1885, January 20th Thomas PARRY

Conduit, William (asst)
1911, January 31st George NEWTON
1911, October 17th Francisco Carlos
  GODHINO & Francis HILL

Critchell, Henry (asst)
1940, December 10th Karl Heindrich
  MEIR
1940, December 10th Jose WALDBERG

1942, January 30th Arthur PEACH
1942, April 15th Cyril JOHNSON
1942, July 7th Jose Estelle KEY
1942, July 7th Alphonse Louis Eugene
TIMMERMAN
1942, September 10th Harold Oswald
MERRY
1942, November 6th Herbert Heram
BOUNDS
1943, January 26th Franciscus Johannes
WINTER
1943, March 24th William Henry
TURNER
1943, April 29th August SANGRET
1943, November 19th Terence CASEY
1943, December 22nd John Joseph
DORGAN
1945, March 8th Karl Gustav HULTEN
1945, December 19th John AMERY
1946, September 6th David Baillie
MASON
1946, September 6th Sydney John
SMITH
1946, November 1st Arthur Robert
BOYCE
1946, November 19th Arthur RUSHTON
1947, February 27th Walter Graham
ROWLAND
1948, December 9th Clifford Godfrey
WILLS

Cross, Stanley
1940, July 31st Udham SINGH
1940, December 10th Karl Heindrich
MEIR
1940, December 10th Jose WALDBERG
1940, December 17th Charles VAN DER
KEIBOOM

Cross, Stanley (asst)
1933, June 8th Jack Samuel PUTTNAM
1934, May 4th Frederick William
PARKER & Albert PROBERT
1935, January 1st Frederick
RUSHWORTH
1936, June 30th Frederick Herbert
Charles FIELD
1937, December 30th Frederick
NODDER
1938, November 1st George BRAIN
1939, October 25th Stanley Ernest
BOON & Arthur John SMITH
1940, February 7th Peter BARNES &
James RICHARDS
1940, July 11th William APPLEBY &
Vincent OSTLER
1940, August 8th George Edward
ROBERTS
1941, September 19th Eli RICHARDS

Cunliffe, Thomas (asst)
1958, August 12th Matthew KAVANAGH
1958, December 17th Brian CHANDLER

1959, May 14th Michael George TATUM
1959, August 14th Bernard Hugh
WALDEN

Dernley, Syd (asst)
1949, December 14th Benjamin
ROBERTS
1949, December 14th John WILSON
1950, March 9th Timothy John EVANS
1950, March 29th Piotr
MAKSIMOWSKI
1950, July 7th Zbigniew GOWER &
Roman REDEL
1950, July 13th Ronald Douglas
ATWELL
1950, November 14th Patrick George
TURNAGE
1950, November 23rd Norman
GOLDTHORPE
1950, December 19th Nicholas
Persoulious CROSBY
1951, April 25th Joseph BROWN &
Edward Charles SMITH
1951, April 26th James VIRRELS
1951, May 8th James INGLIS
1951, July 19th Dennis Albert MOORE
1951, July 19th Alfred George
REYNOLDS
1952, January 1st Horace CARTER
1952, April 25th Alfred BURNS &
Edward Francis DEVLIN
1952, July 22nd Frank BURGESS
1952, October 23rd Donald Neil SIMON
1952, December 17th John Kenneth
LIVESEY
1952, December 23rd Leslie Terrence
GREEN

Dickinson, George (asst)
1949, August 4th Rex Harvey JONES &
Robert Thomas MACKINTOSH

Ellis, John
1907, January 1st John DAVIES
1907, April 2nd Edwin James MOORE
1908, August 4th Thomas SIDDLE
1908, August 19th Edward JOHNSTONE
1909, March 30th Edmund Walter
ELLIOT
1909, July 6th Alexander EDMUNSTONE
1910, August 9th John Alexander
DICKMAN
1910, November 15th Thomas
RAWCLIFFE
1910, November 22nd Henry
THOMPSON
1910, November 23rd Hawley Harvey
CRIPPEN
1910, November 24th William
BROOME
1910, December 21st Noah WOOLF
1911, January 4th William SCANLAN
1911, January 31st George NEWTON

1911, May 9th Thomas SEYMOUR
1911, May 24th Michael COLLINS
1911, June 20th Arthur GARROD
1911, July 19th William Henry PALMER
1911, October 17th Francisco Carlos
GODHINO
1911, October 17th Edward HILL
1911, November 15th Frederick Henry
THOMAS
1911, December 6th Michael FAGAN
1911, December 12th Walter MARTYN
1911, December 12th John Edward
TARKENTER
1911, December 14th Henry PHILLIPS
1911, December 15th Joseph
FLETCHER
1911, December 19th George William
PARKER
1911, December 21st Charles COLEMAN
1912, March 6th Myer ABRAMOVICH
1912, March 19th John WILLIAMS
1912, March 9th
1912, April 18th Frederick Henry
SEDDON
1912, July 23rd Arthur BIRKETT
1912, October 1st Sargent PHILP
1912, December 10th William Henry
BEAL
1912, December 18th Alfred John
LAWRENCE
1913, January 13th Albert RUMENS
1913, January 29th John WILLIAMS
1913, February 4th Eric James
SEDGEWICK
1913, February 25th George
CUNLIFFE
1913, July 8th Henry LONGDEN
1913, July 9th Thomas FLETCHER
1913, August 13th James RYDER
1913, August 14th Hugh McCLAREN
1913, October 2nd Patrick HIGGINS
1913, November 26th Augustus John
PENNY
1913, November 27th Frederick Albert
ROBERTSON
1913, December 17th Ernest Edwin
KELLY
1914, February 26th George BALL
1914, March 10th Josiah DAVIS
1914, March 12th James HONEYANDS
1914, March 24th Robert UPTON
1914, March 25th Edgar Lewis BINDON
1914, May 14th Joseph SPOONER
1914, June 16th Walter James WHITE
1914, July 28th Herbert BROOKER
1914, August 11th Percy Evelyn
CLIFFORD
1914, November 4th Charles FREMD
1914, November 10th John Francis
EAYRES
1914, November 12th Arnold WARREN
1914, December 23rd George
ANDERSON

1915, August 11th Frank STEELE
1915, August 13th George Joseph SMITH
1915, August 17th George MARSHALL
1915, November 16th William
Benjamin REEVE
1915, December 1st Young HILL
1915, December 1st John James
THORNLEY
1916, January 1st Lee KUN
1916, March 8th Frederick HOLMES
1916, March 29th Reginald HASLAM
1916, August 3rd Roger David
CASEMENT
1916, August 16th William Alan BUTLER
1916, September 6th Daniel SULLIVAN
1916, December 12th Fred BROOKS
1916, December 19th James Howarth
HARGREAVES
1916, December 20th Joseph DEANS
1917, March 21st Thomas CLINTON
1917, March 29th Leo George
O'DONNELL
1917, April 10th Alexanda BAKERLIS
1917, April 17th William James
ROBINSON
1917, May 16th Thomas McGUINESS
1917, August 16th William Thomas
HODGSON
1917, December 19th Thomas COX
1918, February 12th Arthur Harry
Victor DE STAMIR
1918, February 21st Joseph JONES
1918, March 2nd Louis Marie Joseph
VOISON
1918, March 5th Verney ASSER
1918, March 9th Louis VAN DER
KERK-HOVE
1918, December 17th William ROONEY
1919, February 19th Joseph ROSE
1919, July 10th Henry PERRY
1919, July 22nd John CROSSLAND
1919, July 31st Thomas FOSTER
1919, August 8th Henry Thomas GASKIN
1919, October 7th Frank George
WARREN
1919, November 11th James ADAMS
1919, November 26th Ambrose QUINN
1919, November 26th Ernest Bernard
SCOTT
1919, December 3rd Djang Djing
SUNG
1920, January 6th David CAPLAN
1920, January 6th Hyman PURDOVICH
1920, March 23rd William HALL
1920, April 13th Frederick Rothwell
HOLT
1920, April 14th Thomas CALER
1920, May 11th Herbert Edward
SALISBURY
1920, May 11th William WADDINGTON
1920, May 26th Albert James FRASER
1920, May 26th James ROLLINS

1920, June 16th Frederick William STOREY
1920, June 22nd William Thomas ALDRED
1920, July 27th Arthur Andrew GOSLETT
1920, August 11th James ELLOR
1920, November 1st Kevin Gerald BARRY
1920, November 30th Cyril Victor Tennyson SAUNDERS
1920, December 30th Samuel WESTWOOD
1920, December 31st Charles COLCLOUGH
1921, March 2nd George Arthur BAILEY
1921, March 14th Patrick MORAN
1921, March 14th Thomas WHELAN
1921, March 14th Bernard RYAN
1921, March 14th Frank FLOOD
1921, March 14th Patrick DOYLE
1921, March 14th Thomas BRYAN
1921, April 5th Frederick QUARMBY
1921, April 26th Thomas TRAYNOR
1921, April 25th
1921, May 24th Thomas WILSON
1921, August 16th Lester HAMILTON
1921, December 22nd Edward O'CONNOR
1922, February 21st William HARKNESS
1922, March 23rd William SULLIVAN
1922, March 24th Edward Ernest BLACK
1922, April 7th Percy James ATKINS
1922, April 11th Frederick Alexander KEELING
1922, April 18th Edmund Hugh TONBRIDGE
1922, May 30th Hyram THOMPSON
1922, May 31st Herbert Rouse ARMSTRONG
1922, June 7th Henry Julius JACOBY
1922, August 10th Reginald DUNN
1922, August 10th Joseph O'SULLIVAN
1922, August 11th Elijah POUTNEY
1922, August 19th Thomas Henry ALLAWAY
1922, September 5th William James YELDHAM
1922, December 19th William RIDER
1923, January 3rd George Frederick EDISBURY
1923, January 9th Edith Jessie THOMPSON
1923, March 28th George PERRY
1923, April 5th Bernard POMROY
1923, April 10th Frederick George WOOD
1923, June 11th John Henry SAVAGE
1923, July 4th Rowland DUCK

1923, July 24th William GRIFFITHS
1923, August 8th Albert BURROWS
1923, October 10th Susan NEWELL
1923, October 30th Phillip MURRAY
1923, November 1st Frederick William Maximillian JESSE
1923, November 29th William DOWNES
1923, December 28th John William EASTWOOD

Ellis, John (asst)

1901, December 7th John & John Robert MILLER
1902, March 18th Richard WIGLEY
1902, May 6th George WOOLFE
1902, December 16th William BROWN
1902, December 30th George PLACE
1903, July 7th Charles HOWELL
1903, July 14th Samuel Herbert DOUGAL
1903, August 11th William Joseph TUFFIN
1903, December 2nd Charles Wood WHITTAKER
1903, December 15th William HAYWOOD
1903, December 29th John GALLAGHER
1903, December 29th Emily SWANN
1904, March 29th Henry JONES
1904, August 2nd George BREEZE
1904, August 16th Samuel HOLDEN
1904, December 21st Eric LANGE
1905, April 25th John FOSTER
1905, May 23rd Albert & Alfred STRATTON
1905, August 1st Ferat Mahomed BENALI
1905, August 15th Arthur DEVEREUX
1905, November 7th William George BUTLER
1905, December 5th William YARNOLD
1905, December 6th Henry PARKINS
1905, December 27th Frederick William EDGE
1905, December 28th George SMITH
1905, December 29th John SILK
1906, February 27th John GRIFFITHS
1906, November 13th Frederick REYNOLDS
1906, December 27th Walter MARSH
1907, July 16th William Edwin SLACK
1907, August 13th Richard Clifford BRINKLEY
1908, August 4th Thomas SIDDLE
1908, December 15th Henry Taylor PARKER
1908, December 30th Noah Percy COLLINS
1909, March 12th Thomas MEADE
1909, May 8th William Joseph FOY
1909, July 3rd John EDMUNDS
1909, August 17th Madar Dal DHINGRA
1909, December 7th John FREEMAN
1910, February 22nd Joseph WREN
1910, February 23rd

334

1910, March 1st George Henry PERRY
1910, March 24th William BUTLER

Fry, William (asst)
1905, December 20th Samuel CURTIS

Heath, Samuel (asst)
1884, March 3rd Catherine FLANAGAN
  & Margaret HIGGINS
1884, March 5th

Incher, George
1875, March 30th John STANTON
1877, July 31st Henry ROGERS
1881, February 22nd James WILLIAMS

Incher, George (asst)
1876, May 23rd Giovanni CACCARIS,
  Pascaler CALADIS, Matteo CORGALIS
  & George KADI

Johnstone, S (asst)
1945, March 19th James Herbert
  LEHMAN
1947, March 31st Joseph McMANUS

Jones, *
1883, December 18th Joseph POOLE

Kirk, Harry
1950, November 23rd Norman
  GOLDTHORPE

Kirk, Harry (asst)
1940, December 10th Karl Heindrich
  MEIR & Jose WALDBERG
1941, August 6th Karl Theo DRUEKE &
  Werner Heindrich WALTI
1942, April 30th Frederick James AUSTIN
1942, June 25th Gordon Frederick
  CUMMINS
1942, July 7th Jose Estelle KEY
  Alphonse Louis Eugene
  TIMMERMAN
1942, September 10th Samuel
  DASHWOOD & George
  SILVEROSA
1942, November 3rd Duncan Alexander
  Croall SCOTT-FORD
1943, February 10th Ronald ROBERTS
1943, September 10th Trevor ELVIN
1944, March 16th Oswald JOB
1944, July 26th James GALBRAITH
1944, August 8th William Alfred COWLE
  William George Frederick MEFFEN
1945, October 31st Ronald Bertram
  MAURI
1945, December 29th Robert BLAINE
1946, April 2nd Marion
  GRONDKOWSKI & Henryk
  MALINOWSKI
1946, October 16th Neville George
  Clevely HEATH

1946, November 13th Frank Joseph
  FREIYER
1947, January 30th Albert SABIN
1947, March 18th Harold HAGGER
1947, March 26th Frederick William
  REYNOLDS
1947, April 15th David John WILLIAMS
1947, June 20th Eric Charles BRIGGS
1948, January 7th George Henry
  WHELPTON
1948, November 18th Stanley Joseph
  CLARKE
1949, January 12th Margaret ALLEN
1949, March 22nd Kenneth
  STRICKSON
1949, March 29th James FARRELL
1949, June 21st Bernard Alfred Peter
  COOPER
1949, August 4th Rex Harvey JONES
Robert Thomas MACKINTOSH
1949, August 10th John George HAIGH
1949, August 16th William John DAVIES
1949, December 14th Benjamin
  ROBERTS
John WILSON
1950, January 6th Daniel RAVEN
1950, April 19th Albert Edward JENKINS
1950, July 7th Zbigniew GOWER &
  Roman REDEL
1950, July 11th George Finlay BROWN
1950, July 13th John WALKER

Lumb, Albert (asst)
1911, December 19th George William
  PARKER
1912, March 6th Myer ABRAMOVICH
1912, March 9th John WILLIAMS
1912, March 9th
1912, July 23rd Arthur BIRKETT
1912, October 1st Sargent PHILP
1912, November 26th Gilbert Oswald
  SMITH
1913, January 29th Edward HOPWOOD
1913, April 23rd Walter William SYKES
1913, November 26th Augustus John
  PENNY
1913, December 31st George Frederick
  LAW

Maldon, Charles (asst)
1886, February 8th James BAKER, James
  MARTIN & Anthony Ben RUDGE

Mann, Lionel (asst)
1925, April 15th Henry GRAHAM
Thomas Henry SHELTON
1925, September 4th Lawrence FOWLER
1926, November 16th James LEAH
1927, March 29th James Frederick
  STRATTON
1927, August 3rd Frederick Stephen
  FULLER

1927, August 3rd James MURPHY
1927, September 2nd Arthur HARNETT
1928, January 27th Daniel DRISCOLL &
Edward ROWLANDS
1928, April 12th Frederick LOCK
1928, November 20th William Charles
BENSON
1929, February 27th William John
HOLMYARD
1930, April 8th Sydney Harry FOX
1931, August 5th Oliver NEWMAN &
William SHELLEY

Marwood, William
1872, April 1st William Frederick
HORRY
1874, December 29th Robert TAYLOR
1874, January 5th Charles DAWSON
1874, January 5th Edward GOUGH
1874, January 5th William THOMPSON
1874, June 29th Frances STEWART
1874, August 10th John MacDONALD
1874, August 24th James Henry GIBBS
1874, August 31st Henry FLANAGAN
1874, August 31st Mary WILLIAMS
1874, October 13th John Walter
COPPEN
1874, November 16th Thomas SMITH
1874, December 28th Hugh DALEY
1874, December 29th Robert TAYLOR
1875, January 4th James CRANWELL
1875, March 24th John McDAID
1875, March 29th Richard COATES
1875, March 30th John MORGAN
1875, April 9th John RUSSELL
1875, April 19th Alfred Thomas HEAP
1875, April 26th William HALE
1875, July 27th Jeremiah CORKERY
1875, August 2nd Michael GILLINGHAM
1875, August 2nd William McHUGH
1875, August 2nd Elizabeth PEARSON
1875, August 9th Peter BLANCHARD
1875, August 11th Joseph Phillip LE
BRUN
1875, August 16th Mark FIDDLER
1875, August 16th William
McCULLOUGH
1875, September 6th William BAKER
1875, September 6th Edward COOPER
1875, October 5th Patrick DOCHERTY
1875, October 19th David WARDLAW
1875, December 21st Henry
WAINWRIGHT
1875, December 22nd John William
ANDERSON
1875, December 23rd Richard
CHARLTON
1876, March 28th George HUNTER
1876, April 4th Thomas FORDRED
1876, April 10th George HILL
1876, April 24th Edward DEACON
1876, April 25th Joseph WEBBER
1876, April 26th John DALY

1876, May 23rd Giovanni CACCARIS,
Pascaler CALADIS, Matteo CORGALIS
& George KADI
1876, May 31st Thomas BARR
1876, July 26th John WILLIAMS
1876, August 1st James PARRIS
1876, August 14th William FISH
1876, August 14th Richard
THOMPSON
1876, August 21st Steven McKEOWN
1876, August 25th Christos Emanuel
BAUMBOS
1876, August 25th Thomas CROWE
1876, August 29th John EBLETHRIFT
1876, December 11th Charles
O'DONNELL
1876, December 14th Robert
BROWNING
1876, December 19th Silas BARLOW
1876, December 20th John GREEN
1876, December 21st William
FLANAGAN
1877, January 2nd Isaac MARKS
1877, March 12th Francis TIDBURY
Henry TIDBURY
1877, March 26th William CLARK
1877, March 27th John McKENNA
1877, April 2nd James BANNISTER
1877, April 17th Frederick Edwin BAKER
1877, August 13th Henry LEIGH
1877, July 31st John Henry STARKEY
1877, August 14th Caleb SMITH
1877, August 21st John GOLDING
1877, August 21st Patrick McGOVERN
1877, October 15th John LYNCH
1877, November 12th Thomas
Benjamin PRATT
1877, November 19th William
HUSSELL
William HASSELL
1877, November 20th Henry MARSH
1877, November 21st Thomas GREY
1877, November 23rd Cadwaller JONES
1877, November 27th James SATCHELL
1877, November 27th John SWIFT
1877, November 27th John UPTON
1878, February 4th George PIGGOTT
1878, February 11th James CAFFYN
1878, February 12th James TRICKETT
1878, February 13th John BROOKS
1878, April 1st Henry ROWLES
1878, April 15th Vincent Knowles
WALKER
1878, May 31st Eugene Marie
CHANTRELLE
1878, July 29th Charles Joseph REVELL
1878, July 30th Robert VEST
1878, August 12th Thomas CHOLERTON
1878, August 15th Selina WADGE
1878, October 3rd William McDONALD
1878, October 8th Thomas SMITHERS
1878, November 12th Patrick John
BYRNE

Marwood, William   Executioner Index   Morris, Herbert (asst)

1878, November 18th Joseph GARCIA
1878, November 19th James McGOWAN
1878, November 25th Henry GILBERT
1879, January 10th Thomas CUNCEEN
1879, February 4th Stephen GAMBRILL
1879, February 10th Enoch WHISTON
1879, February 11th William McGUINESS
1879, February 25th Charles Frederick PEACE
1879, March 24th James SIMMS
1879, May 12th Edwin SMART
1879, May 20th William COOPER
1879, May 26th Catherine CHURCHILL
1879, May 27th John D'ARCY
1879, May 28th Thomas JOHNSON
1879, July 29th Catherine WEBSTER
1879, August 11th Annie TOOKE
1879, August 25th James DILLEY
1879, August 26th John RALPH
1879, December 3rd Henry BEDINGFIELD
1880, January 5th Charles SURETY
1880, January 16th Martin McHUGO
1880, February 17th William CASSIDY
1880, March 2nd Hugh BURNS
1880, March 2nd Patrick KEARNS
1880, March 22nd John WINGFIELD
1880, April 14th Peter CONWAY
1880, May 10th William DUMBLETON
1880, May 11th John Henry WOOD
1880, July 27th Thomas BERRY
1880, August 16th John WAKEFIELD
1880, November 16th William BROWNLESS
1880, November 22nd William Joseph DISTON
1880, November 27th
1880, November 29th Thomas WHEELER
1880, November 69th
1880, December 13th William HERBERT
1880, December 13th George PAVEY
1881, February 21st William STANWAY
1881, February 28th Albert ROBINSON
1881, May 17th Albert MOORE
1881, May 23rd James HALL
1881, May 31st Joseph Patrick McENTIRE
1881, August 15th Thomas BROWN
1881, August 23rd George DURLING
1881, November 21st Alfred GOUGH
1881, November 28th John Aspinall SIMPSON
1881, November 29th Percy LEFROY
1882, January 30th Charles GERRISH
1882, January 31st
1882, February 13th Richard TEMPLETON
1882, April 28th George Henry LAMSON
1882, May 16th Thomas FURY

1882, May 22nd William George ABIGAIL
1882, May 23rd Osmond Otto BRAND
1882, August 21st William TURNER
1882, September 11th Francis HYNES
1882, September 22nd Patrick WALSH
1882, November 13th William Meager BARTLETT
1882, November 28th Edward WHEATFALL
1882, December 4th Bernard MULLARKEY
1882, December 12th Charles TAYLOR
1882, December 15th Patrick CASEY
1882, December 15th Miles JOYCE
1882, December 15th Patrick JOYCE
1883, January 2nd Louisa Jane TAYLOR
1883, January 15th Patrick HIGGINS
1883, January 17th Michael FLYNN
1883, January 17th Thomas HIGGINS
1883, January 23rd James BARRETT
1883, January 23rd Sylvester POFF
1883, February 12th Abraham THOMAS
1883, February 19th James ANDERSON
1883, April 30th Timothy O'KEEFE
1883, May 7th Thomas GARRY
1883, May 8th Patrick CAREY
1883, May 14th Joseph BRADY
1883, May 18th Daniel CURLEY
1883, May 21st Joseph WEDLAKE
1883, May 21st George WHITE
1883, May 23rd Henry MULLEN
1883, May 23rd Martin SCOTT
1883, May 28th Michael FAGAN
1883, June 2nd Thomas CAFFREY
1883, June 9th Timothy KELLY
1883, August 6th James BURTON

Marwood, William (asst)
1873, August 26th Thomas Hartley MONTGOMERY
1873, September 8th James CONNOR

Mills, Seth (asst)
1921, August 16th Lester HAMILTON
1922, March 24th Edward Ernest BLACK
1922, April 11th Frederick Alexander KEELING
1922, August 10th Reginald DUNN
1922, August 10th Joseph O'SULLIVAN
1923, January 9th Frederick Edward Francis BYWATERS
1923, July 24th William GRIFFITHS
1923, December 28th John William EASTWOOD

Morris, Herbert (asst)
1939, October 10th Leonard George HUCKER
1940, October 31st Stanley Edward COLE
1940, December 17th Charles VAN DER KEIBOOM

1941, April 4th Samuel MORGAN
1942, March 11th Harold Dorian
TREVOR
1942, July 21st Arthur ANDERSON
1942, September 10th Samuel
DASHWOOD & George SILVEROSA
1942, October 6th Patrick William
KINGSTON
1943, January 27th Harry DOBKIN
1943, April 6th Gordon Horace
TRENOWORTH
1943, December 29th Thomas JAMES
1944, February 2nd Christos GEORGIOU
1944, June 6th Ernest James Harman
KEMP
1945, January 31st Arthur THOMPSON
1945, March 17th Cubia JONES &
Robert L PEARSON
1945, April 7th William HARRISON
1945, May 8th George Edward SMITH
1945, September 7th Thomas Eric
RICHARDSON
1945, December 21st James McNicol &
John Riley YOUNG
1946, March 19th Arthur CLEGG
1946, July 17th Thomas HENDREN
1951, January 4th Frank GRIFFIN

Phillips, Thomas
1939, March 25th Harry ARMSTRONG
1940, March 27th Ernest Edmund
HAMERTON

Phillips, Thomas (asst)
1922, March 23rd William SULLIVAN
1922, June 7th Henry Julius JACOBY
1923, January 5th Lee DOON
1923, January 9th Edith THOMPSON
1923, April 10th Frederick George
WOOD
1925, March 31st William Frederick
BRESSINGTON
1925, April 22nd John Norman Holmes
THORNE
1925, December 15th Samuel
JOHNSON
1926, March 9th George THOMAS
1926, March 24th Eugene DEVERE
1926, August 10th James SMITH
1926, November 22nd SAMANDA,
Hashan
1926, November 2nd: SAMANDER
1927, August 3rd Frederick Stephen
FULLER & James MURPHY
1927, December 6th William Meynell
ROBERTSON
1928, January 27th Daniel DRISCOLL &
Edward ROWLANDS
1928, January 31st James GILLON
1928, June 6th Frederick STEWART
1928, July 27th William John MAYNARD
1929, November 26th John MAGUIRE
1931, March 10th Alfred Arthur ROUSE

1931, August 5th Oliver NEWMAN &
William SHELLEY
1932, February 23rd William Harold
GODDARD
1932, April 28th Thomas RILEY & John
Henry ROBERTS
1933, July 25th Frederick MORSE
1934, January 3rd Roy GREGORY
1934, May 4th Frederick William
PARKER & Albert PROBERT
1935, October 29th Raymond
BOUSQUET
1936, July 15th Charlotte BRYANT
1937, July 27th Philip Edward Percy
DAVIS
1937, August 17th Frederick George
MURPHY
1938, March 8th Walter SMITH
1938, March 20th Charles James
CALDWELL
1938, July 19th William James
GRAVES
1939, March 29th William Thomas
BUTLER
1940, February 7th Peter BARNES &
James RICHARDS

Pierrepoint, Albert
1941, October 31st Antonio MANCINI
1941, December 3rd John Ernest SMITH
1941, December 10th Karel Richard
RICHTER
1942, March 11th Harold Dorian
TREVOR
1942, June 25th Gordon Frederick
CUMMINS
1942, July 7th Jose Estelle KEY &
Alphonse Louis Eugene
TIMMERMAN
1942, July 21st Arthur ANDERSON
1942, September 10th Samuel
DASHWOOD & George SILVEROSA
1942, October 6th Patrick William
KINGSTON
1942, November 3rd Duncan Alexander
Croall SCOTT-FORD
1942, December 31st Johannes Marius
DRONKERS
1943, January 26th Franciscus Johannes
WINTER
1943, January 27th Harry DOBKIN
1943, March 31st Dudley George
RAYNOR
1943, April 29th August SANGRET
1943, August 3rd Gerald Elphinstone
ROE
1943, September 24th Charles Eugene
GAUTHIER
1943, November 19th Terence CASEY
1944, February 2nd Christos GEORGIOU
1944, March 16th Oswald JOB

1944, June 6th Ernest James Harman KEMP
1944, June 23rd Pierre Richard Charles NEUKERMANS
1944, July 12th Joseph Jan VANHOVE
1945, January 9th Horace Beresford GORDON
1945, January 30th Andrew BROWN
1945, March 8th Karl Gustav HULTEN
1945, October 6th Heinz BRUELING & Joachim GOLTZ & Erich Pallme KOENIG & Josef MERTENS & Kurt ZUEHLSDORFF
1945, October 31st Ronald Bertram MAURI
1945, November 16th Arnim KUEHNE & Emil SCHMITTENDORF
1945, December 19th John AMERY
1945, December 21st John Riley YOUNG
1945, December 21st James McNICOL
1945, December 29th Robert BLAINE
1946, January 3rd William JOYCE
1946, January 4th Theodore John William SCHURCH
1946, January 31st Michael NIESCIOR
1946, March 19th Arthur CLEGG
1946, April 2nd Marion GRONDKOWSKI & Henryk MALINOWSKI
1946, July 17th Thomas HENDREN
1946, August 7th Walter CLAYTON
1946, September 6th Sydney John SMITH David Baillie MASON
1946, October 16th Neville George Clevely HEATH
1946, November 1st Arthur Robert BOYCE
1946, November 13th Frank Joseph FREIYER
1946, November 19th Arthur RUSHTON
1946, December 10th John Fleming McCready MATHIESON
1947, February 27th Walter Graham ROWLAND
1947, March 18th Harold HAGGER
1947, March 26th Frederick William REYNOLDS
1947, March 31st Joseph McMANUS
1947, April 15th David John WILLIAMS
1948, February 3rd Evan Haydn EVANS
1948, February 6th Stanislaw MYSZKA
1948, February 19th Walter John CROSS
1948, November 18th Stanley Joseph CLARKE
1948, November 19th Peter GRIFFITHS
1948, November 24th William M GAMBON
1948, December 2nd George RUSSELL
1949, January 12th Margaret ALLEN
1949, January 27th George SEMINI
1949, March 22nd Kenneth STRICKSON
1949, March 29th James FARRELL
1949, April 21st Harry LEWIS

1949, June 21st Bernard Alfred Peter COOPER
1949, July 28th Sydney Archibald Frederick CHAMBERLAIN
1949, August 4th Rex Harvey JONES & Robert Thomas MACKINTOSH
1949, August 10th John George HAIGH
1949, August 16th William John DAVIES
1949, September 28th William Claude Hodson JONES
1949, December 30th Ernest Soper COUZINS
1950, January 6th Daniel RAVEN
1950, March 8th James Frank RIVETT
1950, March 9th Timothy John EVANS
1950, March 28th George KELLY
1950, March 29th Piotr MAKSIMOWSKI
1950, April 19th Albert Edward JENKINS
1950, July 7th Zbigniew GOWER & Roman REDEL
1950, July 11th George Finlay BROWN
1950, July 13th Ronald Douglas ATWELL
1950, August 16th Albert PRICE
1950, October 30th Paul Christopher HARRIS
1950, November 28th James Henry CORBITT
1950, December 14th Edward Isaac WOODFIELD
1950, December 16th James Ronald ROBERTSON
1950, December 19th Nicholas Persoulious CROSBY
1951, January 4th Frank GRIFFIN
1951, January 26th Nenad KOVASEVIC
1951, April 3rd William Arthur WATKINS
1951, April 25th Joseph BROWN & Edward Charles SMITH
1951, April 26th James VIRRELS
1951, May 8th James INGLIS
1951, May 9th William Edward SHAUGHNESSY
1951, June 12th John DAND
1951, July 3rd Jack WRIGHT
1951, July 19th Dennis Albert MOORE
1951, July 19th Alfred George REYNOLDS
1951, September 15th Robert Dobie SMITH
1951, October 24th John O'CONNER
1951, December 11th Herbert Leonard MILLS
1952, January 1st Horace CARTER
1952, January 15th Alfred BRADLEY
1952, February 26th Herbert Roy HARRIS
1952, April 12th James SMITH
1952, May 7th Ajit SINGH

1952, May 27th Backary MAUNEH
1952, May 29th Peter Gallagher
DEVENEY
1952, July 8th Harry HUXLEY
1952, July 15th Thomas EAMES
1952, July 22nd Frank BURGESS
1952, August 12th Oliver George
BUTLER
1952, September 3rd Mahmood Hussain
MATTAN
1952, September 5th John Howard
GODAR
1952, September 30th Raymond Jack
CULL
Dennis George MULDOWNEY
1952, October 9th Peter Cyril JOHNSON
1952, October 23rd Donald Neil SIMON
1952, December 12th Eric
NORTHCLIFFE
1952, December 17th John Kenneth
LIVESEY
1952, December 23rd Leslie Terrence
GREEN
1953, January 2nd James John ALCOTT
1953, January 26th George Francis SHAW
1953, January 28th Derek William
BENTLEY
1953, February 24th Miles William
GIFFARD
1953, May 19th John Lawrence TODD
1953, July 15th John Reginald Halliday
CHRISTIE
1953, July 30th Philip HENRY
1953, September 18th Louisa May
MERRIFIELD
1953, October 20th John Owen
GREENWAY
1953, November 17th Joseph
Christopher REYNOLDS
1953, December 17th Stanislaw JURAS
1953, December 22nd Alfred Charles
WHITEWAY
1953, December 23rd George James
NEWLANDS
1954, January 8th Czeslaw KOWALSKI
1954, January 26th Desmond Donald
HOOPER
1954, April 14th James Reginald
DOOHAN
1954, April 20th Michael MANNING
1954, April 23rd John LYNCH
1954, April 28th Thomas Ronald Lewis
HARRIES
1954, June 17th Kenneth GILBERT &
Ian Arthur GRANT
1954, June 22nd Milton TAYLOR
1954, June 23rd George Alexander
ROBERTSON
1954, August 11th William Sanchez de
Pina HEPPER
1954, August 12th Harold FOWLER
1954, September 1st Rupert Geoffrey
WELLS

1954, December 15th Styllou Pantopiou
CHRISTOFI
1955, April 14th Sydney Joseph CLARKE
1955, May 2nd James ROBINSON
1955, June 21st Richard GOWLER
1955, July 13th Ruth ELLIS
1955, July 26th Frederick Arthur CROSS
1955, July 27th Norman William GREEN

Pierrepoint, Albert (asst)
1932, December 29th Patrick
McDERMOTT
1933, April 7th Harold COURTNEY
1933, June 20th Richard
HETHERINGTON
1933, December 28th Stanley HOBDAY
1934, May 4th Frederick William
PARKER & Albert PROBERT
1934, December 19th Ethel Lillie MAJOR
1935, July 10th Walter Osmond
WORTHINGTON
1936, April 16th Dorothea Nancy
WADDINGHAM
1936, December 16th Christopher
JACKSON
1937, February 4th Maz Mayer HASLAM
1937, June 17th John HORNICK
1938, June 8th Jan MAHOMED
1938, July 12th Alfred Ernest RICHARDS
1939, January 7th Dermot SMYTH
1939, March 25th Harry ARMSTRONG
1939, June 7th Ralph SMITH
1940, February 7th Peter BARNES &
James RICHARDS
1940, July 11th William APPLEBY &
Vincent OSTLER
1940, July 31st Udham SINGH
1940, September 10th John William
WRIGHT
1940, November 26th William Henry
COOPER
1940, December 10th Karl Heindrich
MEIR & Jose WALDBERG
1941, January 7th David DOHERTY
1941, April 23rd Henry GLEESON
1941, August 6th Karl Theo DRUEKE
Werner Heindrich WALTI
1941, December 18th Patrick KELLY
1941, December 23rd Thomas William
THORPE
1942, May 1st Harold HILL
1942, September 2nd Thomas Joseph
WILLIAMS
1942, October 28th William Ambrose
COLLINS
1943, March 12th David COBB
1943, June 2nd Bernard KIRWAN
1943, June 25th Harold A SMITH
1943, August 12th William O'SHEA
1944, August 8th William Alfred
COWLE & William George Frederick
MEFFEN

1944, August 11th Eliga BRINSON & Willie SMITH
1944, October 12th Madison THOMAS
1944, December 1st Charles KERINS
1945, January 8th Ernest Lee CLARK & Augustine M GUERRA
1945, June 15th Aniceto MARTINEZ

Pierrepoint, Henry
1902, March 18th Richard WIGLEY
1902, December 16th William BROWN
1902, December 30th George PLACE
1903, August 11th William Joseph TUFFIN
1903, December 15th William HAYWOOD
1904, December 22nd Joseph FEE
1905, August 1st Ferat Mahomed BENALI
1905, August 15th Arthur DEVEREUX
1905, November 7th William George BUTLER
1905, November 14th Pasha LIFFEY
1905, December 5th William YARNOLD
1905, December 6th Henry PARKINS
1905, December 20th Samuel CURTIS
1905, December 27th Frederick William EDGE
1905, December 28th George SMITH
1905, December 29th John SILK
1906, February 27th John GRIFFITHS
1906, April 10th Harry WALTERS
1906, August 7th Edward GLYNN
1906, August 9th Thomas Acomb MOUNCER
1906, November 13th Frederick REYNOLDS
1906, November 27th Edward HARTIGAN
1906, December 4th Richard BUCKHAM
1906, December 27th Walter MARSH
1907, February 19th Thomas CONNAN
1907, March 26th Joseph JONES
1907, July 16th William Edwin SLACK
1907, August 7th Charles PATERSON
1907, August 13th Richard Clifford BRINKLEY
1907, August 14th Rhoda WILLIS
1907, November 5th William George Charles AUSTIN
1907, November 20th William DUDDLES
1907, December 13th George STILLS
1908, March 5th Joseph HUME
1908, March 24th William LOWMAN
1908, March 24th Joseph William NOBLE
1908, May 12th John RAMSBOTTOM
1908, July 28th Fred BALLINGTON
1908, August 4th Thomas SIDDLE

1908, August 5th Matthew John DODDS
1908, August 20th John BERRYMAN
1908, November 12th James PHIPPS
1908, December 2nd James NICHOLLS
1908, December 3rd John William ELLWOOD
1908, December 8th William BOULDREY
1908, December 15th Henry Taylor PARKER
1908, December 30th Noah Percy COLLINS
1909, January 6th John Esmond MURPHY
1909, February 23rd Jeremiah O'CONNOR
1909, March 2nd John HUTCHINSON
1909, March 12th Thomas MEADE
1909, March 30th See LEE
1909, April 14th Joseph Edwin JONES
1909, May 8th William Joseph FOY
1909, May 20th Marks REUBENS
1909, July 3rd John EDMUNDS
1909, July 9th Walter DAVIS
1909, July 20th William HAMPTON
1909, August 3rd Mark SHAWCROSS
1909, August 10th Julius WAMMER
1909, August 17th Madar Dal DHINGRA
1909, August 19th Richard JUSTIN
1909, December 7th John FREEMAN
1909, December 8th Abel ATHERTON
1909, December 14th Samuel ATHERLEY
1910, January 4th Joseph HEFFERMAN
1910, February 15th William MURPHY
1910, February 22nd Joseph WREN
1910, February 23rd
1910, March 1st George Henry PERRY
1910, March 24th William BUTLER
1910, May 25th Thomas William JESSHOPE
1910, June 14th James Henry HANCOCK
1910, July 12th Thomas CRAIG
1910, July 14th Frederick FOREMAN

Pierrepoint, Henry (asst)
1901, November 19th Marcel FAUGERON
1901, December 3rd Patrick McKENNA
1902, April 29th Charles Robert EARL
1902, July 30th John BEDFORD
1902, August 13th George HIBBS
1902, September 30th John MacDONALD
1902, November 11th Henry WILLIAMS
1902, December 2nd Henry McWIGGINS
1903 February 3rd Amelia SACH & Annie WALTERS
1903, March 3rd Edgar EDWARDS
1903, April 7th George CHAPMAN

1903, May 13th William George HUDSON
1903, December 1st Bernard WHITE
1903, December 29th Henry Bertram STARR
1904, March 29th James Henry CLARKSON
1904, May 31st Pong LUN
1904, May 31st William KIRWAN
1904, July 13th Samuel ROWLEDGE
1904, August 16th John Thomas KAY
1904, December 13th Conrad DONOVAN & Charles WADE
1904, December 28th Arthur JEFFRIES
1905, February 28th Edward HARRISON
1905, March 29th Ernest HUTCHINSON
1905, April 26th Albert BRIDGEMAN
1905, May 23rd Albert & Alfred STRATTON
1905, June 20th Alfred John HEAL
1905, August 9th William Alfred HANCOCKS

Pierrepoint, Thomas
1910, August 9th John Roper COULSON
1910, December 29th Henry ISON
1911, December 28th George LOAKE
1912, November 5th Robert GALLOWAY
1912, November 26th Gilbert Oswald SMITH
1913, January 29th Edward HOPWOOD
1913, March 19th Edward Henry PALMER
1913, April 23rd Walter William SYKES
1913, June 24th William Walter BURTON
1913, July 22nd John Vickers AMOS
1913, August 13th Frank GREENING
1913, November 4th Frederick SEEKINGS
1913, December 31st George Frederick LAW
1914, November 10th Henry QUARTLEY
1915, July 15th Robert ROSENTHAL
1915, August 10th Walter MARRIOT
1915, December 22nd Harry THOMPSON
1915, December 29th John William McCARTNEY
1917, March 27th John William THOMPSON
1917, April 18th Robert GADSBY
1917, December 18th William CAVANAGH
1918, December 17th John William WALSH
1919, January 7th Benjamin Hindle BENSON
1919, January 8th Percy George BARRETT
1919, January 8th George Walter CARDWELL
George Walter CALDWELL
1920, January 6th Louis MASSEY

1920, March 10th William WRIGHT
1920, April 16th Miles McHUGH
1920, May 6th Thomas Hargreaves WILSON
1920, November 30th James RILEY
1920, December 30th Edwin SOWERBY
1921, January 7th George Edmund Freeman Quentin LEVER
1921, February 4th Jack Alfred FIELD
1921, February 4th William Thomas GRAY
1922, March 21st James Hutton WILLIAMSON
1922, August 17th Simon McGEOWN
1922, December 13th Frank FOWLER & George R ROBINSON
1923, January 5th Lee DOON
1923, April 3rd Daniel CASSIDY
1923, August 8th Hassan MUHAMED
1923, December 12th Thomas DELANEY
1923, December 15th Peter HYNES
1924, January 2nd Matthew Frederick Atkinson NUNN
1924, March 13th Jeremiah GAFFNEY
1924, June 18th William Horsley WARDELL
1924, July 30th Abraham GOLDENBERG
1924, August 1st Felix McMULLEN
1924, September 3rd Patrick Herbert MAHON
1924, December 9th William George SMITH
1924, December 17th Arthur SIMS
1925, February 24th William Grover BIGNELL
1925, March 31st William Frederick BRESSINGTON
1925, April 15th Henry GRAHAM
1925, April 15th Thomas Henry SHELTON
1925, April 22nd John Norman Holmes THORNE
1925, June 10th Hubert Ernest DALTON
1925, July 28th Cornelius O'LEARY
1925, August 5th Michael TALBOT
1925, August 5th Annie WALSH
1925, September 3rd Alfred Davis BOSTOCK
1925, September 3rd Wilfred FOWLER
1925, September 4th Lawrence FOWLER & John KEEN
1926, January 7th Lorraine LAX
1926, February 17th Herbert BURROWS
1926, March 2nd Ignatius Emanuel Nathanial LINCOLN
1926, March 9th Henry THOMPSON
1926, June 24th Louie CALVERT
1926, July 15th James MYLES
1926, August 10th James SMITH
1926, August 12th Charles Edward FINDEN
1926, August 11th

1926, November 16th James LEAH
1926, November 24th James McHUGH
1926, December 3rd Charles
HOUGHTON
1926, December 9th Henry McCABE
1927, January 5th William Cornelius
JONES
1927, April 27th William KNIGHTON
1927, September 2nd Arthur HARNETT
1927, December 6th William Meynell
ROBERTSON
1927, December 29th William O'NEILL
1928, January 3rd Frederick FIELDING
1928, January 4th Bertram KIRBY
1928, January 6th John Thomas DUNN
1928, January 7th Samuel CASE
1928, January 31st James Joseph POWER
1928, April 10th George Frederick Walter
HAYWARD
1928, May 31st William KENNEDY
1928, June 28th Walter BROOKS
1928, July 25th Albert George ABSALOM
1928, July 27th William John MAYNARD
1928, August 8th William SMILEY
1928, August 10th Norman ELLIOTT
1928, August 29th Gerard TOAL
1928, December 6th Chung Yi MIAO
1929, January 4th Charles William
CONLIN
1929, March 12th Joseph Reginald
Victor CLARKE
1929, April 4th George Henry
CARTLEDGE
1929, April 25th John COX
1929, August 7th James JOHNSON
1929, August 7th Arthur Leslie
RAVENEY
1929, November 26th John MAGUIRE
1930, April 8th Samuel William
CUSHNAN
1930, April 22nd William Henry
PODMORE
1930, June 11th Albert Edward
MARJERAM
1931, January 3rd Victor Edward
BETTS
1931, February 4th Frederick GILL
1931, March 10th Alfred Arthur ROUSE
1931, April 16th Francis LAND
1931, July 31st Thomas DORNAN
1931, August 4th David O'SHEA
1931, December 10th Henry Daniel
SEYMOUR
1931, December 15th Solomon STEIN
1932, January 13th Edward CULLENS
1932, February 3rd George Alfred RICE
1932, March 9th George Thomas POPLE
1932, April 27th George Emmanuel
MICHAEL
1932, April 28th Thomas RILEY
1932, April 28th John Henry ROBERTS
1932, May 18th Charles James COWLE

1932, December 29th Patrick
McDERMOTT
1933, February 2nd Jeremiah HANBURY
1933, April 7th Harold COURTNEY
1933, June 20th Richard
HETHERINGTON
1933, July 25th Frederick MORSE
1933, December 6th Ernest Wadge
PARKER
1933, December 19th William BURTOFT
1933, December 28th Stanley HOBDAY
1934, January 3rd Roy GREGORY
1934, January 5th John FLEMING
1934, February 6th Ernest BROWN
1934, April 6th Lewis HAMILTON
1934, May 3rd Reginald Ivor HINKS
1934, May 4th Frederick William
PARKER & Albert PROBERT
1934, December 19th Ethel Lillie
MAJOR
1935, January 1st Frederick
RUSHWORTH
1935, February 7th David Maskill
BLAKE
1935, May 9th John Stephenson
BAINBRIDGE
1935, May 30th John Harris BRIDGE
1935. June 25th Arthur Henry
FRANKLIN
1935, July 10th Walter Osmond
WORTHINGTON
1935, July 16th George HAGUE
1936, April 16th Dorothea Nancy
WADDINGHAM
1936, May 21st Buck RUXTON
1936, July 14th George Arthur BRYANT
1936, July 15th Charlotte BRYANT
1936, August 5th Wallace JENDEN
1936, December 16th Christopher
JACKSON
1937, February 4th Max Mayer
HASLAM
1937, February 10th Andrew Anderson
BAGLEY
1937, June 17th John HORNICK
1937, July 27th Philip Edward Percy
DAVIS
1937, August 12th Horace William
BRUNT
1937, August 13th Leslie George
STONE
1937, November 18th John Thomas
ROGERS
1937, December 7th Ernest John MOSS
1937, December 30th Frederick NODDER
1938, March 8th Walter SMITH
1938, March 20th Charles James
CALDWELL
1938, May 26th Robert William
HOOLHOUSE
1938, June 8th Jan MAHOMED
1938, July 12th Alfred Ernest RICHARDS
1938, July 19th William James GRAVES

1938, July 26th William PARKER
1938, November 1st George BRAIN
1939, January 7th Dermot SMYTH
1939, February 8th John DAYMOND
1939, March 29th William Thomas
BUTLER
1939, June 7th Ralph SMITH
1939, October 10th Leonard George
HUCKER
1939, October 25th Stanley Ernest
BOON & Arthur John SMITH
1940, February 7th Peter BARNES
James RICHARDS
1940, April 24th William Charles
COWELL
1940, July 11th William APPLEBY
Vincent OSTLER
1940, August 8th George Edward
ROBERTS
1940, September 10th John WRIGHT
1940, October 31st Stanley Edward COLE
1940, November 26th William Henry
COOPER
1940, December 24th Edward SCOLLEN
1941, January 7th David DOHERTY
1941, February 11th Clifford HOLMES
1941, March 6th Henry Lyndo WHITE
1941, April 4th Samuel MORGAN
1941, April 23rd Henry GLEESON
1941, July 9th George Johnson
ARMSTRONG
1941, July 23rd David Millar JENNINGS
1941, July 31st Edward Walker
ANDERSON
1941, August 6th Karl Theo DRUEKE
Werner Heindrich WALTI
1941, September 4th John SMITH
1941, September 19th Eli RICHARDS
1941, November 12th Lionel Rupert
Nathan WATSON
1941, December 18th Patrick KELLY
1941, December 23rd Thomas William
THORPE
1942, January 30th Arthur PEACH
1942, March 25th David Roger
WILLIAMS
1942, April 15th Cyril JOHNSON
1942, April 30th Frederick James
AUSTIN
1942, May 1st Harold HILL
1942, June 24th Douglas EDMONDSON
1942, September 2nd Thomas Joseph
WILLIAMS
1942, September 10th Harold Oswald
MERRY
1942, October 28th William Ambrose
COLLINS
1942, November 6th Herbert Heram
BOUNDS
1943, February 10th Ronald ROBERTS
1943, March 12th David COBB
1943, March 24th William Henry
TURNER

1943, April 6th Gordon Horace
TRENOWORTH
1943, June 2nd Bernard KIRWAN
1943, June 25th Harold A SMITH
1943, July 10th Charles Arthur
RAYMOND
1943, August 3rd William QUAYLE
1943, August 12th William O'SHEA
1943, September 10th Trevor ELVIN
1943, December 14th Lee A DAVIS
1943, December 15th Charles William
KOOPMAN
1943, December 22nd John Joseph
DORGAN
1943, December 29th Thomas JAMES
1944, February 3rd Mervin Clare
McEWEN
1944, February 10th John H WATERS
1944, March 16th Ernest Charles DIGBY
1944, April 13th Sydney James
DELASALLE
1944, May 26th Wiley HARRIS
1944, July 12th John Gordon
DAVIDSON
1944, July 26th James GALBRAITH
1944, August 8th William Alfred
COWLE & William George Frederick
MEFFEN
1944, August 11th Eliga BRINSON &
Willie SMITH
1944, October 12th Madison THOMAS
1944, December 1st Charles KERINS
1945, January 8th Ernest Lee CLARK
& Augustine M GUERRA
1945, January 31st Arthur THOMPSON
1945, March 13th Arthur HEYS
1945, March 17th Cubia JONES &
Robert L PEARSON
1945, March 19th James Herbert
LEHMAN
1945, April 7th William HARRISON
1945, May 8th George Edward SMITH
1945, June 15th Aniceto MARTINEZ
1945, September 5th Howard Joseph
GROSSLEY
1945, September 7th Thomas Eric
RICHARDSON
1946, January 8th William BATTY
1946, February 8th John LYON
1946, March 5th Charles Edward
PRESCOTT
1946, April 6th Patrick CARRAHER
1946, April 9th Harold BERRY
1946, April 24th Martin Patrick
COFFEY
1946, May 28th Leonard HOLMES
1946, August 10th John CALDWELL

Pierrepoint, Thomas (asst)
1906, April 10th Harry WALTERS
1906, August 9th Thomas Acomb
MOUNCER
1907, August 7th Charles PATERSON

Pierrepoint, Thomas (asst)

1907, August 14th Rhoda WILLIS
1907, November 5th William George
Charles AUSTIN
1907, November 20th William DUDDLES
1907, December 13th George STILLS
1908, March 24th William LOWMAN
Joseph William NOBLE
1908, August 5th Matthew John DODDS
1908, November 12th James PHIPPS
1908, December 2nd James NICHOLLS
1908, December 3rd John William
ELLWOOD
1909, March 2nd John HUTCHINSON
1909, March 30th See LEE
1909, April 14th Joseph Edwin JONES
1909, May 20th Marks & Morris
REUBENS
1909, July 9th Walter DAVIS
1909, July 20th William HAMPTON
1909, August 3rd Mark SHAWCROSS
1909, December 14th Samuel
ATHERLEY
1910, January 4th Joseph HEFFERMAN
1910, November 15th Thomas
RAWCLIFFE
1911, May 9th Thomas SEYMOUR
1911, May 24th Michael COLLINS
1911, October 17th Francisco Carlos
GODHINO
1911, October 17th Edward HILL
1911, November 15th Frederick Henry
THOMAS
1912, April 18th Frederick Henry
SEDDON
1913, July 9th Thomas FLETCHER
1914, March 10th Josiah DAVIS
1914, June 16th Walter James WHITE
1914, July 28th Herbert BROOKER

Plant, Samuel (asst)

1961, February 9th George RILEY
1961, May 26th Victor John TERRY
1961, September 7th Hendryk NEIMASZ
1961, December 20th Robert Andrew
McGLADDERY
1962, October 12th Oswald Augustus
GREY
1963, August 15th Henry John BURNETT

Pollard, Henry (asst)

1925, April 15th Henry GRAHAM
Thomas Henry SHELTON
1925, August 14th Arthur Henry BISHOP
& William John CRONIN
1925, September 3rd Wilfred FOWLER
1926, March 23rd Lock Ah TAM
1928, January 4th Bertram KIRBY
1928, January 6th Sydney Bernard
GOULTER
1928, January 7th Samuel CASE
1928, May 31st Frederick Guy BROWNE
1928, July 25th Albert George ABSALOM
1928, August 13th Allen WALES

1929, March 12th Joseph Reginald
Victor CLARKE
1930, June 11th Albert Edward
MARJERAM
1931, August 12th William John
CORBETT
1931, June 3rd Alexander
ANASTASSIOU
1932, March 9th George Thomas POPLE
1932, April 27th George Emmanuel
MICHAEL
1932, November 23rd Ernest
HUTCHINSON
1933, August 10th Varnavas Loizi
ANTORKA
1934, May 3rd Reginald Ivor HINKS
1935, March 13th George Frank
HARVEY
1935, October 30th Allan James
GRIERSON
1936, July 14th George Arthur BRYANT
1937, November 18th John Thomas
ROGERS
1946, November 19th Arthur RUSHTON

Rickard, Royston (asst)

1953, July 30th Philip HENRY
1953, December 17th Stanislaw JURAS
1953, December 18th John Francis
WILKINSON
1954, June 17th Kenneth GILBERT &
Ian Arthur GRANT
1954, August 11th William Sanchez de
Pina HEPPER
1955, July 13th Ruth ELLIS
1957, December 4th Dennis HOWARD
1959, April 28th Joseph CHRIMES
1959, October 9th Francis Joseph
HUCHET
1959, November 5th Guenther Fritz Erwin
PODOLA
1960, September 1st John Louis
CONSTANTINE
1960, November 10th Francis Robert
FORSYTH
1961, July 25th Samuel McCLAUGHLIN
1962, April 4th James HANRATTY
1963, December 17th Russell PASCOE
1964, August 13th Gwynne Owen EVANS

Riley, Alex (asst)

1938, July 26th William PARKER
1940, March 27th Ernest Edmund
HAMERTON
1940, July 11th William APPLEBY &
Vincent OSTLER
1941, July 23rd David Millar JENNINGS
1943, August 3rd William QUAYLE
1943, September 24th Charles Eugene
GAUTHIER
1943, December 14th Lee A DAVIS
1944, February 10th John H WATERS

1944, May 26th Wiley HARRIS
1944, June 23rd Pierre Richard Charles
    NEUKERMANS
1944, August 8th William Alfred COWLE
William George Frederick MEFFEN
1945, November 16th Arnim KUEHNE,
    Emil SCHMITTENDORF
1946, January 3rd William JOYCE
1946, January 4th Theodore John
    William SCHURCH
1946, April 2nd Marion
    GRONDKOWSKI & Henryk
    MALINOWSKI

Robinson, * (asst)
1925, August 5th Michael TALBOT
1925, August 5th Annie WALSH
1926, November 24th James McHUGH
1926, December 9th Henry McCABE
1927, December 29th William O'NEILL

Robinson, Harry (asst)
1958, May 6th Vivian Frederick TEED
1959, May 8th Ronald Henry
    MARWOOD
1960, November 10th Norman HARRIS
1961, March 29th Jack DAY
1961, June 29th Zsiga PANKOTAI
1963, December 17th Dennis John
    WHITTY
1964, August 13th Peter Anthony ALLEN

Scott, Thomas
1892, January 12th James HEANEY
1892, April 4th James CAMPBELL
1892, April 19th Daniel HANDLEY
1893, January 6th John BOYLE
1893, July 10th Edward LEIGH
1893, August 15th John Thomas HEWITT
1893, September 2nd James REILLY
1894, August 17th John GILMOUR
1895, August 20th Thomas BOND
1898, January 14th Patrick HESTOR
1898, April 5th Wilfrid F KENNY
1899, January 7th Patrick HOLMES
1899, January 10th Thomas KELLY
1899, January 13th Philip KING
1900, April 10th Patrick DUNPHY
1901, January 11th William WOODS
1901, March 7th John TOOLE

Scott, Thomas (asst)
1892, August 16th James TAYLOR
John George WENZEL
1893, March 16th Albert MANNING
1893, March 28th William WILLIAMS
1893, December 21st Frederick
    WYNDHAM
1895, June 18th James CANNING
1895, July 2nd Henry TICKNER
1895, December 17th Elijah
    WINSTANLEY

Smith, George
1872, August 13th Christopher
    EDWARDS
1872, August 12th
1873, January 7th Edward HANCOCK
1873, August 4th Henry EVANS
1873, August 16th Laurence SMITH
1873, August 20th
1873, August 19th Edward WALSH
1873, August 26th Thomas Hartley
    MONTGOMERY

Smith, George (asst)
1868, August 13th Thomas WELLS
1868, September 8th Alexander Arthur
    MACKAY
1872, August 13th Francis BRADFORD,
    Thomas MOORE & James TOOTH

Smith, Harry (asst)
1951, July 3rd Jack WRIGHT
1952, March 21st Takir ALI
1952, April 25th Alfred BURNS &
    Edward Francis DEVLIN
1952, May 27th Backary MAUNEH
1952, August 12th Oliver George
    BUTLER
1952, September 30th Raymond Jack
    CULL & Dennis George
    MULDOWNEY
1953, January 2nd James John ALCOTT
1953, February 24th Miles William
    GIFFARD
1953, July 15th John Reginald Halliday
    CHRISTIE
1954, January 5th Robert William
    MOORE
1954, April 22nd Albert George HALL
1954, June 17th Kenneth GILBERT & Ian
    Arthur GRANT
1954, September 1st Edward REID
1955, March 29th William Arthur SALT
1955, May 4th Winston SHAW
1957, July 23rd John Willson VICKERS
1958, September 3rd Frank STOKES
1958, September 30th Ernest Raymond
    JONES

Speight, * (asst)
1884, December 8th Ernest
    EWERSTADT & Arthur SHAW

Stanhouse, *
1879, August 25th Joseph PRISTORIA

Stewart, Robert
1958, May 6th Vivian Frederick TEED
1958, December 17th Brian CHANDLER
1959, May 14th Michael George TATUM
1964, August 13th Peter Anthony ALLEN

Stewart, Robert (asst)
1951, July 19th Dennis Albert MOORE

1951, July 19th Alfred George REYNOLDS
1952, January 15th Alfred BRADLEY
1952, February 26th Herbert Roy HARRIS
1952, April 25th Alfred BURNS & Edward Francis DEVLIN
1952, July 15th Thomas EAMES
1952, September 3rd Mahmood Hussain MATTAN
1952, September 5th John Howard GODAR
1952, September 30th Raymond Jack CULL & Dennis George MULDOWNEY
1952, December 12th Eric NORTHCLIFFE
1953, September 18th Louisa May MERRIFIELD
1953, November 17th Joseph Christopher REYNOLDS
1954, January 26th Desmond Donald HOOPER
1954, April 20th Michael MANNING
1954, April 23rd John LYNCH
1954, April 28th Thomas Ronald Lewis HARRIES
1954, June 22nd Milton TAYLOR
1954, September 1st Rupert Geoffrey WELLS
1955, April 14th Sydney Joseph CLARKE
1955, June 21st Richard GOWLER
1955, July 12th Kenneth ROBERTS
1955, July 26th Frederick Arthur CROSS
1955, July 27th Norman William GREEN
1955, August 9th Ernest Charles HARDING
1955, August 12th Alec WILKINSON
1960, November 10th Norman HARRIS
1960, December 22nd Anthony Joseph MILLER
1963, December 17th Dennis John WHITTY

Taylor, Edward (asst)
1915, August 13th George Joseph SMITH
1915, December 22nd Harry THOMPSON
1916, March 29th Reginald HASLAM
1916, August 16th William Alan BUTLER
1918, March 2nd Louis Marie Joseph VOISON
1917, April 10th Alexanda BAKERLIS
1917, August 16th William Thomas HODGSON
1919, February 19th Joseph ROSE
1919, July 31st Thomas FOSTER
1919, November 26th Ernest Bernard SCOTT
1919, December 3rd Djang Djing SUNG
1920, April 16th Miles McHUGH

1920, July 27th Arthur Andrew GOSLETT
1920, August 11th James ELLOR
1920, November 30th James RILEY
1920, December 30th Edwin SOWERBY
1921, March 2nd George Arthur BAILEY
1922, May 31st Herbert Rouse ARMSTRONG
1922, August 19th Thomas Henry ALLAWAY
1925, August 14th Arthur Henry BISHOP & William John CRONIN
1925, November 12th Hubert George BLOYE

Thompson, * (asst)
1894, April 2nd Margaret WALBER
1894, August 14th Paul KOEZULA

Underhill, John (asst)
1961, January 27th Wasyl GNYPIUK
1961, July 6th Edwin Albert Arthur BUSH
1962, November 28th James SMITH

Wade, Robert (asst)
1896, June 9th Henry FOWLER, Albert MILSOM & William SEAMAN
1899, November 28th Charles SCOTT

Wade, Steve
1946, March 26th Arthur CHARLES
1947, January 3rd Stanley SHEMINANT
1947, January 30th Albert SABIN
1947, June 20th Eric Charles BRIGGS
1948, January 7th George Henry WHELPTON
1948, December 9th Clifford Godfrey WILLS
1948, December 30th Arthur George OSBORNE
1949, June 2nd Dennis NEVILLE
1949, December 14th Benjamin ROBERTS
John WILSON
1950, March 30th Walter SHARPE
1950, July 13th John WALKER
1950, November 14th Patrick George TURNAGE
1952, February 6th Alfred MOORE
1952, March 21st Takir ALI
1952, December 24th Herbert APPLEBY
1953, December 18th John Francis WILKINSON
1954, January 5th Robert William MOORE
1954, January 27th William LUBINA
1954, April 22nd Albert George HALL
1954, September 1st Edward REID
1955, March 29th William Arthur SALT
1955, May 4th Winston SHAW
1955, July 12th Kenneth ROBERTS

1955, August 2nd Corbett Montague ROBERTS
1955, August 9th Ernest Charles HARDING
1955, August 12th Alec WILKINSON

Wade, Steve (asst)
1941, July 9th George Johnson ARMSTRONG
1941, August 6th Karl Theo DRUEKE
1941, August 6th Werner Heindrich WALTI
1941, October 31st Antonio MANCINI
1941, December 10th Karel Richard RICHTER
1942, March 25th David Roger WILLIAMS
1942, July 7th Jose Estelle KEY
1942, July 7th Alphonse Louis Eugene TIMMERMAN
1942, September 10th Samuel DASHWOOD & George SILVEROSA
1942, December 31st Johannes Marius DRONKERS
1943, March 31st Dudley George RAYNOR
1943, July 10th Charles Arthur RAYMOND
1943, August 3rd Gerald Elphinstone ROE
1943, December 15th Charles William KOOPMAN
1944, February 3rd Mervin Clare McEWEN
1944, March 16th Ernest Charles DIGBY
1944, July 12th Joseph Jan VANHOVE
1945, January 9th Horace Beresford GORDON
1945, January 30th Andrew BROWN
1945, March 13th Arthur HEYS
1945, September 5th Howard Joseph GROSSLEY
1945, October 6th Heinz BRUELING & Joachim GOLTZ & Erich Pallme KOENIG & Josef MERTENS & Kurt ZUEHLSDORFF
1945, December 21st James McNICOL John Riley YOUNG
1946, January 31st Michael NIESCIOR
1946, August 7th Walter CLAYTON
1948, February 6th Stanislaw MYSZKA
1948, December 2nd George RUSSELL
1950, October 30th Paul Christopher HARRIS
1950, December 16th James Ronald ROBERTSON
1951, September 15th Robert Dobie SMITH
1952, April 12th James SMITH
1952, May 29th Peter Gallagher DEVENEY
1953, January 26th George Francis SHAW

Warbrick, William (asst)
1893, August 16th John DAVIS
1893, December 19th Henry RUMBOLD
1895, June 4th William MILLER
1895, December 24th Henry WRIGHT
1896, February 4th William James MORGAN
1896, February 25th Alfred CHIPPERFIELD
1896, June 9th Henry FOWLER
1896, June 9th Albert MILSOM
1896, June 9th William SEAMAN
1896, July 21st Frederick BURDEN
1896, July 21st Philip MATTHEWS
1896, July 21st Samuel Edward SMITH
1896, August 5th William PUGH
1896, August 11th John ROSE
1896, August 11th Samuel WILKINSON
1900, January 9th Louisa Josephine MASSET
1900, December 4th Joseph HOLDEN
1905, August 15th Thomas George TATTERSALL
1905, November 7th William George BUTLER
1910, August 9th John Roper COULSON

Willis, William
1920, March 10th William WRIGHT
1920, December 30th Marks GOODMARCHER
1921, April 25th Thomas TRAYNOR
1921, April 25th
1923, January 9th Frederick Edward Francis BYWATERS
1923, February 8th William ROONEY
1924, April 8th Francis Wilson BOOKER
1924, May 8th Michael PRATLEY
1924, August 13th John HORNER
1925, May 26th Patrick POWER
1925, August 5th James WINSTANLEY
1925, August 11th James MAKIN
1925, December 15th Samuel JOHNSON
1926, January 5th John FISHER
1926, March 16th William Henry THORPE
1926, March 23rd Lock Ah TAM
1926, April 13th George SHARPES

Willis, William (asst)
1906, August 7th Edward GLYNN
1906, November 27th Edward HARTIGAN
1907, January 1st John DAVIES
1907, March 26th Joseph JONES
1907, April 2nd Edwin James MOORE
1908, July 28th Fred BALLINGTON
1908, August 19th Edward JOHNSTONE
1908, December 8th William BOULDREY
1909, January 6th John Esmond MURPHY

Willis, William (Asst) Executioner Index Wilson, Robert (Asst)

1909, February 23rd Jeremiah
O'CONNOR
1909, March 30th Edmund Walter
ELLIOT
1909, December 8th Abel ATHERTON
1910, February 15th William MURPHY
1910, March 1st George Henry PERRY
1910, May 25th Thomas William
JESSHOPE
1910, July 12th Thomas CRAIG
1910, August 9th John Alexander
DICKMAN
1910, November 22nd Henry
THOMPSON
1910, November 23rd Hawley Harvey
CRIPPEN
1910, November 24th William BROOME
1910, December 21st Noah WOOLF
1910, December 29th Henry ISON
1911, January 4th William SCANLAN
1911, December 14th Henry PHILLIPS
1911, December 28th George LOAKE
1912, December 18th Alfred John
LAWRENCE
1912, December 29th William Wallace
GALBRAITH
1913, January 13th Albert RUMENS
1913, January 29th John WILLIAMS
1913, July 8th Henry LONGDEN
1913, July 22nd John Vickers AMOS
1913, August 14th Hugh McCLAREN
1913, October 2nd Patrick HIGGINS
1913, November 27th Frederick Albert
ROBERTSON
1914, February 26th George BALL
1914, March 12th James HONEYANDS
1914, March 24th Robert UPTON
1914, May 14th Joseph SPOONER
1914, November 10th John Francis
EAYRES
1915, August 10th Walter MARRIOT
1916, December 12th Fred BROOKS
1916, December 19th James Howarth
HARGREAVES
1917, March 27th John William
THOMPSON
1917, December 19th Thomas COX
1918, February 21st Joseph JONES
1918, March 5th Verney ASSER
1918, December 17th John William
WALSH
1919, July 10th Henry PERRY
1919, August 8th Henry Thomas GASKIN
1920, January 6th Louis MASSEY
1920, March 10th William WRIGHT
1920, April 13th Frederick Rothwell
HOLT
1920, April 14th Thomas CALER
1920, May 26th Albert James FRASER
1920, May 26th James ROLLINS
1920, November 30th Cyril Victor
Tennyson SAUNDERS

1921, February 4th Jack Alfred FIELD &
William Thomas GRAY
1921, April 26th Thomas TRAYNOR
1921, April 25th
1922, March 21st James Hutton
WILLIAMSON
1922, May 30th Hyram THOMPSON
1922, September 5th William James
YELDHAM
1922, December 19th William RIDER
1923, June 11th John Henry SAVAGE
1923, October 10th Susan NEWELL
1924, June 18th William Horsley
WARDELL
1924, July 30th Abraham GOLDENBERG
1924, August 12th Jean-Pierre VAQUIER
1924, September 3rd Patrick Herbert
MAHON
1925, April 15th Henry GRAHAM
1925, April 15th Thomas Henry
SHELTON
1926, January 7th Lorraine LAX
1926, March 9th Henry THOMPSON
1926, April 13th George SHARPES
1926, July 27th Johannes Josephus
Cornelius MOMMERS
1926, June 27th

Wilson, Robert (asst)
1920, December 30th Samuel
WESTWOOD
1923, July 4th Rowland DUCK
1924, May 8th Michael PRATLEY
1925, April 2nd George William
BARTON
1925, August 5th James WINSTANLEY
1925, August 14th Arthur Henry BISHOP
William John CRONIN
1925, September 3rd Alfred Davis
BOSTOCK & Wilfred FOWLER
1926, January 5th John FISHER
1927, August 12th John ROBINSON
1928, January 27th Daniel DRISCOLL
1928, January 27th Edward
ROWLANDS
1928, January 31st James Joseph POWER
1928, May 31st William KENNEDY
1928, August 10th Norman ELLIOTT
1929, February 20th Frank
HOLLINGTON
1930, April 8th Samuel William
CUSHNAN
1931, February 4th Frederick GILL
1931, July 31st Thomas DORNAN
1931, August 5th Oliver NEWMAN &
William SHELLEY
1932, January 13th Edward CULLENS
1932, May 4th Maurice FREEDMAN
1933, February 2nd Jeremiah HANBURY
1933, October 11th Robert James KIRBY
1934, February 6th Ernest BROWN
1934, November 14th John Frederick
STOCKWELL

1935, April 2nd Leonard Albert
  BRIGSTOCK
1935, June 25th Arthur Henry
  FRANKLIN

1936, August 5th Wallace JENDEN
1937, February 10th Andrew Anderson
  BAGLEY
1948, February 3rd Evan Haydn EVANS

Hanged Index

This is a cumulative index, encompassing
Volumes I, II and III of the Hangman's Record.

Erroneous dates of hangings, and names of victims,
executioners and people hanged, have been corrected in the
relevant indexes. For easy reference, updated entries include
the information as originally given, *shown in italics.*

* = given name unknown

ABIGAIL, William George
1882, May 22nd

ABRAMOVICH, Myer
1912, March 6th

ABSALOM, Albert George
1928, July 25th

ADAMS, James
1919, November 11th

ADDINGTON, Richard
1871, July 31st

ALCOTT, James John
1953, January 2nd

ALDRED, William Thomas
1920, June 22nd

TAKIR, Ali
1952, March 21st

ALLAWAY, Thomas Henry
1922, August 19th

ALLCOCK, Joseph
1896, December 23rd

ALLEN, Margaret
1949, January 12th

ALLEN, Peter Anthony
1964, August 13th

ALLEN, Thomas
1889, April 10th

ALT, Henry
1885, July 13th

AMERY, John
1945, December 19th

AMOS, John Vickers
1913, July 22nd

ANASTASSIOU, Alexander
1931, June 3rd

ANDERSON, Arthur
1942, July 21st

ANDERSON, Edward Walker
1941, July 31st

ANDERSON, George
1914, December 23rd

ANDERSON, James
1883, February 19th

ANDERSON, John William
1875, December 22nd

ANDREWS, Frederick James
1899, May 3rd

ANSELL, Mary Ann
1899, July 19th

ANTORKA, Varnavas Loizi
1933, August 10th

APPLEBY, Herbert
1952, December 24th

APPLEBY, William
1940, July 11th

APTED, Harold
1902, March 18th

ARMSTRONG, George Johnson
1941, July 9th

ARMSTRONG, Harry
1939, March 25th

ARMSTRONG, Herbert Rouse
1922, May 31st

ARROWSMITH, William
1888, March 28th

ASHTON, Charles William
1903, December 22nd

ASSER, Verney
1918, March 5th

ATHERLEY, Samuel
1909, December 14th

ATHERTON, Abel
1909, December 8th

ATKINS, Percy James
1922, April 7th

ATWELL, Ronald Douglas
1950, July 13th

AUSTIN, Frederick James
1942, April 30th

AUSTIN, William George Charles
1907, November 5th

BACKHOUSE, Charles Benjamin
1900, August 16th

BAGLEY, Andrew Anderson
1937, February 10th

BAILEY, Edwin
1874, January 12th

BAILEY, George Arthur
1921, March 2nd

BAINBRIDGE, John Stephenson
1935, May 9th

BAINS, John
1886, February 9th

BAKER, Frederick Edwin
1877, April 17th

BAKER, James
1886, February 8th

BAKER, William
1875, September 6th

BAKERLIS, Alexanda
1917, April 10th

BALL, George
1914, February 26th

BALLINGTON, Fred
1908, July 28th

BANBURY, John James
1892, October 11th

BANNISTER, James
1877, April 2nd

BARLOW, Silas
1876, December 19th

BARNES, Peter
1940, February 7th

BARR, Thomas
1876, May 31st

BARRETT, James
1883, January 23rd

BARRETT, Percy George
1919, January 8th

BARRY, Kevin Gerald
1920, November 1st

BARTLETT, Leir Richard
1888, November 13th

BARTLETT, William Meager
1882, November 13th

BARTON, George William
1925, April 2nd

BANTON, James
1886, November 30th
BARTON, James

BATTY, William
1946, January 8th

BAUMBOS, Christos Emanuel
1876, August 25th

BEAL, William Henry
1912, December 10th

BEDFORD, John
1902, July 30th

BEDINGFIELD, Henry
1879, December 3rd

BELL, Edward
1899, July 25th

BENALI, Ferat Mahomed
1905, August 1st

BENNETT, Herbert John
1901, March 21st

BENSON, Benjamin Hindle
1919, January 7th

BENSON, William Charles
1928, November 20th

BENTLEY, Derek William
1953, January 28th

BERGIN,James Joseph
1900, December 27th

BERRY, Ann
1874, January 12th

BERRY, Harold
1946, April 9th

BERRY, Thomas
1880, July 27th

BERRY,Elizabeth
1887, March 14th

BERRYMAN, John
1908, August 20th

BETTS, Victor Edward
1931, January 3rd

BETTS, William
1897, December 16th

BEVAN, Thomas Henry
1887, August 16th

BIGGADYKE, Priscilla 1868, December 28th	**BOUNDS, Herbert Heram** 1942, November 6th
BIGNELL, William Grover 1925, February 24th	**BOUSQUET, Raymond** 1935, October 29th
BINDON, Edgar Lewis 1914, March 25th	**BOWES, John** 1900, December 12th
BIRKETT, Arthur 1912, July 23rd	**BOWLING, George** 1890, July 29th
BISHOP, Arthur Henry 1925, August 14th	**BOWSER, Joseph** 1897, July 27th
BLACK, Edward Ernest 1922, March 24th	**BOYCE, Arthur Robert** 1946, November 1st
BLAINE, Robert 1945, December 29th	**BOYLE, John** 1893, January 6th
BLAKE, David Maskill 1935, February 7th	**BRADFORD, Francis** 1872, August 13th
BLANCHARD, Peter 1875, August 9th	**BRADLEY, Alfred** 1952, January 15th
BLEWITT, Charles Oliver 1900, August 28th	**BRADSHAW, Robert** 1891, August 19th
BLOXHAM, Thomas 1887, February 14th	**BRADY, Joseph** 1883, May 14th
BLOYE, Hubert George 1925, November 12th	**BRAIN, George** 1938, November 1st
BOLTON, William James 1902, December 22nd	**BRAND, Osmond Otto** 1882, May 23rd
BOND, Thomas 1895, August 20th	**BRAY, Peter** 1883, November 19th
BOOKER, Francis Wilson 1924, April 8th	**BREEZE, George** 1904, August 2nd
BOON, Stanley Ernest 1939, October 25th	**BRESSINGTON, William Frederick** 1925, March 31st
BOSTOCK, Alfred Davis 1925, September 3rd	**BRETT, Frederick** 1889, December 31st
BOSWELL, Joseph 1890, March 11th	**BRIDGE, John Harris** 1935, May 30th
BOSWELL, Samuel 1890, March 11th	**BRIDGEMAN, Albert** 1905, April 26th
BOULDREY, William 1908, December 8th	**BRIGGS, Eric Charles** 1947, June 20th
BOULTON,Thomas 1885, August 17th	**BRIGSTOCK, Leonard Albert** 1935, April 2nd

354

BRINKLEY, Richard Clifford 1907, August 13th	**BRUNT, Horace William** 1937, August 12th
BRINSON, Eliga 1944, August 11th	**BRYAN, Thomas** 1921, March 14th
BRITLAND, Mary Ann 1886, August 9th	**BRYANT, Charlotte** 1936, July 15th
BROOKER, Herbert 1914, July 28th	**BRYANT, George Arthur** 1936, July 14th
BROOKS, Fred 1916, December 12th	**BUCKHAM, Richard** 1906, December 4th
BROOKS, John 1878, February 13th	**BULL, William** 1871, April 3rd
BROOKS, Walter 1928, June 28th	**BULMER, Charles** 1889, January 1st
BROOME, William 1910, November 24th	**BURDEN, Frederick** 1896, July 21st
BROWN, Albert Edward 1886, May 31st	**BURGESS, Frank** 1952, July 22nd
BROWN, Andrew 1945, January 30th	**BURNETT, Henry John** 1963, August 15th
BROWN, Ernest 1934, February 6th	**BURNS, Alfred** 1952, April 25th
BROWN, George Finlay 1950, July 11th	**BURNS, Hugh** 1880, March 2nd
BROWN, Henry 1897, January 5th	**BURRETT, William** 1900, October 3rd
BROWN, Joseph 1951, April 25th	**BURROWS, Albert** 1923, August 8th
BROWN, Thomas 1881, August 15th	**BURROWS, Herbert** 1926, February 17th
BROWN, William 1902, December 16th	**BURTOFT, William** 1933, December 19th
BROWN, William 1903, December 16th	**BURTON, James** 1883, August 6th
BROWNE, Frederick Guy 1928, May 31st	**BURTON, William Walter** 1913, June 24th
BROWNING, Robert 1876, December 14th	**BURY, William Henry** 1889, April 24th
BROWNLESS, William 1880, November 16th	**BUSH, Edwin Albert Arthur** 1961, July 6th
BRUELING, Harry 1945, October 6th	**BUTLER, Oliver George** 1952, August 12th

355

BUTLER, William
1910, March 24th

BUTLER, William Alan
1916, August 16th

BUTLER, William George
1905, November 7th

BUTLER, William Thomas
1939, March 29th

BUTT, Charles Edward
1874, January 12th

BYRNE, Patrick John
1878, November 12th

BYWATERS, Frederick Edward Francis
1923, January 9th

CACCARIS, Giovanni
1876, May 23rd

CADOGEN, Timothy
1901, January 11th

CAFFREY, Thomas
1883, June 2nd

CAFFREY, Thomas
1883, June 2nd

CAFFYN, James
1878, February 11th

CALADIS, Pascaler
1876, May 23rd

CALDWELL, Charles James
1938, March 20th

CALDWELL, John
1946, August 10th

CALER, Thomas
1920, April 14th

CALLAGHAN, Jeremiah
1902, December 12th

CALVERT, Louie
1926, June 24th

CAMPBELL, James
1892, April 4th

CAMPBELL, Michael
1871, April 24th

CAMPION, James
1904, April 14th

CANNING, James
1895, June 18th

CAPLAN, David
1920, January 6th

CARDWELL, George Walter
1919, January 8th
CALDWELL, George Walter

CAREY, Patrick
1883, May 8th

CARLSEN, August
1896, December 22nd

CARR, Andrew
1870, July 28th

CARRAHER, Patrick
1946, April 6th

CARTER, Horace
1952, January 1st

CARTER, John
1893, December 5th

CARTLEDGE, George Henry
1929, April 4th

CASE, Samuel
1928, January 7th

CASEMENT, Roger David
1916, August 3rd

CASEY, Terence
1943, November 19th

CASEY, Patrick
1882, December 15th

CASSIDY, Daniel
1923, April 3rd

CASSIDY, Peter
1884, August 19th

CASSIDY, William
1880, February 17th

CAVANAGH, William
1917, December 18th

CHADWICK, William Matthew
1890, April 15th

CHALMERS, George
1870, October 4th

356

CHAMBERLAIN, Sydney Archibald Frederick
1949, July 28th

CHAMBERLAIN, Thomas
1874, March 30th
1874, March 31st

CHAMBERS, William
1902, December 4th

CHANDLER, Brian
1958, December 17th

CHANTRELLE, Eugene Marie
1878, May 31st

CHAPMAN, George
1903, April 7th

CHARD-WILLIAMS, Ada
1900, March 6th

CHARLES, Arthur
1946, March 26th

CHARLTON, Richard
1875, December 23rd

CHIPPERFIELD, Alfred
1896, February 25th

CHOLERTON, Thomas
1878, August 12th

CHRIMES, Joseph
1959, April 28th

CHRISTIE, John Reginald Halliday
1953, July 15th

CHRISTOFI, Styllou Pantopiou
1954, December 15th

CHURCHER, William
1902, July 22nd

CHURCHILL, Catherine
1879, May 26th

CLARK, Ernest Lee
1945, January 8th

CLARK, William
1877, March 26th

CLARKE, George
1888, March 27th

CLARKE, Joseph Reginald Victor
1929, March 12th

CLARKE, Stanley Joseph
1948, November 18th

CLARKE, Sydney Joseph
1955, April 14th

CLARKSON, James Henry
1904, March 29th

CLAYDON, Alick
1901, December 13th

CLAYTON, Walter
1946, August 7th

CLEGG, Arthur
1946, March 19th

CLEWES, Thomas
1889, January 1st

CLIFFORD, Percy Evelyn
1914, August 11th

CLINTON, Thomas
1917, March 21st

COATES, Richard
1875, March 29th

COBB, David
1943, March 12th

COFFEY, Martin Patrick
1946, April 24th

COLCLOUGH, Charles
1920, December 31st

COLE, Stanley Edward
1940, October 31st

COLEMAN, Charles
1911, December 21st

COLLINS, Michael
1911, May 24th

COLLINS, Noah Percy
1908, December 30th

COLLINS, William
1871, August 17th

COLLINS, William Ambrose
1942, October 28th

CONLIN, Charles William
1929, January 4th

CONNAN, Thomas
1907, February 19th

CONNOR, James
1873, September 8th

CONSTANTINE, John Louis
1960, September 1st

CONWAY, John
1891, August 20th

CONWAY, Peter
1880, April 14th

COOK, George Samuel
1893, July 25th

COOPER, Bernard Alfred Peter
1949, June 21st

COOPER, Edward
1875, September 6th

COOPER, William
1879, May 20th

COOPER, William Henry
1940, November 26th

COPPEN, John Walter
1874, October 13th

CORBETT, William John
1931, August 12th

CORBITT, James Henry
1950, November 28th

CORGALIS, Matteo
1876, May 23rd

CORKERY, Jeremiah
1875, July 27th

CORRIGAN, Thomas
1874, January 5th

COTTON, John
1898, December 21st

COTTON, Mary Ann
1873, March 24th

COULSON, John Roper
1910, August 9th

COURTNEY, Harold
1933, April 7th

COUZINS, Ernest Soper
1949, December 30th

COVINGTON, Arthur
1895, December 3rd

COWDREY, Thomas
1903, December 16th

COWELL, William Charles
1940, April 24th

COWLE, Charles James
1932, May 18th

COWLE, William Alfred
1944, August 8th

COX, John
1929, April 25th

COX, Thomas
1917, December 19th

CRAIG, Thomas
1910, July 12th

CRANWELL, James
1875, January 4th

CREAM, Thomas
1892, November 15th

CRIPPEN, Hawley Harvey
1910, November 23rd

CRONIN, John
1886, January 12th

CRONIN, William John
1925, August 14th

CROSBY, Nicholas Persoulious
1950, December 19th

CROSS, Frederick Arthur
1955, July 26th

CROSS, Phillip Henry Eustace
1888, January 10th

CROSS, Walter John
1948, February 19th

CROSSLAND, John
1919, July 22nd

CROSSLEY,William
1894, July 31st

CROWE, Thomas
1876, August 25th

CROWTHER, Samuel
1888, December 11th

CROZIER,Samuel
1899, December 5th

CUDWORTH, Moses
1892, August 18th

CULL, Raymond Jack
1952, September 30th

CULLENS, Edward
1932, January 13th

CUMMINS, Gordon Frederick
1942, June 25th

CUNCEEN, Thomas
1879, January 10th

CUNLIFFE, George
1913, February 25th

CURLEY, Daniel
1883, May 18th

CURRELL, Thomas William
1887, April 18th

CURTIS, Samuel
1905, December 20th

CUSHNAN, Samuel William
1930, April 8th

DAINTON, Henry
1891, December 15th

DALEY, Hugh
1874, December 28th

DALEY, Thomas
1898, December 13th
1898, December 14th

DALGLEISH, James
1876, December 19th

DALTON, Hubert Ernest
1925, June 10th

DALY, John
1876, April 26th

DALY, Mary
1903, January 9th

DAND, John
1951, June 12th

DANIELS, George Nathaniel
1888, August 28th

D'ARCY, John
1879, May 27th

DASHWOOD, Samuel
1942, September 10th

DAVIDSON, John Gordon
1944, July 12th

DAVIES, Frederick
1890, August 26th

DAVIES, John
1907, January 1st

DAVIES, Richard
1890, April 8th

DAVIES, William John
1949, August 16th

DAVIS, John
1893, August 16th

DAVIS, Josiah
1914, March 10th

DAVIS, Lee A
1943, December 14th

DAVIS, Philip Edward Percy
1937, July 27th

DAVIS, Walter
1909, July 9th

DAWSON, Charles
1874, January 5th

DAY, Jack
1961, March 29th

DAY, Thomas Lyons
1883, November 13th

DAYMOND, John
1939, February 8th

DE STAMIR, Arthur Harry Victor
1918, February 12th

DEACON, Edward
1876, April 24th

DEANS, Joseph
1916, December 20th

DELANEY, Arthur Thomas
1888, August 10th

DELANEY, Thomas
1923, December 12th

DELASALLE, Sydney James
1944, April 13th

DELVIN, Henry
1890, September 23rd

DETHERIDGE, Jonah
1869, August 12th

DEVENEY, Peter Gallagher
1952, May 29th

DEVEREUX, Arthur
1905, August 15th

DEVERE, Eugene
1926, March 24th

DEVLIN, Edward Francis
1952, April 25th

DEWS, Alfred
1894, August 21st

DHINGRA, Madar Dal
1909, August 17th

DICKMAN, John Alexander
1910, August 9th

DIGBY, Ernest Charles
1944, March 16th

DILLEY, James
1879, August 25th

DISTON, William Joseph
1880, November 22nd
1880, November 27th

DOBELL, Charles
1889, January 2nd

DOBKIN, Harry
1943, January 27th

DOCHERTY, James
1902, December 30th

DOCHERTY, Patrick
1875, October 5th

DODDS, Matthew John
1908, August 5th

DOHERTY, David
1941, January 7th

DOLAN, John
1869, March 22nd
1869, March 23rd

DONOVAN, Conrad
1904, December 13th

DOOHAN, James Reginald
1954, April 14th

DOON, Lee
1923, January 5th

DORGAN, John Joseph
1943, December 22nd

DORNAN, Thomas
1931, July 31st

DOUGAL, Samuel Herbert
1903, July 14th

DOWDLE, Michael
1899, December 6th

DOWNES, William
1923, November 29th

DOWNEY, Michael
1885, January 16th

DOYLE, Patrick
1921, March 14th

DRISCOLL, Daniel
1928, January 27th

DRONKERS, Johannes Marius
1942, December 31st

DRUEKE, Karl Theo
1941, August 6th

DUCK, Rowland
1923, July 4th

DUCKWORTH, Cross
1893, January 3rd

DUDDLES, William
1907, November 20th

DUFFY, James
1903, December 8th

DUKES, William
1889, December 24th

DUMBLETON, William
1880, May 10th

DUNN, John Thomas
1928, January 6th

DUNN, Reginald
1922, August 10th

DUNPHY, Patrick
1900, April 10th

DURLING, George
1881, August 23rd

DUTTON, Henry
1883, December 3rd

DYER, Amelia Elizabeth
1896, June 10th

DYER, Charles Samuel
1904, April 5th

EAMES, Thomas
1952, July 15th

EARL, Charles Robert
1902, April 29th

EASTWOOD, John William
1923, December 28th

EAYRES, John Francis
1914, November 10th

EBLETHRIFT, John
1876, August 29th

EDGE, Frederick William
1905, December 27th

EDISBURY, George Frederick
1923, January 3rd

EDMONDSON, Douglas
1942, June 24th

EDMUNDS, John
1909, July 3rd

EDMUNSTONE, Alexander
1909, July 6th

EDWARDS, Christopher
1872, August 13th
1872, August 12th

EDWARDS, Edgar
1903, March 3rd

EDWARDS, Edgar
1928, December 11th

EDWARDS, Thomas
1892, December 22nd

EGGLESTON, Frederick
1892, March 17th

ELKINS, Samuel
1894, July 18th

ELLIOT, Augustus
1872, December 9th

ELLIOT, Edmund Walter
1909, March 30th

ELLIOTT, Norman
1928, August 10th

ELLIS, Joseph Robert
1896, August 25th

ELLIS, Ruth
1955, July 13th

ELLOR, James
1920, August 11th

ELLWOOD, John William
1908, December 3rd

ELVIN, Trevor
1943, September 10th

EMERY, Samuel George
1894, December 11th

EVANS, Evan Haydn
1948, February 3rd

EVANS, Henry
1873, August 4th

EVANS, Timothy John
1950, March 9th

EWERSTADT, Ernest
1884, December 8th

FAGAN, Michael
1883, May 28th

FAGAN, Michael
1911, December 6th

FAIRCLOUGH-BARROW, Thomas
1902, December 9th

FARRELL, James
1949, March 29th

FAUGERON, Marcel
1901, November 19th

FAWCETT, Edward Henry
1891, August 25th

FEE, Joseph
1904, December 22nd

FENTON, Frederick William
1894, April 4th

FIDDLER, Mark
1875, August 16th

FIELD, Frederick Herbert Charles
1936, June 30th

FIELD, Jack Alfred
1921, February 4th

FIELDING, Frederick
1928, January 3rd

FINDEN, Charles Edward
1926, August 12th
1926, August 11th

FISH, William
1876, August 14th

FISHER, John
1926, January 5th

FLANAGAN, Catherine
1884, March 3rd
1884, March 5th

FLANAGAN, Henry
1874, August 31st

FLANAGAN, William
1876, December 21st

FLEMING, John
1934, January 5th

FLETCHER, Joseph
1911, December 15th0

FLETCHER, Thomas
1913, July 9th

FLOOD, Frank
1921, March 14th

FLYNN, Michael
1883, January 17th

FOLEY, Edmund
1921, June 7th

FORDRED, Thomas
1876, April 4th

FOREMAN, Frederick
1910, July 14th

FORSYTH, Francis Robert
1960, November 10th

FOSTER, John
1905, April 25th

FOSTER, Thomas
1919, July 31st

FOWLER, Frank
1922, December 13th

FOWLER, Harold
1954, August 12th

FOWLER, Henry
1896, June 9th

FOWLER, Lawrence
1925, September 4th

FOWLER, Wilfred
1925, September 3rd

FOX, Sydney Harry
1930, April 8th

FOY, William Joseph
1909, May 8th

Frank George WARREN
1919, October 7th

FRANKLIN, Arthur Henry
1935. June 25th

FRASER, Albert James
1920, May 26th

FREEDMAN, Maurice
1932, May 4th

FREEMAN, John
1909, December 7th

FREIYER, Frank Joseph
1946, November 13th

FREMD, Charles
1914, November 4th

FULLER, Frederick Stephen
1927, August 3rd

FURY, Thomas
1882, May 16th

GADSBY, Robert
1917, April 18th

GAFFNEY, Jeremiah
1924, March 13th

GALBRAITH, James
1944, July 26th

GALBRAITH, William Wallace
1912, December 29th

GALLAGHER, John
1903, December 29th

GALLOWAY, Robert
1912, November 5th

GAMBON, William M
1948, November 24th

GAMBRILL, Stephen
1879, February 4th

GARCIA, Joseph
1878, November 18th

GARNER, Philip
1894, April 3rd

GARROD, Arthur
1911, June 20th

GARRY, Thomas
1883, May 7th

GASKIN, Henry Thomas
1919, August 8th

GAUTHIER, Charles Eugene
1943, September 24th

GELL, John Alfred
1888, May 15th

GEORGIOU, Christos
1944, February 2nd

GERRISH, Charles
1882, January 30th
1882, January 31st

GIBBONS, Patrick
1892, August 17th

GIBBS, James Henry
1874, August 24th

GIFFARD, Miles William
1953, February 24th

GILBERT, Henry
1878, November 25th

GILBERT, Kenneth
1954, June 17th

GILL, Frederick
1931, February 4th

GILLINGHAM, Michael
1875, August 2nd

GILLON, James
1928, January 31st

GILMOUR, John
1894, August 17th

GIOVANNI, Valeri
1901, July 9th

GLEESON, Henry
1941, April 23rd

GLYNN, Edward
1906, August 7th

GNYPIUK, Wasyl
1961, January 27th

GODAR, John Howard
1952, September 5th

GODDARD, William Harold
1932, February 23rd

GODHINO, Francisco Carlos
1911, October 17th

GODWIN, John
1874, May 25th

GOLDENBERG, Abraham
1924, July 30th

GOLDING, John
1877, August 21st

GOLDTHORPE, Norman
1950, November 23rd

GOLTZ, Joachim
1945, October 6th

GOODALE, Robert
1885, November 30th

GOODMARCHER, Marks
1920, December 30th

GORDON, Horace Beresford
1945, January 9th

GORRIE, Daniel Stewart
1890, June 10th

GOSLETT, Arthur Andrew
1920, July 27th

GOUGH, Alfred
1881, November 21st

GOUGH, Edward
1874, January 5th

GOULTER, Sydney Bernard
1928, January 6th

GOWER, William
1889, January 2nd

GOWER, Zbigniew
1950, July 7th

GOWLER, Richard 1955, June 21st	**GROVE, Henry** 1900, May 22nd
GRAHAM, Henry 1925, April 15th	**GUERRA, Augustine M** 1945, January 8th
GRANT, Ian Arthur 1954, June 17th	**GUNNING, Thomas** 1904, July 26th
GRAVES, William James 1938, July 19th	**GURD, John** 1892, July 26th
GRAY, William Thomas 1921, February 4th	**HAGGER, Harold** 1947, March 18th
GREEN, John 1876, December 20th	**HAGUE, George** 1935, July 16th
GREEN, Leslie Terrence 1952, December 23rd	**HAIGH, John George** 1949, August 10th
GREEN, Norman William 1955, July 27th	**HALE, William** 1875, April 26th
GREENING, Frank 1913, August 13th	**HALL, Albert George** 1954, April 22nd
GREENWAY, John Owen 1953, October 20th	**HALL, Edmund** 1904, December 20th
GREGORY, Roy 1934, January 3rd	**HALL, James** 1881, May 23rd
GREGSON, John 1870, January 10th	**HALL, William** 1920, March 23rd
GREY, Oswald Augustus 1962, October 12th	**HAMER, Emanuel** 1893, November 28th
GREY, Thomas 1877, November 21st	**HAMERTON, Ernest Edmund** 1940, March 27th
GRIERSON, Allan James 1935, October 30th	**HAMILTON, Lester** 1921, August 16th
GRIFFIN, Frank 1951, January 4th	**HAMILTON, Lewis** 1934, April 6th
GRIFFITHS, John 1906, February 27th	**HAMPTON, William** 1909, July 20th
GRIFFITHS, Peter 1948, November 19th	**HANBURY, Jeremiah** 1933, February 2nd
GRIFFITHS, William 1923, July 24th	**HANCOCK, Edward** 1873, January 7th
GRONDKOWSKI, Marion 1946, April 2nd	**HANCOCK, James Henry** 1910, June 14th
GROSSLEY, Howard Joseph 1945, September 5th	**HANCOCKS, William Alfred** 1905, August 9th

HANDLEY, Daniel
1892, April 19th

HANRATTY, James
1962, April 4th

HARDING, Ernest Charles
1955, August 9th

HARGREAVES, James Howarth
1916, December 19th

HARKNESS, William
1922, February 21st

HARMER, George
1886, December 13th

HARNETT, Arthur
1927, September 2nd

HARRIES, Thomas Ronald Lewis
1954, April 28th

HARRIS, Herbert Roy
1952, February 26th

HARRIS, Norman James
1960, November 10th

HARRIS, Paul Christopher
1950, October 30th

HARRIS, Thomas
1884, October 6th

HARRIS, Wiley
1944, May 26th

HARRIS, William
1894, January 2nd

HARRISON, Edward
1905, February 28th

HARRISON, James
1890, August 26th

HARRISON, John
1901, December 24th

HARRISON, William
1945, April 7th

HARTIGAN, Edward
1906, November 27th

HARVEY, George Frank
1935, March 13th

HASLAM, Max Mayer
1937, February 4th

HASLAM, Reginald
1916, March 29th

HAYES, Daniel
1888, April 28th
1888, April 29th

HAYES, John
1873, January 13th

HAYMAN, Robert
1897, February 9th

HAYNES, Thomas
1882, August 22nd

HAYWARD, George Frederick Walter
1928, April 10th

HAYWOOD, William
1903, December 15th

HEAL, Alfred John
1905, June 20th

HEANEY, James
1892, January 12th

HEAP, Alfred Thomas
1875, April 19th

HEATH, Neville George Clevely
1946, October 16th

HEFFERMAN, Joseph
1910, January 4th

HEMMINGS, Edward
1893, April 4th

HENDREN, Thomas
1946, July 17th

HENRY, Philip
1953, July 30th

HEPPER, William Sanchez de Pina
1954, August 11th

HERBERT, William
1880, December 13th

HERDMAN, John
1898, March 14th
1898, March 12th

HESTOR, Patrick
1898, January 14th

HETHERINGTON, Richard
1933, June 20th

HEWITT, Edward
1886, June 15th

HEWITT, John Thomas
1893, August 15th

HEYS, Arthur
1945, March 13th

HIBBS, George
1902, August 13th

HICKEY, Lawrence Maurice
1889, August 7th

HIGGENBOTHAM, Charles Lister
1890, January 7th

HIGGINS, Margaret
1884, March 3rd
1884, March 5th

HIGGINS, Patrick
1883, January 15th

HIGGINS, Patrick
1913, October 2nd

HIGGINS, Thomas
1883, January 17th

HIGHFIELD, Alfred
1900, July 17th

HILL, Edward
1911, October 17th

HILL, George
1876, April 10th

HILL, Harold
1942, May 1st

HILL, John
1885, November 23rd

HILL, Young
1915, December 1st

HINKS, Reginald Ivor
1934, May 3rd

HINSON, Frederick
1869, December 13th

HIRST, Joseph
1896, August 4th

HOBDAY, Stanley
1933, December 28th

HOBSON, Henry
1887, August 22nd

HODGSON, William Thomas
1917, August 16th

HOLDEN, Joseph
1900, December 4th

HOLDEN, Samuel
1904, August 16th

HOLLINGTON, Frank
1929, February 20th

HOLMES, Charles
1872, August 12th

HOLMES, Clifford
1941, February 11th

HOLMES, Frederick
1916, March 8th

HOLMES, Leonard
1946, May 28th

HOLMES, Patrick
1899, January 7th

HOLMYARD, William John
1929, February 27th

HOLT, Frederick Rothwell
1920, April 13th

HONEYANDS, James
1914, March 12th

HOOK, William Thomas
1889, December 31st

HOOLHOUSE, Robert William
1938, May 26th

HOOPER, Desmond Donald
1954, January 26th

HOPWOOD, Edward
1913, January 29th

HORNER, John
1924, August 13th

HORNICK, John
1937, June 17th

HORRY, William Frederick
1872, April 1st

HORSFORD, William
1898, June 28th

HORTON, George
1889, August 21st

HORTON, John

HORTON, John
1886, February 1st

HOUGHTON, Charles
1926, December 3rd

HOWARD, Dennis
1957, December 4th

HOWARTH, Kay
1884, November 24th

HOWE, George William
1898, February 22nd

HOWELL, Charles
1903, July 7th

HUCHET, Francis Joseph
1959, October 9th

HUCKER, Leonard George
1939, October 10th

HUDSON, Benjamin
1873, August 4th

HUDSON, Robert Heseltine
1895, August 13th

HUDSON, William George
1903, May 13th

HUGHES, William
1903, February 17th
1903, February 18th

HULTEN, Karl Gustav
1945, March 8th

HUME, Joseph
1908, March 5th

HUNTER, William
1887, November 14th

HUNTER,George
1876, March 28th

HUSSELL, William
1877, November 19th
HASSELL, William

HUTCHINSON, Ernest
1905, March 29th

HUTCHINSON, Ernest
1932, November 23rd

HUTCHINSON, John
1909, March 2nd

HUXLEY, Harry
1952, July 8th

HYNES, Peter
1923, December 15th

HYNES,Francis
1882, September 11th

INGLIS, James
1951, May 8th

INNES, William
1884, March 31st

INSOLE, Richard
1887, February 21st

IRWIN, William James
1900, August 14th

ISON, Henry
1910, December 29th

JACKSON, Christopher
1936, December 16th

JACKSON, John
1888, August 7th

JACKSON, William
1874, August 18th

JACOBY, Henry Julius
1922, June 7th

JAMES, Thomas
1943, December 29th

JAY, Horace Robert
1885, January 13th

JEFFRIES, Arthur
1904, December 28th

JENDEN, Wallace
1936, August 5th

JENKINS, Albert Edward
1950, April 19th

JENKINS,Ebeneezer Samuel
1889, March 6th

JENNINGS, David Millar
1941, July 23rd

JESSE, Frederick William Maximillian
1923, November 1st

JESSHOPE, Thomas William
1910, May 25th

JOB, Oswald
1944, March 16th

JOHNSON, Cyril
1942, April 15th

JOHNSON, James
1929, August 7th

JOHNSON, John Henry
1877, April 3rd

JOHNSON, John William
1891, December 22nd

JOHNSON, Michael James
1869, March 29th

JOHNSON, Peter Cyril
1952, October 9th

JOHNSON, Samuel
1925, December 15th

JOHNSON, Thomas
1879, May 28th

JOHNSTONE, Edward
1908, August 19th

JONES, Cadwaller
1877, November 23rd

JONES, Cubia
1945, March 17th

JONES, Ernest Raymond
1958, September 30th

JONES, Frederick
1872, January 8th

JONES, Harry Benjamin
1888, August 28th

JONES, Henry
1904, March 29th

JONES, James
1888, March 20th

JONES, James
1896, October 6th

JONES, Joseph
1907, March 26th

JONES, Joseph
1917, February 21st

JONES, Joseph Edwin
1909, April 14th

JONES, Rex Harvey
1949, August 4th

JONES, Thomas
1898, August 3rd

JONES, William Claude Hodson
1949, September 28th

JONES, William Cornelius
1927, January 5th

JOYCE, John
1901, August 20th

JOYCE, William
1946, January 3rd

JOYCE,Miles
1882, December 15th

JOYCE,Patrick
1882, December 15th

JUDGE, Patrick
1886, November 16th

JURAS, Stanislaw
1953, December 17th

JUSTIN, Richard
1909, August 19th

KADI, George
1876, May 23rd

KAVANAGH, Matthew
1958, August 12th

KAY, John Thomas
1904, August 16th

KEARNS, Patrick
1880, March 2nd

KEELEY, Thomas
1902, April 23rd

KEELING, Frederick Alexander
1922, April 11th

KEEN, John
1925, September 4th

KELLY, Ernest Edwin
1913, December 17th

KELLY, George
1950, March 28th

KELLY, John
1904, April 15th

KELLY, Patrick   Hanged Index   LAWSON, Joseph

KELLY, Patrick
1941, December 18th

KELLY, Thomas
1899, January 10th

KELLY, Timothy
1883, June 9th

KEMP, Ernest James Harman
1944, June 6th

KENNEDY, Michael
1872, December 30th

KENNEDY, William
1928, May 31st

KENNY, Wilfrid F
1898, April 5th

KERINS, Charles
1944, December 1st

KESTEVEN, Edmund
1895, March 26th

KEWISH, John
1872, August 1st

KEY, Jose Estelle
1942, July 7th

KIMBERLEY, Henry
1885, March 17th

KING, Jessie
1889, March 11th

KING, Joseph
1887, March 21st

KING, Philip
1899, January 13th

KINGSTON, Patrick William
1942, October 6th

KIRBY, Bertram
1928, January 4th

KIRBY, James
1888, May 7th

KIRBY, Robert James
1933, October 11th

KIRWAN, Bernard
1943, June 2nd

KIRWAN, William
1904, May 31st

KITCHING, Robert
1890, December 30th

KITE, Charles
1884, February 25th

KNIGHT, Cyrus
1894, December 12th

KNIGHTON, William
1927, April 27th

KOENIG, Erich Pallme
1945, October 6th

KOEZULA, Paul
1894, August 14th

KOOPMAN, Charles William
1943, December 15th

KOVASEVIC, Nenad
1951, January 26th

KOWALSKI, Czeslaw
1954, January 8th

KUEHNE, Arnim
1945, November 16th

KUN, Lee
1916, January 1st

LACE, William
1872, August 26th

LACY, William
1900, August 21st

LAMSON, George Henry
1882, April 28th

LAND, Francis
1931, April 16th

LANE, William
1902, August 12th

LANGE, Eric
1904, December 21st

LANGFORD, John
1894, May 22nd

LAW, George Frederick
1913, December 31st

LAWRENCE, Alfred John
1912, December 18th

LAWSON, Joseph
1884, May 27th

LAX, Lorraine
1926, January 7th

LAYCOCK, Joseph
1884, August 26th

LE BRUN, Joseph Phillip
1875, August 12th
1875, August 11th

LEAH, James
1926, November 16th

LEATHERBARROW, Thomas
1887, February 15th

LEATHERBERRY, John C
1944, May 16th

LEE, James
1885, May 18th

LEE, See
1909, March 30th

LEFLEY, Mary
1884, May 26th

LEFROY, Percy
1881, November 29th

LEGGETT, Patrick
1902, November 12th

LEHMAN, James Herbert
1945, March 19th

LEIGH, Edward
1893, July 10th

LEIGH, Henry
1877, August 13th

LEVER, George Edmund Freeman Quentin
1921, January 7th

LEWIS, Harry
1949, April 21st

LEWIS, Joseph
1898, August 30th

LIFFEY, Pasha
1905, November 14th

LINCOLN, Ignatius Emanuel Nathanial
1926, March 2nd

LIPSKI, Israel
1887, August 22nd

LIVESEY, John Kenneth
1952, December 17th

LLOYD, Thomas
1897, August 18th

LOAKE, George
1911, December 28th

LOCK, Frederick
1928, April 12th

LONGDEN, Henry
1913, July 8th

LOWMAN, William
1908, March 24th

LUBINA, William
1954, January 27th

LUN, Pong
1904, May 31st

LYNCH, John
1877, October 15th

LYNCH, John
1954, April 23rd

LYON, John
1946, February 8th

MacDONALD, John
1874, August 10th

MacDONALD, John
1902, September 30th

MACKAY, Alexander Arthur
1868, September 8th

MAGUIRE, John
1929, November 26th

MAHER, Patrick
1921, June 7th

MAHOMED, Jan
1938, June 8th

MAHON, Patrick Herbert
1924, September 3rd

MAIDMENT, Charles
1899, July 18th

MAJOR, Ethel Lillie
1934, December 19th

MAKIN, James
1925, August 11th

MAKSIMOWSKI, Piotr
1950, March 29th

MALINOWSKI, Henryk
1946, April 2nd

MANCINI, Antonio
1941, October 31st

MANNING, Albert
1893, March 16th

MANNING, Michael
1954, April 20th

MANUEL, Peter Thomas Anthony
1958, July 11th

MARJERAM, Albert Edward
1930, June 11th

MARKS, Isaac
1877, January 2nd

MARRIOT, Walter
1915, August 10th

MARSH, Henry
1877, November 20th

MARSH, Walter
1906, December 27th

MARSHALL, George
1915, August 17th

MARSLAND, Thomas
1902, May 20th

MARTIN, James
1886, February 8th

MARTINEZ, Aniceto
1945, June 15th

MARTYN, Walter
1911, December 12th

MARWOOD, Ronald Henry
1959, May 8th

MASON, David Baillie
1946, September 6th

MASON, George
1893, December 6th

MASSET, Louisa Josephine
1900, January 9th

MASSEY, Louis
1920, January 6th

MATHIESON, John Fleming
  McCready
1946, December 10th

MATTAN, Mahmood Hussain
1952, September 3rd

MATTHEWS, Philip
1896, July 21st

MAUNEH, Backary
1952, May 27th

MAURI, Ronald Bertram
1945, October 31st

MAYNARD, William John
1928, July 27th

McCABE, Henry
1926, December 9th

McCARTNEY, John William
1915, December 29th

McCLAREN, Hugh
1913, August 14th

McCLAUGHLIN, Samuel
1961, July 25th

McCONVILLE, John
1869, March 22nd
1869, March 23rd

McCRAE, Andrew George
1893, January 10th

McCULLOUGH, William
1875, August 16th

McDAID, John
1875, March 24th

McDERMOTT, Patrick
1932, December 29th

McDONAGH, Thomas
1923, December 12th

McDONALD, Thomas
1890, December 30th

McDONALD, William
1878, October 3rd

McENTIRE, Joseph Patrick
1881, May 31st

McEWEN, Mervin Clare
1944, February 3rd

McGEOWN, Simon
1922, August 17th

McGILL, Owen
1886, February 22nd

McGLADDERY, Robert Andrew
1961, December 20th

McGOVERN, Patrick
1877, August 21st

McGOWAN, James
1878, November 19th

McGRAVE, John
1875, January 4th

McGUINESS, Thomas
1917, May 16th

McGUINESS, William
1879, February 11th

McHUGH, James
1926, November 24th

McHUGH, Miles
1920, April 16th

McHUGH, William
1875, August 2nd

McHUGO, Martin
1880, January 16th

McKAY, James
1928, January 24th

McKENNA, John
1877, March 27th

McKENNA, Patrick
1901, December 3rd

McKEOWN, Arthur
1889, January 14th

McKEOWN, Steven
1876, August 21st

McKEOWN, William
1893, January 18th

McLEAN, Michael
1884, March 10th

McMANUS, Joseph
1947, March 31st

McMULLEN, Felix
1924, August 1st

McNICHOL, James
1945, December 21st

McWIGGINS, Henry
1902, December 2nd

MEADE, Thomas
1909, March 12th

MEFFEN, William George Frederick
1944, August 8th

MEIR, Karl Heindrich
1940, December 10th

MELLOR, James
1892, December 20th

MELLOR, Thomas
1900, August 16th

MERRIFIELD, Louisa May
1953, September 18th

MERRY, Harold Oswald
1942, September 10th

MERTENS, Josef
1945, October 6th

MEUNIER, Amie Holman
1893, July 19th

MIAO, Chung Yi
1928, December 6th

MICHAEL, George Emmanuel
1932, April 27th

MIDDLETON, Samuel
1902, July 15th

MILLAR, Walter
1870, August 1st

MILLER, Anthony Joseph
1960, December 22nd

MILLER, John
1901, December 7th

MILLER, John Robert
1901, December 7th

MILLER, William
1895, June 4th

MILLS, Herbert Leonard
1951, December 11th

MILSOM, Albert
1896, June 9th

MINAHAN, Daniel
1885, December 7th

MITCHELL, William
1921, June 7th

MOBBS, William
1870, March 28th

**MOMMERS, Johannes Josephus
  Cornelius**
1926, July 27th
1926, June 27th

MONTEAU, Francois
1890, August 27th

MONTGOMERY, Thomas Hartley
1873, August 26th

MOORE, Albert
1881, May 17th

MOORE, Alfred
1952, February 6th

MOORE, Dennis Albert
1951, July 19th

MOORE, Edwin James
1907, April 2nd

MOORE, Robert William
1954, January 5th

MOORE, Thomas
1872, August 13th

MORAN, Joseph
1904, January 5th

MORAN, Patrick
1921, March 14th

MORGAN, John
1875, March 30th

MORGAN, Samuel
1941, April 4th

MORGAN, William James
1896, February 4th

MORIARTY, Daniel
1888, April 28th
1888, April 29th

MORLEY, Joseph
1887, November 21st

MORLEY, Patrick
1895, December 31st

MORSE, Frederick
1933, July 25th

MOSS, Ernest John
1937, December 7th

MOUNCER, Thomas Acomb
1906, August 9th

MUHAMED, Hassan
1923, August 8th

MUIR, James
1892, March 1st

MULDOWNEY, Dennis George
1952, September 30th

MULLARKEY, Bernard
1882, December 4th

MULLEN, Henry
1883, May 23rd

MULLEN, Michael
1875, January 4th

MUNCH, Franz Joseph
1891, July 21st

MURPHY, Frederick George
1937, August 17th

MURPHY, James
1886, November 29th

MURPHY, James
1927, August 3rd

MURPHY, John Esmond
1909, January 6th

MURPHY, William
1910, February 15th

MURRAY, Phillip
1923, October 30th

MYLES, James
1926, July 15th

MYSZKA, Stanislaw
1948, February 6th

NASH, Thomas
1886, March 1st

NEAL, John
1890, March 26th

NEIMASZ, Hendryk
1961, September 7th

NEUKERMANS, Pierre Richard
  Charles
1944, June 23rd

NEVILLE, Dennis
1949, June 2nd

NEWELL, John William
1894, December 10th

NEWELL, Susan
1923, October 10th

NEWLANDS, George James
1953, December 23rd

NEWMAN, Oliver
1931, August 5th

NEWTON, George
1911, January 31st

NICHOLLS, James
1908, December 2nd

NICHOLSON, George
1889, January 8th

NICHOLSON, Thomas
1902, December 16th

NIESCIOR, Michael
1946, January 31st

NOBLE, John
1892, March 29th

NOBLE, Joseph William
1908, March 24th

NODDER, Frederick
1937, December 30th

NORMAN, Henry
1885, October 5th

NORTHCLIFFE, Eric
1952, December 12th

NUNN, George
1899, November 21st

NUNN, Matthew Frederick Atkinson
1924, January 2nd

O'CONNER, John
1951, October 24th

O'CONNOR, Edward
1921, December 22nd

O'CONNOR, Jeremiah
1909, February 23rd

O'DONNELL, Charles
1876, December 11th

O'DONNELL, Leo George
1917, March 29th

O'DONNELL, Patrick
1883, December 17th

O'KEEFE, Timothy
1883, April 30th

O'LEARY, Cornelius
1925, July 28th

O'NEILL, William
1927, December 29th

ORROCK, Thomas Henry
1884, October 6th

OSBORNE, Arthur George
1948, December 30th

O'SHEA, David
1931, August 4th

O'SHEA, William
1943, August 12th

OSTLER, Vincent
1940, July 11th

O'SULLIVAN, Joseph
1922, August 10th

OWEN, John
1870, August 8th

PALMER, Edward Henry
1913, March 19th

PALMER, Edward Richard
1903, November 17th

PALMER, William Henry
1911, July 19th

PARKER, Ernest Wadge
1933, December 6th

PARKER, Frederick William
1934, May 4th

PARKER, George Henry
1901, March 19th

PARKER, George William
1911, December 19th

PARKER, Henry Taylor
1908, December 15th

PARKER, Joseph C   Hanged Index   PRESTON, Thomas

PARKER, Joseph Cornelius 1899, July 11th	**PHILP, Sargent** 1912, October 1st
PARKER, William 1938, July 26th	**PHIPPS, James** 1908, November 12th
PARKINS, Henry 1905, December 6th	**PICKERING, Henry** 1892, June 14th
PARR, John 1900, October 2nd	**PIGGOTT, George** 1878, February 4th
PARRIS, James 1876, August 1st	**PLACE, George** 1902, December 30th
PARRY, Thomas 1885, January 20th	**PODMORE, William Henry** 1930, April 22nd
PASCOE, Russell 1963, December 17th	**PODOLA, Guenther Fritz Erwin** 1959, November 5th
PATCHETT, Leonard 1903, July 28th	**POFF, Sylvester** 1883, January 23rd
PATERSON, Charles 1907, August 7th	**POMROY, Bernard** 1923, April 5th
PATERSON, George 1897, June 7th	**POOLE, Joseph** 1883, December 18th
PAVEY, George 1880, December 13th	**POPLE, George Thomas** 1932, March 9th
PAYNE, Thomas 1887, December 6th	**PORTER, Thomas** 1903, July 21st
PEACE, Charles Frederick 1879, February 25th	**POUTNEY, Elijah** 1922, August 11th
PEACH, Arthur 1942, January 30th	**POWELL, Henry** 1883, November 6th
PEARSON, Elizabeth 1875, August 2nd	**POWER, James Joseph** 1928, January 31st
PEARSON, Robert L 1945, March 17th	**POWER, Patrick** 1925, May 26th
PENNY, Augustus John 1913, November 26th	**PRATLEY, Michael** 1924, May 8th
PERRY, George 1923, March 28th	**PRATT, Thomas Benjamin** 1877, November 12th
PERRY, George Henry 1910, March 1st	**PRESCOTT, Charles Edward** 1946, March 5th
PERRY, Henry 1919, July 10th	**PRESTON, Frederick** 1899, October 3rd
PHILLIPS, Henry 1911, December 14th	**PRESTON, Thomas** 1903, July 21st

375

PRICE, Albert
1950, August 16th

PRISTORIA, Joseph
1879, August 25th

PRITCHARD, Edward
1887, February 17th

PROBERT, Albert
1934, May 4th

PUGH, William
1896, August 5th

PURCELL, Benjamin
1889, December 9th

PURCELL, John
1891, March 13th

PURDOVICH, Hyman
1920, January 6th

PUTTNAM, Jack Samuel
1933, June 8th

QUARMBY, Frederick
1921, April 5th

QUARTLEY, Henry
1914, November 10th

QUAYLE, William
1943, August 3rd

QUINN, Ambrose
1919, November 26th

RADCLIFFE, Thomas
1870, August 15th

RALPH, John
1879, August 26th

RAMSBOTTOM, John
1908, May 12th

RAU, Gustav
1903, June 2nd

RAVEN, Daniel
1950, January 6th

RAVENEY, Arthur Leslie
1929, August 7th

RAWCLIFFE, Thomas
1910, November 15th

RAYMOND, Charles Arthur
1943, July 10th

RAYNOR, Charles
1892, March 17th

RAYNOR, Dudley George
1943, March 31st

READ, James Canham
1894, December 4th

REDEL, Roman
1950, July 7th

REES, David
1888, March 13th

REEVE, William Benjamin
1915, November 16th

REID, Edward
1954, September 1st

REILLY, James
1893, September 2nd

REUBENS, Marks
1909, May 20th

REUBENS, Morris
1909, May 20th

REVELL, Charles Joseph
1878, July 29th

REYNOLDS, Alfred George
1951, July 19th

REYNOLDS, Frederick
1906, November 13th

REYNOLDS, Frederick William
1947, March 26th

REYNOLDS, George
1928, August 3rd

REYNOLDS, Joseph Christopher
1953, November 17th

RICE, George Alfred
1932, February 3rd

RICHARDS, Alfred Ernest
1938, July 12th

RICHARDS, Eli
1941, September 19th

RICHARDS, James
1940, February 7th

RICHARDS, Thomas
1894, November 29th

RICHARDSON, Arthur
1902, March 25th

RICHARDSON, James William
1888, May 22nd

RICHARDSON, Thomas Eric
1945, September 7th

RICHTER, Karel Richard
1941, December 10th

RIDER, William
1922, December 19th

RILEY, George
1961, February 9th

RILEY, James
1920, November 30th

RILEY, Thomas
1883, November 26th

RILEY, Thomas
1932, April 28th

RIVETT, James Frank
1950, March 8th

ROBERTS, Benjamin
1949, December 14th

ROBERTS, Corbett Montague
1955, August 2nd

ROBERTS, David
1886, March 2nd

ROBERTS, Edward
1872, March 18th

ROBERTS, George Edward
1940, August 8th

ROBERTS, John Henry
1932, April 28th

ROBERTS, Kenneth
1955, July 12th

ROBERTS, Ronald
1943, February 10th

ROBERTSON, Frederick Albert
1913, November 27th

ROBERTSON, George
1899, March 28th

ROBERTSON, George Alexander
1954, June 23rd

ROBERTSON, James Ronald
1950, December 16th

ROBERTSON, William Meynell
1927, December 6th

ROBINSON, Albert
1881, February 28th

ROBINSON, George
1922, December 13th

ROBINSON, James
1955, May 2nd

ROBINSON, John
1927, August 12th

ROBINSON, Joseph
1897, August 17th

ROBINSON, Walter
1897, August 17th

ROBINSON, William James
1917, April 17th

ROE, Gerald Elphinstone
1943, August 3rd

ROGERS, Henry
1877, July 31st

ROGERS, John Thomas
1937, November 18th

ROGERS, William
1894, December 12th

ROLLINS, James
1920, May 26th

ROONEY, William
1918, December 17th

ROONEY, William
1923, February 8th

ROSE, John
1896, August 11th

ROSE, Joseph
1919, February 19th

ROSENTHAL, Robert
1915, July 15th

ROUSE, Alfred Arthur
1931, March 10th

ROW, William
1890, March 12th

ROWLAND, Walter Graham
1947, February 27th

ROWLANDS, Edward
1928, January 27th

ROWLEDGE, Samuel
1904, July 13th

ROWLES, Henry
1878, April 1st

RUDGE, Anthony Ben
1886, February 8th

RUMBOLD, Henry
1893, December 19th

RUMENS, Albert
1913, January 13th

RUSHTON, Arthur
1946, November 19th

RUSHWORTH, Frederick
1935, January 1st

RUSSELL, George
1948, December 2nd

RUSSELL, John
1875, April 9th

RUXTON, Buck
1936, May 21st

RYAN, Bernard
1921, March 14th

RYAN, John
1898, November 15th

RYDER, James
1913, August 13th

RYLANDS, Samuel
1889, March 13th

SABEY, Richard
1893, July 18th

SABIN, Albert
1947, January 30th

SACH, Amelia
1903, February 3rd

SADLER, Thomas
1891, August 18th

SALISBURY, Herbert Edward
1920, May 11th

SALMON, Sampson Silas
1901, February 19th

SALT, William Arthur
1955, March 29th

SAMANDA, Hashan
1926, November 22nd
SAMANDER
1926, November 2nd

SAMUELS, William
1886, July 26th
1886, July 27th

SANGRET, August
1943, April 29th

SARGENT, George
1888, August 15th

SATCHELL, James
1877, November 27th

SAUNDERS, Charles
1891, December 23rd

SAUNDERS, Cyril Victor Tennyson
1920, November 30th

SAUNDERS, George
1886, February 16th

SAVAGE, John Henry
1923, June 11th

SCANDRETT, Alfred
1888, March 20th

SCANLAN, William
1911, January 4th

SCHMIDT, Willem
1903, June 2nd

SCHMITTENDORF, Emil
1945, November 16th

SCHNEIDER, John
1899, January 3rd

SCHURCH, Theodore John William
1946, January 4th

SCOLLEN, Edward
1940, December 24th

SCOTT, Charles
1899, November 28th

SCOTT, Ernest Bernard
1919, November 26th

SCOTT, Martin
1883, May 23rd

SCOTT-FORD, Duncan Alexander Croall
1942, November 3rd

SEAMAN, William
1896, June 9th

SEDDON, Frederick Henry
1912, April 18th

SEDGEWICK, Eric James
1913, February 4th

SEEKINGS, Frederick
1913, November 4th

SEMINI, George
1949, January 27th

SEYMOUR, Henry Daniel
1931, December 10th

SEYMOUR, Thomas
1911, May 9th

SHARPE, Walter
1950, March 30th

SHARPES, George
1926, April 13th

SHAUGHNESSY, William Edward
1951, May 9th

SHAW, Arthur
1884, December 8th

SHAW, George Francis
1953, January 26th

SHAW, Winston
1955, May 4th

SHAWCROSS, Mark
1909, August 3rd

SHEEHAN, William
1886, January 20th

SHEILD, Lawrence
1870, May 27th

SHEILD, Margaret
1870, May 27th

SHELLEY, William
1931, August 5th

SHELTON, Thomas Henry
1925, April 15th

SHEMINANT, Stanley
1947, January 3rd

SHEWARD, William
1869, April 20th

SHRIMPTON, Moses
1885, May 25th

SHUFFLEBOTHAM, Joseph Arthur
1901, April 2nd

SIDDLE, Thomas
1908, August 4th

SILK, John
1905, December 29th

SILVEROSA, George
1942, September 10th

SIMMS, James
1879, March 24th

SIMON, Donald Neil
1952, October 23rd

SIMPSON, John Aspinall
1881, November 28th

SIMS, Arthur
1924, December 17th

SINGH, Ajit
1952, May 7th

SINGH, Udham
1940, July 31st

SKEFFINGTON, Thomas
1899, November 15th

SLACK, William Edwin
1907, July 16th

SLANE, Hugh
1873, January 13th

SLOWE, Charles Jeremiah
1903, November 10th

SMART, Edwin
1879, May 12th

SMEDLEY, William
1875, December 21st

SMILEY, William
1928, August 8th

SMITH, Arthur John
1939, October 25th

SMITH, Caleb
1877, August 14th

SMITH, Charles
1887, May 9th

SMITH, Charles
1898, March 22nd

SMITH, Edward Charles
1951, April 25th

SMITH, George
1905, December 28th

SMITH, George Edward
1945, May 8th

SMITH, George Joseph
1915, August 13th

SMITH, Gilbert Oswald
1912, November 26th

SMITH, Harold A
1943, June 25th

SMITH, James
1926, August 10th

SMITH, James
1952, April 12th

SMITH, James
1962, November 28th

SMITH, John
1941, September 4th

SMITH, John Ernest
1941, December 3rd

SMITH, Laurence
1873, August 16th

SMITH, Ralph
1939, June 7th

SMITH, Robert Dobie
1951, September 15th

SMITH, Samuel Edward
1896, July 21st

SMITH, Samuel Henry
1903, March 10th

SMITH, Sydney George
1903, March 9th

SMITH, Sydney John
1946, September 6th

SMITH, Thomas
1874, November 16th

SMITH, Walter
1894, March 27th

SMITH, Walter
1938, March 8th

SMITH, William George
1924, December 9th

SMITH, Willie
1944, August 11th

SMITHERS, Thomas
1878, October 8th

SMYTH, Dermot
1939, January 7th

SOUTHGATE, Frederick
1924, November 27th

SOWERBY, Edwin
1920, December 30th

SOWERY, Alfred
1887, August 1st

SPENCER, Arthur
1891, July 28th

SPENCER, Richard
1873, January 8th

SPICER, Felix
1890, August 22nd

SPOONER, Joseph
1914, May 14th

SQUIRES, Charles
1893, August 10th

STAFFORD, Peter
1889, April 8th

STANTON, John
1875, March 30th

STANWAY, William
1881, February 21st

STARKEY, John Henry
1877, July 31st

STARR, Henry Bertram
1903, December 29th

STEELE, Frank
1915, August 11th

STEIN, Solomon
1931, December 15th

STEWART, Frances
1874, June 29th

STEWART, Frederick
1928, June 6th

STILLS, George
1907, December 13th

STOCKWELL, James
1892, January 5th

STOCKWELL, John Frederick
1934, November 14th

STOKES, Frank
1958, September 3rd

STONE, Leslie George
1937, August 13th

STOREY, Frederick Thomas
1892, January 12th
1891, January 11th

STOREY, Frederick William
1920, June 16th

STRATTON, Albert
1905, May 23rd

STRATTON, Alfred
1905, May 23rd

STRATTON, James Frederick
1927, March 29th

STRICKSON, Kenneth
1949, March 22nd

SULLIVAN, Bartholomew
1891, February 2nd

SULLIVAN, Daniel
1916, September 6th

SULLIVAN, John
1904, July 12th

SULLIVAN, William
1922, March 23rd

SUNG, Djang Djing
1919, December 3rd

SURETY, Charles
1880, January 5th

SWANN, Emily
1903, December 29th

SWIFT, John
1877, November 27th

SWINDELLS, Harry Hammond
1884, November 24th

SYKES, Walter William
1913, April 23rd

TALBOT, Michael
1925, August 5th

TAM, Lock Ah
1926, March 23rd

TARKENTER, John Edward
1911, December 12th

TATTERSALL, Thomas George
1905, August 15th

TATUM, Michael George
1959, May 14th

TAYLOR, Charles
1882, December 12th

TAYLOR, Frank
1896, August 18th

TAYLOR, James
1892, August 16th

TAYLOR, Joseph
1903, January 7th

TAYLOR, Louisa Jane
1883, January 2nd

TAYLOR, Milton
1954, June 22nd

TAYLOR, Robert
1874, December 29th

TAYLOR, William
1869, October 11th

TEED, Vivian Frederick
1958, May 6th

TEMPLETON, Richard
1882, February 13th

TERRY, Benjamin
1887, February 22nd

TERRY, Victor John
1961, May 26th

THOMAS, Abraham
1883, February 12th

THOMAS, Frederick Henry
1911, November 15th

THOMAS, George
1885, December 8th
1885, December 9th

THOMAS, George
1894, February 13th

THOMAS, George
1926, March 9th

THOMAS, Madison
1944, October 12th

THOMPSON, Arthur
1945, January 31st

THOMPSON, Edith Jessie
1923, January 9th

THOMPSON, Harry
1915, December 22nd

THOMPSON, Henry
1910, November 22nd

THOMPSON, Henry
1926, March 9th

THOMPSON, Hyram
1922, May 30th

THOMPSON, John George
1901, December 10th

THOMPSON, John William
1917, March 27th

THOMPSON, Richard
1876, August 14th

THOMPSON, William
1874, January 5th

THORNE, John Norman Holmes
1925, April 22nd

THORNLEY, John James
1915, December 1st

THORPE, Thomas William
1941, December 23rd

THORPE, William Henry
1926, March 16th

THURSTON, John
1886, February 10th

TICKNER, Henry
1895, July 2nd

TIDBURY, Francis
1877, March 12th

TIDBURY, Henry
1877, March 12th

TIMMERMAN, Alphonse Louis Eugene
1942, July 7th

TOAL, Gerard
1928, August 29th

TOBIN, James
1884, August 26th
1884, August 24th

TOBIN, William
1875, April 19th

TODD, John Lawrence
1953, May 19th

TONBRIDGE, Edmund Hugh
1922, April 18th

TOOKE, Annie
1879, August 11th

TOOLE, John
1901, March 7th

TOOTH, James
1872, August 13th

TORR, Elias
1899, August 9th

TRAYNOR, Thomas
1921, April 26th
1921, April 25th

TRENOWORTH, Gordon Horace
1943, April 6th

TREVOR, Harold Dorian
1942, March 11th

TRICKETT, James
1878, February 12th

TUCKER, Joseph
1885, August 3rd

TUFFIN, William Joseph
1903, August 11th

TUFFNEY, Harry
1934, October 9th

TURNAGE, Patrick George
1950, November 14th

TURNER, Alfred William
1891, May 19th

TURNER, Walter Lewis
1891, August 18th

TURNER, William
1882, August 21st

TURNER, William Henry
1943, March 24th

TWISS, John
1895, February 9th

UPTON, John
1877, November 27th

UPTON, Robert
1888, July 17th

UPTON, Robert
1914, March 24th

VAN DER KERK-HOVE, Louis
1918, March 9th

Van DER KEIBOOM, Charles
1940, December 17th

VANHOVE, Joseph Jan
1944, July 12th

VAQUIER, Jean-Pierre
1924, August 12th

VEST, Robert
1878, July 30th

VICKERS, John Willson
1957, July 23rd

VICKERS, Robert Flockheart
1884, March 31st

VINALL, Martin Henry
1869, January 18th

VIRRELS, James
1951, April 26th

VOISON, Louis Marie Joseph
1918, March 2nd

WADDELL, William
1888, December 18th

WADDINGHAM, Dorothea Nancy
1936, April 16th

WADDINGTON, William
1920, May 11th

WADE, Charles
1904, December 13th

WADE, Peter
1884, January 15th

WADELY, Enoch
1887, November 28th

WADGE, Selina
1878, August 15th

WAINWRIGHT, Henry
1875, December 21st

WAKEFIELD, John
1880, August 16th

WALBER, Margaret
1894, April 2nd

WALDBERG, Jose
1940, December 10th

WALDEN, Bernard Hugh
1959, August 14th

WALES, Allen
1928, August 13th

WALKER, John
1950, July 13th

WALKER, Joseph
1887, November 15th

WALKER, Vincent Knowles
1878, April 15th

WALSH, Annie
1925, August 5th

WALSH, Edward
1873, August 19th

WALSH, John William
1918, December 17th

WALSH, Patrick
1882, September 22nd

WALTERS, Annie
1903, February 3rd

WALTERS, Harry
1905, April 10th

WALTI, Werner Heindrich
1941, August 6th

WALTON, Samuel Thomas
1902, December 16th

WAMMER, Julius
1909, August 10th

WARD, Robert
1899, October 4th

WARDELL, William Horsley
1924, June 18th

WARDLAW, David
1875, October 19th

WARREN, Arnold
1914, November 12th

WATERS, John H
1944, February 10th

WATERS, Margaret
1870, October 11th

WATKINS, William Arthur
1951, April 3rd

WATKINS,Charles
1901, July 30th

WATSON, Lionel Rupert Nathan
1941, November 12th

WATT, James
1898, July 12th

WEBBER, Joseph
1876, April 25th

WEBSTER, Catherine
1879, July 29th

WEDLAKE, Joseph
1883, May 21st

WELLS, Rupert Geoffrey
1954, September 1st

WELLS, Thomas
1868, August 13th

WELSH, Joseph
1869, November 15th

WENZEL, John George
1892, August 16th

WEST, Robert
1889, December 31st

WESTWOOD, Samuel
1920, December 30th

WHEATFALL, Edward
1882, November 28th

WHEELER, Mary Eleanor
1890, December 23rd

WHEELER, Thomas
1880, November 29th
1880, November 26th

WHELAN, James
1886, May 31st

WHELAN, Thomas
1921, March 14th

WHELPTON, George Henry
1948, January 7th

WHISTON, Enoch
1879, February 10th

WHITE, Bernard
1903, December 1st

WHITE, George
1883, May 21st

WHITE, Henry Lyndo
1941, March 6th

WHITE, Walter James
1914, June 16th

WHITEHEAD, James Wilshaw
1894, November 27th

WHITEWAY, Alfred Charles
1953, December 22nd

WHITTAKER, Charles Wood
1903, December 2nd

WHITTY, Dennis John
1963, December 17th

WICKHAM, Ernest Walter
1901, August 13th

WIGLEY, Richard
1902, March 18th

WILKES, William
1898, July 19th

WILKINSON, Alec
1955, August 12th

WILKINSON, John Francis
1953, December 18th

WILKINSON, Samuel
1896, August 11th

WILLIAMS, David John
1947, April 15th

WILLIAMS, David Roger
1942, March 25th

WILLIAMS, Henry
1902, November 11th

WILLIAMS, James
1881, February 22nd

WILLIAMS, John
1876, July 26th

WILLIAMS, John
1885, November 23rd

WILLIAMS, John
1912, March 19th
1912, March 9th

WILLIAMS, John
1913, January 29th

WILLIAMS, Mary
1874, August 31st

WILLIAMS, Thomas Joseph
1942, September 2nd

WILLIAMS, William
1893, March 28th

WILLIAMSON, James Hutton
1922, March 21st
WILLIS, Rhoda
1907, August 14th

WILLS, Clifford Godfrey
1948, December 9th

WILSON, John
1949, December 14th

WILSON, Joseph
1892, March 22nd

WILSON, Thomas
1921, May 24th

WILSON, Thomas Hargreaves
1920, May 6th

WILTON, William
1887, August 29th

WINGFIELD, John
1880, March 22nd

WINGROVE, Richard
1895, November 19th
1895, November 13th

WINSTANLEY, Elijah
1895, December 17th

WINSTANLEY, James
1925, August 5th

WINTER, Franciscus Johannes
1943, January 26th

WITHEY, John
1889, April 11th

WOOD, Frederick George
1923, April 10th

WOOD, George Henry
1892, April 26th

WOOD, John Henry
1880, May 11th

WOOD, Walter
1887, May 30th

WOODFIELD, Edward Isaac
1950, December 14th

WOODS, William
1901, January 11th

WOOLDRIDGE, Charles Thomas
1896, July 7th

WOOLF, Noah
1910, December 21st

WOOLFE, George
1902, May 6th

WORTHINGTON, Walter Osmond
1935, July 10th

WORTHINGTON, William
1875, January 4th

WREN, Joseph
1910, February 22nd
1910, February 23rd

WRIGHT, Henry
1895, December 24th

WRIGHT, Jack
1951, July 3rd

WRIGHT, John
1940, September 10th

WRIGHT, William
1920, March 10th

WYNDHAM, Frederick
1893, December 21st

WYRE, Thomas
1888, July 18th

YARNOLD, William
1905, December 5th

YELDHAM, William James
1922, September 5th

YOUNG, Henry William
1887, May 16th

YOUNG, John Riley
1945, December 21st

ZUEHLSDORFF, Kurt
1945, October 6th

'I wish I could have got her mother as well. I would have chopped her into mincemeat and made sausages of her, and then I should have been satisfied.'

William Harris, hanged by James Billington in 1894 for murdering his girlfriend, Florence Clifford, with an axe.

Meet him in…

THE
HANGMAN'S
RECORD
VOLUME ONE 1868-1899
STEVE FIELDING

£14.95 (£17.45 post-free) ISBN 0 900246 65 0

Available now from Chancery House Press

Chancery House Press

Who was hanged in 1901 but is still not officially dead?

Who declared that being sentenced to death was "not as bad as marriage"?

Find out, in….

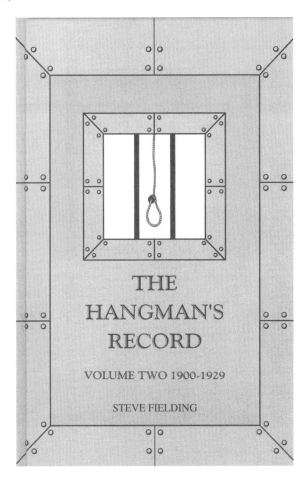

£17.95 (£21.45 post-free) ISBN 0 900246 77 4

Available now from Chancery House Press

Chancery House Press

Order Form

Please send me…

THE HANGMAN'S RECORD **VOL I 1868-1899**   @ £14.95
(£17.95 post free)   ISBN 0 900246 65 0
THE HANGMAN'S RECORD **VOL II 1900-1929**   @ £17.95
(£21.45 post free)   ISBN 0 900246 77 4
THE HANGMAN'S RECORD **VOL III 1930-1964**   @ £26.95
(£30.45 post free)   ISBN 0 900246 81 2
THE HANGMAN'S RECORD **(all 3 books)**   @ £55.00
(£62.75 post free)

I enclose a cheque for ……………… payable to Chancery House Press.

OR

Please charge my credit card (please tick appropriate box).

VISA   MasterCard   AMERICAN EXPRESS

Card no:

Expiry date: …./………. Signature: ……………………………………

and deliver to

Name:
………………………………………………………………...……

Address:
……………………………………………………….………..

……………………………………………………………………..

.

Tel………………………… E-mail: ……………..………………………

Please return this form and payment to:

Chancery House Press, 15 Wickham Road, Beckenham, Kent, BR3 5JS.
Tel: 020 8650 7745   **Fax: 020 8650 0768**
info@chanceryhousepress.co.uk   **www.chanceryhousepress.co.uk**